RE-ENVISIONING PSYCHOLOGY

This book studies the ideological nature of mainstream scientific psychology. It raises critical questions about the dominant forms of psychological theorization and praxis, based on their validity, social relevance and power privileges. *Re-envisioning Psychology* critically interrogates scientific images of the mind, the individual, gender, development, society and culture that mainstream psychology promotes. The issues taken up in this book revolve around the pivotal concerns of psychology's scientific basis, its dominant quantitative research methodology, the construction of the 'individual' as the unit of analysis, the conceptualization of 'social', 'cultural' and 'gender' in relation to individualism, and the understanding of abnormality as shaped by the discourses of medical science and capitalism.

Comprehensive and topical, the book will be useful to students, researchers, and teachers of Psychology, Applied Psychology, Social Work, Gender and Women Studies, and Sociology. It will also be of interest to professional counsellors and psychotherapists.

Parul Bansal is Associate Professor of Psychology at Lady Shri Ram College for Women, India's premier liberal arts college, affiliated to the University of Delhi. She received a BA in psychology from Lady Shri Ram College for Women, and an MA and a doctorate degree in psychology from the University of Delhi. Her teaching career spans over 20 years, during which she has served as the Chair of the Department of Psychology at Lady Shri Ram College for Women twice. In addition, she has been actively involved with curriculum development and course writing at the University of Delhi and the Indira Gandhi National Open University (IGNOU). She has to her credit a well-received research text, *Youth in Contemporary India: Images of Identity and Social Change*, which uses a psychoanalytically informed qualitative research methodology. Her academic and research interests are in psychosocial studies of identity, intimacy, ideology and social change, critical psychology, psychoanalysis and mental health, and qualitative research methodology. She was awarded the Shashikala Singh Gold Medal for being one of the top students at the University of Delhi for her Master's. She has also received an ICSSR Doctoral Fellowship to conduct her PhD work. She has published in several journals of international repute.

"The aim of this book is to 'stir up trouble' – to raise awkward and challenging questions about the standard, mainstream way in which psychology these days gets carried out, gets researched, gets taught and gets promoted. Dr Parul's book makes an excellent and very readable contribution to a growing campaign (mostly but not only among self-defined critical psychologists) to challenge the misguided assumption that the only way to approach psychology is a science, much like physics and chemistry. Instead she argues for re-defining psychology as the study of human being/being human, with all the complexities, nuances and inventiveness operating within people's multiply diverse life-worlds, communities and mindsets. Her critique of the complacency and self-interest of psychologists who confirm to the conventional approach is systematic and thorough – this is a book that will really make its readers think! And there is a real need for it. Increasingly students and early career psychologists are becoming frustrated by the way that psychology's powerful elites (such as supervisors, journal editors and research funders) continue to force their research into the straitjackets of quantitative research methods. This prevents these scholars from asking open-ended research questions and seeking insight into 'what is going on' by using the extraordinary range of alternative and inventive qualitative methods that can be tailored to address particular issues, including the mechanisms of Othering, exclusion and discrimination. This book will give these activists some really powerful ammunition to join the fight – for a re-formed psychology that is reflective, ethical and inclusive. I recommend it to you very highly."

Wendy Stainton Rogers, Professor Emerita, the Open University, UK

"The book offers a comprehensive overview of all the important issues in the rapidly growing field of psychology. It's expanse and depth make it a unique source text providing a rich and engaging picture of the discourses that have been shaping the discipline. A must - have book for students and scholars interested in the themes of psychology in a historical and culturally contextualised perspective."

Girishwar Mishra, Former Professor of Psychology, University of Delhi & Ex. Vice Chancellor, Mahatma Gandhi Antarrashtriya Hindi Vishvavidyalaya, Wardha

"This excellent book puts to deconstruction the science of psychology and unveils in the process the crypted normativisms and normalizations at work in both theory and practice. It unearths the politics at work in psychology. It thus inaugurates a new discourse of psychology."

Prof. Anup Dhar, Fellow, The Hans Kilian and Lotte Köhler Centre for Cultural Psychology and Historical Anthropology, Ruhr-University Bochum

"This book provides a much needed and thorough interrogation of long-standing assumptions of mainstream psychology in order to develop alternative conceptualizations. It provides a definitive impetus to the critical debates about epistemology and methodology to reset the standard ways of understanding human 'being'."

Dr. Nandita Chaudhary, Former Associate Professor at the Department of Human Development and Childhood Studies at Lady Irwin College, University of Delhi & an independent scholar in the field of cultural developmental psychology

"In this book, Parul Bansal builds her arguments on the limits of epistemological foundations of psychology and discusses the shifting axial age of major psychological debates and controversies. She boldly exposes the ideological nature of psychological theories and their political consequences."

Prof. Minati Panda, Professor of Cultural Psychology and Education, Jawaharlal Nehru University

RE-ENVISIONING PSYCHOLOGY

Debating Paradigmatic Foundations

Parul Bansal

LONDON AND NEW YORK

First published 2024
by Routledge
4 Park Square, Milton Park, Abingdon, Oxon OX14 4RN

and by Routledge
605 Third Avenue, New York, NY 10158

Routledge is an imprint of the Taylor & Francis Group, an informa business

© 2024 Parul Bansal

The right of Parul Bansal to be identified as author of this work has been asserted in accordance with sections 77 and 78 of the Copyright, Designs and Patents Act 1988.

All rights reserved. No part of this book may be reprinted or reproduced or utilised in any form or by any electronic, mechanical, or other means, now known or hereafter invented, including photocopying and recording, or in any information storage or retrieval system, without permission in writing from the publishers.

Trademark notice: Product or corporate names may be trademarks or registered trademarks, and are used only for identification and explanation without intent to infringe.

British Library Cataloguing-in-Publication Data
A catalogue record for this book is available from the British Library

ISBN: 978-1-032-74994-5 (hbk)
ISBN: 978-1-032-74993-8 (pbk)
ISBN: 978-1-003-47185-1 (ebk)

DOI: 10.4324/9781003471851

Typeset in Sabon
by Taylor & Francis Books

Dedicated to the ever-loving memory of my mother, Neerja, and the ever-playful spirit of my son, Saarthak

CONTENTS

List of figures	*x*
List of tables	*xi*
List of boxes	*xii*
Acknowledgements	*xiii*

	Why Debate Psychology?: An Introduction	1
1	Is Psychology a Science?	16
2	Should Psychological Research Be Only about Numbers?	51
3	What Is 'Social' about Social Psychology?	88
4	Where Is 'Culture' in Psychology?	132
5	How Is 'Gender' Treated in Psychology?	190
6	What Is 'Abnormal' in Clinical Psychology?	252
7	Why Should We Rethink 'Child' and 'Development' in Psychology?	287

References	*313*
Index	*340*

FIGURES

1.1 Research cycle: deduction and induction	19
1.2 Kuhn's philosophy of scientific revolution	31
3.1 The sociogenesis of social representations	111
4.1 Culture as an independent variable	153
4.2 Culture as a mediator variable	154
4.3 Visual illusions	156
4.4 Berry's ecocultural framework	157
5.1 Models of social interaction in gender-related behaviour	209
6.1 Sociocultural pathways to deviance, distress and disorder	278

TABLES

1.1 Human science and natural science	17
2.1 The philosophical positions of positivism and post-positivism	56
2.2 The philosophical positions of interpretivism and critical research	71
2.3 Two major traditions of scientific research	74
4.1 Comparison between Indian and Western views of psychological functioning	168
5.1 Kohlberg's stages of moral development	227
6.1 Deciding on a categorical or dimensional scale	272

BOXES

1.1 The Feminist Critiques of Science	28
1.2 The Inner World of the Scientist	33
1.3 Is Psychoanalysis a Science?	42
2.1 The Limits of Statistical Reasoning	60
2.2 The Six 'Red Herrings' of Psychological Research	63
2.3 An Example of a Qualitative Research Study	77
3.1 The Intersubjective View of the Self	99
3.2 From Discursive Psychology to a Psychosocial Approach	120
3.3 The Contact Hypothesis: Critical Reflections	128
4.1 Cross-Cultural Research on Kohlberg's Stages of Moral Development	150
4.2 The Indigenization of Psychology in India	170
4.3 Cross-Cultural Equivalence versus Cultural Constitution of Emotions	185
5.1 Discourses Blaming the Media for Body Image-Related Disturbances	200
5.2 Moving Gender beyond Individual Traits	215
5.3 Gender Binarism in Psychology	225
5.4 Why Should There Be a Psychology of Men?	249
6.1 Clinical Psychology in the Context of Medical Discourse	257
6.2 The Split Understandings of Schizophrenia	273
6.3 Women's Reproductive Functions and Mental Health: Does Social Context Matter?	284
7.1 Cultural Variations in Child-Rearing Practices and Its Implications for Social Relationships	305

ACKNOWLEDGEMENTS

Writing saps! Writing also exhilarates! Writing mixes with affect and forms an axis with thinking-feeling. Writing doesn't just represent but also creates ideas, perspectives, experience.

The impulse to write this book stemmed from a vague, unformed feeling of discomfort that I have experienced with the way psychology is carried out, in over two decades of my association with the discipline as a student and an academic. I was fortunate enough to be taught in my undergraduate studies by feisty, well-intentioned and staunch believers of scientific psychology. Subsequently, during my Master's training in psychology, the whole edifice of scientific psychology came under systematic review from various standpoints through the teachings and discussions of some very talented teachers. This at first created huge angst and feelings of being bereft of the power of knowing and doing psychology. *DSM*, Psychological Testing, Experimentation, Objectivity, Truth – everything was circumspect. Mental illness became a myth. Mother's love is a historical construction. The individual is always ever social. Objectivity was nothing but social consensus. The painful unlearning process was accompanied by eager realigning of oneself with the critiques, the alternatives. In my journey as a student and academic, I have been fascinated by and attracted to diverse traditions of critique in social sciences, in general, and psychology, in particular. This book is a milestone in this journey. It is a coming together of my dissatisfaction, my 'not knowing', my enthusiastic explorations of perspectives beyond the mainstream psychology and just sheer love and devotion that I have for academic psychology. Writing this book allowed me to discover new horizons for psychology and forge new alliances with other social sciences and humanities for myself and, hopefully, for the readers too. I am really grateful to all that/ those which/who made it possible.

xiv Acknowledgements

Over the past decade or so, I have been very lucky to engage with bright, enthusiastic and ambitious students whose questions egged me on to think, reflect, and articulate clearly and deeply each day. Their ideas, queries and writings prodded me to engage with the discipline creatively and critically. It is with them in my mind that I decided to put pen to paper (or, literally, fingers on the keyboard). I owe this book to them for keeping me motivated to push the bar, to go beyond the prescribed curriculum, to show them the diversity and incoherence of psychology and human experience. I have tried to replicate the dialogical process of the mutual teaching-learning process in the book too by posing questions throughout the text.

While writing this book, I kept alive in me a host of live models and authors/ thinkers whom I encountered in what I read. Their voices shaped this book via me. My teachers have been the live models who have played a formative role in this. My most and deepest gratitude is to the triumvirate of Professor Rachana Johri (former Professor of Psychology and Dean of School of Undergraduate Studies, Ambedkar University of Delhi), Professor Honey Oberoi Vahali (Professor of Psychology, Ambedkar University of Delhi), and Professor Ashok Nagpal (former Professor of Psychology and Dean of School of Human Studies). I was ushered into rethinking psychology by many other teacher figures: Professor Girishwar Mishra (former Head of Department of Psychology, Delhi University and Vice Chancellor, MGAHV, Wardha), Professor Anand Prakash (former Senior Professor of Psychology at Delhi University), Dr Bimol Akoijam (Associate Professor, Centre for the Study of Social Systems, JNU) and Professor Suneet Varma (Professor of Psychology at Delhi University). Their diverse standpoints in relation to the theory and practice of psychology have been hugely influential.

Then, there are many perspectives and thinkers who have been luminous presences and enabling teachers for me: Erik H. Erikson's psychosocial thinking, Winnicott's emphasis on the coterminous nature of inner and outer reality, Derrida's deconstruction, Foucault's historical critiques and the relation between power and knowledge, Laing's existential phenomenology, the work of Wendy Hollway and Stephen Frosh in psychosocial studies, Ashis Nandy's political psychology, Sudhir Kakar's forays into cultural psychoanalysis, Anup Dhar's work at the intersection of critical theory and psychoanalysis, Judith Butler and queer theory, social constructionism, feminism, discourse analysis, and the like. I am grateful for such a body of thought being accessible to us through digital and print media. They populate and excite my mind constantly.

This deeply meaningful and fulfilling thought-feeling exercise would have not been possible if the world around me was not held reliably and lovingly by my family, colleagues and friends. I dedicate this piece to my late mother, whose loving memories encouraged me to work through my grief in a personally meaningful way and my son Saarthak, who is my source of joy and light. For my father and my sister, who provided the much-needed intellectual-emotional succour and containment throughout, there are no words to express my gratitude at my good fortune. I deeply appreciate my husband and my in-laws for providing me with the space, both mental and physical, required for a project like this which painstakingly comes to fruition. A heartful thank you to my friends Indu and Gunjan for believing in my capabilities.

I owe this book to my college from where I started my journey as a student and academic of psychology – Lady Shri Ram College for Women, University of Delhi. Its highly intellectually stimulating environment has been a deeply nourishing force for me.

I am deeply grateful to the publishers for giving me the opportunity to formulate and coalesce the ideas in the form of this book.

Finally, Mummy, Bade Papa, Amma, Naniji and God – thank you for keeping me in your grace!

15 August 2023

WHY DEBATE PSYCHOLOGY?

An Introduction

A book claiming to discuss the debates in psychology must take a questioning approach. So, the entire book is a series of questions about the discourse of mainstream psychology, its ideological foundations, the alternative discourses and their ideological assumptions, and what they are all trying to accomplish. Let us begin right away by asking searching questions about the nature of this book itself.

What Is This Book About?

A book, much like any other artefact, is open to interpretation of what it is about. Its readers constitute its meanings as much as the author. There is little claim that I can make, as an author, about the pristine originality of the idea behind the book, let alone of the questions, arguments and the deliberations that are encompassed in this text. Debates, critiques and deconstruction are standard academic practices, and a plethora of such work is available in psychology. What this book endeavours to do is to fill a gap – that I experienced as a student and teacher of psychology – of having a textbook that systematically presents under one title the critiques of mainstream psychology, as well as the other forms of psychology that address such critiques, and provides ways of doing psychology differently. It attempts to gather, analyse, reorganize and represent the salient strands of psychological thought that are available as a set of core issues defining psychology as an academic discipline and a practical field. The issues taken up in this book revolve around the pivotal concerns of psychology's scientific basis, its dominant quantitative research methodology, the construction of the 'individual' as the unit of analysis, the conceptualization of 'social', 'cultural', and 'gender' in relation to that, and the understanding of abnormality as it is shaped by the discourses of medical science, individualism and capitalism.

DOI: 10.4324/9781003471851-1

2 Why Debate Psychology? An Introduction

In the light of the above, this book is about mainstream psychology and the critical debates central to its epistemology and methodology. It raises critical questions about the dominant forms of psychological theorization and praxis because of their validity, social relevance and power privileges. It is about how the dominant ideologies of the time create the 'conditions of possibility' for specific forms of psychological images of mind, self and society to exist. It highlights the contested nature of what we call psychology. It reflects and interrupts the dominant theories of psychology given by academic and professional psychologists. It is equally about re-envisioning psychology along paths other than the mainstream. It aims to recover and restore at par the diverse moments and contexts of emergence and application of psychology. It intends to find different linguistic resources and social practices that will create 'conditions of possibility' for practising psychology differently.

The watchwords that form the spirit of this book are 'deconstruction', 'critique', 'fragmentation', 'hybridization', 'pluralism' and 'in-betweenness'. Readers of this text will find the arguments and discourses of this text are drawn from several frameworks: discourse analysis, social constructionism, critical psychology, post-structuralism, psychoanalysis and phenomenology. The first four are kindred approaches conjoined by the emphasis on discourse. Discourse is a notion that is used in various kinds of social sciences in such different contexts and meanings that a formulation of a clear and conclusive definition that would satisfy all its users seems to be an impossible task. For the purposes of this book, a general definition of discourse as 'a particular way of talking about and understanding the world (or an aspect of the world)' (Jørgensen & Phillips, 2002, p. 1) is used. What is common among all the kindred approaches on discourse is that our ways of talking do not neutrally reflect the world but rather play a role in creating and changing it. Since the spirit of the book is to push forward and to engage in a 'critique of critique', the limitation of the notion of discourse is also given sufficient attention. It is argued that discourse largely ignores the role of human subject in the process of the constitution of sense. From a psychological perspective, the concern with human agency and subjective processes in the constitution of sense cannot be ignored. This results in the 'in-between' stance of this book where frameworks, such as psychoanalysis and phenomenology, are drawn upon as much as the discourse-oriented frameworks to carve out the interstitial spaces for the truly psychosocial, psychocultural and psychohistorical forms of enquiry. The critiques discussed in the text are not just internal critiques emanating from within mainstream psychology; rather, they are critiques stemming from divergent frameworks external to the body of mainstream psychological knowledge. Critique is different from criticism. Critique opens up the possibility of rethinking and re-envisioning, which criticism does not allow.

What Are the Aims of the Book?

The overarching aim of the book is to turn a reflexive gaze on what mainstream psychology and psychologists do. This brings the ideological nature of scientific psychology to the fore, which it does not want to admit, due to its stance of scientific objectivity and political neutrality. This exposes the values and assumptions on which the mainstream discipline rests. Another related objective of the book is to critically interrogate scientific images of the mind, the individual, gender, society and culture that the mainstream psychology promotes. It asks the following questions: While operating as a scientific study of an individual, how does mainstream psychology engage with the vital concerns of the social nature of the human mind, the cultural constitution of behaviour and the gendered basis of subjectivity? Are behaviour and development, normal or abnormal, located within the overlapping realities of situation, history and culture? The next endeavour of the book is to tie the two aforementioned aims pivoted on deconstruction and critical enquiry of mainstream psychology to the third objective of re-forming psychology and not just reforming mainstream psychology. The book strives to present other traditions in psychology that are developing the discipline along the lines of diverse epistemologies and methodologies with different implications for the ways of understanding human subjectivity in context.

Why These Debates?

There is no dearth of debates in psychology. There are debates on free will versus determinism, nature versus nurture, the mind–body relationship, man versus machine, the relationship between psychology, religion and spirituality, and many more. The ones discussed in this book have been chosen because they have resulted in paradigmatic shifts in psychology. The debates on the nature of science, the methodological imperatives in psychology and individual–social/cultural dualism are central to the rethinking of psychology as a natural science. Since the 1960s, discontent has been expressed about the narrowness and artificiality of psychological research, the individualism inherent in its conceptualization of the subject matter and the irrelevance of an epistemology based on a particular conception of the natural sciences. This has led to the search for psychologies that are meaning-centred, constructionist, contextual (in terms of context of cognition, social structures, power dynamics, history), linguistically constituted, and reflective on their own ideological foundations. An attempt has been made in the book to represent these terse and complex definitional debates in a simple and precise manner for students to grasp the essentials. These debates are not only theoretical battles fought on the grounds of epistemology. They have profound implications for the practice of psychology in the real world as well. For example, when prejudice against minority groups or work stress is conceived in terms of an 'individual's' cognitive mechanism or psychological problem, we do not

4 Why Debate Psychology? An Introduction

critically engage with the social sources of these maladies. Our psycho-educational and therapeutic efforts are aimed at cognitive restructuring without questioning the histories of oppression and representation of the marginal groups and the exploitative potential of the competitive capitalist institutions of work. Similarly, when we conceive of gender not in terms of our hormones or traits but in terms of what we do by dressing up, talking, sitting and standing, cultivating preference of a kind of musical genre, and so on, it breaks the dichotomous understanding of two genders. It opens up the possibility of conceiving gender in multitudinous ways, according legitimacy to gender diversity and reducing pathologizing of the forms that deviate from hegemonic constructions of feminine femininity and masculine masculinity.

What Are the Critiques of Mainstream Psychology?

For many of us, the term 'mainstream psychology' may itself be startling. Does that mean that there is a 'psychology at the margins' as well? Yes! The discipline of psychology functions as a power structure privileging the notion of the stable and coherent individual as its subject matter and the use of an objectivist, empiricist–rational methodology to study that subject matter. This is the nucleus of mainstream psychology. Ways of understanding human subjectivity in ways not aligned with this nucleus are often ignored, silenced and excluded. The fiercest battle on defining the mainstream and the marginal psychology has been fought on the issue of methodology in psychology. The natural science methodological imperatives such as experimentation and quantification rule the roost in psychology. They marginalize and disempower all other forms of research enquiry. In 2009, a newsletter by the American Psychological Association (APA) reported that an overwhelmingly large number of previous presidents of its Division 5: Quantitative and Qualitative Methods have a strong grounding in quantitative psychology, with about 83% of the speciality ratings assigned to the measurement and statistics speciality. Qualitative psychology is grouped with quantitative psychology and is not considered worthy of a separate division. Fox, Prilleltensky and Austin (2009) describe mainstream psychology as:

> [T]he psychology that universities most often teach and that clinicians, researchers and consultants most often practice. It is the psychology that you most probably studied in your introductory course, presented as a science whose researchers use objective methods to understand human behavior and whose practitioners help individuals cope with distress. Building on their research findings, mainstream psychologists who recognize the societal sources of that distress sometimes propose institutional reforms to help people function more effectively. In short, most psychologists expect to do good.
>
> *(p. 3)*

In spite of their good intentions, mainstream psychologists are burdened with a myopic view of the subject matter, methodological considerations and an ethical mandate to promote human welfare.

Mainstream psychology is challenged on several grounds.

1. *Psychological and methodological individualism*: Individualism is an ideology 'where the individual is a discrete and isolated phenomenon whose actions, thoughts and feelings can be explained as a consequence of internal properties or essences, whose fundamental "nature" can be objectively known and empirically verified' (Nightingale & Cromby, 2001). Mainstream psychology is an anthropology of the isolated, abstract individual (Holzkamp, cited in Tolman, 1994, p. 40). It is ill at ease with the accounts of the individual provided by both sociology and biology. In the case of sociology, there is a movement downwards from social process to the individual. In the case of biology, there is a movement upwards from the level of physiological functions to psychological functions. Psychology attempts to produce models operating at exactly the right level of analysis – that of the individual who is separate from social/cultural surroundings and who is a repository of abstracted behavioural sequences and cognitive mechanisms. This ideology of psychological individualism is exemplified in the procedure of the quantitative method which forms the backbone of academic psychology. In reducing the phenomenon under study to discrete variables, studying people as subjects within controlled experimental settings or as respondents to preset questionnaires and interviews, questions about social structures and their effects are commonly excluded. Methodological individualism in psychology supports such context-stripping, reductionist research practices. In professional practice, the focus on the individual takes the attention away from structural oppression and interventions directed towards it. Clinical psychology 'individualizes' psychological distress and places the onus of change on the individual. It perpetuates the status quo: Why change the social structures when you can change the individual? Too many psychologists identify their tasks in overly narrow terms: helping clients on an individual basis or increasing scientific knowledge about traditionally framed topics using traditional research practices or supporting relatively minor reforms consistent with liberal-to-moderate political values. Individualism limits the potential of human and social change. For example, the liberal, humanist, individualist psychological discourse of 'identity' and 'self-esteem' looks well-meaning. This makes it seem that they reside within the individual, even though their sources are acknowledged to be social. The interventions are all directed towards the individual to help him/her become better at managing them. Thus, it precludes a critical investigation of the social–structural–cultural forces.

6 Why Debate Psychology? An Introduction

Individualism is also responsible for the problematic binaries within which psychological theories are developed. The binarism of psycho-social, psyche–culture, and inner–outer is pervasive in psychology. It sees the individual as separate from the outside, albeit, interacting with the outside. The reciprocal interaction between the mind/individual and the social/cultural retains dualistic thinking, treating the inner and outer as separate realms. Such binary assumptions have been critiqued by the more socially and culturally oriented frameworks in psychology.

2. *Modernist science*: Along with modernism rose the notion of science, linear progress and grand narratives. Psychology has been in the grip of scientism, exaggerated trust in the efficacy of natural science methods applied in all areas of investigation. The natural science model brings assumptions of determinism, empiricism, mechanism, reductionism and essentialism to psychology. It believes in the power of science and technology to move human society and knowledge towards progress. Quite often, the history of psychology is written to present a linear picture of cumulative progress and achievements in mapping the true reality of human nature. 'Conditioning explanations' within behaviourism, the 'Oedipal conflict' within psychoanalysis, the 'information processing mctaphor' within cognitivc psychology, the 'intelligence quotient' and the 'Big Five factors of personality' within individual differences are all examples of grand narratives which are totalizing schemas that order and explain experience. These grand narratives are criticized because they are dominant discourses that exclude other understandings and do not allow for a multiplicity of truths.

3. *Claim to scientific objectivity and political neutrality*: Mainstream psychologists conform to professional norms portraying psychology as an objective science, neutral in values and politics. When compared to other social scientific disciplines, such as anthropology, sociology and history, psychology is especially resistant to acknowledge that personal, professional and political values affect its theoretical reflections, methodological choices and policy recommendations. The discipline is not open to reflexivity, a conscious exploration of how one's values and assumptions affect one's theoretical and methodological goals, activities and interpretations (Fox et al., 2009). Psychology has operated to strengthen certain structures of power and reinforce widely-held stereotypes. For example, evolutionary psychology reinforces the supposed ideas of essential differences between women and men. Psychoanalytic psychology considers homosexuality as a deviant form of human sexuality. Its theories of individual personality, psychological health and happiness create forms of surveillance and self-regulation in everyday life. Professional, academic and popular psychologies tell people about themselves what they have already been taught to be true. While intervention research is the buzzword in psychology, is it really a sign of psychology becoming socially relevant? Do interventions that are

undertaken because they are manageable and fundable within profession-ally convenient time frames hinder more significant possibilities? Does failing to pursue more fundamental solutions discourage work towards more transformative change and promote the status quo?

4. *Methodolatry*: Psychology also suffers from 'method fetishism'. It privi-leges method above all other research considerations (Chamberlain, 2000). Rigid adherence to method functions as the justification for the research claims being made. Such methodolatry leads psychologists to be (among other things) preoccupied with the 'correct' or 'proper methods' and avoid the theoretical, and, in particular, the critical, implications of the research we do. Methodolatry dominates scientific mainstream psychology where positivist methodological assumptions maintain prominence.

5. *Ethnocentrism*: This is the strong tendency to use the standards of one's own group when viewing other groups, that is, to consider one's own group as superior to others. Ethnocentrism enters psychological research at the level of the choice of instruments and interpretations of the findings. Instruments designed in one culture, usually the Western context, are used in other cultures, even though they may not have equivalent meanings in other cultural settings and/or may be irrelevant to understanding the meanings of that culture's processes. Accordingly, the interpretation of data may also suffer from an unreflective imposition of one's own cultural understandings onto the other culture's experience. The choice of research topics based on the priorities of the Western world and the theoretical ideas of behaviour embedded in their ethnocentric notions of psychic functioning also reveals the imperialist nature of psychology.

6. *Androcentrism*: While psychology as a science claims to be 'neutral', 'objec-tive' and 'value-free', it is actually value-laden, taking men as the standard against which women are (mis)measured (Tavris, 1992). Although Erikson himself acknowledged that, for women, the stage of intimacy precedes that of identity, his psychosocial theory outlining the invariant stages of human development presents the identity formation stage as a stage prior to inti-macy. Thus, male development is considered to be the universal model of development, and female development is seen as a 'deviation' from the norm, tacked on as an addendum. Psychology suffers from pervasive sexism. The contribution of women psychologists is often rendered invisible. Stevens and Gardner (1982) state:

The histories written by psychology's academicians are neither accurate nor complete, neglecting as they do the most important contributions made by women ... They do not include Mary Calkin's theory of self nor her method of paired associates, they do not mention Christine Ladd-Fraklin's developmental theory of colour vision ... additionally they fail to mention the monumentally important books of Margaret Washburn on animal behavior ... and they totally ignore Magda Arnold's comprehensive theory of emotions and Margaret's

8 Why Debate Psychology? An Introduction

Harlow's contribution to an understanding of the importance of tactile stimulation in mothering.

(p. 100)

The heterosexist bias is also pervasive in psychology. It discriminates against people who display non-heterosexual behaviours and identities.

How to Re-Form Psychology?

A question that naturally forms in the mind after learning about the critique of mainstream psychology is, 'What are the alternatives, then?' The agenda of conceptualizing alternatives to mainstream psychology is in some way a limiting one because it sees other forms of psychology as 'other', 'relative' to mainstream psychology, thereby not displacing it as the standard against which divergences have to be comprehended. The agenda of this book is more aspirational. It is to reconceptualize 'the' scientific, mainstream psychology as just one form of psychological discourse shaped by specific historical and sociocultural forces, resting on particular ideological foundations and serving certain kinds of economic and political ends. This is a radical critical move because it relativizes and contextualizes mainstream psychology and strips it of its unquestioned power to define knowledge. This deconstruction pulls apart the meanings and assumptions which are fused together to form the ways we know ourselves, so as to let us see ourselves as historically specific products, rather than timeless, incontrovertible given facts. Once this form of relativizing is accomplished, the plural nature of psychology becomes apparent. The plurality of psychology is a resource rather than a liability, the way it is often made to feel. The recognition of the polymorphous nature of psychology allows the proliferation of and respect for the divergent psychologies whose genealogies have been marginalized or excluded from the powerful dominant discourse of mainstream psychology. These psychologies rest on radically different epistemologies than the one on which mainstream psychology rests, developing quite different forms of psychological knowledge. The impulse to re-envision psychology requires the following analytic moves that are discussed in the book:

1. Deconstructing the histories and value assumptions of dominant conceptualizations of mainstream psychological discourse, thereby positioning them as a particular narrative of psychological knowledge.
2. Highlighting a few of the different ways of doing psychology stemming from different ideological presuppositions. Such an analysis is more radically critical because it doesn't exhaust the critique by reducing the vital concern of epistemological diversity to just 'methodological flaws' of scientific psychology, such as poorly representative samples, faulty measurement techniques, misinterpretation of statistical findings and so on, which can be eliminated if psychologists adhere more rigorously to empiricist methods and norms for scientific research. Such a reductionist critique does not challenge the

ideological foundations of evolution, individualism, androsexism, heterosexism, ethnocentrism and logical empiricism on which the discourse of mainstream psychology is founded. It merely reforms the existing. What is being sought is more challenging – a re-formation of psychology. The process of re-forming psychology involves an interminable continuum of critiques – psychoanalytic/phenomenological critique of mainstream psychology, critical/cultural/feminist critique of psychoanalytic, critical critique of cultural and so on. It is not a finished project.

Catalytic dialogues since the 1960s in the social sciences and humanities have made it possible to recognize 'positivist science' and 'mainstream psychology' as situated narratives and practices constructed through social interactions by groups of people who organize themselves as the 'scientists' and 'psychologists', as well as by the lay persons. Seen in this way, scientific psychology becomes a discursive construction that shapes our perceptions of the world and organizes the way we behave towards objects in the world. For example, it makes us believe the following:

- Our behaviour is caused by something called 'traits' that reside within us.
- Psychological tests measure intelligence like a thermometer assesses temperature.
- Men are different from women.
- Members of a religious community will perceive members of other religious community as all the same ('All Hindus are the same') but different from themselves ('Hindus are different from us').
- Schizophrenia is a mental disorder, and it can be treated with antipsychotic medication that will fix the dysfunctional neurochemistry.

The discourse of mainstream psychology gives social, cultural and political power to psychologists to speak the 'truth' and to be believed. Psychologists are believed when they speak of how to understand children's emotional states, the strategies to increase job satisfaction among employees, the treatment for depression, the reasons for an increase in juvenile crime, and the like. The constructionist notion of psychology sees it as a cultural and gendered construction. Scientific psychology is largely a by-product of the Western cultural tradition at a particular time in its historical development. Its suppositions about the nature of knowledge, the character of objectivity, the place of values in the knowledge-generating process and the nature of linguistic representation carry the stamp of a unique cultural tradition. In fact, the suppositions about the nature of human psychology exist *a priori* and inform the character of scientific psychology (Gergen, 1994). This means that psychology as a science is based on certain assumptions concerning the psychological functioning of the individual scientist, such as that the scientist possesses a conscious or observing mind, a capacity for inductive and deductive logic, and so on. Without these assumptions, the science, as we know it, would fail to be intelligible. In this light, the 'universal' scientific psychology is really a Western ethnopsychology.

10 Why Debate Psychology? An Introduction

In what follows is a critical impulse to give fuller expression to specific cultural standpoints reflecting disparate cultural backgrounds and histories. In the same vein, science and psychology are gendered enterprises. Mainstream psychology is referred to as the 'malestream' psychology, as its epistemologies, research foci and methods have been shaped by androcentric assumptions. From the kinds of research questions it asks, to the research design and choice of methods, to the way data are analysed and conclusions are drawn – the knowledge-generating process in psychology is loaded with male-centric ideas. Much like in the case of the cultural construction of 'science' and 'psychology', the suppositions about gender roles and characteristics exist *a priori* and inform the nature of scientific psychology. This means that psychology as a science is based on certain gender-based understandings with which individual scientists and institutions of science and psychology operate. It is in this way that psychological knowledge ends up replicating, supporting and perpetuating the sexist, androcentric and heterosexist notions prevalent in society. Thus follows a need to liberate the range of femininities and masculinities and the range of sexualities to speak for themselves and for the psychological enterprise to develop the capacity to map the gender and sexuality continuum.

What Does a Re-Formed Psychology Look Like?

Perhaps there will not be any singular, coherent, organized form of such a re-formed psychology. It is not a model that will replace the 'old' psychology. Rather, it refers to the diverse practices of engagement with scientific/mainstream psychology through which the dualistic frameworks of individual–social, psyche–culture, nature–nurture, science–common sense in which psychology is caught are transformed. Rather than assuming the pre-given category of the individual (which is rapidly reduced to biological) and using scientific-sounding words, such as 'socialization' and 'interaction', to theorize the relationship between the individual and the social, a radical reconceptualization is done in such a way that implicit dualism is dissolved. The biological individual is not taken as an *a priori* given, on which the social/cultural has later effects. The logic of cause and effect, which ties in with the dualistic thinking, also disappears. In its place, human subjectivity is rethought of as constituted by historically and socially available meanings and practices (not asocial/acultural), plural (and not unitary), dynamic and conflictual (and not stable and coherent) and relational (and not self-contained).

Both scientific psychological perspectives and commonsensical perspectives informing ideas of child development, human potential, suffering, gender roles, sexual behaviour, and so on are seen as possible resources on which people can draw their own understandings and practices for self-regulation. Both individual and social change occur due to the human ability to exploit the spaces of contradiction and incoherence in social discourses to develop diverse responses challenging the status quo. Human desires, anxieties and life historical experiences guide people's choices and discrimination in relation to available discourses. Humans are ineluctably psychosocial as suggested by Hollway and Jefferson (2005):

> We are psychosocial because we are products of a unique biography of anxiety- and desire-provoking life events and the manner in which their meanings have been unconsciously transformed in internal reality. We are psychosocial because such defensive activities affect and are affected by discourses and also because the unconscious defences that we describe are intersubjective processes (that is, they affect and are affected by others). We are psychosocial because the real events in the external, social world are desirously and defensively, as well as discursively, appropriated.
>
> *(p. 149)*

The agency–structure dichotomy also loses its relevance in such a reformulated understanding of human subjectivity. Such accounts of human subjectivities necessitate the use of research methodologies that are process-oriented, context-sensitive, idiographic, experiential as well as oriented to capture the discursive/conversational aspects.

Should the Theories and Practices of 'Old Psychology' Be Abandoned?

It is important to be mindful that different theories and practices function as critical interventions in different geographical contexts and historical moments. Behaviourism, heavily critiqued now, actually popularized the claim that 'all men are born equal' and it is the life experiences which account for differences among them. This claim was progressive at the time in which it emerged. Similarly, a psychological test that can stigmatize a 'failing' student can help rescue a student from a 'special' school. Humanism can be faulted for its individualism but its phenomenological emphasis can be used to contradict experimental findings. Thus, the primary idea is not to supplant the 'old' paradigm but to engage with it critically. The endeavour is to examine systematically and reflexively how dominant accounts of psychology operate ideologically and in the service of power, to draw upon a variety of different theories to disrupt the stories told by academics and professional psychologies, and to create new stories of social change. No one perspective, whether mainstream or critical psychology, can lay claim to the truth. Rather than asking the question, 'Which one is more valid?' (which presumes a fixed conception of truth and reality), it is more appropriate to ask, 'What is it valid for?', which focuses the attention on the political ends and goals of the discourse.

12 Why Debate Psychology? An Introduction

How Is the Book Organized?

The book is composed of seven chapters. Chapter 1 engages with the most fundamental definitional issue for psychology: its scientific nature. It is pivoted on two central questions: what is science?, and, what kind of science is psychology? On the first issue, the notion of science as a singular entity is subverted. The chapter revisits the notion of two models of science as given by Dilthey (1883): the natural science model and the human science model. The characteristics of the natural/positivist science model are explained. The claim of positivist science to be objective is critically examined. The chapter investigates whether there is any 'objective', 'true' reality which has to be discovered and whether science can be free of moral, political and social values. Drawing on the works of philosophers and historians of science, such as Karl Popper, Thomas Kuhn and Paul Feyeraband, the notion of the linear progress of science is reviewed. The spirit of 'epistemological anarchism' (Feyerabend, 1975) is what this book seeks to champion. On the second question, the plural forms of thinking about psychology as a science, through its history, are recovered and presented. A case is made for how psychology has always engaged with both forms of science even though it has been in the grip of the natural/ positivist science. The chapter ends with an examination of whether experimental psychology stands to gain or lose.

Chapter 2 continues with the main concern that the text has to unravel the epistemological suppositions underlying psychological knowledge. The debate on the scientific nature of psychology inevitably leads one to the issue of research methodology in psychology. The parameters of the issue of the qualitative research versus the quantitative research methodology are broadened to implicate not only the type of data and analysis but also the notions of ontology and epistemology. The debate is embedded in the paradigmatic assumptions about reality, knowledge and the means of acquiring knowledge. The chapter begins with a discussion on positivism and its variants, such as logical positivism and post-positivism, which constitute the philosophical rationale underlying natural science, and support quantification. The heterogeneous nature of the philosophical underpinnings underlying qualitative research is detailed, which includes discussions on the premises of interpretivism, critical social sciences and postmodernism. The key characteristics of quantitative and qualitative research are highlighted. The diverse methods and standpoints of qualitative research are outlined, foregrounding the distinction between small q and Big Q methodologies (Kidder & Fine, 1987). The possibility of and the barriers to combining qualitative and quantitative research paradigms are deliberated upon.

One of the most significant concerns in psychology has been the relationship between the individual and the context. Since psychology is the study of the individual in his/her context, there are a variety of contextual approaches in the discipline, such as social psychology, cultural psychology, environmental psychology, ecological psychology, and so on. In Chapter 3, the interface between the individual and the context is reviewed, with a focus on how it is conceptualized within the purview of social psychology. The singular nature of social psychology as popularly understood by students of psychology is deconstructed. In the course of tracing the history of psychological social psychology (PSP), its ideological foundations of individualism, positivism and quantification are revealed. Its relationship with common sense and its dualistic, interactionist conceptualization of the individual and the social, in which the 'social' is positioned as external to the unitary individual, is dwelt upon. Such assumptions led to a paradigmatic crisis in psychological/experimental social psychology that gained momentum in the late 1960s and 1970s. The crisis highlighted the epistemological and methodological problems of this form of social psychology, as well as its lack of social relevance in solving societal problems. The various alternative forms of social psychology enlarge the notion of the social and reorient social psychology to societal concerns. In spite of the differences between these alternatives, they share in common the premise that the individual thought process and social reality are mutually constitutive. Given the striking differences in the epistemological and methodological imperatives of psychological/experimental social psychology and other more socially oriented forms of social psychology, the two most widely-studied topics – attitudes and social categorization – are analysed through different lenses. While the mainstream social psychological theorization sees attitude and social categorization as cognitive mechanisms residing within the individual, the social representation and the discursive psychological frameworks move away from the individualized accounts of attitudes and stresses on the social origins and ideological consequences of representations/discourse.

Continuing the exploration of the relationship between the individual and the context, Chapter 4 discusses this within the purview of culture and psyche. It begins with an untangling of the various conceptual confusions about the concept of culture: Is culture in the mind or is it in the public realm? Can nation be understood as equivalent to culture? How is a cultural explanation different from a social explanation? The focus of the chapter is to understand the role of culture within the different academic streams of psychology, such as the mainstream psychology, cross-cultural psychology, cultural psychology and Indigenous psychology. Beginning with mainstream psychology as a culture-blind and a culture-bound discipline, the chapter goes on to trace the rise of the concept of culture in cross-cultural psychology and social psychology. Through a detailed analysis of the goals, assumptions and frameworks of cross-cultural psychology, the conceptualization of culture and its relationship with psyche within this paradigm are highlighted. By underlining the methodological and conceptual challenges of this paradigm, its adherence to the principle of universality and its inability to change the architectonics of modern psychology are brought to light. Moving to the paradigm of cultural psychology takes us to a more differentiated understanding of culture in which it is not a static, independent variable. Cultural psychology sees mind as ineluctably cultural and culture as

14 Why Debate Psychology? An Introduction

decisively psychological. This works to seek out the psychological foundations of culture and the cultural foundations of mind. Much like the alternative approaches of social psychology, the cultural psychological approach too rejects the dualism of person and context, seeing both as interpenetrating and constitutive of each other. Indigenous psychology is hailed as a revolutionary force decolonizing psychology from its Western imprints and having the potential to unleash a range of dissonant, even dissident, cultural voices.

The aim of Chapter 5 is to understand how gender is understood in psychology. The opening section lays out the foundation with regard to the terminology – sex, gender and sexuality – as it is commonly understood and then this conceptual structure is challenged in the light of later queer and feminist thought. Psychology's adherence to an individualistic, essentialist and dualistic thinking on gender is highlighted throughout the chapter. The sex difference paradigm has attracted special attention as an exemplar of how gender operates in psychology in a highly reductionist, variable-based way rather than as an analytic concept. Psychology lacks research on how gender structures social organization and processes, creating status and power differentials. Freudian psychoanalysis has also been a very influential perspective in shaping the notions of sexual difference. The chapter presents an analysis of the foundational premises of the Freudian theory on gender and desire and its feminist critiques.

The critical thrust of Chapter 6 is to analyse the historical events which led to the rise to power of biopsychiatry and to turn a reflective gaze on the practice of the medical model. In this chapter, the practice of psychiatric classification and diagnosis is reviewed. Symptom-based language, a proliferation of mental disorders, a strict dichotomy between normal and abnormal, and reliability and validity issues are highlighted. Psychiatric diagnosis, the much-exalted practice of psychiatry, loses the personal meaning of illness, the personal and social contexts of the patient, and the mutual collaboration and relationship between the patient and the therapist. Alternative clinical practices such as psychological formulation and illness narratives have been put forward as more egalitarian and transformative mechanisms of therapeutic change. A challenge to the medicalization of madness comes from the direction of social and cultural sources of abnormality. Research is increasingly showing evidence of culture's significance in the aetiology as well as in the manifestation, epidemiology and course of psychopathology. Critical questions are being raised about the feasibility of separating a disorder from the psychic structure that produces it and the social surroundings in which people respond to it. Another powerful challenge to the medical model examined in the chapter is the thesis that psychopathology is a form of social suffering which is both a cause and consequence of several interlinked social problems, such as victimization, poverty, trauma and social isolation.

Chapter 7 attempts to deconstruct the notion of 'child' and 'development' in psychology. The chapter examines why development psychology is so focused on the study of infant and/or the child. It highlights how biology and epistemology meet in the study of the infant. The nature of the developmental explanation or developmentalism is critically analysed. The influential role of the organismic and contextual model in shaping the dominant developmental thinking in psychology is highlighted. The two frameworks are contrasted on various conceptual dimensions. The position of mechanistic and organismic meta-theories on the important theoretical issues of development are analysed The evolution of thinking and research on the nature–nurture debate is examined. Even though development psychology has moved away from a purely naturist position, its conceptualization of context has not only been limited but also problematic. The chapter critiques the understanding of the environment/context from the cultural psychological and post-structuralist/critical psychological standpoints.

1
IS PSYCHOLOGY A SCIENCE?

The first lesson that we learn in psychology is its definition: psychology is a scientific study of human cognition, emotions, motivations and behaviours. The definitiveness of this definition sets the stage for us to understand psychology as a science. It profoundly affects the way the discipline is conceptualized, its goals and methods are set, research is conducted and criteria for worthwhile knowledge are decided. While psychological questions have been deliberated upon from time immemorial in philosophy, psychology as a distinct discipline emerged when it took on the cloak of science. From the formal beginnings of scientific psychology in the nineteenth century to the present day, psychology has striven to be empirical, studying phenomena that are observable and measurable, testing its scientific claims and predicting and controlling behaviour.

Psychological science affects varied facets of our lives. Psychology has scientific responses to various concerns: Why does a person suffer from a phobia? How can she/he be treated? How to bring up children to become intelligent? Are people selfish by nature? Is money the only motivator of work performance? People trust psychological knowledge as valid and reliable because it is based on scientific method. Psychological tests are trusted more than ordinary conversation as revealing the personality of the individual because they are scientific. Many of psychology's scientific concepts, such as schema, traits, superego, achievement orientation, reinforcement, intelligence quotient, schizophrenia and attachment styles have entered the common lexicon. They guide people's behaviours and understanding of the world around them.

What Is Science?

The word 'science' evokes the image of white lab coats, test tubes, chemical concoctions, specimen rats, microscopes, and so on. It brings to mind disciplines such

DOI: 10.4324/9781003471851-2

as physics, chemistry, biology, or zoology, and inventions and discoveries by people such as Newton, Galileo, or Einstein. Thus, the term has come to be synonymous with the study of the natural world. Etymologically, the word 'science' is derived from the Latin word *scientia* meaning knowledge. The word 'science' encapsulates various referents. It refers to an organized and systematic body of knowledge and a system for producing that knowledge. It combines assumptions about the nature of the world; the goals of knowledge; and a set of procedures and techniques and instruments for gaining knowledge.

Science, as a way of producing knowledge, is a human invention and emerged from a major shift in thinking that began with the Age of Reason or the Age of Enlightenment in Western European history, which occurred between the 1600s and the early 1800s. The Enlightenment stood for an emphasis on experiences in the material world, a belief in human progress, a faith in logical reasoning and a questioning of traditional religious authority. Before science, people used other pre-scientific or non-scientific methods to understand the world, such as tradition ('this is what has been done for centuries'), authority ('the church/the king tells us this'), common sense ('everyone believes this') and personal experience ('in my house, I saw this'). These methods are still used but they are secondary to science and are treated with suspicion.

The first form of science to develop was natural science: astronomy and physics. With regard to the study of people and their socio-cultural-historical context, two approaches existed. Wilhelm Dilthey (1883) makes a distinction between *Naturwissenschaften* (the natural science model) and *Geisteswissenschaften* (the human science model) (see Table 1.1 for more details). The natural science model draws on a positivist philosophy of science, emphasizing a causal deterministic perspective favouring a quantitative analysis. The human science model draws on interpretivist philosophy, which emphasizes the study of meaning and privileges qualitative analysis. Seeing human beings as a part of the natural world, psychology largely adopted the positivist, natural science model, although the interpretivist framework never completely disappeared.

TABLE 1.1 Human science and natural science

Human science	Natural science
Interpretation	Explanation
Hermeneutics	Deterministic
Reasons	Causes
Telos, purpose	Efficient cause
Rule-governed	Empirical laws
Historical context	Material context
Internal factors	External factors
Action	Behaviour

Source: Hiles (2001).

18 Is Psychology a Science?

The Natural Science Model

The 'organized and systematic knowledge' that natural science produces is the scientific knowledge which is a generalized body of laws and theories to explain a phenomenon or behaviour of interest. Examples include heliocentrism by Copernicus, the theory of relativity by Einstein, or the cell theory by Matthias Schleiden, Theodor Schwann and Rudolf Virchow. Laws are observed patterns of phenomena or behaviours, while theories are systematic explanations of the phenomenon or behaviour. The 'system for producing the scientific knowledge' is called the scientific method. The scientific method refers to the standardized set of steps for building scientific knowledge, such as how to make valid observations, how to interpret results, and how to generalize those results. The scientific method allows researchers to independently and impartially test pre-existing theories and prior findings, and subject them to open debate, modifications or enhancements. René Descartes established the framework of the scientific method in 1619, and his first step is seen as a guiding principle for many in the field of science today:

> [N]ever to accept anything for true which I did not clearly know to be such; that is to say, to carefully avoid precipitancy and prejudice, and to compromise nothing more in my judgment than what was presented to my mind so clearly and distinctly as to exclude all ground of methodic doubt.
> *(Descartes, 2013, p. 120)*

Evident in the quote above is the emphasis on scepticism as an important element of scientific method. Both theory-building (inductive research) and theory-testing (deductive research) are crucial for the advancement of science. Inductive (theory-building) research is more valuable when there are few prior theories or explanations, while deductive (theory-testing) research is more productive when there are many competing theories of the same phenomenon and researchers are interested in knowing which theory works best and under what circumstances. Inductive and deductive researches are two halves of the research cycle that constantly iterates between theory and observations (Figure 1.1). In science, theories and observations are interrelated and cannot exist without each other. Theories provide meaning and significance to what we observe, and observations help validate or refine an existing theory or construct a new theory.

PAUSE AND THINK

To check whether your thinking is scientific, think of something you follow/believe in, such as a healthy food item. Reflect on the reasons for believing in it. Is your belief/attitude supported by empirical data? Or is common sense, tradition or authority shaping what you believe in?

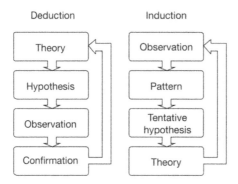

FIGURE 1.1 Research cycle: deduction and induction

Psychology's Assumptions about the Nature of Reality in Positivist Science

Positivism, a philosophy of science, and its derivatives, such as logical positivism and post- positivism, have shaped the assumptions and goals of scientific knowledge in psychology. There are two fundamental assumptions about the nature of reality that positivist science makes. One is determinism: the assumption that all events in the universe, including behaviour, are lawful or orderly. To say behaviour is lawful is to say that behaviour is a function of antecedent events. More loosely, one can say that there is a cause–effect relationship between the past and the present, a continuity between before and after. The second assumption is that this lawfulness is discoverable. Note that the first assumption does not necessarily imply the second assumption. In other words, one can assume that behaviour is lawful without presuming that we will discover this lawfulness.

Goals of Scientific Knowledge

Following are some of the goals of positivist scientific knowledge:

1. Description
2. Explanation
3. Prediction
4. Control.

Let us first look at description. The first step in science is to know 'what' we are studying, that is, to describe. For example, Isaac Newton defined his scientific enterprise as remaining as close as possible to the observable facts of the domain of study (in this case, it was the physics of motion), recording observed regularities in nature and codifying them in the form of laws (he proposed three laws of motion and a law of gravity). His law of gravity states, 'Between any

20 Is Psychology a Science?

two bodies there is a mutually attracting force whose strength is inversely proportional to the square of the distance between them.' This describes the movement of the bodies in the solar system by postulating a force called gravity. For him, description was sufficient to predict the motions of the celestial bodies. He was not bothered about the explanation of his law of gravity, or why it worked (Leahey, 2013). For Newton and the other positivists (led by Auguste Comte) who followed his form of science, description, prediction and control were the only three functions assigned to science. Description, ideally summarized as laws, gave rise to the second function – prediction. Newton's laws help in the prediction of future events, such as eclipses and the return of comets. Prediction from laws made control possible. For example, using Newton's laws, engineers could calculate the thrust required to send satellites into precise orbits around the Earth. Positivism, a philosophy of science developed by Auguste Comte, saw explanation as futile indulgence in metaphysical and theoretical speculation. Science worked according to the positivists by eschewing hypotheses and explanations and sticking to facts.

Dissatisfied with this approach, the contemporary era of philosophical understanding of explanation began with the seminal paper, 'Studies in the Logic of Explanation' in 1948 by two logical positivists, Carl Hempel and Paul Oppenheim. Explanation is a logical argument that tells us why something takes a specific form or occurs. A good explanation depends on a well-developed theory and is confirmed by empirical observation. Explanation is often confused with prediction. Prediction is a statement that something will occur. Explanation implies a logical connection of what occurs in a specific situation to a more abstract or basic principle about 'how things work'. It is easier to predict than to explain, but people are enchanted by the dramatic visibility of the prediction. An explanation has more logical power than prediction because good explanations also predict. By explaining or answering the question 'why?', the researcher shows that one particular situation is a case or instance of the more general principle (Neuman, 2006).

There are several approaches of scientific explanation: the nomological approach, the causal approach, and the pragmatic approach. The causal approach is the best known and most widely used. It argues that the goal of science is to probe deeper into the nature of reality and tell us not merely how nature works as it does but why it works as it does. Philosophers have long debated the idea of cause. Some people argue that causality exists in the empirical world, but it cannot be proved as it lies beyond the reach of observation. Researchers can only try to find evidence for it. We cannot directly verify our hunches about real causes. Others argue that causality is only a mental construction, a way of thinking about the world. It is not something real in the world. Irrespective of this philosophical debate, the idea of causal explanation is psychologically compelling and many researchers pursue causal relationships. Three conditions have to be met to establish causality: (1) temporal order; (2) association; and (3) elimination of plausible alternatives (Neuman, 2006). In themselves, each is a necessary but not sufficient condition to establish causality. The *temporal order* condition means that a cause must come before an effect. *Association* implies the co-occurrence of two events, characteristics or factors, such that when one happens/is present, the other one is likely to happen/be present as well. An association does not have to be perfect (i.e., every time one variable is present, the other also is). *Eliminating alternatives* means that a researcher interested in causality needs to show that the effect is due to the causal variable and not due to something else. Eliminating alternatives is an ideal because eliminating all possible alternatives is impossible. Experimental designs provide a strong way of insulating the experimental variable(s) from the influence of other major variables by controlling them. A simple causal explanation is X causes Y, Y occurs because of X. There can be a more complex causal explanation such as A causes B, B causes C, C causes D, and so on. An example of this can be a causal theory: A rise in unemployment causes an increase in depression. Here, depression is explained in terms of its cause, unemployment. A complete explanation also requires elaborating the causal mechanism. The causal mechanism/theory suggests that when people lose their job (A), they feel a loss of self-worth (B). This leads to feelings of sadness and anhedonia (C). This example illustrates a chain of causes and a causal mechanism. Researchers can also test different parts of the chain. They might test whether unemployment rates and depression occur together, or whether low self-worth leads to feelings of sadness and loss of pleasure. They can also test to rule out an alternative causal factor such as the effect of the possibility of seeking redressal from employers or the state on aggression. Causality can be stated in many ways: X leads to Y, X produces Y, X influences Y, X is related to Y, the greater the X, higher the Y.

Characteristics of Positivist Science

Positivist science is believed to have certain qualities that grant it its privileged position:

- *Objectivity*: Scientific objectivity is a characteristic of scientific claims, methods and results. Objectivity has two interrelated meanings. First, its products – theories, laws, experimental results and observations – constitute accurate representations of the external world. Second, they are not tainted by personal interests, value commitments and perspectives. The philosophical rationale underlying this conception of objectivity is the view that there are facts 'out there' in the world and that it is the task of a scientist to discover, analyse and systematize them.
- *Empiricism*: Francis Bacon is called the father of modern empiricism. This is the belief that sensory experience is the basis of all scientific knowledge. According to this definition, unobservable entities, such as self-concept, free will and atoms, are non-sense and scientifically useless. An expanded understanding of empiricism allows for unobservable entities to be scientifically useful as long as they can be observed and measured directly/

22 Is Psychology a Science?

indirectly. For example, no one has seen a subatomic particle, but scientists have seen and measured a trace it leaves on a photographic plate. Similarly, in psychology, the construct of learning is never observed directly, but is measured in terms of its effects on some aspect of behaviour. To say that an event must have an empirical referent implies that the event is a public one, not a private one. It also implies that the observations are objective and not subjective. Empiricism emphasizes the importance of induction over deduction and causes of behaviour, which are automatic and mechanical, rather than reasons, which are freely chosen. D. N. Robinson (1986) defined it thus:

Empiricism ... is the epistemology that asserts that the evidence of sense constitutes the primary data of all knowledge; that knowledge cannot exist until this evidence has first been gathered; and that all subsequent intellectual processes must use this evidence and only this evidence in framing valid propositions about the real world.

(p. 205)

- *Precision and control*: Science requires observations to be accurate, and, for that, the conditions under which they are made need to be clearly specified and controlled. How the observations will be made also has to be clearly defined. For example, in an experiment studying the relation between the nature of learning material presented and learning, it is important to specify and control all the relevant factors that can influence the relationship, such as varying subject characteristics (age, educational background) and task characteristics (task instructions, difficulty level of different kinds of learning material, manner of presentation of different learning material). It is also important to define which variations of learning material are presented and how learning will be assessed (time taken/trial taken/errors made). This is called operationally defining the constructs, that is, defining constructs in terms of how they will be empirically measured.
- *Replication and generalization*: Replication applies both to the conditions under which data are collected and to the results of scientific tests. Scientists are required to specify the procedures used by them in their research so that other researchers can repeat the study conditions and verify the results. Repeatable results are believed to be reliable and trustworthy. Generalization of results implies the extrapolation of findings beyond the particular situation constructed and the particular sample used in the study.
- *Verification/falsification of scientific theories*: It is important in science to distinguish between claims that are scientific from those that are unscientific. One view on this issue is to stress confirmability/verification of theories as the test of their scientific status. From theories with properly worked-out operational definitions, we can deduce predictions whose confirmation

lends credence to the theory. Good theories will add confirmation, poor ones will not. Falsification, as proposed by Karl Popper (1959), rejects this view as naïve. For Popper, the most important demarcation criterion separating science and pseudoscience was the falsification of scientific claims. According to this view, scientific rationality consists not in seeking to be proved right but in allowing for the possibility of being proved wrong. Popper claimed that if a theory is falsifiable, then it is scientific. Falsified claims are to be replaced by claims that can account for the phenomena that falsified the prior theory, that is, with greater explanatory power.

- *Parsimony*: This implies economy of explanation. Mach summarizes the principle of parsimony as 'complete presentment of the facts with the least possible expenditure of thought' (1960, p. 516). The criteria of parsimony include brevity, the nature and scope of the assumptions held, the role of unobservables and generality. Where two theories account for the same facts and we have no other reason to prefer one over the other, one should prefer the briefer. One should prefer the theory that has fewer assumptions and which is less dependent on its assumptions. The scientific accounts which make use of more observables and fewer unobservables should be used. If one set of principles can account for a multitude of facts, it should be preferred over two separate sets that explain each phenomenon separately.

The Scientific Method

Although science in its spirit is much more than the scientific method, the method has assumed the power to define what it is. The scientific method is the system of producing scientific knowledge. Its chief elements are discussed in brief here:

- *Hypotheses*: A hypothesis is a statement that proposes a relationship between specific factors or variables. The statement 'administration of penicillin cures pneumonia' is a hypothesis that specifies the relationship between two or more observations such as observations regarding the administration of penicillin and observations about the cure of pneumonia. Previous research, experience, chance observation or intuition suggest to the investigator that a logical relationship exists. The variables in the hypothesis are to be stated in precise and measurable terms. A hypothesis is integral to both inductive and deductive forms of science. In the case of the former, the hypothesis may be based on observed regularities in the phenomena of study. In the case of the latter, the hypothesis may be derived from a theory. In both cases, the hypothesis should contain a prediction about its verifiability. For example, if the hypothesis is true, then A should happen when B is manipulated.
- *Testing hypotheses and theories*: Testing hypotheses is at the core of the process of science. Any aspect of the natural world can be described and explained in many different ways. It is the job of science to collect all those plausible descriptions and explanations, convert them into testable and

24 Is Psychology a Science?

verifiable hypotheses, and use scientific testing to filter through them, retaining hypotheses that are supported by the evidence and discarding the others. Scientific testing occurs in two logical steps: (1) if the hypothesis is correct, what would we expect to see?; and (2) does that expectation match what we actually observe? Hypotheses are supported when actual observations (i.e., results of scientific testing) match the expected/hypothesized observations and are contradicted when they do not match. Experiments are one way to test some hypotheses. An experiment is a test that involves manipulating some factor in a system in order to see how that affects the outcome. Ideally, experiments also involve controlling as many other factors as possible in order to isolate the cause of the experimental results. Experiments can be quite simple tests set up in a lab, such as rolling a ball down different inclines to see how the angle affects the rolling time. But large-scale experiments can also be performed in the real world. Experiments are distinguished from other sorts of tests by their reliance on the intentional manipulation of some factors and, ideally, the control of others. For many ideas in science, testing via experiment is impossible, inappropriate or only a part of the picture. In these cases, testing is often a matter of making the right observations. For example, we cannot actually experiment on distant stars in order to test ideas about which nuclear reactions occur within them, but we can test those ideas by building sensors that allow us to observe what forms of radiation the stars emit.

- *Making unbiased observations*: Observations yield what scientists call data. Whether the observation is an experimental result, radiation measurements taken from an orbiting satellite or an infrared recording of a volcanic eruption, they are all data. Scientists analyse and interpret data in order to figure out how those data inform their hypotheses and theories. Do they support one hypothesis over others, help refute a hypothesis or suggest an entirely new explanation? Data become evidence only when they are interpreted in a way that reflects the accuracy or inaccuracy of a scientific hypothesis.

PAUSE AND THINK

List the various research methods in psychology. Think to what extent they meet the goals of science.

REVIEW QUESTIONS

1. What are the differences between scientific knowledge and knowledge based on authority/tradition/common sense?
2. Is explanation the same as prediction?
3. How is law different from theory?

How Objective Is Positivist Science?

The most valued characteristic of positivist science is objectivity. It is considered as ideal for scientific inquiry and is the basis of the authority of science in society. Objectivity, as defined earlier, expresses the idea that the claims, methods and results of science are not, and should not be, influenced by particular perspectives, vested interests and value commitments. The ideal of objectivity has been criticized repeatedly in the philosophy of science, questioning both its value and attainability. There are several problems with the notion of objectivity. Let us examine some such concerns.

- Is there an 'objective', 'real', 'true' reality that has to be discovered?

The natural science model believes so. Reality is real; it exists 'out there' and can be discovered unmediated by human minds and other distortions, such as values and beliefs. Science helps in doing that! Mulkay (1979) said:

> The basic, observational laws of science are considered to be true, primary and certain, because they were built into the fabric of the natural world. Discovering a law is like discovering America, in the sense that both are already waiting to be revealed.
>
> *(p. 2)*

The interpretive approach (this includes hermeneutics, phenomenology, constructionism) holds that social reality is not a given, but rather an accomplishment. It is intentionally constructed by the purposeful actions of interacting social beings. In other words, when you see an apple, there is no 'appleness' in it; rather, what you see as an apple arises from what people in a society define, accept and understand as an apple. What is taken as natural, objective and fixed reality, for example, 12 months in a year, is a social construction which came into being under specific historical circumstances.

- Can science provide the 'real', the 'true' account of the workings of the world?

Yes, says positivist science. Science becomes more faithful to the truth by adding true (experimentally verifiable) and eliminating false (experimentally discredited) facts from scientific theory. Many scientific realists maintain that science does aim to describe the real and true world in a way that is independent of any perspective. Nagel (1986) calls this the 'view from nowhere'. It represents the world as it is, unmediated by human minds and other 'distortions'. Scientists themselves are a divided house on this matter. According to Van Fraassen (1980), realists say that 'science aims to give us, in its theory, a literally true story of what the world is like; and the acceptance of theory

26 Is Psychology a Science?

involves the belief that it is true'. On the other hand, according to anti-realists, 'science aims to give us theories which are empirically adequate; and the acceptance of theory involves only the belief that it is empirically adequate'. The debate between realists and anti-realists continues and is far from settled. It is debatable whether scientific theories can be unequivocally seen as explaining the true world. They may just be useful tools or instruments by which human beings come to grips with nature.

- Are scientific claims and practices free of moral, political and social values?

While the natural science model claims so, several lines of reasoning have been advanced to rebut the claim that science is value-free. Values enter scientific process at any of the four stages: (1) the choice of a scientific research problem; (2) the gathering of evidence in relation to the problem; (3) the acceptance of a scientific hypothesis or theory as an adequate answer to the problem on the basis of the evidence; and (4) the proliferation and application of scientific research results (Weber, 1949).

It is almost universally accepted that the choice of a research problem is often influenced by the interests of individual scientists, funding parties and society as a whole. Similarly, the proliferation and the application of scientific research results are evidently affected by the personal values of journal editors and end users, and there seems to be little one can do about this.

Helen Longino (1996) problematizes the acceptance of values, such as predictive accuracy, scope, unification, explanatory power, simplicity and coherence in science, by stating that these traditional foundational values are not purely objective. Their use imports specific kinds of political and social values into contexts of scientific judgement. She juxtaposes such values with feminist values, such as novelty, ontological heterogeneity, mutuality of interaction, applicability to human needs and diffusion of power, and argues that the use of the traditional values instead of its alternative (e.g., simplicity instead of ontological heterogeneity) can lead to biases. Thus, not every scientist entertains the same list of values. The assessment of scientific theory is a process of judgement where values rather than the mechanical application of rules or algorithms determines which is the best theory.

Science, then, cannot be value-free because no scientist ever works exclusively in the supposedly value-free zone of assessing and accepting hypotheses. Evidence is gathered, and hypotheses are assessed and accepted in the light of their potential for application and fruitful research avenues. Different kinds of value judgements guide these choices and are themselves influenced by their results.

- Is verification/falsification of theories based upon empirical evidence (observations, measurements, tests, experiments)?

Our ability to use scientific claims (theories/hypotheses) to represent all and the only true facts about the world depends on whether these claims can unambiguously be established on the basis of evidence. However, the relation between evidence and scientific hypothesis is not straightforward. First, abstract theories are not tested against naïve observations. They are tested against experimental facts or phenomena which are established using intricate procedures of scientific measurement which themselves are value-laden. Thus, what constitutes evidence is itself not free from perspectives (facts = data + theory). Thomas Kuhn (1962), a historian and philosopher of science, opined that 'observations are theory-laden'. For example, the concepts 'mass' and 'length' have different meanings in Newtonian and relativistic mechanics, so does the concept of 'temperature' in thermo-dynamics and statistical mechanics. In his view, the meaning of observational concepts is influenced by theoretical assumptions and presuppositions. Second, no scientific hypothesis is ever confirmed beyond reasonable doubt – some probability of error always remains. When we accept or reject a hypothesis, there is always a chance that our decision is mistaken (erroneous acceptance/rejection of hypothesis). This corresponds to Type I and Type II errors in statistical inference. Thus, value judgement (the decision to choose a certain level of significance to test the hypothesis) enters scientific reasoning in the 'acceptance/rejection' of scientific theories. Third, crucial experiments do not refute a specific scientific claim, but these are only taken to indicate that there is an error in the entire network of hypotheses. Thus, existing bodies of evidence often underdetermine the choice of rival theoretical accounts.

It is believed that scientific progress is based on the addition of true beliefs and the elimination of false beliefs (based on scientific evidence) in our best scientific theories. By making these theories more and more verisimilar, that is, truth-like, scientific knowledge grows over time (e.g., Popper, 1963). This belief is countered by the thesis of 'incommensurability of different paradigms or scientific theories', problematized independently by Thomas S. Kuhn (1962) and Paul Feyerabend (1962). This argues against a linear and standpoint-independent picture of scientific progress. Literally, this concept means 'having no measure in common'. There are two central aspects of incommensurability. First, not only do the observational concepts in both theories differ but also the principles for specifying their meaning may be inconsistent with each other (as discussed in the example of mass and length above; see Feyerabend, 1975, pp. 269–270). Second, scientific research methods and standards of evaluation change with the theories or paradigms. Not all puzzles that could be tackled in the old paradigm will be solved by the new one – this is the phenomenon of 'Kuhn loss'. According to Feyerabend, the concept of objectivity may be applied meaningfully, only within a particular scientific worldview.

BOX 1.1 THE FEMINIST CRITIQUES OF SCIENCE

Modern science has come under critique from various actors, groups and movements – the anti-colonialists, the counter-culture, environmentalists, anti-militarists and feminists among others. For the feminists, the ways in which gender and science intersect is the site of debate. First, there is the question of who does science, who the leaders and innovators are and who the followers and workers are. The history of science has often made men into heroes while it has silenced, excluded or simply forgotten women. Science historian Margaret Rossiter used the term 'Matilda effect' (named after a forgotten eighteenth-century thinker, Matilda Joslyn Cage) to describe the systematic 'undercutting, undercounting and minimizing' of women in scientific arenas, using examples from antiquity to Nobel laureates such as Rosalind Franklin and Lise Meitner, and scientific encyclopaedias (Rossiter, 1993, p. 325). This had led to the hegemonic association of scientific objectivity and rationality with masculinity. Second, the low priority given to research on women's experience, issues and questions has come under review. Research on male samples and experiences are seen as applicable to all, including women, and, wherever there are deviations, women's subjectivities are tacked on as addenda rather than changing the architectonics of the theoretical edifice. Women's experience is also treated as inferior. Third, feminism conceptualizes the scientific construction of knowledge itself as gendered. It sees science as a heteropatriarchal enterprise mirroring much of the sexual division of labour and gender stereotypes in its knowledge creation. By revealing the sexist, androcentric and heterosexist biases at all stages of scientific research – from question formulation to conclusion – it overthrows the notion of science as value-neutral and objective. Rather, it exposes science as seeped in material and cultural values. Feminists' objections to value-free science have been manifold. The feminist empiricist theory holds that science is not autonomous in practice and is guided by contextual (social, cultural and political) values, on the basis of which the relevance of evidence is determined. The feminist standpoint theory sees knowledge as relative to cultural/social/political 'location', and knowledge as situated, thus posing a direct challenge to the objectivity of science.

Feminist critique has immensely benefitted science. Broadly speaking, it has broken up thought centred on dualisms: subject/object, reason/emotion, nature/culture, men/women, heterosexual/homosexual. It has also argued forcefully for the inclusion of subjective and emotional dimensions of life, both as factors impacting knowledge production and as objects of enquiry. It proposes subjective experience as located at the intersection of class, ethnicity, race, religion, gender and many such social realities. It has also supported the re-envisioning of newer forms of research methodologies.

REVIEW QUESTIONS

1. What does scientific objectivity entail?
2. The value and attainability of scientific objectivity are questionable. Discuss.

How Does Science Progress?

One of the central issues in science has been 'how scientific theories are tested, modified, abandoned and new theories are formed'. There is no consensus among the philosophers of science with regard to this. Three influential positions on this issue are reviewed here.

Karl Popper and Falsification

According to Popper (1959), the growth of human knowledge proceeds from our problems and our attempts to solve them. In order to do so, theories are formulated. If these theories are to explain anomalies which exist with respect to earlier theories, they must go beyond existing knowledge and take a leap of the imagination. For this reason, Popper places special emphasis on the role played by the independent creative imagination in the formulation of theory. The centrality and priority of 'problems' in Popper's account of science are paramount, and it is this which leads him to characterize scientists as 'problem solvers'. The scientist makes observations in the first instance in the context of grappling with a problem. These observations are selectively designed to test the extent to which a given theory functions as a satisfactory solution to a given problem.

In one of his most important books, *The Logic of Scientific Discovery*, Popper (1959) stated that scientific progress requires comparing the new theory with existing ones to determine whether it constitutes an advance upon them. If it does not constitute such an advance, it will not be adopted. If, on the other hand, its explanatory success matches that of the existing theories, and, additionally, it explains some inconsistent phenomenon, or solves some unsolvable problems, it will be considered to constitute an advance upon the existing theories, and will be adopted. Thus, science involves theoretical progress. However, Popper stresses that we ascertain whether one theory is better than another by deductively testing both theories, rather than by induction. For this reason, he argues that a theory is deemed to be better than another, if (while unfalsified) it has greater empirical content, and therefore greater predictive power than its rival.

The method of theory-testing is as follows: Certain singular propositions (hypotheses) are deduced from the new theory. These are predictions, and of special interest are those predictions which are 'risky' (in the sense of being intuitively implausible or contradicting the current or existing theory) and experimentally testable. One then compares them with the results of practical applications and experimentation. If the new predictions are borne out, then the new theory is corroborated (and the old one falsified), and it is adopted as a working hypothesis. If the predictions are not borne out, they falsify the theory from which they are derived. Thus, Popper retains an element of empiricism: For him, scientific method does involve making an appeal to observation. However, unlike traditional empiricists, Popper holds that observation cannot 'determine' theory (i.e., we do not argue or infer from observation to theory), it rather 'delimits' it (it shows which theories are false, not which theories are true). Moreover, he also rejects the empiricist doctrine that empirical observations are, or can be, infallible, in view of the fact that they are themselves theory-laden.

Popper proposed two provocative ideas. First, he repudiated induction as the basis of theory formulation and suggested a hypothetico-deductive method of scientific reasoning. Second, in place of verification of theory, he substituted falsifiability. Scientific theories, for him, are not inductively inferred from experience and neither is scientific experimentation carried out with a view to verifying or finally establishing the truth of theories. For Popper, a theory is scientific only if it is refutable by a conceivable event. Every genuine test of a scientific theory, then, is logically an attempt to refute or to falsify it. In a word, an exception, far from 'proving' a rule, conclusively refutes it. All knowledge is provisional, conjectural, hypothetical – we can never finally prove our scientific theories, we can merely (provisionally) confirm or (conclusively) refute them. At any given time, we have to choose between the potentially infinite number of theories which will explain the set of phenomena under investigation. Faced with this choice, we can only eliminate those theories that are demonstrably false and rationally choose between the remaining, unfalsified theories. Hence, Popper emphasized the importance of the critical spirit to science – for him, critical thinking is the very essence of rationality.

Popper takes 'falsifiability' as his criterion for demarcating science from non-science. On this criterion of demarcation, physics, chemistry and (non-introspective) psychology, among others, are sciences. Psychoanalysis is a pre-science (i.e., it undoubtedly contains useful and informative truths; however, until such time as psychoanalytical theories can be formulated in such a manner as to be falsifiable, they will not attain the status of scientific theories), and astrology and phrenology are pseudo-sciences.

Thomas Kuhn and Normal Science

Kuhn (1962) took a naturalistic approach to science: how do scientists work? He provided a critique of the standard version of scientific progress by stating an ideal scenario of how science ought to develop by the addition of new truths to the stock of old truths, or the increasing approximation of theories to the truth and the correction of past errors. Here, progress is guaranteed by the scientific method. He also objected to Popper's emphasis on criticism and falsification as salient aspects of scientific rationality.

Taking a naturalistic approach to the history of science, Kuhn suggested that the development of a science is not uniform but has alternating 'normal' and 'revolutionary' (or 'extraordinary') phases (see Figure 1.2). Science is a puzzle-solving enterprise. In mature sciences, there is a phase of normal science in which the key theories, instruments, values, metaphysical assumptions and experimental or mathematical techniques (in short, the paradigm) are kept fixed, permitting the cumulative generation of puzzle solutions. On the other hand, in a scientific revolution, the paradigm undergoes revision in order to permit the solution of the more serious anomalous puzzles that disturbed the preceding period of normal science. A paradigm as exemplar fulfils three functions: (1) it suggests new puzzles; (2) it suggests approaches to solving those puzzles; and (3) it is the standard by which the quality of a proposed puzzle solution can be measured (Kuhn, 1962, pp. 38–39). In each case, it is similarity to the exemplar that is the scientists' guide. That normal science proceeds on the basis of perceived similarity to exemplars is an important and distinctive feature of Kuhn's new picture of scientific development. The standards of assessment therefore are not permanent theory-independent rules. In focusing on the commitment to the paradigm as a prerequisite for successful normal science, Kuhn departed from Popper and his depiction of the scientist forever attempting to refute his/her most important theories.

Kuhn's view is that scientists neither test nor seek to confirm the guiding theories during normal science. Nor do they regard anomalous results as falsifying those theories. Rather, anomalies are ignored or explained away if at all possible. It is only the accumulation of particularly troublesome anomalies that

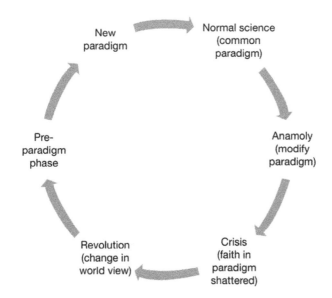

FIGURE 1.2 Kuhn's philosophy of scientific revolution

poses a serious problem for the existing disciplinary matrix. 'Normal science' will find it difficult to continue with confidence until this anomaly is addressed. Kuhn calls this widespread failure in confidence a 'crisis'. The most interesting response to crisis will be the search for a revised paradigm, a revision that will allow the elimination of at least the most pressing anomalies or optimally the solution of many outstanding, unsolved puzzles. Such a revision will be a 'scientific revolution'. The revolutionary phase is particularly open to competition among differing ideas and rational disagreement about their relative merits. The revolutionary search for a replacement paradigm is driven by the failure of the existing paradigm to solve certain important anomalies. Any replacement paradigm has to solve the majority of those puzzles better, or it will not be worth adopting in place of the existing paradigm. Revolutions do bring with them an overall increase in puzzle-solving power. However, Kuhn is quick to deny that this crisis leads to improved nearness of science to the truth. Rather, he favoured an evolutionary view of scientific progress. The evolutionary development of an organism might be seen as its response to a challenge set by its environment. However, that does not imply that there is some ideal form of the organism that it is evolving towards. Analogously, science improves by allowing its theories to evolve in response to puzzles, and progress is measured by its success in solving those puzzles; it is not measured by its progress towards an ideal true theory.

Kuhn also talks about 'incommensurability'. Incommensurability is supposed to rule out the view that science shows an ever-improving approximation to the truth. Theories are incommensurable when they share no common measure. Thus, if paradigms are the measures of attempted puzzle solutions, then puzzle solutions developed in different eras of normal science will be judged by comparison to differing paradigms and so lack a common measure. For example, to many in the seventeenth century, Newton's account of gravitation, involving action at a distance with no underlying explanation, seemed a poor account, in that respect at least, when compared, for example, to Ptolemy's explanation of the motion of the planets in terms of contiguous crystalline spheres. However, later, once Newton's theory was accepted, the lack of an underlying mechanism for a fundamental force was regarded as no objection. Further, Kuhn opined that Einstein's theory of relativity and Newton's theory are incommensurable. We cannot therefore say that the later theory is closer to the truth than the older theory. Kuhn's view that 'mass' as used by Newton cannot be translated by 'mass' as used by Einstein allegedly renders this kind of comparison impossible.

Feyerabend and Epistemological Anarchism

Paul Feyerabend (1975) also opposed Popper's viewpoint which argued in favour of a strongly normative epistemology, a discipline which lays down optimum rules of method for scientists to follow. According to him, science did not develop in accordance with Popper's model. It is not 'irrational', but it contains no overarching pattern. Popper's rules could produce a science, but not the science we now have.

He opined that scientific progress comes through 'theoretical pluralism', allowing a plurality of incompatible theories, each of which will contribute by competition to maintaining and enhancing the testability of the others (Feyerabend, 1963, 1964, 1965). According to Feyerabend's pluralistic test model, theories are tested against one another. He thus idealized what Kuhn called 'pre-paradigm' periods and 'scientific revolutions', occasions when there are many incompatible theories, all forced to develop through their competition with each other. However, he downplayed the idea that theories are compared with one another primarily for their ability to account for the results of observation and experiment. For Feyerabend, this idea was an empiricist myth which disguised the role of aesthetic and social factors in theory choice.

In *Against Method*, Feyerabend (1975) concluded that there are no useful and exceptionless methodological rules governing the progress of science or the growth of knowledge. He undermined the arguments for science's privileged position within culture, and much of his later work was a critique of the position of science within Western societies. Because there is no scientific method, we cannot justify science as the best way of acquiring knowledge. And the results of science do not prove its excellence, since these results have often depended on the presence of non-scientific elements. In most of his work after *Against Method*, he emphasized the 'disunity of science'. Science, he insisted, is a collage, not a system or a unified project. It is a collection of theories, practices, research traditions and worldviews whose range of application is not well determined and whose merits vary to a great extent. All this can be summed up in his slogan: 'Science is not one thing, it is many.' Likewise, the supposed ontological correlate of science, 'the world', also consists not only of one kind of thing but also of countless kinds of things, things which cannot be 'reduced' to one another. In fact, there is no good reason to suppose that the world has a single determinate nature. Rather, we construct the world in the course of our inquiries, and the plurality of our inquiries ensures that the world itself has a deeply plural quality. How the world is 'in-itself' is forever unknowable. In this respect, Feyerabend's last works can be thought of as aligned with 'social constructivism'.

PAUSE AND THINK

According to Kuhn's naturalistic approach, is psychology a pre-science, a normal science or is it undergoing a scientific revolution?

BOX 1.2 THE INNER WORLD OF THE SCIENTIST

Sir Jagadish Chandra Bose was an eminent Indian biologist and biophysicist. He is well known for his pioneering discoveries in plant physiology during the first half of the twentieth century. He researched the mechanism of the seasonal effect on plants, the effect of chemical inhibitors on plant stimuli and the effect

34 Is Psychology a Science?

of temperature. From the analysis of the variation of the cell membrane potential of plants under different circumstances, he hypothesized that plants can 'feel' pain and understand affection. His books include *Response in the Living and Non-Living* (1902) and *The Nervous Mechanism of Plants* (1926). He also subjected metals to a combination of mechanical, thermal, chemical and electrical stimuli and noted the similarities between metals and cells. Bose's experiments demonstrated a cyclical fatigue response in both stimulated cells and metals, as well as a distinctive cyclical fatigue and recovery response across multiple types of stimuli in both living cells and metals.

Ashis Nandy, a sociologist and political psychologist, has in his book, *Alternative Sciences: Creativity and Authenticity in Two Indian Scientists* (Nandy, 1980) attempted to trace the links between Bose's science to the dynamics of his motivational patterns, the distinctive concept of Indian science and the needs of modern science in his time. This analysis provides a deep understanding of how social realities come to be reflected in the scientist's personality and worldview.

In one of his lecture demonstrations at the Royal Institute in London in 1901, Bose said:

> I have shown you this evening the autographic records of the stress and strain in both the living and the non-living ... They show you the waxing and waning pulsations of life – and climax due to stimulants, the gradual decline in fatigue, the rapid setting in of death rigor from the toxic effects of poison. It was when I came on this mute witness of life and saw an all-pervading unity that binds together all things – it was then for the first time I understood the message proclaimed on the banks of the Ganges thirty centuries ago – 'they who behold the One, in all the changing manifoldness of the universe, unto them belongs eternal truth, unto none else, unto none else.'
>
> *(Nandy, 1972)*

Bose formulated the Indigenous philosophical position of non-duality, the oneness of existence and the singleness of experience into a scientific idiom and a research ideology. It won him many admirers and supporters among Indian and Western elites. It helped the Indian intelligentsia to accept their Indianness which was made into a controversial inheritance by colonialism. It induced the West, beset by the acute problem of moral ethics and of scientific ethics in the inter-war years, to find in the East a plausible alternative lifestyle – harmonious, placid, secure and holistic. Nandy suggested that Bose's work was also shaped by his lifelong struggle with his own aggressiveness and the anxieties they aroused. In Bose's work were found a persistent obsession with death, anger, cruelty and suffering. The pain of a poisoned leaf, the suffering of a metal strip injured manually and cured medically, these were the data Bose worked with. Perhaps, Bose's science was his restitutive effort to feel the pain of the victim, cope with his violence by renouncing violence, by aggressively protecting one's likely victims (Nandy, 1980).

REVIEW QUESTIONS

1. What does Kuhn mean by 'theory-ladenness of observations'?
2. How does Popper differ from traditional empiricists?
3. How does the incommensurability of different paradigms or scientific theories argue against a linear progressive trend of science?
4. Is science irrational, according to Kuhn and Feyerabend?

Can Psychology Be a Science?

Before psychology became an experimental science due to the work of psychophysicists, many thinkers such as Galileo, Kant and Comte had proclaimed that psychology could never be a science. Galileo, the great astronomer, believed that consciousness could never be studied by objective methods of science. His work marked a major philosophical shift concerning man's position in the world. Before him, humans had a prominent position in the world. He opined that the most human experiences – pleasures and disappointments, passions and ambitions, and auditory, visual and olfactory experiences – had secondary status, and we cannot have true knowledge of them, just opinions and illusions. Thus, for him, it was the physical reality, not subjective reality, that could be and should be studied scientifically. Immanuel Kant was a rationalist and his ideas have exerted a considerable influence on psychology. He defined psychology as the introspective analysis of the mind and believed that psychology thus defined could not be scientific. This was so because, first, he believed that the mind itself could never be objectively studied because it is not a physical thing. Second, the mind is constantly changing and is not still waiting to be analysed; thus it cannot be reliably studied using introspection. Third, the act of introspection influences what we are studying, thus limiting the value of what is found through introspection. Auguste Comte, the father of positivism, believed that psychology as 'the introspective analysis of the mind' was metaphysical nonsense because introspection examined only private experience. Introspective data were not like sense experiences that can be shared with other individuals. For him, scientific data were worthy of trust as they were publicly observable. In his hierarchy of sciences (from the one developed first to the one developed last) specified as mathematics, astronomy, physics, chemistry, physiology, biology and sociology, psychology did not appear.

Against the weight of such anti-views, it is indeed ironic that psychology did emerge as a scientific discipline and that too as a positivist experimental science. The scientific achievements of the seventeenth and eighteenth centuries allowed ancient philosophical questions to be examined in new, more precise ways. Much had been learnt about the physical world, and the time was ripe to use the scientific method for the study of the human mechanisms through which the physical world was represented in consciousness. Evidence about the discrepancy between

36 Is Psychology a Science?

physical reality and the psychological experience of that reality was piling up. For example, in 1760, van Musschenbroek discovered that if complementary colours such as yellow and blue are presented in proper proportions on a rapidly rotating disc, an observer sees neither yellow nor blue but grey. For the natural scientists, this mismatch between physical events and perception was of great concern, as their task was to accurately describe and explain the physical world. Because the most likely source of this discrepancy was the responding organism, the physical scientist had reason to be interested in the new science of physiology, which studied the biological processes by which humans interact with the physical world. The work of early physiologists in the area of the human sensory apparatus and the nervous system provided the link between mental philosophy and the science of psychology. The advances in knowledge of the natural sciences and the widespread belief in the applicability of scientific methods used in these sciences to investigate questions of individual psyche led to the emergence of psychology as a new science. The founders of this new science hoped that by taking a path to the mind through physiology, what had been speculative philosophy and religion might become naturalistic science. Helmholtz, a physiologist, showed that the principle of conservation of energy applied to living organisms as well. With his concept of unconscious inference, he also concluded that the mind embellished sensory experience. Ernst Heinrich Weber and Gustav Theodor Fechner were the first to measure how sensations vary systematically as a function of physical stimulation. Their work demonstrated that mental events could be studied experimentally and the ground was laid for the founding of psychology as an experimental science. As an emerging discipline in the nineteenth century, psychology claimed to be a natural science for two main reasons (Leahey 2013):

1. Since human beings are part of the natural world, it seems reasonable that natural science should encompass them. Psychology took physics to be its role model.
2. The authority of science was growing in the nineteenth century and it seemed no discipline could be respected if it was not a science.

Psychology wanted to be an experimental science because it was experimentation (as an embodiment of scientific method) that separated natural philosophy from the modern science. The controlled study of the phenomena in the laboratory made possible careful observation and abstraction of causal relations. It also aided precise testing of deductions from the observed laws (hypothesis testing). Psychology, thus, has been extremely method-driven, in its pursuit of scientific knowledge.

What Kind of Science Is Psychology?

Conceptually, psychology was founded several times and each time a distinct way of thinking about psychology as a science has come about (Leahey, 2013).

Psychology as a Science of Consciousness

Wilhelm Wundt, widely credited as the father of scientific psychology, applied the method of 'experimental introspection' (in contrast to the philosophical method of armchair introspection) to the study of consciousness (a philosophical concern of the past). This psychology sought to achieve the twin goals of discovering the elements of thought and discovering the laws by which mental elements combine into more complex mental experiences. In experimental introspection, observers were exposed to standard, repeatable situations and were asked to describe the resulting experience. The experimenter organized the situation and collected what the observer reported about his/her conscious experience. Because the ability to control the stimulus, systematic variation and duplication were possible, this held out the promise for the discovery of basic elements of thought and laws of combining them.

Gestalt psychologists – Max Wertheimer, Kurt Koffka and Wolfgang Kohler – rebelled against Wundt's elementalism. For them, the investigation of conscious experience through the introspective method was a worthwhile project, but they disagreed that conscious experience could be studied meaningfully in terms of elements. They believed that humans experienced the world in terms of intact configurations called gestalts. Gestalts were objective, physically real, natural self-organizations discoverable in (and not imposed on) experience and in the brain. The brain and experience were isomorphic in nature. The brain, Kohler said, is a dynamic field of self-organizing force fields reflecting the physical gestalts and giving rise to the gestalts of experienced objects. 'In a sense, gestalt psychology has since become a type of application of field physics to essential parts of psychology and brain physiology' (Kohler, 1969, p. 115). While structuralism used the language of elements borrowed from chemistry, gestalt psychology borrowed analogies from field theory in the realm of electromagnetism for the scientific study of consciousness. The gestaltists gave several definite principles of perceptual organization which are cited in psychology textbooks even today. They used a scientific phenomenological approach to describe the object under study (holistic, immediate conscious experience) to make an experimental investigation of its functional relations and finally to formulate a theory that serves as an explanation.

The experimental psychology of consciousness was a product of Germany. It did not fit with the spirit of the United States. The pioneering US spirit was prepared to accept only the viewpoint that was new, practical and unconcerned with the abstract analysis of the mind. The evolutionary theory caught the imagination of the intelligentsia there and created a psychology that was uniquely American. Science, concern for practicality, emphasis on the individual, and the adaptation focus of evolutionary theory combined into the formation of the 'school of functionalism'. The functionalists pursued a psychology of adaptation and were interested in understanding the function of the mind, what the mind is for, rather than the structure or what the mind is.

38 Is Psychology a Science?

They wanted psychology to be a practical science rather than a pure science, and they sought to use psychology to find solutions in the realms of education, personal life, industry, and so on. They were eclectic in their use of methods and embraced mental testing and animal experimentation along with introspection. In the work of the American functionalists, emphasis on experimentation shifted from conscious experience to the determination of responses by stimulus conditions. Meanwhile, the mental testing movement was also growing in the hands of James McKeen Cattell in America, Alfred Binet in France and Charles Spearman in Britain. They helped develop tests of intelligence that measured higher-order functions, such as intelligence, directly. William James, a major proponent of functionalism, proposed radical empiricism by which all consistently reported aspects of human experience (and not just consciousness) are worthy of study. He suggested the use of both scientific and philosophical approaches to the study of human behaviour and thought. Gradually, functionalism drifted towards what was later called the behaviourist position.

Psychology as a Science of Behaviour

An important precursor of behaviourism was objective psychology in Russia. Ivan Sechenov, a Russian physiologist, sought to explain consciousness in terms of physiological processes triggered by external events. He strongly believed that the traditional approach of understanding psychological phenomena using introspective analysis had led nowhere. The only valid approach to the study of psychology involved the objective methods of physiology. Works of other physiologists such as Ivan Pavlov and Vladimir M. Bekhterev laid the foundation of a scientific study of human behaviour by seeking to understand the relationship between environmental influences and overt behaviour. John B. Watson, usually credited as the father of behaviourist psychology, fully elaborated a stimulus–response psychology. In his major work, *Psychology from the Standpoint of a Behaviourist*, Watson explicated the scientific project of his psychology as:

> The goal of psychological study is the ascertaining of such data and laws, that given the stimulus, psychology can predict what the response will be; or, on the other hand, given the response, it can specify the nature of the objective stimulus.
>
> *(1919, p. 10)*

Watson expunged consciousness from the study of psychology and advocated a study of objective, observable behaviour which can be measured. Behaviourism and neo-behaviourism (the works of Edward Chace Tolman, Clark Leonard Hull, Edwin Ray Guthrie and B. F. Skinner) have maximally subscribed to the precepts of science. In their strict adherence to experimentation, operational definitions for abstract concepts such as habit and drive, a hypothetico-deductive method and mathematical axioms to define behaviours, behaviourists perhaps came closest to fulfilling the scientific ideals of psychology as embodied in positivism and logical positivism (discussed in detail in Chapter 2).

The return of the mind in psychology led to the development of cognitive psychology and the decline of behaviourism. 'Cognitive psychology' is a part of an interdisciplinary network devoted to studying the cognitive processes: cognitive science. Cognitive science embraces philosophy, psychology, artificial intelligence, neuroscience, linguistics and anthropology. The schema theory has tried to respond to the problem of meaning that led to the downfall of behaviourism. The parallel distributed processing theory (or the new connectionism) offers a form of a computational and neurological theory of mind. Cognitive psychology uses experimental methods, computational modelling and functional brain imaging techniques.

Psychology as a Science of the Unconscious

This form of psychology did not come from experimental or academic psychology. Nor did it come from the tradition of empiricism and associationism as so much of other psychology had. Rather, it emerged from clinical practice. The concerns of its developer, Sigmund Freud, were to develop a theory of psychopathology, techniques of treatment of psychopathology and a general theory of psychic functioning. There is no doubt that Freud shared the goal of the other founders of psychology – to create a psychology that was a science like any other (Freud appropriated the archaeological metaphor of excavating the unconscious to discover the obscure past and integrate it into the self, present ego). But he did not undertake to construct an experimental psychology of the unconscious, nor did he welcome attempts to verify his ideas experimentally. Rather than experimental testing, he regarded therapeutic success as the distinguishing mark of scientific truth. He regarded the talk of his patients as scientific data and the analytic session as a scientifically valid method of investigation. Such a dismissal of experimental methodology served to isolate psychoanalysis from academic psychology. It is often considered an unscientific theory and is critiqued on the grounds of biased observations, low precision in defining its concepts and lack of falsifiability. In its defence, it has been argued that psychoanalytic theory is a series of plausible propositions, usually logical, though at times contradictory, that have been offered as an explanation for phenomena observed in clinical work (Harrison, 1967). As such, they are a series of hypotheses; all of them should be tested, if possible. Some have been exhaustively tested and demonstrated to be established fact, such as the existence of unconscious mental functioning. Others have been tested but not found to be unambiguously valid and still others cannot be tested at our current level of knowledge, despite possessing considerable explanatory value, such as the theory of libidinal and aggressive drives.

40 Is Psychology a Science?

Psychology as a Humanist Science

'Humanistic psychology' also grew out of psychotherapy like psychoanalysis. It valued emotional feeling and intuition and questioned the authority of reason. Humanistic psychologists called for a human science which would study humans as aware, choosing, valuing, emotional and unique beings in the universe. Traditional science does not do this and must therefore be rejected. They tended to privilege qualitative, phenomenological methods rather than experimental, quantitative methods to assess the 'whole, consciously experiencing person'. 'Positive psychology', founded by Seligman and Csikszentmihalyi, has furthered the aims and goals of humanistic psychology but by using more rigorous, quantitative and reductionist methods.

The Myth of Psychology as an Experimental Science

Psychology has never been exclusively an experimental science at any point in its history, perhaps with the exception of behaviourism. Wundt, who founded an experimental science of psychology, also believed that individual experimental psychology could not be a complete psychology. The higher mental processes, which are reflected in human culture, could be studied only through historical analysis and naturalistic observation. According to Wundt, the nature of the higher mental processes could be deduced from the study of such cultural products as religion, social customs, myths, history, language, art and law. His extensive studies on these topics culminated in his 10-volume work, *Völkerpsychologie* ('group' or 'cultural' psychology). Wundt said that experimental psychology penetrates only the 'outworks' of the mind; *Völkerpsychologie* reaches deeper into the transcendental ego. William James echoed similar sentiments that science cannot embrace all that can be known about human beings. He advocated the use of both natural and philosophical approaches. His penchant for pragmatism – the principle that any belief, thought or behaviour must be judged by its consequences – led him to admit all forms of experience as valid and worthy of study. He said:

> Pragmatism is willing to take anything, to follow either logic or the senses and to count the humblest and most personal experiences. She will count mystical experiences if they have practical consequences. She will take a God who lives in the very dirt of private fact – if that should seem as a likely place to find him.
>
> *(James, [1907] 1975, pp. 38–39)*

He campaigned against methodolatry and distorting phenomena for the sake of methodology.

The Current Status of Psychology as a Science

In a nutshell, psychology has been scientific in the broad sense of the word. It puts the commonsensical notions of the world to the test. From the inception of scientific psychology, structured methods such as observations, psychological tests and interviewing have been applied to its subject matter to create systematic and logically consistent forms of knowledge. Scientific psychological knowledge is largely based on empirical observations and valid explanatory inferences which are trustworthy and reliable. Some of the research traditions in psychology have been interpretive, hermeneutic and largely qualitative in nature, while others have been experimental, statistical and quantitative.

The choice of method for psychologists in many domains of research has been the experimental method, the linchpin positivist scientific method, which requires precise definitions and measurements of variables of interest and control over extraneous variables. The preference for this method of data collection imports within psychology the positivist assumptions of 'essentialism' (that reality is real and exists 'out there', waiting to be discovered), 'empiricism' (data are only that which can be sensed by our sense organs or collected through our objective instruments and tools; hunches and intuition are not data), 'determinism' (events are caused, and it is possible to have laws explaining the causation) and 'measurement' (attributes such as intelligence, short-term memory and perceptual illusions can be quantified in the same way as water, temperature, velocity and mass). It also holds out the promise of attaining a predictive and controlling power over psychological phenomena. These assumptions are not unique to the experimental method only. The other scientific methods used in psychology, such as structured observations, questionnaires and interviews, also subscribe to them.

Through its historical development, psychologists have borrowed conceptual frameworks developed in sciences, such as physics, physiology and mathematics, to characterize psychological functioning. Salient examples include the search for laws like Newton's laws of gravity to understand properties of consciousness by structuralists, the notion of a psychological field as akin to an electromagnetic field to analyse the multiple interacting factors acting upon the individual, used by Kurt Lewin; to understand humans as energy systems and apply the law of conservation of energy to psychic energy propounded by Helmholtz and used by Freud; the computer metaphor to explain the functioning of the mind accepted by cognitive psychologists; the search for neural/physiological correlates of behaviour and experience by physiologically oriented behaviourists like Watson and contemporary neuropsychologists; and the application of mathematical models to psychological terms by Clark Hull.

The science of psychology is pervasive and affects diverse domains of life. As practitioners of applied science, psychologists serve as consultants to communities and organizations, diagnose and treat people, and teach future psychologists and those who will pursue other disciplines. They construct and analyse

42 Is Psychology a Science?

tests of intelligence and personality. Many psychologists work as healthcare providers. They assess behavioural and mental functions and well-being. Other psychologists study how human beings relate to each other and to machines, and work to improve these relationships. The strides made in educational assessments are helping students with learning disabilities. Psychological science helps educators understand how children think, process and remember – helping to design effective teaching methods. Psychological science contributes to justice by helping the courts understand the minds of criminals, the role of memory in the construction of eyewitness testimony and the limits of certain types of evidence or testimony. Through research, it strives to create evidence-based strategies that solve problems and improve lives. The application of psychological research can decrease the economic burden of disease on governments and society as people learn how to make choices that improve their health and well-being.

PAUSE AND THINK

Psychology is called a behavioural science. Find out what behavioural science is and how psychology is a behavioural science.

BOX 1.3 IS PSYCHOANALYSIS A SCIENCE?

For Freud, it was evident that psychoanalysis is an evolution-based biological science, a science of the mind within the biological body, to be firmly anchored in its physiological and chemical matrix, as our knowledge increases (Wallerstein, 2009). However, Freud did not feel the need to make use of the formal systematic research by which science necessarily claims to grow. When the American psychologist Saul Rosenzweig wrote to Freud in 1934, describing his laboratory support for some of Freud's central psychoanalytic concepts, Freud responded dismissively, stating that such confirmatory evidence was not needed as psychoanalysis rested on a wealth of positive clinical research. Freud was convinced of the scientific nature of psychoanalytic concepts and theory, but he did not have faith in the conventional scientific method. The scientific status of psychoanalysis has been a matter of much debate. While much critique has been directed towards the method of psychoanalysis, some argue against psychoanalytic knowledge being called scientific. Karl Popper (1963) dismissed psychoanalysis as a pre-science. Adolf Grünbaum (1984) subjected Freud's writings to a detailed logical analysis, and pointed out that Freud's conclusions do not always follow from his data. He also argued that data were elicited and shaped by the analyst's own implicit or explicit demands that the patient's associations conform with the analyst's predetermined theory. He declared that to secure legitimate status as a science, psychoanalytic findings would need extra-clinical confirmation outside the individual consulting room, via experimental or epidemiological means. The hermeneutic critique removes psychoanalysis from the world of science entirely as it believes that the project of investigating the meaning of human behaviour cannot qualify as science. There is a significant position in contemporary psychoanalysis led by André Green that declares it is not a science at all in the usual sense and there is not even a psychology which can later be developed as a science. In this view, it is a unique and *sui generis* discipline, relying only on the conceptualizing of the findings that emerge in the psychoanalytic consulting room.

Currently, many are still trying to place psychoanalysis as a biologically and cognitively based natural science, after Freud's disposition. There is enormous growth in the field of neurosciences and hectic attempts are being made to bridge conceptualizations between the two disciplines. There is even a journal by the name of *Neuro Psychoanalysis*. A large number of authors see psycho-analysis as a human/behavioural science, debating about what kind of research has the potential to advance it as a science. A letter by Mary Target to *The New Scientist*, dated 27 October 2010, responding to an article on the scientific status of psychoanalysis by Mario Bunge, included 54 signatories who were distinguished researchers in psychoanalysis in the science faculties of the lead-ing world universities, who have acquired major public grants and have pub-lished papers in high-impact, peer-reviewed scientific journals. On this ground, it can be argued that psychoanalysis is becoming a science. There is an expan-sion of research methodologies used in psychoanalysis now – the clinical, con-ceptual and empirical in whatever mixture or the parallelism of qualitative and quantitative approaches, depending on the suitability to the research hypoth-esis under scrutiny. An example of the expansion of the clinical methodology is the work of Kachele, Schachter and Thomäs (2009), who developed the single case study and have significantly improved the rigour and objectivity of infer-ences drawn from it. They presented the case history in 80 pages, followed by a 130-page analysis with the evidential record of 517 audiotaped sessions avail-able to other researchers. A number of such databases now exist. Wallerstein (2009) argues that for psychoanalytic research to be counted as research and not just search, it should be systematic, and, to the extent possible, observable and replicable.

Positivist Psychology: Winner or Loser?

Positivism can be understood as the study of social reality using the conceptual framework, the techniques of observation and measurement, the instruments of mathematical analysis and the procedures of inference of the natural science. The conceptual framework consists of cause and effect, empirical verification, and explanation. The techniques of observation and measurement imply the use of quantitative variables, even for qualitative phenomena, such as mental abil-ities and psychological states (attitude measurement, intelligence tests, etc.).

Mathematical analysis makes use of statistics and mathematical models. The procedures of inference are the inductive process, whereby specific observations give rise to general laws; the use of theory to predict outcomes; and extrapolation from the sample to the whole population (Corbetta, 2003, p. 13).

Psychology works according to the logic of positivism. Experimentation, an empirical research procedure to test hypotheses under controlled conditions, is widely believed by the scientifically-minded psychologists to be the route to becoming positivist science. Although much research has moved beyond the confines of laboratory experiment, the positivist logic is still central to how psychological enquiry is conceived and conducted. As a positivist science, psychology gains its credibility among the natural sciences, but it also loses a great deal.

Limiting the Scope of Psychology

The dominance of positivism has isolated many traditions within psychology, such as psychoanalysis, humanism and existentialism, as their precepts were not amenable to operational definitions and scientific experimentation. This has also led to the exclusion of phenomena such as extrasensory perception and spiritual experiences, to name but a few, from the scientific study of psychology. This is a violation of the radical empiricist spirit of William James, which supported the study of all valid forms of human experience. In order to fit the bill of 'scientific knowledge', research on subjective states, such as happiness, well-being, faith, illness, ego, *rasa* (flavour, sentiment, emotion), *ahankar* (arrogance), transcendence, undertaken within positive psychology, transpersonal psychology and Indian psychology, operates within the logic of operationalization and developing structured questionnaires to map these complex states, losing out on the essence of such experiences. Similar problems afflict studies of culture and psychology in which cultural processes are packaged as static variables which can then be manipulated to assess their impact on behaviour.

The Problem of Meaning

Problems of placing mind and meaning are replete in psychology. It can be seen in Watson's physiological views on language and thinking. To be consistent, in his behaviouristic view, Watson had to reduce language and thinking to some form of behaviour and nothing more: 'Saying is doing – that is, behaving.' He claimed that thinking is subvocal or implicit speech which can be detected in minute movements of the tongue and larynx. This contention was widely opposed. Instances abound of how one has a meaning to be expressed in one's mind/thought but does not have the word required for it. This questions whether thought equals speech. Similarly, one can recite a familiar passage with no sense of its meaning. So, then, can speech equal thought?

The use of the computer and the brain as analogies to the mind has also run into the 'problem of intentionality and meaning'. Cognitive psychology is the study of mental representation, that is, a study of how the external world is symbolized in the mind. When the mind is understood as a machine-like computer or in terms of the brain and its neural networks, it becomes difficult to explain how the meaning of a word like 'apple' is understood by the machine or neuron. They understand only the syntax, that is, the form of the word 'apple' (i.e., it is a five-letter word, the unique formation of the shape of the alphabets) and store them as a set of 0s or 1s in binary machine language or in some other physiological code in the brain. However, the computer machine can do intelligent things with the word 'apple', such as find the occurrence of 'apple' in every file, give related meaning for the word, substitute 'apple' for 'orange'. It may appear that the computer knows the semantic meaning of the word 'apple', but, actually, the computer is operating only on the syntax of 0s and 1s. Similarly, when we play chess with a computer, we are likely to attribute intentional stance to it, such as it is trying to defeat me, it wants to capture my pawn, and so on. But what is going on inside the computer is not intentional at all. It does not try or want; it simply carries out formal computations on patterns of 0s and 1s. So, are the intentional folk psychological theories that suggest that human beings have thoughts and wants really redundant because the only scientifically acceptable theories in human cognitive psychology will be those that treat human information processing just like a computer's (Leahey, 2013)?

Ignoring the Moral-Ethical Dimensions of Life

Many of psychology's central questions – what is human nature, is it inherently evil or virtuous? What is a good life? What constitutes deviant behaviour? – are all implicated in moral debates and raise significant ethical dilemmas. When fields such as positive psychology and clinical psychology have attempted to give scientific responses to these questions, they fall short.

Reductionism

The discipline of psychology is often critiqued for methodolatry – the obsession with a particular method of investigation (experimentation in this case) and the willingness to disfigure a phenomenon to preserve the sanctity of the method of inquiry. Psychology, in a bid to be an experimental discipline, has often resorted to reductionism. Ebbinghaus' work on memory is a good example of this. He developed nonsense syllables (a three-letter word: consonant–vowel–consonant) to study retention and forgetting of material as a function of time and conditions of learning (massed versus distributed). The reason for developing nonsense syllables was to ensure the uniformity of stimulus condition so that the meaningfulness of the learning material did not act as a confounding variable. However, it is well known that nonsense syllables set up a variety of associations,

46 Is Psychology a Science?

thereby reiterating that it is impossible to rid stimuli of meaning so long as they remain capable of arousing any human response. This added an element of artificiality to the experimental situation, making it rather a study of the establishment and maintenance of repetition habits. It also ignored factors such as subjective attitude and predetermined reaction tendencies, which also affect recall responses besides the experimental manipulation.

Psychology uses the 'language of variables', a phrase coined by Paul F. Lazarsfeld, the principal exponent of the neopositivist empirical methodology in sociology. Every construct has been reduced to a range of properties and attributes called variables, and social phenomena are analysed in terms of the relationships between variables. The variables with their neutral character and objectivity became substitutes for social reality and there was no longer any need to recompose the original construct again. For example, the construct 'self' has been reduced to a psychometric assessment of the self concept with its various dimensions such as social self, physical self, and so on. In this way, psychological research became 'depersonalized' and the language of variables, with the measurement of concepts, the distinction between independent and dependent variables, the quantification of their interrelations and the formulation of a causal model, provided a formal instrument that allowed scientifically-minded psychological researchers to go beyond the vagueness of the everyday language.

The Limitations of the Experimental Method

The Social Psychology of the Experimental Method

Experiment is considered to be the objective method of empirical research in psychology. To regard experiment as objective involves two related assumptions: (1) the researcher's influence on the participant's behaviour (the outcome of the experiment) is limited to the design-related features of the experiment, such as which hypothesis to be tested, how the variables are to be operationalized, which design to use; and (2) the only factors which influence the participant's behaviour are the objectively defined variables manipulated by the experimenter.

However, these two assumptions do not hold true in human experimentation. The truth is that the influence of the experimenter extends far beyond the design of the experiment. Rosenthal and Rosnow (1969) have conducted a number of classic pieces of research on the influence of the experimenter on research results and discovered three problems:

1. The biosocial characteristics of the researcher: age, sex, race and appearance.
2. The psychosocial factors of the researcher: research experience, anxiety levels, social skills, friendly versus putting-off demeanour.
3. The experimenter's expectancy effect (the Rosenthal effect): experimenters who have a hypothesis in mind may end up validating it simply because of their belief about how the results will turn out. The hypothesis then

becomes a self-fulfilling prophecy. Expectancy effects work even with non-human subjects. In one study, Rosenthal and Fode (1963) randomly assigned groups of rats to different experimenters. Half of the experimenters were told that their rats were 'maze bright' and the other half were told that they were 'maze dull'. The rats were, in fact, randomly chosen. At the end of the five days, the rats who were believed to be better performers in fact became better performers, learning mazes more quickly than their supposedly less-intelligent counterparts. Rosenthal suggested that experimenters' expectancies of the subjects resulted in different treatment of the two groups of rats, which in turn led to better performance among the rats labelled 'maze bright'.

The participants also do not passively respond only to the experimenter manipulation. They can also affect the objectivity of research according to who they are and how they behave. A recurrent criticism of psychology is that it usually employs white male undergraduate students for its research. It is a science of white male American undergraduates. Psychological knowledge explains their behaviour the best. Also important is the idea that many participants are volunteers. This practice immediately produces ethical problems, and the nature of the sample, i.e., the types of people investigated, is not representative. The types of people who choose to take part in psychology studies tend to be younger, brighter, friendlier, less conventional or authoritarian, but with a strong need for approval (Rosenthal, 1965). These factors limit the generalizability of the results. Weber and Cook (1972) identified four roles that volunteering participants being studied might adopt:

1. The faithful participants try to react to the situation as naturally as possible.
2. The cooperative participants try to discover the hypothesis being tested so that they can do their best to help prove it.
3. The negativist participants try to discover the hypothesis in order to disprove it.
4. The evaluatively apprehensive participants who believe that the experimenter is capable of uncovering some hidden truth about them and do what they can to avoid being evaluated negatively.

Orne (1962) also stressed that participants attempt to make sense of the research, and will always formulate their own version of what the hypotheses or aims of the study are. In some cases, subjects are anxious to confirm what they think are the desired outcomes of the study, and much work has been done on the power of these 'demand characteristics' in experiments. Thus, we cannot just assume that the independent variable is identical for every participant, and exerts a standard effect on everyone.

The evaluative scenario of research also affects the behaviour of the participants. Human participants are often affected by the knowledge that they are being observed and this knowledge changes the way they normally behave. This is called the Hawthorne effect.

48 Is Psychology a Science?

The Problem of Validity

Psychological experimentation suffers from the problem of internal and external validity. Modelling itself on natural science, psychology attempts to overcome the problem of the complexity of human behaviour by using experimental control. This involves isolating an independent variable and ensuring that extraneous variables (variables other than the independent variable that can influence the dependent variable) do not affect the outcome. The question that begs an answer is: Is it possible to control all the extraneous variables? While it is relatively easy to control the more obvious situational variables, this is more difficult with participant variables (such as gender and culture), either for practical reasons (such as availability of groups) or because it is not always obvious exactly what the relevant variables are. Ultimately, it is up to the experimenter's judgement and intuition what he/she believes is important and possible to control. Even if complete control were possible (in other words, if we could guarantee the internal validity of the experiment), a fundamental dilemma would still remain. The greater the degree of control over the experimental situation (internal validity), the more different it becomes from real-life situations (the more artificial it becomes and the lower its external/ecological validity). The generalization of findings beyond the research situation and the applicability of the results to explain real-life behaviour become less confident. Experimental studies study individuals in an ahistorical, ungendered and acultural fashion. Stripped of the context, the behaviour loses its meaning.

The Power Differential in Experimental Research

Criticisms of traditional empirical methods (especially the laboratory experiment method) have focused on their artificiality, including the often unusual and bizarre tasks that people are asked to perform in the name of science. What makes the lab experiment such an unnatural and artificial situation is the fact that it is almost totally structured by one participant – the experimenter. This relates to power differences between experimenters and their subjects, which is as much of an ethical as a practical issue. Traditionally, participants have been referred to as subjects, implying something less than a person, a dehumanized and depersonalized object. There is a continual tension between the attempt by the 'subjects' to understand and control the research and the ways in which the demands of the situation limit their room for manoeuvre. While psychologists agonize about deception or the depersonalization of those subjects they treat like objects, they also find themselves faced with the (to them) unbearable prospect of being open about the hypotheses and giving the game away. The discussions in the literature of informed consent, debriefing and minimizing harm are all ways of trying to solve the problem without letting the subject win the battle.

The Problem of Causal Explanation

Shadish, Cook and Campbell (2002), in what is arguably the most detailed and sophisticated presentation of the case for experimental research, highlight one of its significant limitations. They state:

> The unique strength of experimentation is in describing the consequences attributable to deliberately varying a treatment. We call this causal description. In contrast, experiments do less well in clarifying the mechanisms through which and the conditions under which that causal relationship holds – what we call causal explanation.
>
> *(p. 9)*

For this goal, the other methods of psychology, which are process-oriented, are needed.

REVIEW QUESTION

In what ways has the positivist-experimental perspective helped in furthering the aim of psychology as a scientific discipline?

Final Comments

So, what do we conclude about the question: Is psychology a science? In spite of doubts being raised about the amenability of its subject matter to be scientific, psychology is a science. It is a science in the broader sense of the word, that is, in terms of being a systematic body of knowledge having theories, using research (in different research paradigms) to advance knowledge claims. It is a systematic study of human motives, affects, thinking and action in a context. The verdict is more fractured on the question: What kind of science is psychology? Psychology has struggled to be like a natural science, thus embracing the positivist–experimental tradition of science. The influence of this tradition on psychological research and the subsequent generation of knowledge has been pervasive. However, it is important to critically engage with the expressed values of positivist science, such as objectivity, realism and the primacy of hypothetico-deductivism. Its relevance to human sciences such as psychology must be questioned. Also, it is also important to recognize that there have always been spaces in the discipline where non-experimental interpretivist work has been carried out. As a science, psychology is both nomothetic (developing general laws about how the mind works) and idiographic (pursuing the individualized workings of these laws in the specific endowments and life experiences of individuals). It draws on the hard sciences, such as neurosciences, computational sciences and engineering sciences, and also on the social sciences, such as sociology, economics, politics and history.

50 Is Psychology a Science?

Its hermeneutic nature also forges an affinity with literature. As a science, its optimal research posture should be expansive to encourage an admixture or parallelism of empirical and conceptual approaches and qualitative and quantitative methodologies. Psychology as a science is committed to scepticism and systematic research on all the kinds of experiences and realities that animate human life. The security of its scientific identity lies in its open embrace of its hybrid nature of its subject matter as well as the methods of inquiry.

2

SHOULD PSYCHOLOGICAL RESEARCH BE ONLY ABOUT NUMBERS?

Research is at the heart of all forms of systematic knowledge. This is a disciplined enquiry that results in the advancement of knowledge, and, thus, it shapes the form and content of the knowledge of whatever we are curious about, be it the universe and the celestial bodies, rocks and chemicals, plants and animals, the human body and the human mind, or the historical context and social structures. At this point of human evolution, researched knowledge enjoys unparalleled power that hearsay, common sense and traditional knowledge do not. When we think of research, most of us think of the following elements: a problem that sparks research, a tool to collect data, a sample on which data are collected and research findings. What misses our attention is that this research process is based on the researcher making certain practical and theoretical choices, and the researcher is a part of a research community. Such choices are governed by the paradigm of research in which a researcher is located. Guba and Lincoln (1994, p. 116) state, 'No inquirer, we maintain, ought to go about the business of inquiry without being clear about just what paradigm informs and guides his or her approach.' Research on anything will yield findings that mirror the paradigm's research concerns, its values and assumptions and its procedures for observing or measuring. Psychological research is no exception. The quantitative research paradigm is the foundation on which psychology as a positivist science stands. It shapes the dominant research priorities and knowledge generated in psychology. The interpretivist science model is at the margins of psychology.

Quantification has been the chief feature of scientific psychology. The psychological literature is replete with instances of mathematical axioms, for example, reaction potential $(ER) = SHR \times D$, reporting intelligence and personality traits in terms of T scores, mapping opinions and attitudes on a five-point Likert scale, using factorial designs, regression analysis, analysis of

DOI: 10.4324/9781003471851-3

52 Should Psychological Research Be Only about Numbers?

variance and checking for significance of results. A research methodology course in psychology is mostly about hypothesis testing and statistical techniques. The quantification imperative in psychology goes beyond merely the use of the numbers in research. It dovetails with the positivist ideals of the detached neutrality of the researcher, the replication of results, generalization and objectivity. Thus, to frame the debate of research methodology as quantitative or qualitative is itself reductionist because what is at stake is more than just the form of data but includes the paradigmatic assumptions and research strategy.

What Is Positivism?

The term 'positivism' dominates the qualitative–quantitative debate. There are many misunderstandings associated with it. It often is used as a pejorative term. Some writers imply that positivism equals statistics. It does not. Positivism is an epistemology. Epistemology is a branch of philosophy concerned with the theory of knowledge. It attempts to provide answers to the question: How, and what, can we know? Epistemology is the basis of our understanding of what kinds of things it is possible for us to find out.

By the nineteenth century, Newtonian science was deeply entrenched and was being applied to the study of human nature and human affairs. This gave rise to the 'positive philosophy' of Auguste Comte. Positivism began as a social theory and became a philosophy of science. Comte described human history as passing through three stages: (1) the theological stage, (2) the metaphysical stage, and (3) the scientific stage. Each stage was defined by the characteristic way people explained events in the world around them and a characteristic form of government. During the 'theological stage', people explained phenomena by positing unseen supernatural entities such as angels, demons, gods, and so on. Government was run by priests who had the power to communicate with the gods and control them. During the 'metaphysical stage', explanations were based on unseen essences, principles, causes or laws. Society was ruled by refined aristocrats and philosopher elites who were in touch with the higher things of arts and philosophy. In the 'scientific stage', the third and highest stage of development, scientific description is emphasized over explanation and prediction, and control of natural phenomena becomes all important. In this stage, scientists will rule, specifically sociologists who, armed with the Newtonian science of society, would have the same absolute and accurate power over society as natural scientists over nature. Ernst Mach, a German physicist, elaborated positivism as a foundational philosophy for science. He insisted that science should concentrate only on what could be known with certainty. On the debate over reality and the scientific legitimacy of atoms, he asked, 'Have you ever seen an atom?' He was sceptical of theory and opined that theory should never aspire to truth; at best, it can serve the pragmatic functions of prediction and control.

Common Assumptions of Positivism

There are many different versions of positivism. Bryman (2004, p. 11) summarizes several common assumptions of positivism as follows:

1. Methods and procedures of the natural science are appropriate to the social sciences (methodological monism/naturalism).
2. Only phenomena and knowledge confirmed by the senses can be warranted as knowledge (phenomenalism/empiricism).
3. Knowledge can be produced by the accumulation of verified facts that provide the basis for laws – empirically established regularities of events (inductivism).
4. Theories are used to generate testable predictions/hypotheses and to explain laws (deductivism).
5. Science must be conducted in a way that is value-free and thus objective; there is a clear distinction between science and normative statements (what is and what should be).

Positivism assumes that there is a world out there (an external reality) separate from our descriptions of it. Such a position is also referred to as the 'correspondence theory of truth' because it suggests that phenomena directly determine our perceptions of them and that there is, therefore, a direct correspondence between things and their representation. It is this epistemological assumption that underlines the notions of detached neutrality, objectivity of facts and use of quantification.

Logical Positivism

At the end of the nineteenth century, the positivism of Comte and Mach combined with the developments in logic and mathematics to produce a movement called logical positivism. It was founded by the Vienna Circle, a gathering of philosophers, such as Rudolf Carnap, Otto Neurath and Hans Hahn, around the University of Vienna and the Café Central. They conceded that science could incorporate unseen hypothetical concepts into its theories but wanted to do it without lapsing into metaphysical speculation. Logical positivism devoted the utmost attention to the methodological problems in every science, to the logical analysis of their language and to the procedures by which empirical verification could be achieved (Corbetta, 2003). With logical positivism, the language of variables and operationalism entered social research.

Logical positivism divided the language of science into three sets of terms: (1) observation terms, (2) theoretical terms and (3) mathematical terms. 'Observation terms' were the bedrock of science, which referred to directly observable properties of nature and constituted descriptions of nature. Generalizations from data gave rise to laws of nature specified as axioms that contained

54 Should Psychological Research Be Only about Numbers?

theoretical terms (atoms, force, magnetic fields) connected by logico-mathematical terms. An example of an axiom/law of nature is F = ma. Here, force, mass and acceleration are 'theoretical terms' which cannot be observed directly. Thus, logical positivists gave meaning and epistemological significance to these terms via operational definitions. Operational definitions defined theoretical terms in terms of procedures linking them to observation terms. For example, mass is defined as an object's weight at sea level. Thus, theories consisted of axioms whose terms (theoretical terms) are explicitly defined by reference to observation terms. In line with anti-realism, observations do not provide evidence for the existence of inferred/unobservable entities; rather, they define those entities.

Logical positivism seemed to offer a specific recipe for doing science in any field of study. First, operationally define one's theoretical terms, be it mass or hunger. Second, state one's theory as a set of axioms (e.g., F = ma) from which predictions can be drawn. Third, carry out experiments to test the predictions. Finally, revise one's theory as the observations warrant (Leahey, 2013). Logical positivism expanded the aims of science to include explanation and equated explanation with prediction. This is called the Hempel and Oppenheim model of explanation or the covering law model of explanation in which explanations are deductions from scientific laws and they help to make predictions. Logical positivism opened the doors of science to theory about which positivism was wary. Theories were interconnections among axioms and were accepted in science because they predicted and explained events. If theories helped us to achieve these goals, we retain them as useful; if they fail, we discard them. In the anti-realist strain of logical positivism, theories were merely tools by which human beings came to grips with nature. They were not invested with the power of providing the true picture of the world.

Positivism and logical positivism insisted on the absolute separation of theory and data. Data/observation constituted the basis of science and was conceived of as separate from theory. This allowed the scientists to believe in the value-neutrality of their data. This view was regarded as flawed and simplistic. The objection has been that perception is inevitably influenced by people's expectations and values. Also, the determination of what to observe (data collection) in a given situation is determined by a theory. Theory provides the overall framework within which facts take their place. The idea of observation being theory-laden, as suggested by Kuhn (1962), was discussed in Chapter 1. It is often argued that positivism does not adequately describe the nature of the natural sciences. Perhaps only certain aspects of physics seem to conform to the tenets of positivism, and it is no coincidence that the doctrine of operationalism was largely formulated within the context of that discipline by Bridgman (1927).

Psychology and Logical Positivism

Psychology, however, was greatly influenced by the rigorous, formal ideals of logical positivism from the 1930s to the 1960s. S. S. Stevens (1939) was the psychologist who brought operational definition to psychology. This promised to settle all debates about psychological terminology by claiming that all terms that could not be operationally defined were scientifically meaningless. By this standard, behaviourism was the only scientific psychology as theoretical terms could only be linked to observables like classes of behaviour and not to mental entities. For example, in Hull's system, drive strength (D) was defined in terms of hours of deprivation of food, water, and so on (the more deprivation, the greater the drive strength); habit strength (SHR) was based on the number of reinforced pairings between stimulus and response (the more reinforced pairings, the stronger the habit).

What Is Post-Positivism?

A new philosophic-scientific spirit arose out of the developments in the natural sciences and physics in particular during the early twentieth century. Quantum mechanics, Einstein's special and general theories of relativity, and Heisenberg's principle of uncertainty are some of the cornerstones of new physics that introduced elements of probability and uncertainty to areas, such as the concept of causal law, the objectivity of the external world and even the classical categories of time and space. Theories were no longer expressed in terms of deterministic laws, but of probability (Corbetta, 2003). Another important element introduced into the scientific methodology by this evolution of positivism is the concept of falsification, suggested by Popper (discussed in detail in Chapter 1). This states that a theory cannot be positively confirmed by data. Positive proof is impossible because the same data may be compatible with other theoretical hypotheses. Empirical validation can only take place by demonstrating that the data do not contradict the hypotheses and, therefore, that the theory and data are merely compatible. This position gives rise to the sense of the provisional nature of any theoretical statement, since it is never definitively proven. In disjunction with positivism is another feature of post-positivism which is a widespread conviction that empirical observation, the very perception of reality, is not an objective picture, but is theory-laden. In other words, the act of understanding remains conditioned by the social circumstances and the theoretical framework in which it takes place.

So, what of positivism survives today? Positivism has lost its certainties. Post-positivism has come a long way from the naïve interpretation of the deterministic laws of the original positivism. However, the empiricist spirit of positivism is still alive in its reformulated form. The empiricist approach continues to rest on the cornerstones of operationalization, quantification and generalization. The operational procedures, the ways of collecting data, the measurement operations and the statistical analyses have not fundamentally changed (Table 2.1 explains the differences between positivism and post-positivism further).

56 Should Psychological Research Be Only about Numbers?

TABLE 2.1 The philosophical positions of positivism and post-positivism

	Positivism	*Post-positivism*
Ontology	*Naive realism*: There exists an objective social reality, external to human beings, whether they are studying or performing social acts. This social reality is given and knowable.	*Critical realism*: The reality is given and exists as external to human beings. But reality is only imperfectly knowable as the causal laws are probabilistic.
Epistemology	*Dualist and objective*: The researcher and the object of research are independent entities (dualism). The researcher can study the object of research without influencing it or being influenced by it (objectivity). Natural laws specifying cause and effect can be known.	*Modified dualism and objectivity*: The strict separation between researcher and object of research is no longer sustained. It is acknowledged that the researcher influences the object of study and objectivity can only be approximated. The intent remains of formulating laws, even if limited in scope, probabilistic and provisional.
Methodology	*Experimental and manipulative*: Experimentation founded on manipulation and control of the variables and detachment of the observer from the object of study	*Modified experimental and manipulative*: Experimental methodology, operationalism and statistical analysis remain important. Replication of results is sought. Qualitative methods are admitted.

Source: Corbetta (2003).

REVIEW QUESTIONS

1. Compare and contrast positivism and logical positivism.
2. How does positivism differ from post-positivism?
3. What is the role of operationalism in positivism?

What Is the Quantification Imperative in Psychology?

Quantification and science have been inseparable since the times of the ancient Greek, pre-Socratic Pythagoreans (around 500 BC). Mapping and measuring physical events and experiences in terms of numbers are the basis for the objectivity of science. Physics, among the sciences, has had spectacular success in terms of expressing its findings in terms of mathematics from the times of Isaac Newton. Mathematics, specifically the probability theory, laid down the foundations of the discipline of statistics. In the eighteenth century, statistics was primarily conceived as the science of the state – the collection and analysis of the facts of a country, such as its wealth, land, population, data useful for governance. Later, its use expanded to sciences, such as astronomy and thermodynamics, which used it for the presentation and analysis of data. The development of statistical reasoning is closely associated with the development of inductive logic and scientific method. Psychology's fascination with natural sciences and scientific method has led to an unquestioning adherence to measurement, concepts of variables and operational definitions and the use of statistical theory of hypothesis testing by psychologists. This constitutes the core of the quantitative imperative in psychology.

In psychology textbooks today, references to personality tests of many sorts, intelligence quotients (IQs), ability and aptitude measures, or attitude scales feature heavily as do physiological measures, such as blood pressure, brain rhythms, positron emission tomography (PET) scans. While all of these measure qualities ascribed to the data (usually called variables in the quantitative context), they are quantified in that they are assigned numerical values or scores. The magnitude of the numerical value indicates the extent to which each individual possesses the characteristic or quality. One very common form of quantification method used in psychological research is the Likert scale (in which participants are asked to indicate their agreement with a statement on a scale of 1–5, assessing strongly agree, agree, neutral, disagree and strongly disagree). The current dominant psychological research has remained substantially determinedly quantitative in style, in spite of the fact that psychology has never been at any point in its modern history monolithically quantitative in nature. Alternative voices have regularly been heard, both criticizing and offering alternatives to quantification.

The History of Quantification in Psychology

The growth of psychology into a major academic discipline was possible because of the growth of quantification. Historically, many decisive moments in psychology ushered in quantification of the previously unquantifiable:

- 'Psychophysics' and the works of German psychologists, such as E. H. Weber, G. T. Fechner and Wilhelm Wundt, found ways of quantifying subjective perceptual experiences.
- Psychometricians, such as Francis Galton and James McKeen Cattell, spearheaded the 'testing movement'. James Mckeen Cattell introduced the term 'mental tests' in 1890 and argued:

Psychology cannot attain the certainty and exactness of the physical sciences, unless it rests on a foundation of experimentation and measurement. A step in this direction could be made by applying a series of mental tests and measurements to a large number of individuals.

58 Should Psychological Research Be Only about Numbers?

- The Stanford–Binet test of intelligence (Terman, 1916) became the gold standard in mental testing throughout the twentieth century. IQ is one of the most widely used quantitative indexes of psychological functioning. Charles Spearman and Louis Thurstone made important contributions to the theory and application of 'factor analysis', a statistical method used extensively in the development of psychological tests and psychological theories, such as the factor theories of intelligence and the trait theories of personality.
- Louis Thurstone's methods of measuring attitudes in social psychology and the more familiar methods today of Likert were methodological breakthroughs that allowed the development of empirical social psychology.
- Karl Pearson, who originated the idea of the correlation coefficient, introduced the term 'variable' into psychology. This term has its origins in nineteenth-century mathematics, especially in the field of statistics. Edward Tolman, who is probably best remembered for his cognitive behavioural theory of learning and motivation, was the first to make extensive use of the word 'variable' in psychology in the 1930s, when he discussed independent variables and dependent variables together with his new idea of intervening variables. Experimental psychologists like Robert Woodworth encouraged the use of the concepts of 'independent variable and dependent variable' to replace the terminology of stimulus–response. The increasing prominence of this concept led to the reconstruction of psychological phenomena in terms of measurable and mathematical entities. So, constructs such as personality, anxiety, intelligence, self-esteem, ego defence, social conformity, prejudice and happiness became variables which could be measured and whose values could vary. Variables are what we create when we try to study and measure psychological constructs. In short, they are measurable forms of constructs.
- Percy Williams Bridgman (1927) coined the term 'operationalization' to refer to steps/operations we take to measure the variable in question. In psychology, the concept was introduced by S. S. Stevens. Psychologists today believe that the best way of defining the nature of our variables is to describe how they are measured. For example, there are various ways in which we could operationalize the concept or variable of anxiety. We could manipulate it by putting participants in a situation which makes them anxious and compare that situation with one in which they do not feel anxious. We could assess anxiety by asking them how anxious they are, getting other people to rate how anxious they seem to be or measuring some physiological index of anxiety, such as their heart rate. These are different ways of operationalizing anxiety; if all of them are measuring anxiety, they should relate to one another. Operationalization has its benefits. It does succeed in allowing precise and explicit measurements of the variables. However, the cost is that it privileges the measurement issue over the conceptual issue. It reduces the responsibility of the researcher to explicate the theoretical and conceptual nature of the concepts that are

being measured. Danziger and Dzinas (1997) studied the prevalence of the term 'variables' in four major psychological journals published in 1938, 1949 and 1958. They found that variables ceased to be merely a technical aspect of how psychological research is carried out but became a statement or theory of the nature of psychological phenomena. They wrote:

When some of the texts we have examined here proceeded as if everything that exists psychologically exists as a variable, they were not only taking a metaphysical position, they were also foreclosing further discussion about the appropriateness of their procedures to the reality being investigated.

(Danziger & Dzinas, 1997, p. 47)

Another important concern is whether the operational definition is wholly adequate and captures the conceptual essence of the construct under measurement. This is the issue of construct validation that applies to both psychological tests and experimentation.

- Karl Popper, a philosopher of science, introduced the 'hypothetico-deductive approach' to scientific reasoning. In psychological research, a hypothesis is used far more commonly than in disciplines such as sociology, economics and other related disciplines. It is a concept which is derived from natural sciences such as physics, chemistry and biology, which have influenced mainstream psychology more than social and human sciences. The aims of a great deal of research in psychology are more precisely formulated in terms of a hypothesis – a tentative statement of the relationship between two or more variables. A hypothesis can be causal or non-causal. In the case of true experimental designs where the causal variable is manipulated, participants are randomly assigned to conditions and everything else is held constant, the hypothesis is causal, indicating that one variable is causing the other. For example, frustration causes aggression. In correlational and cross-sectional research, the hypothesis is non-causal, implying that the two variables are interrelated without indicating that one variable is causing the other. For example, frustration is associated with aggression. Hypothesis testing exemplifies the approach of scientific psychology. The use of causal hypothesis in true/randomized experimental designs to ascertain the causality of relationships is the ideal form of research design in psychology. Measurement of psychological constructs in the form of variables through operationalization has led to the increased use of independent, dependent, intervening, moderator and mediator variables. Once the variable can be measured, all forms of mathematical operations can be performed on it and that is where statistical techniques and hypothesis testing dominate psychological research. Psychological variables are used to map various kinds of relationships (casual/non-causal) among psychological phenomena aimed at unravelling the regularities of

60 Should Psychological Research Be Only about Numbers?

patterns (laws) and explanations for those patterns (theory). Quantitative research is better at accomplishing the former rather than the latter. The obsession in scientific psychology with searching for causal relationships in data using randomized laboratory experiments, which are highly contrived and simplified research scenarios, has frequently been debated and found to be counter-productive in a practical sense.

PAUSE AND THINK

Identify and operationally define the independent and dependent variables in the following hypothesis: Boys are more likely than girls to commit acts of bullying. How will you conceptualize the variable of 'bullying'? What will be the indicators of bullying which as a researcher you will try to see in boys and girls?

BOX 2.1 THE LIMITS OF STATISTICAL REASONING

Statistics is integral to quantitative research in psychology. While it is useful, its proper usage and limitations of applicability are often ignored. A few examples will clarify this. The first example involves Stevens' theory of level of measurement, which provides four levels of measurement: nominal, ordinal, interval and ratio. This is actually a hierarchy from the least powerful data to the most powerful data. Thus, variables measured in a manner indicative of a ratio scale are at the highest level of measurement and contain more information, all other things being equal. The mathematical procedures that can be applied to each type of measurement differ. The mathematical operations that are appropriate for one type of measurement may be inappropriate for another. One consequence of this is that the sort of statistical analysis that is appropriate for one sort of variable may be inappropriate for a different type of variable. Choosing a statistical technique appropriate to the sort of data one has is one of the skills that has to be learnt when studying statistics in psychology. With respect to psychological measures, it is difficult to find examples of interval and ratio data on which everyone would agree. Can we say that the person with an IQ of 140 is twice as intelligent as a person with an IQ of 70, which will make it a ratio scale of measurement? Or can we say that the difference between an IQ of 70 and 75 is the same as the difference between an IQ of 135 and 140, which will make it an interval scale of measurement? Even if in terms of numbers involved, it means the same, can we be sure, in terms of what we are actually interested in, that is, intelligence, that the difference has the same psychological implications (in terms of adaptive functioning, learning potential) at both ends of the data? This confounding of psychological meaning with mathematical meaning is a major problem in the use of quantification and statistics in psychology (Howitt & Cramer, 2011). It is not surprising that researchers usually treat any measures they make involving scores as if they were interval data. This is done without questioning the status of their measures in terms of Stevens' theory. This makes possible the use of powerful parametric tests. Because otherwise the scores should be regarded as ordinal data, according to Stevens' theory, as there is no way of showing that these scores are on an equal interval scale. Non-parametric statistics were frequently advocated in the past for psychological data at the ordinal level. Unfortunately, many powerful statistical techniques are excluded if one chooses the strategy of using non-parametric statistics.

Another example of the limited applicability of statistics comes from hypothesis testing in statistical analysis. This deals with a simple question: Are the trends found in the data simply the consequence of chance fluctuations due to sampling? Statistical analysis in psychology is guided by the Neyman–Pearson hypothesis testing model. In this model, two statistical hypotheses are offered: (1) that there is no relationship between the two variables that we are investigating (this is known as the null hypothesis), and (2) that there is a relationship between the two variables (this is known as the alternate hypothesis). The researcher is required to choose between the null hypothesis and the alternate hypothesis. They must accept one of them and reject the other. Since we are dealing with probabilities, we do not say that we have proved/disproved the hypothesis. This form of statistical testing of hypothesis is not all there is to hypothesis testing. Research hypotheses are tested in other ways in addition to statistically. There may be alternative explanations of our findings which perhaps fit the data even better; there may be methodological flaws in the research that statistical analysis is not intended to, and cannot, identify; or there may be evidence that the hypotheses work only with certain groups of participants, for example. Therefore, significance testing is only a minimal test of a hypothesis: There are many more considerations when properly assessing the adequacy of our research hypothesis. However, it is standard practice to evaluate the worth of a research hypothesis merely on the basis of statistical hypothesis testing.

How Are Positivism and Quantitative Research Related?

What is the impact of positivism and the scientific method on quantitative research in psychology? A general commitment to the scientific method and to positivism, in particular, has shaped the following characteristic concerns of quantitative research (Bryman, 2004):

- *Concern with concepts/variable and their measurement.* In line with the positivist's emphasis on empiricism, quantitative research is relatively unconcerned with theory and rather uses concepts (conceptual empiricism) as the central focus of research. Thus, the social world tends to be broken

62 Should Psychological Research Be Only about Numbers?

down into manageable packages – social class, caste prejudice, religiosity, job satisfaction, aggression, and so on. The literature review about previous research in relation to a particular concept or cluster of concepts is often used as a substitute for a prior body of theory. Hypotheses, when constructed, are often not derived from a theory as such but from a body of empirical research related to a concept. The principle of operationalism then insists that these concepts should be measurable, that is, be rendered observable. The measurement of concepts tends to be undertaken through the use of questionnaire devices or some form of structured observation, the latter being particularly prevalent in experimental research.

- *Concern with causality.* Questions of causality greatly preoccupy the exponents of qualitative research. The frequent use of the terms 'independent variable' and 'dependent variable' by quantitative researchers is evidence of the widespread tendency to employ causal imagery in investigations. The preoccupation with causality can be readily seen as a consequence of the tendency among quantitative researchers to seek to absorb the methods and assumptions of the natural scientist which have tended to be interpreted in positivist terms. The main aim of experimental designs is to maximize what Campbell (1957) calls 'internal validity', the extent to which the presumed cause really does have an impact on the presumed effect. Central to the exercise of establishing internal validity is the ability to rule out alternative explanations of a posited causal relationship. Experimental designs are invariably depicted in the textbooks on research methods as particularly effective in the context of establishing definitive causal connections. Within such a frame of reference, non-experimental research, such as cross-sectional survey research, may appear to be inadequate, by virtue of the researcher's inability to manipulate aspects of the social environment and observe the effects of such intervention.

- *Concern with generalization.* The quantitative researcher is invariably concerned with establishing the generalizability of the results of a particular investigation beyond the confines of the research location. By verifying generality, the quantitative researcher draws nearer to the law-like findings of the sciences. Among survey researchers, this preoccupation manifests itself in a great deal of attention being paid to sampling issues and, in particular, the representativeness of samples. Researchers who employ experimental designs are preoccupied with problems of generalization too. This topic is often referred to as the problem of external validity, which denotes the extent to which the findings (which may be internally valid) can be generalized beyond the experiment (Campbell, 1957).

- *Concern with replicability.* The belief in the importance of replication among scientists has led to a view among quantitative researchers that such activities should be an ingredient in the social sciences too. Replication serves two purposes: (1) establishing a base for generalization of the findings, and (2) ensuring that research is bias-free. Replication can provide a means of checking the extent to which findings are applicable to other contexts. In addition, it is often seen as a means of checking the biases of the investigator.

- *Concern with individualism*. In the methods of quantitative research, especially the survey method, the individual is treated as the focus of inquiry. The assumption in survey research is that responses of discrete individuals can be aggregated to form overall measures for the sample. This form of aggregate psychology engenders a view of society as if it 'were only an aggregation of disparate individuals' (Blumer, 1948, p. 546). In this view, the social world is also seen as separate from the individuals.

PAUSE AND THINK

Design a study using questionnaires measuring the variables of 'self-efficacy' and 'academic achievement'. Check how each of the characteristics of quantitative research mentioned above applies to such a research study. How will the variables be defined and measured? What kind of causal relationship will be hypothesized? In what way is individualism reflected in this research? To what extent can this study be replicated and generalized?

BOX 2.2 THE SIX 'RED HERRINGS' OF PSYCHOLOGICAL RESEARCH

Hiles (2001) has proposed six red herrings of psychological research, typical of the natural science model. He builds on the conceptualization of Giorgi (1994) who suggested three stark contrasts in the context of the natural science model. A red herring is something that misleads or distracts from the main path or goal. While they are accepted as basic requirements of 'good research', Hiles suggests that there is nothing necessary about them. In fact, they serve to limit our understanding of the phenomenon. These six 'red herrings' are as follows:

1. *Laboratory.* This isolates the phenomenon of interest from its context.
2. *Causal analysis.* This imposes a deterministic analysis on a phenomenon, thereby simplifying and/or distorting understanding.
3. *Measurement.* This adopts quantitative descriptions and loses out on nuanced, rich descriptions.
4. *Hypothetico-deductive method.* By using a confirmatory, theory-driven approach, exploration is minimized.
5. *Objectivity/replication.* This discounts the observer, only repeatable phenomena are of interest.
6. *Narrowing the field of study.* This leads to expediency, leading to functional blindness.

Why Was the Need for Qualitative Research Felt?

As discussed in Chapter 1, the debate between the natural science model and the interpretivist science model is older than psychology itself. It was imported into psychology because of the insistence of the newly emerging discipline to be a natural science while wanting to study human experience. Because of a fundamental contradiction between the subject matter and the methodology of psychological research, the discipline has remained in a state of conflict between the two models of knowledge. While the positivist/natural science model gained control of psychology, the human science model has always lurked in its shadow, critiquing the former as ill-suited to psychological phenomena and offering its own insights.

Contrary to popular belief, qualitative research did not emerge in the 1960s and the 1970s. In the textbooks of research methodology prior to the mid-1970s, there was a clear awareness of the difference between qualitative and quantitative research. However, most of these discussions were centred on the technical adequacy of qualitative research techniques, such as participant observation, and quantitative research techniques, such as experimentation and social survey. The usual tendency was to appraise qualitative research techniques from the standpoint of scientific method and the natural science model, making them look wanting and not so useful.

In general, techniques of participant observation are extremely useful in providing initial insights and hunches that can lead to more careful formulations of the problem and explicit hypotheses. However, they are open to the charge that findings may be idiosyncratic and difficult to replicate. Therefore, many social scientists prefer to think of participant observation as being useful at a certain stage in the research process rather than being an approach that yields a finished piece of research (Blalock, 1970).

Since the 1970s, there has been a systematic and self-conscious intrusion of broader philosophical issues into discussions about the methods of research. The pivotal point of much of the controversy has been the appropriateness of the natural science model to the social sciences (see Chapter 1 for a detailed discussion). It was argued that the scientific method procedures were inadequate and inappropriate when studying people. They failed to take into account the differences between people and the objects of natural sciences (see Chapter 1 for a detailed discussion on the pitfalls of positivist psychology regarding the limitations of the quantitative research methodology).

A qualitative research methodology, in which participant observation and unstructured interviewing were seen as central data-gathering tools, was proposed since it allowed for a better and closer appreciation of the special character of humans as objects of study. The salience of qualitative research grew with the formation of a philosophical rationale for qualitative research and a challenge to quantitative research. The promotion of self-reflection engendered by the writings of philosophers like T. S. Kuhn (1962) and the diffusion of ideas associated with phenomenology from the late 1960s further helped to bring the subterranean tradition of qualitative research into the open. Increasingly, the terms 'quantitative research' and 'qualitative research' came to signify much more than types of data and ways of gathering data: They came to denote divergent assumptions about the nature and processes of research in the social sciences. It is unfortunate that the terms 'quantitative' and 'qualitative' seem to imply quantification or the absence of it as the central issue since the issues are much wider in their scope. A number of alternative terms have been offered for the two types of research paradigms. For example, Guba and Lincoln (1982) propose a contrast between rationalistic (i.e., quantitative) and naturalistic (i.e., qualitative) paradigms, while Evered and Louis (1981) use a contrast between 'inquiry from the outside' and 'inquiry from the inside'. What is implied in all these alternative terminologies is that qualitative research is an approach to the study of the social world which seeks to describe and analyse the culture and behaviour of humans and their groups from the point of view of those being studied.

What Are the Philosophical Underpinnings of Qualitative Research?

Guba and Lincoln (1982) refer to quantitative and qualitative research as resting on divergent paradigms, and hence assumptions, about the proper study of social life. According to such formulations, qualitative research derives from a different cluster of intellectual commitments than quantitative research. Historically speaking, the intellectual roots of qualitative research are in the sociological ideas of verstehen (comprehension), phenomenology, symbolic interactionism and ethnomethodology, which together are taken to constitute the interpretivist approach to research.

Verstehen

In general, the German philosopher Wilhelm Dilthey is credited with the first critical attack on Comtean scientism in the name of the difference of the human sciences from the natural sciences. In his *Introduction to the Human Sciences*, Dilthey (1883) draws a famous distinction between 'sciences of nature' and 'sciences of the spirit', basing the difference between them precisely on the relationship that is established between the researcher and the reality studied. Indeed, in the natural sciences, the object studied consists of a reality that is external to the researcher and remains so during the course of the study; thus, knowledge takes the form of explanation (cause–effect laws, etc.). In the human sciences, by contrast, there is no such detachment between the observer and the observed. Knowledge can be obtained only through a totally different process, that of 'comprehension' (verstehen). According to Dilthey, we explain nature, whereas we understand the life of the mind.

Max Weber (1904) brought the concept of verstehen into sociology at the turn of the twentieth century, and revised Dilthey's original position. While

66 Should Psychological Research Be Only about Numbers?

adopting the principle of verstehen, Weber wanted to preserve the objectivity of social science both in terms of its being independent of value judgements and in terms of the possibility of formulating statements of a general nature, even when an 'orientation towards individuality' is adopted. Regarding the first point, throughout his life, Weber reiterated the need for the historical and social sciences to be free from any value judgement whatsoever. He maintained the distinction between knowledge and judgement. However, he suggested that values would inevitably affect the choice of the objects of study, thus taking on a guiding role for the researcher. Regarding the second point, Weber believed that even when we start with the individual and the subjective sense of his/her action, we can attain objective knowledge that has general characteristics (Corbetta, 2003). According to Weber, social sciences are no different from natural sciences on the basis of their object of study (human versus natural objects) or on the basis of their goal to study social phenomena in their individuality (because social sciences also aim to generalize) but on the basis of 'orientation towards individuality' captured by the method of verstehen:

> Verstehen is the rational comprehension of the motivations underlying behaviour. It is 'interpretation': understanding the purpose of the action and grasping the intentional element in human behaviour. The ability to identify with others, which is inherent in Verstehen, is also channelled towards rational interpretation: putting oneself into the other person's position so as to 'understand'. This involves understanding the motivations of actions, the subjective meaning that individuals attribute to their own behavior because every action, even the most apparently illogical, has its own inner rationality, its own interior 'sense'.
>
> *(Corbetta, 2003, p. 22)*

Through an inductive process, an ideal type is formed which is based on forms of social action that are recurring in human behaviour. Weber exemplified ideal types with reference to social structures (e.g., capitalism), institutions (e.g., bureaucracy, the church and the sect, forms of power) and individual behaviour (e.g., rational behaviour). The regularities that the researcher pursues and identifies in order to interpret social reality are not 'laws' in the positivist sense. Instead of laws, then, we have causal connections, or rather, to use Boudon's (1984) expressions, mere possibilities or opportunity structures.

Weber's work anticipated practically all the themes that were subsequently developed in the rich vein of sociological theory and research that gave rise to approaches such as phenomenological sociology (Husserl and Schutz), ethnomethodology (Garfinkel and Cicourel) and symbolic interactionism (Mead and Blumer), which became established in American sociology from the 1960s onwards. Together, they constitute the paradigm of 'interpretivism' that provides the philosophical rationale for qualitative research. Let us look at each one of them briefly.

Phenomenology

Phenomenology is a philosophy initiated by Edmund Husserl. To build a secure basis of knowledge, Husserl (1927) decided to start with the problem of how objects and events appeared to consciousness since nothing could be spoken or witnessed if it did not come through someone's consciousness. Phenomenology is the study of human experience and the way in which the things are perceived as they appear to consciousness. The phenomenological investigation begins with that which first appears in straightforward experience (description of the immediate experience), hence the call to the 'things themselves'. If, for instance, you were in a garden looking at a red rose, the rose would be the initial focus of experience, standing out within your sensory field. However, this is not all there is to an experience. The second move is towards the 'how' of experiencing (the reflexive nature of the experience itself). If you return to the flower in the garden and attend to it in your conscious awareness, then how it appears is revealed. Although it was first present to you simply as a rose, you now experience it as a sign of beauty and freshness, as giving out a fragrance, and so on. The final stage is to move to the 'I' that is experiencing and the way in which it (the person) emerges through reflective experience as a consequence of that experience. The 'I' does not reveal the world in advance of experience, but instead reveals itself through engagement with all that it encounters in the world. That is, phenomenologists focus on the experience of the world of people and, through this, come to understand the person in the act of perceiving. Recognizing that our subjective experience of the world is filtered through an unquestioning acceptance of its form and content (what he called 'the natural attitude'), Husserl (1927) advocated that the observer needs to bracket this dense web of prior understandings in order to grasp subjective experience in its pure, uncontaminated form. This bracketing of the immediate comprehension of the world is referred to as the 'phenomenological reduction'. For example, from the natural attitude, we see everything at face value: There is simply this rose, this tree, this house. In a phenomenological inquiry, any individual object necessarily belongs to multiple 'essential species', or essential structures of consciousness. By phenomenological reduction, the rose you notice is both unique and at the same time reveals a common structure or essence that is 'rose', which can apply equally well to a wider horizon of possible roses.

Schutz (1967) was concerned about extending Weber's notion of verstehen by making use of Husserl's phenomenology. He viewed the constructs that people use in order to render the world meaningful and intelligible to them as the key focus of a phenomenologically grounded social science. To quote Schutz:

> The world of nature as explored by the natural scientist does not 'mean' anything to molecules, atoms and electrons. But the observational field of the social scientist – social reality – has a specific meaning and relevance structure for the beings living, acting, and thinking within it ... The thought objects

constructed by the social scientist, in order to grasp this social reality, have to be founded upon the thought objects constructed by the common-sense thinking of men, living their daily life within the social world.

(1962, p. 59)

This view entails that any attempt to understand social reality by the social scientist must be grounded in people's experience of that social reality. The social scientist must grasp individuals' interpretive meanings which provide the motivational background to their actions. Even while moving away from mundane and unproblematic accounts provided by the social actors in order to create 'second-order constructs' of actors' comprehension of social reality, these second-order constructs must retain a basic allegiance to the actors' own conceptions of the social world – their 'typifications', to use Schutz's nomenclature. Schutz was aware that the phenomenological research of social reality working could rarely embrace its full extent and complexity. Since we always start out by accepting the existence of that world, there is doubt as to whether the phenomenological reduction is a feasible first step in the analysis of social reality. Accordingly, the dubbing of a particular piece of research or the philosophical basis of qualitative research as 'phenomenological' very often is interpreted as being indicative of little more than a commitment to the actor's perspective.

Ethnomethodology

Ethnomethodology was one of the chief routes by which phenomenological ideas made inroads into the social sciences. The term was coined by Garfinkel (1967) to denote an approach to the study of social reality that takes people's practical reasoning and the ways in which they make the social world sensible to themselves as the central focus. The field has been very influenced by the works of Schutz and has made substantial use of participant observation, unstructured interviewing and conversation analysis.

Symbolic Interactionism

Symbolic interactionists view social life as an unfolding process in which the individual interprets his or her environment and acts on the basis of that interpretation. Herbert Blumer depicts symbolic interactionism as resting on three premises:

The first premise is that human beings act toward things on the basis of the meanings the things have for them ... The second is that the meaning of such things is derived from, or arises out of, the social interaction that one has with one's fellows. The third premise is that these meanings are handled in, and modified through, an interpretative process used by the person in dealing with the things he encounters.

(1969, p. 2)

The first premise can be exemplified by the notion of the 'definition of the situation' in symbolic interactionism. W. I. Thomas' famous dictum – 'If men define situations as real, they are real in their consequences' – sums up the notion of 'definition of the situation'. According to Thomas, before the individual acts, 'there is always a stage of examination and deliberation' (1931, p. 41) which informs the direction of the act. The second tenet can be understood with the help of the two facets of social self – 'I' and 'Me' – which was forged by G. H. Mead (1934), probably the most influential of the early symbolic interactionist thinkers. The 'Me' contains our views of ourselves as others see us, developed through a history of social interactions, an idea neatly captured in Cooley's (1902) notion of the 'looking-glass self'. The 'I' comprises the untrammelled urges of the individual. Through the 'Me', we see ourselves as others see us, and, in adopting this stance, we are reflecting on the tenability of a particular line of action, as viewed by others. In these two premises, action and interaction are viewed as part of a process. We do not 'simply' act, but we act on the basis of how we define the situation at hand and how we think others will view our actions. Thus, interaction entails a continuous process of mutual interpretation of the nature of situations and how we believe our actions will be received. The third premise underscores the need to examine actors' interpretations. There is a widely accepted link between symbolic interactionism and participant observation. However, Blumer (1969) has mentioned other methods also as consistent with symbolic interactionism, including individual and group interviews, letters and diaries, and listening to conversations. Symbolic interactionist ideas form the bedrock of the social constructionism perspective in social sciences.

Premises of the Interpretivist Paradigm

There are various commonalities among these various perspectives, constituting the paradigm of interpretivism: First, an assertion that there is a fundamental 'ontological' difference between natural sciences and social sciences; second, the claim that methods to study natural and social reality must be different; and, third, a conviction that 'individual action endowed with meaning' must be seen as the core of every social phenomenon and of the researcher's work. Unlike Weber, who operated on a macro-sociological level in an attempt to understand macro-structural phenomena, such as the economy, the state, power, religion and the bureaucracy, the latter perspectives moved towards a 'micro' perspective. If society is built on the interpretations of individuals and if it is their interaction that creates structures, then it is the interaction of individuals that one must study in order to understand society. This conviction opened up a completely new area of sociological research, the study of everyday life, which had formerly been disregarded as non-scientific.

70   Should Psychological Research Be Only about Numbers?

The Rise of Critical Social Sciences

The 1960s were a time of upsurge in Western societies: The civil rights movement, student protests, racial conflicts in urban settings, struggles against poverty and inequality, and the rise of feminism. New theoretical perspectives emerged, such as the neo-Marxian and neo-Weberian approaches, critical theory and other new radical perspectives. This led to the development of the critical paradigm approach to social research which is also aligned with qualitative research. The key feature of the critical approach is a desire to put knowledge into action and a belief that research is not value-free. The critical approach has an activist orientation and favours action research. Praxis is the ultimate test of how good an explanation is in the critical approach. All the approaches see a mutual relationship between abstract theory and concrete empirical evidence, but the critical approach goes further to inform how theory can be used to take the specific real-world actions directed towards advancing social change, and how experiences of engaging in action for social change can be used to reformulate the theory. This is referred to as the theory-praxis link. It gives social research a strong connection to political/moral issues. The researcher can decide to ignore the powerless and help those with power and authority in society or advance social justice and empower the powerless (Neuman, 2006). The aim of the critical approach is to reveal and deconstruct the multi-layered nature of social reality. It takes as its starting point the reality consisting of interpretations and meanings derived from social interaction (as in the case of the interpretivist approach). But then it moves deeper to explore which structures of power and control sustain and reproduce these social interpretations. For example, an interview of a woman talking about her husband's cancer using the language of symptoms, course, duration, recurrence, and so on reveals the presence of a biomedical discourse (mediated through doctors, Internet sites, medical magazines) within which she has made sense of his illness. The critical approach will attempt to explore why this discourse shapes her understanding by investigating the links of this discourse to powerful structures of global science and the commercial interests of the pharmaceutical industry which dominate the way disease and treatment are looked at in modern urban contexts. The critical paradigm is considered the third paradigm of research after positivism and interpretivism (see Table 2.2 for differences between interpretivist and critical social sciences).

Postmodernism and the Social Sciences

Yet another heterogeneous intellectual movement that supports qualitative research endeavours is postmodernism. It challenges modernism and chiefly reason and science. Its critique and positive agenda can be summed up in the following four points (Corbetta, 2003):

1. Rejection of general theories that perpetuate the hegemonic goals of Western culture; promotion of multiple theoretical approaches and languages and defence of the fragmentary and non-unitary nature of scientific explanation.
2. Rejection of features of scientific knowledge, such as rationality, linearity and simplicity; appreciation of paradoxes, contradictions, alternative and incompatible multifaceted outlooks.
3. Rejection of the cumulative nature of science; exaltation of differences, multiplicity of local and contextual truths.
4. Exaltation of the 'other', differences, minorities, identification with the oppressed, assumption of 'power' as an explanatory category as the basis of all social relationships and structures.

TABLE 2.2 The philosophical positions of interpretivism and critical research

	Interpretivism	*Critical research*
Ontology	*Constructivism and relativism*: The world is not given, rather, it is constructed by the meanings attributed by individuals (constructivism). An absolute, single, universal reality does not exist. There are multiple realities, each shared by a community of people (relativism).	*Reality has multiple layers*: There is an empirical reality which we can observe with our senses. This surface reality is generated by structures and causal mechanisms that operate at deeper levels. These deeper structures existed before we experience or think about them and have real effects on people.
Epistemology	*Non dualism and reflexivity*: The separation between the researcher and object of study is not present (non-dualism). Objectivity is no longer the ideal. Rather, the awareness of how the researcher and the object of research are shaping each other is inculcated (reflexivity).	*The relation between the researcher and the object of research is imbued by power dynamics*: Special attention is paid to how processes of inequality, discrimination, control, etc. may be entering the research interaction and subsequent knowledge generation
Methodology	*Empathic interaction*: Between the researcher and the object of study to understand the participants' perspective	*Praxis*: Explaining the hidden structures of power and changing the world by penetrating them. The researcher sees the social world simultaneously from inside outward (from a subjective point of view of the people being studied) and from the outside inward (from the viewpoint of external forces that act on people). Knowledge should erode ignorance, enlarge insights about underlying structures and bring about social change.

Source: Corbetta (2003).

REVIEW QUESTIONS

1. Explain the premises of critical social sciences.
2. What is the importance of postmodernism in the study of social reality?

What Are the Characteristics of Qualitative Research?

Qualitative research is primarily understood in terms of the nature of its data. It is largely believed to be descriptive and making use of 'soft' data consisting of words and images, which include interview transcripts, observational records, field notes and reflective journals, personal documents, such as diaries and letters, public documents, such as government records, newspaper articles and advertisements, visual forms, such as photographs, documentaries and TV series, and cultural narratives, such as children's literature, films and folktales. While this is true, a better understanding of it is to see it as constituting a wide yarn of research methods and approaches of data analysis aimed at engaging with the participants' viewpoint. 'Research methods' primarily include semi-structured and unstructured interviewing, participant observation and focus groups. Methods of data analysis include thematic analysis, interpretive phenomenological analysis, discourse analysis, conversation analysis, narrative analysis and grounded theory. Strictly speaking, there are qualitative methodologies rather than a qualitative methodology. According to Bryman (2004), there are certain shared concerns that different qualitative researchers pursue:

- *Capturing the participant's perspective*: The most fundamental characteristic of qualitative research is to view events, actions, values, or behaviours from the perspective of the people who are being studied. This requires being sensitive to the different perceptions and understandings of people placed in different locations within the social reality/institution being researched, such as teachers and students in a school. This requires a sustained period of involvement by the researcher and a preparedness to empathize with those who are being studied. A close relationship between the researcher and the researched is accepted in this mode of research.
- *Providing thick descriptions of the social reality*: Qualitative researchers provide detailed descriptions of the social settings they investigate. This involves attending to minute details of everyday life, using all the senses because of their capacity to help one understand what is going on in a particular context. Clearly, the researcher needs to first construct accurate, sensitive and comprehensive descriptions of what is happening, why and with what consequences in the research setting. From thick descriptions, analysis and interpretation can be built.
- *Attention to context*: All descriptions and derived meanings are contextual and particular to the research situation. Thus, in qualitative research, the

patterns of influence on the research setting are identified and an account is developed as to how these patterns have played their part in the outcome of the study. Context implies several meanings. At one level, it implies that the meanings that people ascribe to their own and others' behaviour have to be set in the context of the values, practices and underlying structures of the social entities (tribes or corporate organizations) and the time frame. At another level, it implies that the process of research in itself sets up a context in which the meaning of a behaviour is generated. The observations of the participant researcher and/or the interviewing by the qualitative researcher also shape the nature of the data that emerge. All meaning is indexical, which means that it will change as the occasion changes.

- *Commitment to reflect process*: The general image that qualitative research conveys about the social order is one of interconnection and change. Research is conducted in naturally occurring settings which are 'open systems' where conditions continuously develop and interact with one another to give rise to a process of ongoing change. It aids us in understanding how a life, a community or an organization takes on a particular character.
- *Flexibility and lack of structure*: Since the avowed aim of qualitative research is to arrive at an 'insider's view' of social reality (reality as it appears from the view of the participants of the social reality), it favours a research strategy which is relatively open and unstructured. Rather than carrying out a questionnaire or an observation schedule, the researcher enters the field with broad research questions and aims and explores their relevance in the field context. Rather than imposing prior and possibly inappropriate frames of reference on the people to be studied, the researcher adopts a predominantly open approach. It allows the researchers access to unexpectedly important topics which might not have been visible had they foreclosed the domain of study using structured research strategy.
- *Role of theory and concepts*: In line with the above approach, qualitative researchers usually refrain from using already existing theoretical frameworks because they may act as blinkers for the researcher and may not fit with the participants' perspectives. Unlike quantitative research, qualitative research does not have hypothesis testing as its explicit aim. Does this mean that qualitative research does not use any concepts in the beginning of research? Does it also imply that qualitative research is not suitable to generate or test theoretical claims? Not really. Certainly qualitative research is not as theory-driven and hypothetico-deductive in its character as quantitative research. However, it does use social scientific concepts as sensitizing concepts that provide a 'general sense of reference and guidance in approaching empirical instances' in the field (Blumer, 1954, p. 7). In this model, a concept provides a set of general signposts for the researcher in his/her contact with the real world. Sensitizing concepts retain close contact with the complexity of social reality and may take on various forms. They are not treated as having fixed empirical referents and precise operational definitions. Qualitative research can generate theory in the course of

74 Should Psychological Research Be Only about Numbers?

data collection and analysis. The grounded theory approach of Glaser and Strauss (1967) is one such example of qualitative theory development approach. It can also use its data to verify the assumptions of theory (see Table 2.3 for differences between human and natural science research).

The set of considerations that should be used to justify the choice of qualitative research is as follows:

1.   The paradigm/perspective being adopted.
2.   A research question that focuses on an exploratory and/or descriptive approach.
3.   The emphasis on meaning rather than measurement.
4.   A focus on subjective experience rather than behaviour.
5.   The need to respect the uniqueness and context of the data collected.

PAUSE AND THINK

Choose a topic to study, such as 'life satisfaction', 'identity', 'gender roles', for which questionnaires are available for quantitative measurement. Think about what you want to know about these constructs. Then study the available questionnaires and note the conceptual understandings underlying such constructs. Reflect on whether the questionnaire approach enables you to understand the constructs the way you wanted to. Write down the limitations imposed by the quantification approach on the way these topics can be studied.

TABLE 2.3 Two major traditions of scientific research

Human science research	Natural science research
Subjectivity: Study of lived experience, acknowledgement of values, findings emerge from shared experience between researcher and participants, several truths may compete and yet co-exist	*Objectivity*: Study of 'the' truth, reality is lawful, science is value-free, use of scientific method to expand knowledge
Knowledge: It is constructed and historically situated, it is local, holistic and context-specific	*Knowledge*: It is discovered, it is universal, context-free, there is linearity of progress in knowledge accumulation
Meaning: The emphasis is on understanding, narrative accounts, etc.	*Causal explanation*: Mechanical, deterministic models
Grounded theory: Theories are developed from data after the data collection, *a posteriori* reasoning, 'real-world' research	*Hypothesis-driven:* Predictive, laboratory study, isolation and control of variables, experimental approach, *a priori* reasoning
Qualitative: Data are collected in the form of descriptions, discourse, themes, content, etc.	*Quantitative*: Data are collected in the form of numbers
Interpretation: Hermeneutics	*Interpretation*: Statistical: descriptive and inferential

Source: Hiles (2001).

REVIEW QUESTIONS

1. Reflect on the philosophical rationale of qualitative research.
2. 'Phenomenology is the cornerstone of qualitative research.' Discuss.
3. Compare the characteristics of quantitative research with qualitative research.

Is Qualitative Research One or Many?

These shared keynotes among qualitative methodologies should not blind us to the fact that there are important differences between them as well. Kidder and Fine (1987) distinguish between two meanings of qualitative research: Big Q/small q. 'Big Q' refers to open-ended, inductive research methodologies that are concerned with theory generation and the exploration of participants' meanings. The characteristics listed above describe the 'Big Q' methodology. 'Small q' refers to using non-numerical data in hypothetico-deductive designs. For example, using a short interview along with a structured psychological test to embellish the researcher-defined/tool-defined categories.

Differing Standpoints of Qualitative Research

Qualitative research takes different positions in relation to the nature of reality, reflexivity and critical language awareness (Willig, 2013). On the matter of the nature of reality, Reicher (2000) identified two types of approaches to qualitative research: experiential and discursive. Experiential research is realist in its view of reality, as it takes people's cognitions and emotions as real and is aimed at gaining an understanding of people's experiences, ways of thinking and actions. By contrast, discursive research is social constructionist, as it takes reality to be constructed and language to be the vehicle of constructing versions of reality. Madill, Jordan and Shirley (2000) suggested a continuum of positions with naïve realism on one end and radical constructionism on the other, with contextual constructivism in the middle. Some forms of qualitative research adopt a critical realist position. Others adopt a contextual constructionist position where the assumption is that all knowledge is necessarily contextual and standpoint-dependent. This means that different perspectives generate different versions of understandings of the same phenomenon. As a result, such research is concerned with completeness rather than accuracy of representation. Radical constructionism challenges the notion of representation itself. Here, knowledge is seen as a social construction and the focus of research is the discursive resources and practices that constitute knowledge.

Some kinds of qualitative research make both personal and epistemological 'reflexivity' central to the research process, and it forms an integral part of the research report. Personal reflexivity involves reflecting how the researcher's own values, social identities, experiences and curiosity have shaped the research.

Epistemological reflexivity encourages reflection upon how the research question, design of the study and the assumptions of the researchers define and limit the outcome of research. Could the research questions be investigated differently? Qualitative researchers take different positions on the extent to which language constructs versions of reality. At one end of the continuum, researchers argue that language constructs social reality and research should aim at studying ways in which such constructions are produced, how they change across cultures and history and how they shape people's experiences. At the other end of the continuum are qualitative researchers who believe that the link between thought–emotion is complex and language is transparent, and language merely describes 'what is going on' in a particular setting.

Range of Qualitative Methods

An examination of a range of journals and research methods textbooks offers a disturbingly wide range of 'qualitative methods'. Some of them are as follows:

- Interviewing: Semi-structured/narrative
- Single case study
- Focus groups
- Conversation analysis
- Discourse analysis
- Narrative analysis
- Interpretive phenomenological analysis
- Q methodology
- Action research
- Grounded theory
- Feminist research
- Diary method
- Cooperative inquiry
- Biographical methods
- Participative inquiry
- Ethnomethodology
- Naturalistic/field study
- Integral inquiry
- Intuitive inquiry
- Organic inquiry
- Transpersonal inquiry
- Exceptional experience
- Memory work
- Psychosocial research
- Psychoanalytic research
- Ethnography

BOX 2.3 AN EXAMPLE OF A QUALITATIVE RESEARCH STUDY

This qualitative research exemplifies the various keynotes of qualitative research in psychology. The work endeavours to understand the vicissitudes of self in a displaced community – the uprooted and exiled Tibetans. As a qualitative researcher, Vahali (2009) immersed herself in the context of the study. This was facilitated by several field visits and prolonged stays in Dharamshala, a Tibetan settlement in India, by the researcher. In order to develop a holistic and comprehensive understanding of the experience of refugeehood, several generations and groups of Tibetan refugees were studied – the elderly Tibetan refugees, the middle generation, the younger Tibetan generation, torture survivors and ex-political prisoners. The work proceeded with the help of narratives, life profiles and interviews, memories, biographies and autobiographies. This allowed close engagement with the lived reality and experience of the Tibetan participants. In order to have an insider's perspective of the participants' and community's life-world, the researcher familiarized herself with Chinese and Tibetan history, politics and sociology as well as Tibetan art, literature, opera and other folk practices. It also entailed developing an understanding of Buddhism, as it is the dominant religious faith among Tibetans. The researcher, while trying to listen to the psychological, the particular nuance in the life-stories of participants, also attempted to relate whatever they said to the larger and more extended theme of refugeehood and exile. In making this leap from the individual to the abstract, the ideas and perspectives of various thinkers were drawn upon. The text is rich in grounding interpretations in concrete examples (in the form of long conversations and stories) and reflexive moments where the researcher sensitively draws on her own comprehension of the participants' narratives to offer meanings of their lives. A particularly shining example of reflexivity is provided by her in bearing witness to the testimonies of long- term ex-political prisoners and young torture survivors of the Tibetan community:

> Prior to my encounter with Tibetans, in upholding egalitarian ideals, I had strongly affirmed the ideological premises of communism. And though at all levels, this work questioned my Marxist inclinations, yet nowhere was it as difficult for me to hold my ground, as it was during the phase when I was listening to Tibetan torture survivors. Weighed down by a double force (firstly, the very nature of torture testimonies and secondly by the fact that the Communist torture-reformer's presence represented a forceful subversion of my socialist beliefs), my initial reactions to the survivors' evocations were 'purely' emotional. In their narrations, as Communism was repeatedly sketched through dark and brutal strokes, I, in turn, lived through an intense phase of self-despair. How could an ideology that had inspired to create a beautiful world, end up in so much of violence and brutality? In what ways was the revolution any better than the preceding feudal system? ... While throughout the day, I remained preoccupied with the

> task of listening to survivors, during night many sequences of violence and torture from their lives would haunt me in the form of nightmares ... As far as my conscious emotions were concerned, I came to vehemently question and even despise many of the Communists' stances ... I had almost 'become the victim'. Unable to preserve my separate place, position and perspective, for a long while, like the torture survivors, I too needed other listeners to whom I could narrate their stories and thus deal with my sense of guilt.
>
> *(Vahali, 2009, pp. 300–301)*

What Are the Critiques of Qualitative Research?

Qualitative research is often accused of being subjective, merely descriptive, not having adequate checks to ensure reliability and validity and being unable to generalize. How are these issues responded to and resolved?

Qualitative Research Is Subjective

Qualitative research does not make claims to be 'objective', but it does offer a different way of working through the relationship between objectivity and subjectivity. Subjectivity is a resource, not a problem in qualitative research. Objectivity and subjectivity are always defined in relation to one another, and the positivists assume that the relationship is like a conceptual zero-sum game in which the reduction of subjectivity will lead to an increase in the other, the production of a fully objective account. In qualitative research, on the other hand, to get to an objective account of the phenomenon in question, it is important to explore the ways in which the subjectivity of the researcher impacts the definition of the problem to be studied and the way the researcher interacts with the data to produce a particular type of meaning. This is what is called reflexivity, personal and epistemological. Research is always carried out from a standpoint and the pretence of value-neutrality in quantitative research is disingenuous (for a fuller discussion on the objectivity of science, see Chapter 1). To say that research will not have any effects is denying the fact that the activity of studying something will always change it, will affect it.

Qualitative Research Is Merely Descriptive

Description is unfairly condemned as the lowest expression of research. Rather, it is a cornerstone of good quality research. Qualitative research does a good job of providing an accurate, sensitive and comprehensive descriptive foundation of the phenomena under study. It can provide in-depth and detailed descriptions of people, processes, inter-relationships, settings and situations. Quantification encourages premature abstraction from the subject matter of research and a concentration on numbers and statistics rather than concepts.

Human experience and interaction are far too complex to be reduced to a few variables, as is typical in quantitative research. Qualitative methods provide a more complete understanding of the subject matter of the research. Besides, qualitative research does not only provide rich descriptions. 'It also supports other research outcomes like interpretation (developing new concepts, refining old concepts, clarifying and understanding complexity, developing theory), verification of assumptions and theories and evaluation of practices, processes and innovations' (Peshkin, 1993).

Qualitative Research Is Atheoretical

The specification of theory at the outset of research tends to be disfavoured in such research because of a possibility of premature closure on the issues to be investigated. Emphasis on capturing the phenomenal data and contextual understanding are the reasons why qualitative researchers are disinclined to instil theoretical elements into their research. However, this is not to say that it is completely atheoretical. Researchers express their commitment to grand theoretical ideas such as symbolic interactionism, Marxism, and so on.

Qualitative researchers are also often accused of not supporting explanatory concepts and theory generation. This is not true. In the grounded theory approach of Glaser and Strauss (1967), theories are derived from the fieldwork process, refined and tested through it and gradually elaborated into a higher level of abstraction towards the end of the data collection process. Sometimes qualitative researches use the stringent approach of using deviant/negative cases to test emerging theory.

Qualitative Research Suffers from the Problem of Validity

The problem of validity is also referred to as the problem of interpretation in qualitative research. In testing-based research, validity refers to the degree to which what has been measured corresponds with other independent measures obtained by different research tools. The correlation between a test and other tests of the same thing, for example, would be a measure of how far that test is measuring what it claims to be measuring. In experiments, internal validity refers to a study's ability to determine if a causal relationship between independent variable(s) and dependent variable(s) is true. For example, in intervention studies, it is important to know whether observed changes (improved test scores, reduced symptomology) can be attributed to the intervention programme (i.e., the cause) and not to other possible causes (sometimes described as 'alternative explanations' for the outcome). Experimental research suffers from low ecological validity which is usually high in the case of qualitative research because of its emphasis on researching in natural settings and gaining insiders' view.

80 Should Psychological Research Be Only about Numbers?

The essence of validity in qualitative research is different. 'From a qualitative research perspective, validity implies whether research captures participants' meanings and viewpoints.' Lincoln and Guba (1985) coined the term 'credibility' to imply this sense in the context of qualitative research. What is debatable is whether qualitative researchers can really provide accounts from the perspective of those whom they study, and how to evaluate the validity of their interpretations of their perspectives. In other words, the issue of credibility is why one interpretation has been advanced rather than any other, and whether it is genuinely consistent with the participants' perspective. There are some methodological ways that can help resolve this debate (Lincoln & Guba, 1985).

1. *Prolonged engagement.* Researchers should remain in the field for a sufficiently long period of time to learn or understand the culture, social setting or phenomenon of interest. This involves spending adequate time, observing various aspects of a setting, speaking with a range of people and developing relationships with members of the culture. This helps in the development of rapport and trust which facilitates understanding and co-construction of meaning between researchers and members of a setting.

2. *Persistent observation.* The purpose of persistent observation is to identify those characteristics and elements in the situation that are most relevant to the problem or issue being pursued and focusing on them in detail. If prolonged engagement provides scope, persistent observation provides depth.

3. *Triangulation.* Researchers can make use of multiple sources of data collection and observations to get a better understanding of what is happening in reality. A single method can never adequately shed light on a phenomenon. Using multiple methods can help facilitate a deeper understanding. Qualitative researchers generally use this technique to ensure that an account is rich, robust, comprehensive and well developed. Janesick (1994) lists five types of triangulation: (a) data triangulation (use of several data sources); (b) investigator triangulation (use of several researchers or evaluators); (c) theory triangulation (use of multiple perspectives to interpret a single set of data); (d) methodological triangulation (use of multiple methods to study a single problem); and (e) interdisciplinary triangulation (drawing on the methods and insights of several disciplines).

4. *Peer debriefing.* This is a process in which the researcher works with one or several colleagues who hold an impartial view of the study. The peers can examine the researcher's transcripts, final reports and research methodology. Through this investigation, the peers may detect overemphasized or underemphasized points, vague descriptions, general errors in the data, or biases or assumptions in the data which are then communicated back to the researcher. This feedback enhances credibility and ensures validity. Peer debriefing will also help the researcher become more aware of his/her own views regarding the data.

5. *Negative/deviant case analysis.* This involves searching for and discussing elements of the data that do not support or appear to contradict patterns or explanations that are emerging from the data analysis. Deviant case analysis is a process for refining an analysis until it can explain or account for a majority of cases. Analysis of deviant cases may revise, broaden and confirm the patterns emerging from data analysis.

6. *Member checking.* The researcher can submit a version of his/her findings to the participants and seek their verification of his/her interpretations of their worlds. This is also called respondent validation. This gives participants the opportunity to correct errors and challenge what are perceived as wrong interpretations and also provides the opportunity to volunteer additional information which may be stimulated by the playback process. In addition, it provides respondents with the opportunity to assess the adequacy of the data and the preliminary results as well as to confirm particular aspects of the data.

7. *Thick descriptions.* Intricate and detailed descriptions of the patterns of interactions, sequences of events and conversations along with field notes can be provided as data for the readers to engage in. This is helpful in allowing the reader to formulate his/her hunches about the perspectives of the people who have been studied and how adequately the researcher has interpreted people's behaviour in the light of the explication of their systems of meaning. This also provides a vantage point to the reader to formulate alternative accounts of interpretation.

The methods described above to enhance the 'credibility'/'trustworthiness' of the qualitative research are based on a positivist understanding of validity which is a reduction of systematic bias and the approximation to truth. A more radical re-envisioning of the concern of validity is the shift from the question of 'Is this research valid?' to 'What is this research valid for?' (Aguinaldo, 2004). Through a social constructionist lens, notions of 'truth' and 'objectivity' are problematic as research findings are always already situated and partial. Thus, it asks, 'Upon what grounds can we say that one research claim is better, that is, more valid than another?' From this vantage point, scientific research and its empirical claims are rhetorical in nature. Scientists use the linguistic repertoires and discursive strategies institutionalized within the conventions of scientific writing to assert their research claims as 'fact' and to subvert the scientific and lay claims of others. From a social constructionist position, validity becomes not a determination (i.e., 'is valid' versus 'is not valid') but as an interrogation of multiple and sometimes contradictory functions that any particular research representation may serve (Aguinaldo, 2004). Research facts become research claims. They are not policed in accordance with whether they approximate the truth and reality, as these are themselves seen to be fragmented, multiple and contradictory. Rather the research claims are envisioned as 'narratives' that are premised upon certain kinds of ontological and epistemological positions, such

82 Should Psychological Research Be Only about Numbers?

as realist (that assumes an objective world), critical (which foregrounds political structures that shape the social world within uneven social relations), deconstructive (which emphasizes the social construction of narratives and liberates multiple possibilities of experiential realities), and so on. Validity becomes a reflexive exercise on the part of the researcher to make explicit her/his own research positions. It becomes a process of actively promoting a critical reading and rereading of any given research representation. The goal of validation becomes to discover and anticipate how a particular research narrative 'does', 'can' or 'might' function to incite and foreclose, emancipate and oppress when applied to different times and contexts and evaluated from different social locations.

Qualitative Research Is Not Replicable

Reliability in quantitative research is the extent to which the same results will be obtained if the research is repeated. A qualitative researcher does not claim that his/her work is perfectly replicable:

> It is certainly possible to repeat the work that has been described but that repetition will necessarily also be a different piece of work: different by virtue of the change in the researcher, informants and meanings of the research tools over time.
>
> *(Kvale, 1994, p. 150)*

Reliability in qualitative research can take the form of 'inter-researcher agreement' (among researchers conducting similar research in the field) over process and findings of a research study. It also implies a requirement on the part of the researcher to 'develop consistent habits of handling the data'. Audit trails, which are transparent records of research steps taken from the start of the research project to the reporting of the findings, can help in this process. Lincoln and Guba (1985, p. 316) state, 'Since there can be no validity without reliability, a demonstration of validity is sufficient to establish the reliability.' They use the term 'dependability' to refer to reliability in qualitative research.

Qualitative Research Is Not Able to Generalize the Results of the Research

Generalizability/external validity relates to how the findings of one study can be applied to other participants and settings. Sampling techniques and sample size are often used to guarantee the strength of claims made for the generalizability of the results by quantitative research. A good practice in this form of research is to use probability sampling techniques, ensuring representativeness and large samples to collect data. In qualitative research, sample sizes are usually small because of the time-consuming and intensive effort involved in the nature of data collection. Lincoln and Guba (1985) suggest that 'transferability' of results requires 'thick descriptions and careful analysis of key parameters of the research setting' so that transferability of results generated from one research setting to another research setting can be assessed. Another possible approach to the problem of generalizability is through the 'examination of a number of similar cases by more than one researcher', whereby the overall investigation assumes the framework of 'team research', such as that found in much qualitative research. The cases can also be chosen on the basis of their typicality. Thus, every case is typical of a certain cluster of characteristics, other factors being comparable. This procedure is one way of approaching the summation of case studies so that generalization may be extracted as evidence is accumulated. Others like Yin (1994) oppose such a view of generalization in case study research and propose that 'case studies can give rise to theoretical insights that may be generalizable'. Stake (1994, p. 245) sums up the argument:

> [Whereas] the single or a few cases are poor representation of a population of cases and poor grounds for advancing grand generalization ... Case studies are of value in refining theory and suggesting complexities for further investigation, as well as helping to establish the limits of generalizability.

It is important to appreciate that the quality of a study in each paradigm should be judged by its own paradigmatic imperatives. When judging (testing) qualitative work, Strauss and Corbin (1990, p. 250) suggest that the 'usual canons of "good science" ... require redefinition in order to fit the realities of qualitative research'. Conceptualizations of objectivity, reliability, validity and generalizability are laden with many problems of their own in quantitative research. Importantly, they do not fit with the interpretivist/qualitative conceptions:

> Qualitative research has its own standards of rigour and thoroughness. It is not, as if, because qualitative research acknowledges that multiple interpretations exist, all interpretations are considered to be equally valid, irrespective of the soundness of methodological process adopted. Many evaluative criteria for assessing the 'goodness' of qualitative methodologies have been proposed.
> *(Henwood & Pigeon, 1992; see also Lincoln & Guba, 1985)*

Some of them have been reviewed above. Others include 'coherence' (analysis should be characterized by integration and coherence such as in the shape of a story/narrative, a framework, a map) and 'resonance with readers' (readers should feel an appreciation and expansion of understanding of the subject matter; Elliott et al., 1999).

Is Qualitative Research All Good?

Certainly not! Qualitative research has its own shortcomings. Many of its epistemological assumptions are difficult to be actualized in practice. Delay in

84 Should Psychological Research Be Only about Numbers?

the use of theoretical reflection until a later stage of research so as to allow data to emerge through the eyes of participants represents significant problems in the implementation of qualitative research. How possible it is to perceive reality as others perceive it? Many researchers find it difficult to conduct qualitative research, as it does not provide the researcher with certainty. The research process has less clear signposts, and the phases of data generation and data analysis are cyclical. Methodolatry and the non-reflexive stance of the researcher, which the qualitative research paradigm has heavily critiqued, often seep into its own practice. Qualitative researchers often are constrained within the 'methodological straitjacket' and do not explicitly discuss the reasons for the choice of their positions of epistemology, theoretical perspective, methodology and method. The positivist paradigm critiques the qualitative research paradigm for reasons such as its results are provisional and tentative; it is concerned with description and explanation but not with prediction; and it aims at generating interpretation and not cause–effect sequences.

However, qualitative research offers certain 'opportunities' to do research which are not possible within quantitative research:

- It is a method of preference for exploring a topic or problem that has not been previously researched. Because it does not require firm preconceptions about which variables will be important and how will they be related, it can be used profitably in research settings where there is lack of clarity about what research questions should be asked and what the key theoretical issues are.
- It permits analysis of the ways in which real-life contexts affect the phenomena under investigation (e.g., presence of a teacher on a student's behaviour, the effect of institutionalization on mental patients, the impact of joint family living on conjugality of newly-wed couples).
- Qualitative research permits the holistic analysis of complex, dynamic and exceptional phenomena. A period of observation or a series of interviews typically yields a vast repository of data about a multitude of interacting aspects of the topics studied. It permits consideration of fine distinctions, exceptions and complex patterns of interrelationships in analysis. Qualitative research treats internal contradictions, pauses and absences in people's talk as valuable pointers to areas of tension, difficulty and conflict. Rather than discarding deviant or exceptional cases, they are used to reflect on cultural norms that are circumvented by them and the reasons for and consequences of transgressing these.
- It is a suitable method for gaining partial access to the subjective perspectives of others, be it the psychological core of an experience, latent and irrational meanings of actions or multiple conflicting inner voices constituting one's identity.
- As a scientific discipline, psychology has tended to deny the aesthetic dimension of research and to ignore the aesthetic dimension of human

experience. Qualitative research marks its return. Crafting a case study can be an experience akin to painting a portrait in which dominant features, idiosyncratic elements and an overall balance and coherence of the whole image are given due consideration. Listening to participants is also a process of registering the distinctive tonalities, rhythms, convergences and dissonances in participants' narratives.

The choice of qualitative and quantitative research methodology should be dictated by the aims and objectives of the research and not by the personal whims and tastes of individual researchers. Both have their benefits and scope of relevance.

PAUSE AND THINK

Search for a qualitative research study in a journal. Read it closely to infer the characteristics of qualitative research. Identify the limitations of the study.

Can Qualitative and Quantitative Research Approaches Be Combined?

The question of the integration of qualitative and quantitative research approaches depends upon the extent to which they constitute divergent models of the research process. The epistemological version of debate (positivism versus interpretivism) does not readily admit a blending of qualitative and quantitative research since the two traditions are deemed to represent highly contrasting views about how social reality should be studied (see Tables 2.1 and 2.2). The technical version of the debate much more readily accommodates an integration of the two since it looks at the two traditions as methods of data collection. In this latter position, each method – qualitative and quantitative – has its own advantages and limitations and is better suited for some kinds of research problems and data analysis. There are studies that use methods of participant observation and survey together and those that present some findings of an ethnographic study in a quantitative way. Questions are also raised about one-to-one correspondence between epistemology and method. Can an interview method not have positivist leanings? Can social surveys not provide insights into questions of meanings?

The issue of integration of the two approaches also raises the concern about the 'similarities between the two'. The emphasis on their epistemological difference runs the risk of failing to give attention to these commonalities. Both are empirical and emphasize systematic, planned research. Each approach says research must be public and its process must be explicit, open to scrutiny by other researchers. Neither sees research as static, fixed or close; rather, it is evolving, asking new questions and pursuing leads. They also share some common problems. One is reactivity – the awareness in the participant that he/she is being studied and the reaction it generates in him/her towards the researcher and the research instruments. It affects the experimenter and the ethnographer alike. While experimental tradition tries to deal with this problem through the use of double-blind procedures and one-way mirrors, ethnographers try to minimize it by prolonged immersion in the site of fieldwork to reduce their 'stranger' value. The second is the issue of the representativeness of the sample. Quantitative research is concerned with establishing that respondents are representative of a wider population so that the generalizability of the findings can be enhanced. The issue takes on a different hue in the case of qualitative research, as here the focus is more on the typicality of the person's experience and actions. However, it is still important to know how representative the 'typical' account is. For example, qualitative researchers sometimes display a concern that the people with whom they come into contact may be marginal to the social setting and thus provide a selective version of reality.

There are many ways in which qualitative and quantitative research can be combined. One is triangulation. Denzin (1970, p. 310) treats triangulation as an approach in which 'multiple observers, theoretical perspectives, sources of data, and methodologies' are combined. In this context, qualitative and quantitative research may be viewed as different ways of examining the same research problem, thereby enhancing validity. Yet another way is in which qualitative research acts as a precursor to the formulation of problems and the development of instruments for qualitative research. Sometimes the researcher uses quantitative methods of data collection in predominantly qualitative studies because of the researcher's assessment that qualitative data will not allow a full account of all the relevant issues. Thus, survey data are used along with ethnographic/interview data. The quantitative methods may give a macro picture and reflect on structural elements of the field. The qualitative methods provide the micro details and help to reflect on the processual aspects of the data. Quantitative research procedures are also used to demonstrate that qualitative analysis was reasonably representative of the whole. Another important reason for combining the two research approaches is that qualitative research may facilitate the interpretation of the relationship between variables. It is helpful in providing an understanding of the processes and mechanisms that produce statistical relationships.

While integration of approaches and methods seems like a good research strategy, there are several barriers to this integration. One is the view that qualitative and quantitative research traditions are based on fundamentally opposing epistemological positions. Another obstacle is cost in terms of time, effort and money in combining both strategies. Third, rarely do the two methods have an equal role in an investigation. Usually, one approach prevails as the major source of data and analysis. Fourth, the methodological competence and inclination of researchers also play an important role in the possibility of combining the two traditions.

REVIEW QUESTIONS

1. Which is better, qualitative research or quantitative research?
2. Suggest ways in which qualitative and quantitative research can be combined.

Final Comments

What does the above discussion tell us about the relevance of quantification in psychology? Dale Boesky (2002, p. 445) has reminded us of a seemingly self-evident dictum enunciated by Aristotle more than 2000 years ago: 'The same degree of precision is not to be sought for in all subjects ... It is a mark of an educated man to look for precision in each class of things just so far as the subject admits.' While encouraging us to seek precision and perhaps quantification as far as our knowledge permits, this famous quotation also issues a warning 'but not to go further'. The arguments about the limits of applicability of the positivist–experimental paradigm and the quantification imperative in psychology, as outlined in Chapter 1 and the present chapter, converge on an understanding that psychological research should not be exclusively quantitative in nature.

It is also important to recognize that, historically, psychological research has not been exclusively quantitative – not in its epistemology, not in its methods and not in its data. Description, qualitative methods and interpretation have always been used in psychology. The quantification imperative, expressed in terms of large samples and statistical analysis, has not been the traditional preoccupation of psychologists, including behaviourists. Experiments by Watson and Rayner (Little Albert in 1920) and by Jones (Little Peter in 1924)—are two sterling examples of single case experimentation in the history of psychological research in abnormal psychology. Ebbinghaus' famed investigation on memory in 1885 had only himself as an experimental subject. Besides, interview and observations have been significant research techniques used in several classic researches, such as Piagetian studies, Adorno's work on authoritarian personality, Milgram's destructive obedience studies, Hawthorne interviews on human relations, Robert White's work on normal personality, to name but a few. Qualitative research methods continue to be used with profit in several fields of psychology, notably, clinical psychology, developmental psychology, personality and cultural psychology.

The discipline of psychology shows no signs of becoming purely positivist or purely interpretivist or purely critical in its orientation. As Lev Vygotsky (1978, p. 65) said, 'The search for method becomes one of the most important problems of the entire enterprise of understanding the uniquely human form of psychological activity.' As long as there is a plurality of epistemological foundations of psychological knowledge, there will be and should be use of multiple research methods and strategies. An 'as well as' stance rather than an 'either/or' stance supporting the balanced interplay of causal and interpretive perspectives seems most promising.

3

WHAT IS 'SOCIAL' ABOUT SOCIAL PSYCHOLOGY?

Psychology as a discipline, by definition, is about the person, but what makes us who we are? A part of the answer is that it is our traits, weaknesses or flaws that determine our actions. However, it is equally true that words, actions or the mere presence of other people also can affect us. Social psychology, as a sub-discipline of psychology, is entrusted with the task of answering this question by weighing up the relative strength of the 'inner' and 'outer' forces in shaping a person's behaviour. It is a contextual approach that attempts to study how the social situation affects human behaviour. Naomi Weisstein summarizes the power of social situation and, thus, the need for psychology as 'social' as:

> If subjects under quite innocuous and non-coercive social conditions can be made to kill other subjects and under other types of social conditions will positively refuse to do so; if subjects can react with a state of physiological fear or by becoming euphoric because there is somebody else around who is euphoric or angry because there is somebody else around who is angry, if a student becomes intelligent because teachers expect them to be intelligent and rats run mazes better because experimenters are told that the rats are bright, then it is obvious that a study of human behavior requires, first and foremost, a study of the social context within which people move, the expectation as to how they will behave, and the authority which tells [them] who they are and what they are supposed to do.
>
> *(1993, p. 203)*

Social psychology is assumed to be a unitary body of knowledge. Perhaps nothing is further from the truth. There are many social psychologies. Distinctions are drawn according to disciplinary positioning (between psychological social psychology (PSP) and sociological social psychology (SSP)), location

DOI: 10.4324/9781003471851-4

(between American and European social psychology) and contents (between experimental psychology, on the one hand, and discursive, critical and social constructionist social psychology, on the other). Each of these social psychologies addresses the question of 'social' differently.

How Has Psychological Social Psychology Developed?

What we, as students of psychology, understand today as modern social psychology is a particular form of social psychology called the psychological social psychology (PSP). It is considered to have a short history, tracing its beginnings from the twentieth century. But issues of social psychological relevance have echoed throughout history, in literature and in the works of Aristotle and Machiavelli. The question, 'How does the social situation impact human behaviour?', has been an abiding one. However, there is something different about modern social psychology which is not found in these other writings and that is a high value on the 'scientific approach' which becomes a linchpin of the discipline of psychology. The most obvious sign of the allegiance to science was the commitment to the collection of empirical data, particularly from 'controlled' experiments.

Roots

PSP, which is now mostly American in its character, has its main roots in two movements in European psychology: German *Völkerpsychologie* and French and Italian work on 'crowd psychology'. The German psychologist Wilhelm Wundt, who is widely regarded as the founder of psychology, had a hand in the early development of what would become social psychology. In 1862, Wundt proposed that there should be two branches of psychology: physiological psychology and *Völkerpsychologie* (literally translated as the psychology of ordinary people). *Völkerpsychologie* dealt with the cultural and communal products of human nature, which includes religions, languages and mythologies. It proposed that people who belong to particular social groups tend to think in a collective rather than individual manner, to hold the same opinions and beliefs and to share the same values. Its theories proposed a link between culture and language. Wundt, for example, suggested that the vocabulary and grammar of a particular language profoundly affect the way people think and perceive the social world, and hence argued that language can provide a unifying medium for group identity and membership. He proposed that historical and comparative methods rather than experimentation were more applicable for the study of such concerns. The French theorist, Gustave Le Bon, in his book, *The Crowd: A Study of the Popular Mind* ([1895] 1977), suggested the idea of a 'group mind' which in many ways was a parallel to the thesis in *Völkerpsychologie*. Another influential theorist in the field was Tarde, who in his book, *The Laws of Imitation* (1890), speculated about the impact of elite groups on general populations.

90 What Is 'Social' about Social Psychology?

These European traditions were incompatible with the new behaviourist perspective emerging in the United States during the early years of the twentieth century. Thus, PSP in America, which would become the intellectual core of the discipline, developed largely outside the realm of these influences.

The Rise of Social Psychology in America

From the perspective of science, contemporary social psychology originated in America with the first experiments on a social psychological topic. An American psychologist at Indiana University, Norman Triplett, is generally credited with having conducted the first empirical social psychological study. In 1895, Triplett asked the following question: 'How does a person's performance of a task change when other people are present?' The question was prompted by Triplett noticing that a bicycle racer's speed was faster when he was paced by other cyclists than when he raced alone. He devised a social scientific experiment to answer this question and the results were published in 1898. In 1908, English psychologist William McDougall published the first text on social psychology, arguing for a scientific approach to psychology and, crucially, for studying the impact of social processes on instincts, the processes by which societies move from 'primitive' to 'civilized'. Central to McDougall's theorizing was the primacy of instincts. He took as his fundamental axiom that human action arises out of biologically pre-programmed instincts, but that this conduct is modulated through the influence of social regulations operating in the society to which a person belongs and, in civilized societies, by an individual's socially acquired self-control. Walther Moede (1920) wrote a pamphlet on 'experimental group psychology' in which he opposed the nineteenth-century European tradition of 'crowd psychology' (associated with Gustave Le Bon), which was more philosophical. The experiments he suggested involved setting up groups in the laboratory in various controlled ways so that the effects of group membership on thinking and feeling could be established. Moede influenced Floyd Allport, whose series of investigations at Harvard University in the 1920s into whether group membership influences people's judgements definitively launched North American experimental social psychology. Allport published an influential social psychology text in 1924, which bore the stamp of individualism, behaviourism and scientism. In his book, *Social Psychology*, he stated:

> I believe that only within the individual can we find the behavior mechanisms and consciousness which are fundamental in the interactions between individuals ... There is no psychology of groups which is not essentially and entirely a psychology of individuals ... Psychology in all its branches is a science of the individual.

> *(Allport, 1924, p. 4)*

What Is 'Social' about Social Psychology? **91**

Allport's brand of social psychology emphasized how the person responds to stimuli in the social environment, with the group merely being one of many such stimuli. He extolled the virtues of the experimental method in studying such topics as conformity, non-verbal communication and social facilitation.

Another methodological development that greatly aided the development of individual-centric social psychology within psychology was the rise of social psychometrics, the measurement of reported attitudes, opinions, beliefs and behaviours. In the late 1920s, the American social psychologist Emory Bogardus developed the 'social distance scale', one of the first attitude scales to assess attitudes towards the various racial and ethnic groups on a set of questions varying according to social distance.

Growth and Expansion of the Field

During the first three decades of the twentieth century, Allport's conception of social psychology emphasized basic research, with little consideration given to addressing specific social problems or broader issues bearing on reform. However, by the mid-1930s, the discipline was poised for further growth and expansion. This was the time when a significant number of social psychology's most distinguished thinkers fled from Europe to America to escape Nazism. They were trained in gestalt psychology and were instrumental in bringing back the emphasis on cognitive and thought processes in behaviourist social psychology. The trinity of Kurt Lewin, Fritz Heider and Leon Festinger had a great influence on the development of PSP. Lewin is generally considered the 'founding father' of experimental social psychology, and he developed the field theory based on gestalt principles. He proposed that behaviour is influenced by the 'psychological field' or 'social climate', thereby taking a broader view of the social. He also believed that social psychology should be dedicated to social reform and introduced the term 'action research' to describe research engaged in intervening in real social problems. Heider believed that people are naïve psychologists trying to understand the social world and developed the attribution theory which helped explain how people assign the causes of behaviour to internal (personality characteristics) or external characteristics (situational factors). Leon Festinger's theory of cognitive dissonance asserted that people's thoughts and actions are motivated by a desire to maintain cognitive consistency. His theories and research are credited with renouncing the previously dominant behaviourist view of social psychology by demonstrating the inadequacy of stimulus–response conditioning accounts of human behaviour. Festinger is also credited with advancing the use of laboratory experimentation in social psychology, although he simultaneously stressed the importance of studying real-life situations. Theodor Adorno, another émigré from Germany to America (albeit for a short time), studied the psychological parameters of the authoritarian personality. Muzafer Sherif from Turkey developed a range of elegant experimental studies on social norms, cohesion and social judgement. He combined an experimental approach with observation in the studies of boys' camps.

The Society for Experimental Psychology and the Society for Personality and Social Psychology were founded in 1965 and 1974, respectively. A number of different journals were also established, including the *Journal of Personality and Social Psychology* and the *Journal of Experimental Social Psychology*.

The tradition of social psychology within psychology has been largely American, even if it had its roots in and influences from Europe. As experimentation became the distinguishing marker of this discipline, it came to be known as experimental social psychology. This was the primary method of distinguishing social psychology from social philosophy. In its pursuit to be a science, it turned away from commonsensical knowledge. It is based on the individual as its conceptual object and sees the social as a separate entity influencing the individual. That is the reason why investigating processes, such as conformity, persuasion, obedience, formation of group norms and their effects on people, have been the key areas of research in PSP. The field, since the 1970s, has been beset with questions and critiques regarding the methods, subject matter, theoretical approach, real-world significance and future directions of the field.

PAUSE AND THINK

Identify the key experimental studies on social psychological topics such as pro-social behaviour and aggression. In what way is the 'social situation' defined in these studies?

What Is Psychological/Experimental Social Psychology?

According to Gordon Allport (1954), social psychology is best defined as the discipline that uses scientific methods in 'an attempt to understand and explain how the thought, feeling and behavior of individuals are influenced by the actual, imagined, or implied presence of other human beings'. Myers and Spencer (2006) define social psychology as the 'scientific study of how people think about, influence, and relate to one another'. Baron, Byrne and Branscombe (2007) defined social psychology as 'the scientific field that seeks to understand the nature and cause of individual behaviour and thought in social situations'.

The experimental tradition in social psychology bears the stamp of scientism and behaviourism and can be traced to the writings of Floyd Allport. In 1937, psychologist Stuart Henderson Britt aptly summed up the nature of experimental social psychology: 'Social Psychology of the "present" can be typified by one word: empirical. The empirical method may be characterized by three important techniques: the experimental method; the use of first hand observations; and the employment of statistics' (Britt, 1937, p. 464).

In spite of the waning of the behaviourist influence in psychology, social psychology has continued to use experimentation as its key method throughout its history, such as in the works of Kurt Lewin and Leon Festinger (influenced by gestalt psychology) and Henri Tajfel (who argued that the social bases of experimentation must be understood). The classic and well-known research studies of social psychology, such as Festinger's work on cognitive dissonance, Solomon Asch's conformity research and Stanley Milgram's work on obedience to authority, were experimental in nature. The first book called *Experimental Social Psychology* was published by Murphy and Murphy (1931). None of the studies included in it were experimental, but all were based on the hypothetico-deductive method. Hogg and Vaughan explain what holds experimental social psychology together:

> The scientific method dictates that no theory is 'true' simply because it is logical and makes internal sense. On the contrary, a theory is valid on the basis of its correspondence with fact. Social psychologists construct theories from data and/or previous theories and then conduct empirical research in which data are collected to test the theory.
>
> *(1998, p. 3)*

Social psychology studies a range of social behaviours. To classify its subject matter, William Doise (1986) suggested four levels of analysis: intrapersonal, interpersonal, group and inter-group. The *intrapersonal level* involves a focus on social cognition, the cognitive processes and structures that influence and are influenced by social behaviour. The focus is on the ways in which people think about and make sense of their social behaviour and that of others. Topics included are person perception and stereotyping, social judgement, attitude and attitude change. The *interpersonal level* deals with our relations with other individuals, such as interpersonal attraction, aggression, pro-social behaviour, communication. *Group processes* include pressures to conform and obey, the emergence of a leader, group cohesiveness and decision-making, cooperation–competition, the behaviour of mobs and an audience. At the level of *inter-group relations*, the key topics are social identity processes, social and self-categorization, prejudice and out-group bias, inter-group conflict.

From the above definitions, the following features of the field can be identified:

- It is scientific.
- The level of analysis is the 'individual in the context of the social situation'.
- The social situation has profound effects on human behaviour.
- It seeks to understand the nature and causes of individual behaviour in social situations.

Social Psychology Is Scientific

Social psychology uses the scientific method to study social phenomena. This distinguishes it from philosophy. Let us try to understand the difference

94 What Is 'Social' about Social Psychology?

between scientific social psychology and philosophy. In 1663, the Dutch philosopher Benedict Spinoza offered a highly original insight. He proposed that if we love someone whom we formerly hated, that love would have been stronger if hatred had not preceded it. Spinoza's proposition was logically worked out. His logic is impeccable. But how to be sure that it holds up? Does it always hold up? What are the conditions under which it does or does not? These are empirical questions, meaning that their answers have to be derived from experimentation or measurement rather than by personal opinion. There are several plausible reasons for certain social behaviours. In order to know which of them is most likely and under what conditions, social psychology relies on scientific method.

Social psychologists assert that their understandings are not commonsensical. Common sense and folklore suggest various contradictions, such as 'out of sight is out of mind' and 'absence makes the heart grow fonder' or 'birds of a feather flock together' and 'opposites attract'. Which one is true? To answer questions like these, the social psychologist makes a hypothesis under which one outcome or the other will occur. Then a well-designed experiment is carried out which specifies the conditions under which one or the other is more likely to take place.

While experimentation is the method of choice in psychology, another quantitative tradition is social psychometrics, which also bolsters the claim of social psychology as a science. It is perhaps one of the most widely used techniques in social psychology. With a measuring device of this kind, whole populations can be sampled to discover prevailing attitudes and behaviours in the areas of concern.

Following from its conviction that the scientific method is the only valid means to gain knowledge, social psychology regards this knowledge as objective – unaffected by ideology and hence neutral in its values. Since science, in its view, makes it possible to get at 'the facts' (and facts are facts, irrespective of politics, values, and so on), scientific social psychology places itself outside of and unaffected by ideology. The scientific emphasis also imports into social psychology the valued goals of science, that is, causal explanations based on hypothetico-deductive testing of theory, prediction and control. (For detailed discussion of the issues of objectivity and goals of scientific psychology, see Chapter 1.) It also asserts that the basic psychological processes are universal, and they transcend time and cultural location.

The Level of Analysis Is the 'Individual in the Context of the Social Situation'

Social psychologists attempt to identify the psychological processes within individuals (such as cognitive dissonance, social motives, tendency to comply, attributions) to explain their behaviour in social situations. For example, to answer a social psychological question – Why does a person act violently in a particular situation? – the social psychologist will try to identify the psychological processes that trigger aggression. One such process can be frustration.

Further questions requiring scientific testing are: Does frustration always precede aggression? If people are feeling frustrated, under what conditions will they vent their frustration with an overt, aggressive act? What factors might preclude an aggressive response by a frustrated individual? Besides frustration, what other factors might cause aggression? Sociologists interested in studying aggression are more likely to ask the question: How does a society (or a group within a society) produce aggression in its members? The answer to this question is likely to be sought in macro-environmental factors, such as social and institutional inequalities.

The individual–society interface in psychology is well explained by the analogy of the ocean and sea creatures by Wendy Stainton Rogers. She explains:

> Social psychology has an image of the social world as something like an ocean, in which people swim like sea creatures. They may sometimes act together – like shoals of fish. They may even work cooperatively together and communicate (like dolphins do). But these are going on within the social world – the creatures are immersed in it, and it affects what they can do. It is an ocean with tides and currents that buffet and sweep the creatures along. Mostly these currents merely set them in motion in a particular direction and they still have volition about where they go (after their dinner, for example). Sometimes, though, the current may be so strong that it cannot be resisted. Crucial to this image of the social world is that the creatures and the ocean are separate from one another. The psychological processes going on in their minds interact with the social forces going on outside, and this interaction determines what they do.
>
> *(2003, p. 6)*

Social psychology is defined by this individual–society dualism. Its explanations of social behaviour are the ones that take into consideration the individual-level factors (such as arousal, cognitions, motivations) or the ones that look at the interaction between individual and social factors (such as conformity pressures on people). The social is positioned as external to the individual; as a set of variables that influences a relatively independent, unitary individual.

The Social Situation Has Profound Effects on Human Behaviour

Most of us believe that it is our personalities that explain our behaviour. However, that is not the case. Ross and Ward (1996) demonstrated that when competitive students were called to play the 'Wall Street Game', approximately two-thirds of them responded competitively. But when it was called the 'Community Game', only a third responded competitively. The name of the game sent a powerful message about how the players should behave. It alone conveyed a social norm about what kind of behaviour was appropriate in this situation. Since the social situation is important for social psychologists, a significant question that arises is, what is meant by the social situation? The behaviourist approach will be to specify the objective properties of the situation, such as how rewarding it is to people, and then document the behaviours that follow from these objective properties. This takes a more static view of the environment and leans towards social determinism of behaviour, allowing little role for human agency. The gestalt and cognitive perspectives have shifted the focus on how people perceive, comprehend and interpret the social world. Kurt Lewin said:

> If an individual sits in a room trusting that a ceiling will not come down, should only his 'subjective probability' be taken into account for predicting behavior or should we also consider the 'objective probability' of the ceiling's coming down as determined by the engineers? To my mind, only the first has to be taken into account.
>
> *(1943, p. 5)*

A social situation in which a young woman is enjoying a party with drinking and smoking can be construed as she is either a woman with low morals or a fun-loving woman with modern sensibilities. A person's behaviour towards her will be contingent upon the kind of interpretation that he or she has formed of her. This emphasis on the meaning of the situation puts the focus back on the individual and allows scope for negotiation and reformulation of the construal of the situation.

What constitutes a social situations in social psychology? Gordon Allport defined any kind of actual, imagined and implied presence of another as a social situation. This suggests that social interaction among people is not necessary for a situation to be called social. Social facilitation research has investigated the effects of the mere presence of others on people's performance. Social psychological research also explores such behaviours that are governed by internalized attitudes and norms. For example, whether individuals will be more likely to intervene to address acts of littering and graffiti when alone or when others are present is a social psychological question. Such research has revealed that people who had strong views against littering prevented/confronted/expressed disapproval of littering even when no one else was present (Chekroun & Brauer, 2002). This is an instance which highlighted that the presence of others (the bystander effect) does not play a crucial role in influencing pro-social behaviour when the situation is relevant (holding strong views against littering).

Seeking to Understand the Nature and Causes of Individual Behaviour in Social Situations

Howitt, Billig and Cramer (1989) suggested a useful way of understanding the behaviour to be explained and the explanatory concepts in social psychology in terms of the referent and the explanation. The 'referent' is the thing to be explained, which may or may not be social. For example, social referents include friendships, conformity, social attitudes and language that are specifically concerned with interaction between people. Non-social referents include visual perception, intelligence, information processing. 'Explanations' may include concepts which are broadly social or non-social in nature. Who becomes a leader can have both social and non-social explanations. Social explanations emphasize social mechanisms and interactions between people. For example, leaders share dominant attitudes in the group. Non-social explanations for leadership emphasize individual qualities, such as high intelligence and high need for achievement as important features of being a leader. The two concepts (intelligence and achievement) used are psychological but not particularly social psychological as they are not concerned with processes which have any necessary origins in social activity. There are four possibilities based on this:

1. *Referent social/explanation social*: An example of this is conformity to group pressures which is a social referent as it describes a pattern of relationship within the group. Some of the concepts used in the explanation of conformity, such as group cohesiveness and influence of norms, are social too. The PSP differs in its study of conformity pressures from sociologically-oriented social psychology on the ground that the former sees the referent (conformity) as a characteristic of an individual and attempts to understand the causes and conditions accounting for why an individual conforms. The latter asks what are the group/societal-level processes creating pressures to conform in its members.

2. *Referent social/explanation non-social*: For the same example of conformity, there are a few non-social concepts that are used to explain it, such as the motives of wanting to be liked and to be right. A large amount of PSP work that attempts to explain the social dimensions of our life, such as forming social judgements about others (interpersonal perception and attribution), our views on affirmative action policy (attitudes and prejudice), persuading others to quit smoking (persuasion and compliance), feeling attracted or aggressive towards others (interpersonal attraction and aggression) and offering to volunteer for a good cause (pro-social behaviour), are explained using non-social intrapersonal variables, such as schemas, categorization, heuristics, cognitive errors and biases. This constitutes research in one of the most influential areas of social psychology called social cognition. Non-social explanations are advanced for not only intra-personal and inter-personal levels of analysis but also for group and inter-group levels of analysis. Tajfel's work on inter-group prejudice using the perceptual mechanism of categorization to explain prejudice against groups of which one is not a member is an example of a social referent and non-social explanation. There is nothing social psychological about the idea that categorization is a basic perceptual process.

3. *Referent non-social/explanation social*: For areas of psychology where referents are non-social, such as intelligence, mental disorder and language

development, explanations can be social. Most psychologists acknowledge the influence of sociocultural forces on psychological processes. This suggests that there is not a complete disjunction between the social psychological and the psychological. However, the social psychological literature does not typically include these areas of study as they are not essentially social psychological in nature, that is, they do not directly try to explain relationships between people.

4. *Referent non-social/explanation non-social*: Where both referents and explanations are non-social, it cannot even be remotely considered to be social psychological in nature. Examples include understanding individual differences in intelligence in terms of genetic factors rather than in terms of differences of cultural privilege.

Social psychology attempts to explain social behaviour in terms of the following:

1. *Actions and characteristics of other persons*: The behaviouristic viewpoint stresses the importance of objective conditions of the situation, such as how and what other people say and do as determiners of our behaviour. For example, reacting with anger towards those who jump the queue.

2. *Cognitive processes*: The social cognition perspective suggests that our thinking determines what we do in social situations. For instance, those people who attribute the queue-jumping behaviour of others to deliberate hostile intentions are more likely to aggressively criticize them than those who see it as occurring due to some emergency situation.

3. *Ecological factors*: Physical factors such as crowding, temperature, privacy and other related factors affect our social behaviours too. In the case of aggression, high temperatures and overcrowding also contribute to high levels of aggression.

4. *Cultural variables*: Culture as the sum of our values, beliefs, practices, art and language impacts our behaviour. The non-Western cultures, such as India and Japan, inhibit the expression of direct aggression against elders in our social relationships (Roland, 1998).

5. *Biological and evolutionary processes*: Genetics, hormonal and neurotransmitter functioning, brain structure and neuronal activity as well as our evolutionary inheritance also affect our behaviour. Aggressive behaviour is explained as due to hormonal secretions as well as in terms of its adaptive value in evolution.

REVIEW QUESTIONS

1. Identify the European and American roots of experimental social psychology.
2. Trace the influence of Floyd Allport on experimental social psychology.

BOX 3.1 THE INTERSUBJECTIVE VIEW OF THE SELF

Experimental social psychology assumes that there is a separation between two entities: the 'person' and the 'situation' (or context) in which that person operates. Persons are seen as individuals, self-contained beings who are influenced by internal forces (instincts, motives, values, cognitions) and by external forces (the social situation, the group). The individual is seen as 'pre-formed' and the situation is seen as an objective 'frame' which exerts an independent causal effect on the person. An inter-subjective view of the self, encapsulated in Heidegger's notion of being-in-the-world, challenges this separation.

According to this view:

- A person is never in a situation that is not subject to social influence, and hence separating them creates an artificial partition, dividing up that which is inseparable. As long as they are conscious, people are always in the state of being-in-the-world, or, as the famous functionalist thinker William James might have put it, they are always immersed in a flow of consciousness about the world, a flow of consciousness on which the world (either/both immediately present or imagined) always-ever impinges.
- A situation is never simply an objectively present set of environmental conditions. It always-ever influences people's thoughts, experiences and actions through its significance to and meaningfulness for them. In simple words, people are always-ever influenced by the situation through the way that they construe that situation.
- A person is never simply just 'there' as a timeless entity, but is constantly constructed, moment by moment, through the immanent possibilities presented by the situations that they are 'in', which are continually transformed and negotiated by the person.

(Stainton Rogers (2003, p. 248)

What Is the Crisis in Experimental Social Psychology?

The 1970s witnessed a crisis brewing in experimental social psychology. Several psychologists voiced their concerns regarding the current and future state of their discipline. Many of them concluded that social psychology had become frivolous (Ring, 1967), directionless (Elms, 1975) and socially irrelevant (Silverman, 1971). What were the core debates that constituted this crisis?

Epistemological Problems

One of the most forceful epistemological attacks on social psychology came from Kenneth Gergen (1973) when he claimed, 'social psychology as history'. He argued that social psychology can never be a science because the subject matter it deals with (human social behaviour) is largely culturally and historically specific. Unlike the physical sciences, general laws of human behaviour cannot be established definitively because they fluctuate with changing cultural and historical circumstances. Social psychology is thus, at best, a 'historical inquiry'.

Another location of epistemological challenge has been the thesis of 'self-contained individualism' inherent in most of social psychology's theories (dissonance theory, game theory, equity theory, attitude theory, theories of socialization and personality). 'The individualism of social psychology is largely attributed to the joint forces of experimentation and positivism which came to dominate the discipline' (Augoustinos et al., 2014, p. 4). These forces led to the demise of interest in collective phenomena in which early psychologists such as Wundt and McDougall were interested. Following the cognitive turn in general psychology, the 1970s and 1980s witnessed a similar turn in social psychology when the focus of research shifted from the observation of behaviours to the investigation of cognitive processes. It was an attempt to establish 'meaning' as the central concept in psychology. However, it is the information processing which is being studied, not meanings. The new approach to the study of social cognition based on the cognitive theories of information processing and retrieval is highly individualistic and non-social. The concept of cognition has been reduced from thinking to information processing and one where the study of the contents of cognition (what people think about or know of social contexts) has been replaced by the study of how information processing functions without social contents. This social psychology, which is information processing-oriented, is a study of how isolated individual information processors manage to make sense of the social stimuli presented to them.

However, the information-processing model runs into several problems when the stimuli are as complex as people (Cantor & Mischel, 1977; Hastie & Kumar, 1979). Social behaviour has a normative and moral character. Human beings are not simply rational processors of information, but are engaged in social performances designed to present acceptable personae in terms of the norms of their culture (Garfinkel, 1967; Goffman, 1974). Judgements of responsibility attribution do not necessarily have the character of 'naïve scientists' searching for causality (Heider, 1958; Kelley, 1971), but are more likely to be personal accounts of what are taken to be acceptable reasons for action within a culture. The social context thus plays a significant role in determining how responsibility is attributed. For example, the fundamental attribution error, that is, the tendency to attribute causality to the disposition of the person rather than the situational factor, may not simply be an error of judgement. Its pervasiveness suggests that it is motivated by a strong individualistic ideological tradition in the Western societies or social representation that views the individual at the centre of all cognition, action and process (Lukes, 1973). Thus, Moscovici (1972) does not view these errors in simple cognitive terms but as grounded in socially shared representations.

The information-processing view has also pushed out the motivational and affective aspects of social cognition and action. As distinct from Lewin's or Festinger's motivated social actor, the human being within the information-processing metaphor is reduced to a 'lonely machine cognizing information inputs' with the only motivation being to achieve rational understanding. There is no mention of other motivations, such as the achievement of satisfying goals and motivation to have pleasure, power or friendship, which were historically the earliest explanatory notions in social psychology.

Problems of Method

A very visible concern leading up to a declaration of a crisis was dissatisfaction with the dominance of laboratory experimentation. Experimentation in social psychology gained prominence in the 1920s and 1930s, when social psychology had begun moving towards disciplinary status as a sub-field of general psychology. In the early 1960s, however, the experimental method came under considerable scrutiny in the social psychological literature. It was argued that the artificiality of the contrived experimental environment did not and could not adequately simulate human social experience. Another line of critique began to examine the social nature of experimentation by looking at what kind of other factors, besides the experimental manipulation and participants' response, are operative in the experimental situation. Rosenthal and Orne were two most significant researchers in this field. By the 1970s, an entire research field had opened up devoted to the topic of social psychology of experimentation (for a detailed discussion of this, see Chapter 1).

Moghaddam and Harré (1992) reinterpreted 'experiment as a drama' in which the experimenter is the dramatist and the experimental participant is the character who performs the role of both the audience and performer. Unlike the understanding in a controlled experiment in which the participant's behaviour is believed to be contingent on only the experimental manipulation, in the 'experiment as drama' metaphor, the participant's performance is seen as requiring improvisation evolving from his or her interpretation of the dramatic situation as well as his or her role within it. They said that it is important to ask the participant the following: 'What was it that you meant to do and how did you mean to do it? What did you think was going on and who did you think were the prime movers?' (Moghaddam & Harré, 1992, p. 27). The goal of the experimenter is not to try to identify causes for behavioural events but to achieve an understanding of the participant's interpretations of the unfolding drama and knowledge of the norms in terms of which appropriate actions are taken. The results will be explicit formulations of that knowledge, perhaps in the form of a set of rules or as scripts.

Confronted with such radical critiques of experimentation, some authors began to examine methods of eliminating the intrusive variables, such as demand characteristics and experimenter's expectancy effects (e.g., by using

102 What Is 'Social' about Social Psychology?

double-blind procedures, one-way mirrors, etc.). On the other hand, others began a re-examination of some of social psychology's most robust and classic findings as a result of experimental conditions. Rosenberg's (1965) reinterpretation of cognitive dissonance findings serves as one apt example. He demonstrated that the participants' actions to reduce cognitive inconsistencies when made to behave in ways inconsistent with their attitudes or cognitions might have been due to participants' desire to confirm or disconfirm the experimenter's hypotheses. Other researchers agreed with Rosenthal and argued that once the 'contaminants' were removed from these classic studies, the demonstrated effects also disappeared.

Reinterpretation of Milgram's Studies on 'Obedience to Authority'

Another set of experimental studies that have invited a lot of attention is the Milgram's 'obedience to authority' series conducted in the 1960s. Stanley Milgram required experimental subjects (teachers) to administer electric shocks to people (learners) who were, in fact, Milgram's accomplices, that is, stooges. The studies purported to be about the effects of punishment on learning. Participants/teachers were told to increase the voltage whenever the learner made a mistake. The main measure used in the study was the point at which the participants stopped delivering electric shocks on a 30-point incremental scale of intensity. If they subjected the learners to shocks all the way through the scale to the maximum level, they were designated 'obedient'; if they refused to continue to administer electric shocks at any earlier point, they were regarded as having 'disobeyed'. Although no actual shocks were administered, learners/ stooges in the various experiments either could be seen or were heard to react as if they had received electric shocks. When participants objected to administering the shocks (which most did), they were told to continue and this instruction became increasingly stern and insistent. Although the proportion of participants proceeding to give the highest level of shock varied under different conditions (e.g., immediacy of the victim to the participant administering the shocks and the authority of the experimental context), Milgram found that 65% continued to administer the highest level of shock on the display, even when they heard the (supposed) recipient begging them to stop, screaming in pain and eventually going silent. In this experiment, Milgram was interested in the three-party situation 'in which one agent commands another to hurt a third', which he regarded as a significant theme in human relations (Milgram, 1974). He claimed explicitly, 'we are not dealing with the personal power of the experimenter ... but with the consequence of social structure for action' (Milgram, 1974, p. 131). The experiment was designed to condense the elements present when obedience occurs in the larger world which entails experiencing the concurrent operations of antagonistic forces within oneself. In the context of the experiment, the antagonistic forces were the pressure to obey the experimenter and the belief that one should not harm others. Thus, according to Milgram, the methodological success of the obedience to authority studies was centred on whether participants were successfully deceived into believing that the learners were receiving dangerous shocks. Successfully deceiving most of his participants was critical because as the subject believes he or she is transmitting painful shocks to the learner, the essential manipulatory intent of the experiment is achieved. This raised significant ethical and methodological criticisms of the experiments.

Let us first look at the 'ethical critiques'. Observations during the experiment demonstrated the palpable stress that participants/teachers experienced: 'There were powerful reactions of tension and emotional strain in a substantial proportion of the participants. Persons were observed to sweat, tremble, stutter, bite their lips, and groan as they found themselves implicated' (Milgram, 1974, p. 112). In one case, the experiment had to be stopped because a participant's seizure was 'so violently convulsive' (Milgram, 1974, p. 113). Baumrind (1964) argued, 'I do regard the emotional disturbance described by Milgram as potentially harmful because it could easily effect an alteration in the subject's self-image' (p. 422). Other ethical criticisms directed at these experiments were a failure to obtain the participants' informed consent, supplanting their right to withdraw, potentially inflicting on them physiological and psychological harm, and the provision of a disingenuous and potentially inadequate debriefing session.

The 'methodological critique' of the studies was that 'it was not an experiment about obedience. It was an experiment about trust' (Harré, 1979, p. 105). Mixon (1972, 1976, 1989) argued that many of Milgram's participants' were tense because they were confronted with an extremely ambiguous, confusing and uncertain situation. That is, the information coming from both the experimenter and learner were mutually contradictory – the shocks were apparently harmful but not dangerous, the learner was screaming in agony but the experimenter looked calm. 'No wonder many subjects showed such stress. What to believe?' Mixon (1989, p. 33) argued, 'the right thing to do depends on which actor (the learner or the experimenter) is believed'. Mixon concluded:

> The extreme emotional reactions of many of the participants are due not to certain knowledge that they are inflicting serious harm, but to the fact that they cannot be certain. The evidence of their senses tells them they are, but background expectations and the expert responsible for the well-being of the participants tell them that they are not.
>
> *(1989, p. 94)*

According to Mixon, 'increasingly large chunks of the social and physical world that we live in can be understood only by experts' (1989, p. 35), and therefore most participants resolved the stressfully ambiguous situation by placing their trust in the authority figures' word that the learner would not be hurt.

Mixon's and Harré's arguments about trust raise the question not only of the different interpretations of 'facts' (experimental results) but of the meaning of research scenarios and how these affect the behaviour of the participants. Milgram's operational model of obedience to authority was undertheorized. He asked, what happens when these two forces – obedience and a belief that one should not harm others – come into opposition? The meanings of obedience and disobedience to different participants are not included in the investigation. Trust is a response to power and the trust that nobody would be harmed invoked by a research scenario could have been a crucial element in producing an outcome which he did not consider. Looked at from the vantage point of trust, the chief manipulatory intent of the experimenter, which is to make the participant/teacher believe in the victim's/learner's increasingly mounting suffering is not met. Another problem has been the averaging and universalizing tendency of statistical analysis which has meant that the 40%t or so (and in certain conditions over half) of the participants who disobeyed have been rendered almost invisible in social psychology.

The critique of method is not limited to experimentation. The discursive social psychological approach has subjected psychometrics to severe critique. The assumption in psychometry that every participant understands the attitudinal object equivalently is brought under scrutiny. It disallows a unique and variable construction of the attitudinal object by each respondent. Also, the questionnaire-based approach does not permit an independent description of the attitudinal object (immigration, alcohol use, global warming, homosexuality) as it is primarily interested in the evaluation of the attitudinal object (whether one agrees or disagrees, likes or dislikes). The artificiality of the psychometric measurement in terms of a fixed and unitary meaning of attitudinal object is challenged by discursive psychology.

Running through the practices of quantitative research methodology is the issue of power relations and situated knowledge. Although these issues affect interview and observation methods too, the problem has been most acute in experimental social psychology. The objectification of the participants in experimental and questionnaire-based research is obvious. The researcher retains the power to interpret people's experience in a reductive fashion. There is little attention paid to how evidence and interpretations of the evidence have come to be produced, within what assumptions and power relations. Knowledge production needs to be situated at the level of each and every piece of research. Who is providing the data? What have participants been told about the research? What do they make of what they have been told? What differences in social identity may be salient in the relationship between researcher and researched (sex, age, race, caste, class, religion, sexuality, occupational role) and with what effects? What are the salient features of each participant that situates them socially, and what difference will this make to how they make sense of the research task? It also needs to be situated at the level of historical changes in culture, values and salient social issues (Hollway et al., 2010).

The Problem of Relevance

Social psychology was heavily influenced by the turmoil created by the Second World War. It took upon itself to study socially relevant issues created by war, such as prejudice, authoritarianism, leadership and group processes. Kurt Lewin, a Jewish–German émigré to America, was a lifelong advocate of the idea that psychology should be relevant to social reform. By the 1970s, however, the optimism had begun to wane. Silverman (1971) argued that, despite serious external pressures to produce results relevant to pressing social problems, social psychology had not produced much data that were relevant to social ills. Deutsch (1975) noted that after Lewin's death, there remained few influential voices that advocated the integration of theory, research and social action. The outcome was an academic social psychology that held application and action in low self-esteem and remained confined within the university. Many see the problem of relevance as a direct outgrowth of the problem of method – the artificiality of experimentation. Even classic studies in the field that seemed to be highly socially relevant were not immune to such critiques. Milgram's obedience studies were one such example. Diana Baumrind explained,

> [F]ar from illuminating real life, as he claimed, Milgram in fact appeared to have constructed a set of conditions so internally inconsistent that they could not occur in real life. His application of his results to destructive obedience in military settings or Nazi Germany ... is metaphorical rather than scientific.
>
> *(1985, p. 171)*

Critical social psychologists take a different route to critiquing the lack of social reform in scientific social psychological work. They do not find such work 'political' enough. Ian Parker states:

> Social psychology should be about changes in the real world. It should also, though, be concerned with how people can collectively change the order of things for themselves. Unfortunately, social psychology as an academic institution is structured in such a way as to blot out that which is most interesting about social interaction (language, power and history) and to divert attention from efforts to deconstruct its oppressive functions in a practical way.
>
> *(1989, p. 1)*

Little has been written of the crisis since the 1970s. So does this mean that the debates and issues of social psychology have been resolved? Not quite. The questions disappeared from the centre stage because the discipline lost interest in them.

106 What Is 'Social' about Social Psychology?

PAUSE AND THINK

Pick any classic social psychological experimental study and analyse how experimentation is a social psychological situation.

What About Other Forms of Social Psychology?

A review of the history and the present state of PSP reveals that the social does not have the status in this form of social psychology that might be expected. Flick points out:

> [N]either current textbooks nor the discussions in most social psychological journals offer answers to questions such as: What part do social and collective attributions play in everyday life, and how can they be studied psychologically? What social discourses of racism circulate in everyday life? How does social development or the social construction of knowledge proceed? ... Which psychological concepts can explain how ideologies function? Which forms of social memory can be studied in a culture? How do representations of selfhood vary in different cultures? ... What is the relevance of everyday knowledge for research in social psychology, and what is the relevance of social psychology for everyday knowledge?
>
> *(1998, p. 1)*

A number of other traditions of social psychology have made these questions the central concerns of study. These traditions include: the SSP, European social psychology and discursive/critical/social constructionist social psychology.

Sociological Social Psychology (SSP)

This tradition originated in North America but within sociology, and is sometimes also referred to as microsociology. SSP has long constituted an area of specialization within sociology, but it has been less intellectually and organizationally coherent than PSP. Sociologists have always been keenly interested in understanding the relationship between the social and the individual as is represented in the distinction between individual and collective representations made by Durkheim in the early days of sociology. However, social psychologists within sociology have been beset by twin pressures to distinguish themselves and their work from their counterparts within psychology and also to defend themselves against the charge of not being really or sufficiently 'sociological' (House, 1977). Both *Völkerpsychologie* and crowd psychology stimulated the development of SSP. Tarde's work, for example, was highly influential for the sociologist Edward Alsworth Ross who published his text, *Social Psychology: An Outline and Source Book*, in 1908 (the same year that William McDougall published his text on PSP). Ross defined the discipline of SSP as the study of the 'planes and currents that come into existence among men in consequence of their association' (1908, p. 1). It took various forms which are discussed below.

Symbolic Interactionism

A potent form of SSP emerged during the 1920s and 1930s as a more 'social' alternative to the psychological and experimental social psychology of Floyd Allport and others. This was fashioned by the symbolic interactionism of George Herbert Mead, Charles Holton Cooley and W. I. Thomas. Mead elucidated:

> We are not in social psychology building up the behaviour of the social group in terms of the behaviours of the separate individuals composing it, rather we are starting out with a given social whole of complex social activity, into which we analyze (as elements) the behaviours of each of the separate individuals composing it.
>
> *(1934, p. 7)*

In line with their emphasis on understanding social life by understanding the processes through which individuals interpret situations and construct their actions with respect to others' reactions, symbolic interactionist research has focused on aspects of social life where this process of cognitive interpretation and behavioural construction is most evident and important. These include socialization and development of self, deviant behaviour, collective behaviour and face-to-face interaction. Symbolic interaction has tried to find a place for itself by critiquing the view that social life (1) could be adequately understood in terms of S-R (stimulus–response) relationships involving little or no cognitive mediation (behaviourism) and/or (2) could be understood without even taking into account the intentions, beliefs and needs of individuals (sociologism). Along with these positions, symbolic interactionism has rejected a variety of other ideas (e.g., quantification and causal theorizing associated with experimentation and macrosocial concepts and phenomena).

Symbolic interactionism is a micro-level theoretical framework which developed to provide an understanding of the operation of society from the 'bottom up' rather than 'top down', in which macro-level institutions and social structures were believed to define and constrain the individual. It conceived the individual as agentic, autonomous and integral in creating their social world. The basic premise of this perspective is that people make sense of their world on the basis of the meanings they have for the physical and social objects involved in the situation and these meanings are 'social', that is, constructed

108 What Is 'Social' about Social Psychology?

and reconstructed through interactions with others. For example, the act of giving roses rather than daffodils by a man to a woman involves understanding of the symbolic significance of roses and their exchange between two people of opposite genders. The meaning of this situation and action has emerged through the interactions one has had with others in the society.

Symbolic interactionism provides a unique social psychological view of social life, as meanings are neither seen as inherent in the person's mind nor in the objects of the world. Meanings emerge through interactions people have with each other and they are constantly reinterpreted. Understanding social behaviour requires an interpretive perspective that examines how situations are defined on an ongoing basis and how behaviours are changing and are unique to each and every social encounter.

One of the most famous interactionist studies was provided by Becker (1953) in his work on becoming a marijuana user, where he showed how 'feeling high' when using marijuana is a social construction rather than a physiological, internal motivational state caused by the drug. Becker revealed that in marijuana users, feeling high requires both the presence and recognition of the drug's symptoms, and recognition of the drug's symptoms is constructed socially through interactions with others. Applied more broadly, Becker's study shows how role behaviours are socialized and acquired through interactions with others. Becker's marijuana study had a massive influence, not only for symbolic interactionists but on the field of sociology. Traces of symbolic constructionism can be found in ethnomethodology (developed by Garfinkel) and dramaturgy (developed by Goffman).

Ethnomethodology

This is the study of how people make sense of the world and the commonsensical methods people use in their everyday lives. For ethnomethodology, what is of utmost importance in understanding social life is the forms of common-sense knowledge and practical reasoning that people use to make sense of their circumstances and find ways of acting within them. A methodological problem that Garfinkel initially faced was how to make forms of common-sense reasoning available for empirical research. He dealt with this problem by approaching the phenomenon indirectly in situations where it had ostensibly broken down. Successfully disrupted situations should enable one to infer the absence of some essential procedure and, by working backwards, elucidate its importance in normal circumstances. In light of these considerations, Garfinkel developed the well-known 'breaching experiments'. In these breaching experiments, Garfinkel (1967) instructed his confederates to demand that subjects explain and clarify the meaning of their most casual remarks, to act as boarders in their own homes, to act on the assumption that subjects had some hidden motive, and so forth. Following is one such example of the breaching experiment in which the taken-for-granted meaning is breached:

The subject waved his hand cheerily.

SUBJECT: How are you?
CONFEDERATE: How am I in regard to what? My health, my finance, my schoolwork, my peace of mind, my...
SUBJECT: (Red in the face and suddenly out of control.) Look! I was just trying to be polite. Frankly, I don't give a damn how you are.

The outcomes of his demonstrations were indeed dramatic. Instead of yielding a state of bewilderment or 'cognitive anomie', subjects typically reacted with marked hostility, displaying acute anger, sanctioning the confederates and attributing various negative motivations to them. Taken together, these reactions served as evidence that societal members orient to tacit methods of reasoning in ordinary life. Moreover, the hostile reactions suggested that, within the domain of everyday life, sense-making procedures have an underlying normative/moral dimension. That is, these procedures are treated as mutually relevant and binding and powerful sanctions can be mobilized against those who violate these and the trust that they embody.

Dramaturgical Sociology

In dramaturgical sociology, social interaction is understood in terms of the 'life as a theatre' metaphor. Individuals can be seen as performers, audience members and outsiders who operate within particular social spaces/stages. It is argued that the elements of human actions are dependent on time, place and audience. The theory suggests that a person's identity is not a stable and independent psychological entity, but rather it is constantly remade as a person interacts with others. According to Goffman (1959), how we present ourselves to others is aimed at 'impression management' which is a conscious decision on the part of the individual to reveal certain aspects of the self and to conceal others, as actors do when performing on stage. As on the stage, people play certain roles, use certain scripts, utilize costumes, expressions and actions to give a particular impression to others. He argues that the dramaturgical element of social interaction is ubiquitously present. In a work scenario, where one set of individuals have to appraise the quality of the work accomplishments of the other set of individuals, the latter set has to manage impressions that their work is indeed meeting the standards. The set of individuals attempting to control/direct others by means of example, manipulation, exchange, authority, punishment or coercion must be able to keep strategic secrets from others and mask their power effectively in a way that conveys effectively what they want done, what they are prepared to do to get it done and what they will do if it is not done. Culture also operates by providing a framework of values and appearances with regard to customs, politeness, decorum, and so on.

110 What Is 'Social' about Social Psychology?

Social Representations

The contemporary site where much of SSP operates is social representations. Moscovici introduced the theory of social representations into social psychology with his study of the appearance and diffusion of psychoanalysis in French public life in the 1950s. His investigations involved a study of the mass media in France in the 1950s and a questionnaire survey of over 2,000 respondents from different social classes. It was evident that psychoanalytic concepts and ways of thinking had entered everyday life, and it was also clear that only some aspects of the theory were retained in these representations and that the perception of the theory differed from group to group. Social representation theory suggests that what people know and how they know depend on the particular social groups to which they belonged. A social representation is traditionally understood as a system of values, ideas and practices which aims to make something unfamiliar familiar. It provides an instrument to cope with and classify new phenomena and changes in phenomena that are already known. They come about, take shape and circulate in and through our communications and interactions with others of our group. It is through this communicative process that we build a picture of particular issues and of our social world. These representations are shared among groups of people so they allow a common basis for us to understand each other and thus provide a degree of cohesiveness that bonds particular social groups together. Social representations do not account for the behaviour of individuals per se, but only for the behaviour of individuals qua members of social groups (Moscovici, 1982). The fact that they have been collectively elaborated makes these representations valid systems of knowledge for groups as a whole and individual members.

To sum up, in SSP, we see a return to the systematic study of everyday life and common-sense knowledge to understand how people behave in social situations. Across the diverse traditions of the micro-sociological perspective, the consensus is that social meanings are generated through social interactions and communications. The focus is not on what is going on within the head of the individual in response to the social situation; rather, it is on what kinds of social meanings are being constituted and how (see Figure 3.1).

European Social Psychology

As compared to American experimental psychology, European psychology is distinguished by the greater emphasis on contextual determinants of behaviour, both before and after the upheavals caused by the Second World War. Reflecting on numerous early US visitors to his research group in Oxford, in the UK, soon after the Second World War, Argyle (2001) wrote:

> All were a great source of stimulation, information and help. Our group became an important channel for the transfer of American social Psychology to Britain. And yet we kept our distance from American social

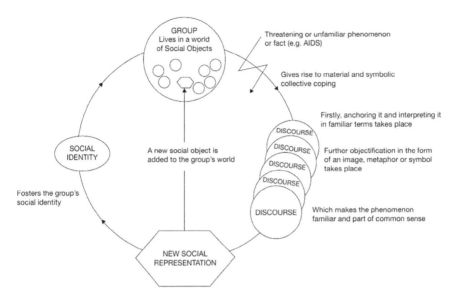

FIGURE 3.1 The sociogenesis of social representations
Source: Adapted from Wagner et al. (1999).

psychology. They had colonized us, perhaps intentionally, but we altered the message. We were impressed by their ingenious and well-designed experiments, but we found them too artificial, insufficiently related to real behavior. We could not see how this kind of research could be applied to real problems. We were looking at a different way of doing it. The way we favoured could also be found in several places in the US, but not in the mainstream.

(pp. 340–341)

In the post-war decades, this dissatisfaction with American social psychology led to the formulation of distinctive theories that focused upon social identity, social representation and minority influence, each of which has been vigorously pursued in centres of excellence that are spread across differing regions of Europe. On the theme of risky shift in groups and group polarization, Moscovici and Zavalloni (1969) argued that the risky shift was simply one manifestation of the general tendency, identified by Le Bon, for groups to become extreme. They argued that whenever a cultural value is relevant to a group discussion or group decision, whether that value be risk, democracy, favouring the in-group or evaluating national icons, the views of group members will become more extreme. The group will polarize. They showed that high school students in France discussing the French president, Charles de Gaulle, or American tourists produced polarized evaluations – positive in the case of de Gaulle, negative in the case of American tourists. The year 1969 marked the publication of Argyle's social psychology textbook, *Social Interaction*, and Tajfel's (1969) chapter, 'Social and Cultural Factors in Perception', in the *Handbook of Social Psychology*. Argyle focused principally on interpersonal and small-group interaction, especially non-verbal communication (Argyle & Dean, 1965), while Tajfel was beginning to develop the research that led to the creation of social identity theory.

The social identity theory proposed by Henri Tajfel and its subsequent development into self-categorization theory (Tajfel & Turner, 1979; Turner et al., 1987) have proved to be distinctly popular among European social psychologists, especially in psychology. Tajfel was a vocal critic of conducting experiments 'in a vacuum' and argued for a greater role of small and large group affiliations in determining social behaviours. Researchers in this tradition continue to use experimental methods, but they test predictions that emphasize the impact of group affiliations in real-world settings. Researchers who study social representations have mostly abandoned experimental methods and rely more on observations, interviews and media analysis to elucidate the way in which one or another concept, such as health, illness, the European Union and the individual, is socially represented. Work on social representations is widespread in Europe and Latin America. While the perspective has enjoyed more popularity within sociology, it is being taken up by social psychologists within psychology and connections are being forged between it and social identity theory (Breakwell, 1993).

Since the 1970s, the UK has been the hub of intellectual activity within social psychology responding to the 'crises' in psychological/American/experimental social psychology. What started out as a social psychology with a socio-centred focus branched out in different directions. For Jonathan Potter and Margaret Wetherell (1987), it was becoming 'discursive social psychology' which they introduced in their classic text, *Discourse and Social Psychology: Beyond Attitudes and Behaviour*. They introduced discourse analysis into social psychology, drawing on two different traditions, one European and the other American. 'European discourse analysis' originated in the work of Michel Foucault, whose historical work studied the emergence and effects of discourses (systems of meaning), such as madness, punishment and sexuality. This macro socio-historical approach was complemented by the 'American microsociology tradition' which focused on micro-interactions and the production of meanings in everyday interaction. For the likes of Henriques, Wendy Hollway, Valerie Walkerdine and Ian Parker, it was turning into critical social psychology. In the influential text, *Changing the Subject: Psychology, Social Regulation and Subjectivity*, Henriques et al. (1984) critiqued the discourses rooted in the notion of a unitary rational subject from three standpoints, namely, (1) critical theory and post-structuralist interrogations of the foundations of the discourses of modernity; (2) feminist challenges to the phallocentric and masculine model of subjectivity privileged in Western theory; and (3) the postcolonial questioning of the ideologies of imperialism and racism.

Discursive/Critical/Social Constructionist Social Psychology

The combination of discursive, critical social psychology and social constructionism is a critique of experimental social psychology which is the intellectual core of PSP. It refers to a set of ideas and developments from discourse analysis, conversation analysis and rhetoric. It is a broadly constructionist perspective and is commonly, though not always, associated with a relativist rather than a realist positivist epistemology that is still commonplace in experimental social psychology (Potter, 1998). It takes people to be constructing their worlds through their accounts and descriptions. The world is not already constructed by God or Nature; rather, it is constituted in one way or another as people talk it, write it, argue it and undermine it. What it implies is that when people talk about an object, event or social phenomenon, they are not merely describing it; rather, they are constructing a version of it. The version that gets constructed depends on the function or purpose of the account that has been put together. For example, when we think of an Indian celebrity, for example, Salman Khan, a well-known actor in the Mumbai film industry, he has been constructed variously as, for example, one of the most successful actors in the industry, as a criminal, as a bad boy with a golden heart, as an unfortunate victim of celebrity status, and so on. None of these versions gets us any closer to what Salman Khan is objectively like! When the contexts in which these constructions are generated are studied, the diverse purposes of these constructions are understood.

Discursive social psychology researches the particular constructions (accounts and descriptions) of the phenomena (celebrityhood in the above example) as well as how these descriptions are built according to the purpose/context of use. Discursive social psychology, thus, sees language or discourse as not just a means to express what is going on inside the mind, that is, language is not just a representation. Language is not merely descriptive and reflective of cognitive entities and processes. Discourse analysis is not attempting 'to recover events, beliefs and cognitive processes from participants' discourse, or treat language as an indicator or signpost to some other state of affairs' (Potter & Wetherell, 2003, p. 352). Rather, it is a social action. Each of the constructions surrounding Salman Khan is accomplishing the function of idealizing him, of making him seem more or less accountable for a deed done, accuse him or justify his actions. The central idea is that we talk purposefully (that talk has a function) and what we say varies according to the purpose of the talk and/or what we are trying to achieve. Important to note is that when we say speakers talk purposefully, this does not necessarily mean that speakers talk with specific intentions. It may well be the case that a particular construction of an issue emerges as the speakers tried to reflect and make sense of a topic/issue, or that a particular account of justifying an a0act occurs without deliberation or intent. Variation according to the function of talk can also make talk inconsistent, fragmented and contradictory.

There are two main strands of discourse analysis: discursive practices and discursive resources. The analysis of 'discursive practices' is best seen in the

114 What Is 'Social' about Social Psychology?

work of Potter and Wetherell (1987). This form of analysis responds to the research questions: What is this person, in this part of the conversation, seeking to achieve? What discursive practices are they using to do so? The analysis of 'discursive resources' works at a different level. Instead of looking at the strategic use of discourse within a particular piece of text, it takes a broad brush perspective. It examines how discourses work across situations and settings as a social and cultural resource. This work draws extensively on Foucauldian analysis of the relationship between power and knowledge. This form of analysis responds to the research questions: What discourses operate in relation to this topic? Where do they come from? How and why were they constructed? How are they deployed and what can they be used to achieve?

To illustrate the way the locus of psychological processes changes from the 'internal' to a 'social' domain in discursive psychological perspective, Gergen notes, 'to hold an attitude is to occupy a particular position in a conversation' (Potter & Wetherell, 1987), to possess an identity is to play a part in a relational configuration (Davies & Harré, 1990), to have an emotion is to perform appropriately in a relational scenario (Gergen & Gergen, 1988), and to possess a memory is to act according to a socially negotiated rule (Middleton & Edwards, 1990).

Discourse analytic theory is different from social representations in being distinctively anti-cognitive. Rather than focusing on the nature of people's knowledge about social domains and the cognitive processes (anchoring and objectification) involved in its generation, discourse analysis focuses on the language in text and talk to comprehend (1) the function of talk in a context and the strategies used (pauses, sniffs, use of the phrase 'you know', etc.) to execute those functions, and (2) the different linguistic constructions of reality and how they interact and compete with each other.

Critical Social Psychology

Critical psychology and critical social psychology have their foundations in the critiques of modernity, structuralism, colonialism and patriarchy. Thus, postmodernism, post-structuralism, postcolonialism and feminism have played a significant role in its development. These discourses have challenged the idea of a self-contained, self-defining, conscious and rational individual which is the unit of analysis of scientific psychology. The critiques question the 'truth' of this notion of the individual. No theory is innocent, cross-culturally or historically valid. They emphasize that all conceptions of individuals are a product of historically-specific practices of social regulation. The idea of the autonomous individual is also criticized as a very masculine notion. There is a new emphasis on relationship and its centrality to the self. These critiques have fundamentally changed the way of thinking about individuals and their relationship with social structures. Within critical social psychology, the individual is re-thought of as (Henriques et al., 1984, p. 3):

- socially and historically located (situatedness)
- relational (influence of others within oneself)
- dynamic and conflictual (change and tensions between people's plural identities)
- embodied (bodies expressing social meaning)
- discursive (positioned in socially available meanings and practices).

Critical social psychology argues against the possibility of value-free theory and in favour of greater reflexivity on the part of scientists who themselves speak from a social location of gender, ethnicity, social class and sexual orientation. It turns the gaze of the psychologists back on the discipline to interrogate how psychology operates as a power structure shaping people's practices and understandings of themselves through its expert knowledge and recommendations to governments and other institutions (Parker, 2007).

Social Constructionism and Social Psychology

Kenneth Gergen (1973) proposes a social constructionist version of social psychology in which he argues that social psychology is primarily a historical enquiry. Unlike the natural sciences, social psychology deals with facts and phenomena that are largely non-repeatable and which fluctuate markedly over time. Gergen proposes two reasons for the historical dependency of psychological theory. One is the feedback loop that science and society constitute. Through the multifarious channels of communication, social psychological knowledge has entered people's lives, and this dissemination has itself altered the character of causal relations in social interaction. For example, conformity research treats the conformist as a social sheep that lets go of their own personal convictions to agree with other's erroneous opinions. Thus, models of social conformity sensitize us to the factors that might lead us into actions that are socially unacceptable. In effect, knowledge insulates against the future efficacy of these same factors. Similarly, knowledge about attitude change may sensitize one into guarding against factors that can potentially influence one's behaviour. Thus, psychological sophistication liberates us from our behavioural implications. May (1971, p. 100) stated: 'Each of us inherits from society a burden of tendencies which shapes us willy-nilly; but the capacity to be conscious of this fact saves us from being strictly determined.' The second line of thinking is that the observed regularities and the major theoretical principles are firmly wedded to historical circumstances. Gergen (1973) cites the example of research on the prediction of political activism. He opines that the variables that successfully predicted political activism during the early stages of the Vietnam War are dissimilar to those that successfully predicted activism during later periods. The conclusion is that factors motivating activism have changed over time and a new theory of political activism will invalidate the older findings. Thus, social psychological research cannot develop cumulative forms of knowledge, as a lot of social behaviour is due to historically contingent factors, and it is more

116 What Is 'Social' about Social Psychology?

important to capture such processes 'in flight' and during specific periods of history rather than look for universalities.

According to Gergen (1973), social psychologists should see their discipline as playing an important role as a sensitizing device rather than forcing contrived forms of predictions or offering apologies for not being able to make reliable predictions. He opines that it is imperative to develop a continuum of historical durability, with phenomena highly susceptible to historical influence at one extreme and the more stable processes at the other. Social psychologists can then research the range of factors potentially influencing behaviour under various conditions. Research may also provide some estimate of the importance of these factors at a given time.

PAUSE AND THINK

Select a newspaper report on a clash between a separatist group and the Indian Army. Pay close attention to the specific words, descriptions and account of the violence that are presented in it. Try to understand what the report is trying to do. Who is the victim? Who is the perpetrator? How are the reasons for violence assigned?

REVIEW QUESTIONS

1. Discuss the various traditions that constitute microsociology.
2. How does discursive psychology expand the notion of 'the social'?
3. How does critical psychology challenge the psychological notion of 'the person'?
4. What is the central thesis of social constructionism in the context of social psychology?

What Is the Common Ground for the Other Forms of Social Psychologies?

Flick (1998) coined the phrase 'psychology of the social' to refer to a body of theory and research that reorients social psychology to social questions and re-establishes links with contemporary social issues. He sees it as an integrative framework of social representation theory, discursive psychology, cultural models and cultural–historical models, attempting to enlarge the notion of the social. The three perspectives – social representations, discursive and critical social psychology inhabiting the 'psychology of the social' space – have in common their position on the relationship between science and commonsensical knowledge, idiographic versus nomothetic research orientations, as well as the theory of the individual–society interface. With respect to these matters, the three perspectives take very different positions compared to experimental/PSP. In the process, they respond to the crisis that beset experimental social psychology.

Position on the Relationship Between Science and Common Knowledge

The three perspectives view social psychology as a science, a rigorous and systematic form of inquiry, but deny that the scientific method is the only or even the best way to be rigorous and systematic. These forms of social psychology are underwritten by the ontological, epistemological and methodological imperatives of the interpretivist and critical paradigms of research rather than the positivist (for detailed discussions of these paradigms, see Chapter 2). There is no rigid distinction between common sense and science, according to the non-positivist paradigms. Rather, the researchers in these paradigms view common sense as the stockpile of everyday theories people use to organize and explain events in the world. It becomes critical for them to understand common sense because it contains the meanings that people use when people engage in routine social interactions. Kelley has argued for the interpenetration of science and common sense:

> We are all members of the common culture and users of the common language long before we become scientific psychologists. Insofar as we address our scientific efforts to the behavioural phenomena encompassed by common terms and beliefs, they inevitably influence the concepts and theories we develop for our scientific purposes.
>
> *(1992, p. 4)*

Gergen (1973), Sampson (1988) and Parker (1990) have all pointed out the need to recognize the social, historical and ideological origins of psychological concepts. Common-sense representations thus influence scientific knowledge. Moscovici (1982) and Gergen (1973) have also presented convincing arguments for how scientific knowledge in modern societies is actually 'science made common' through the media and publication technology. Thus, the relationship between academic and common-sense understandings of constructs such as attitudes must be seen as dialectical (Howarth, 2006).

Unlike the positivist social psychology, the view of social reality is constructionist in nature for these perspectives. It, therefore, does not ask the question, Which version of reality is true?, as this is unanswerable. Social reality is the symbolic world of meanings and interpretations. It is not some 'thing' that may be interpreted in different ways; it is those interpretations. From this viewpoint, there is no independent 'benchmark' that can be used to establish which social reality is 'true'. It does not privilege scientific knowledge over commonsensical knowledge. Rather, questions arise: What actions does a particular version of social reality make possible? In what ways does it enable/constrain what people can do? Who gets their own way? Who gets exploited?

118 What Is 'Social' about Social Psychology?

Science is also seen as one of the versions of social reality and the effort is to understand the practices through which scientific findings are produced and the implications of scientific research. Thus, scientific knowledge is not considered to be value-free. For instance, the cognitive tradition of scientific social psychological theorization sees racism and prejudice as the natural outcome of universal mental processes of categorization and stereotypical association. In doing so, it naturalizes race and takes race categories as reflecting natural points of difference – 'whiteness' and 'blackness'. It takes an ideological position that these points of difference are *a priori*. It does not engage in critical examination of why black is inferior and discriminated against, and how these group differences have come about. In doing so, it precludes understanding how group differences are a social product, the outcome of historical patterns of exploitation and representation (Durrheim et al., 2009).

Idiographic Explication Rather Than Nomothetic Explanations

Based on the assumption that knowledge is constructed and contingent, the sociological/discursive/critical forms of social psychology seek to produce idiographic explications rather than nomothetic explanations. An explication does not seek to account for cause and effect since it is believed that such linearity is a gross simplification. Instead, explication teases out the particular social and cultural conventions that govern social interaction in particular circumstances and that mediate the ways people make and interpret meaning and significance in a particular situation. It relies on another form of reasoning beyond induction and deduction called abduction. Both induction and deduction assume a stable, consistent world where regularities in nature will be found which can then be used to develop hypotheses about causal relationships. However, often there are deviations, unusual and surprising findings – the data that do not fit with our beliefs. Abduction operates in this sphere. Abductive research involves either homing in on disjunctions and discrepancies chanced upon or creating conditions where researchers can be surprised. The researcher has to make sense of what can account for this anomaly. According to C. S. Peirce's explanation in the seventh of his 'Lectures on Pragmatism', the logical structure of abduction is the following ([1903] 1997):

- The surprising fact C is observed.
- But if A were true, C would be a matter of course.
- Hence, there is a reason to suspect that A is true.

The key to understanding it properly is to realize that the trigger of abduction is the surprising character of the fact referred to in the first premise, and the 'motor' is the work of imagination in the second premise. In the second premise, one discovers that if some hypothesis were true, it would render the surprising fact to be a matter of course, something normal, reasonable and thus something not surprising. If this is the case, it is reasonable to think that A is true. Abduction is the act of insight that puts different elements together in the form of a new suggestion. Not only are detective stories full of abductive reasoning but our everyday lives also contain many examples of its effective use. Medical diagnoses, for instance, follow its structure: from certain surprising symptoms and a classification of diseases, some particular disease is chosen to make those symptoms reasonable. Research in these perspectives uses qualitative methods rather than experimentation and psychometric tools.

Position on the Individual–Society Interface

In PSP, the individual and the social are seen as separate, as is reflected in the metaphor of the ocean and sea creatures suggested by Stainton Rogers. The social influences the individual. The endeavour is to understand the information-processing activity (attitudes, attributions, schemas, categorization) taking place within the individual in response to the social stimulus. The focus of social psychology mostly was on individual cognition, emotion and behaviour in relation to various social stimulus, such as the presence of another individual, the judgements of other group members or the presentation of a persuasive message.

In contrast to this, the sociological/discursive/critical social psychology takes the position that the individual is already social. It is not enough to accept that there is a social world in which an individual lives and may influence the way the individual behaves. Instead, the need is to understand how 'society constitutes and inhabits the very core of whatever passes for personhood: each is interpenetrated by the other' (Sampson, 1988, p. 17). Individual thought processes and social reality must be understood as mutually interdependent, constitutive and transformative. Here the individual is a product of her/his social environment and produces that environment in constantly dynamic ways. Stainton Rogers, Stenner and Gleeson put it like this:

> [P]eople are inexorably part of, involved with, and inseparable from the circumstances that make up their world. To conceive of our selves (or whatever is denoted by the words 'I' and 'Me') as the 'inside' and the world as the 'outside' (a collection of stimuli) is to fail to recognize the extent to which we exist alongside-and-within the world. It is through and against our everyday involvements and engagements with the circumstances of our worlds (especially including other people) that we come to know ourselves.
>
> *(1995, p. 55)*

Moscovici (1984, p. 950) asserts: 'what counts is not the separateness of individual representations but the transformation each individual imposes on group representation and the converse'. The focus of research is not the internal cognitive structure of subjective knowledge that helps the individual to act in the world, but the

120 What Is 'Social' about Social Psychology?

contents of the stocks of knowledge within different groups and how they are generated through social interaction among people within groups in specific contexts. The focus of analysis then changes from individual cognitions (schemas, attributions, attitudes) to the social representations, discourses, their meanings and effects.

Stainton Rogers (2003) suggests the image of music making as a metaphor for meaning making social interaction. This image is in contrast to the image of sea creatures and ocean discussed above in the context of PSP. Music making exists when and because people are making it. She states:

> All sorts of things may contribute to the music that is played and how it is performed. The musical instruments available, the skills and expertise of the players and singers ... all of these will have an effect. Where and when historically the music is played will make a difference. Sometimes there will be a need to please a paying audience. Even, sometimes, there may be political constraints on what can be performed ... There can be different kinds of orchestras, musical bands and choirs throughout history and across the world, each making different kinds of music – from gamelan to rock, plainchant to jazz.
>
> *(Stainton Rogers, 2003, p. 8)*

BOX 3.2 FROM DISCURSIVE PSYCHOLOGY TO A PSYCHOSOCIAL APPROACH

Social psychology is caught in the dilemma of individual–society dualism. Which forces – inner and outer – are mainly responsible for forming the person? Discursive psychology emphasizes outer forces, specifically following the idea that people's identities are formed through their positioning in discourses. The founders of discursive psychology, Potter and Wetherell, and those who followed their lead rejected the person as the object of inquiry and established the inadequacy of cognitive accounts of mental life. However, it leaves many questions unanswered: How to recognize the agency of the subject positioned in the discourse? How does the external world get transformed into identity? How should we theorize subjectivity? Who is the speaker? Wetherell (2003, p. 114) points out, 'discourse analysts rarely sample the discourse of one individual' with the consequence that 'we need to do more to examine the person as yet a further site where meaning gets organized'. Hollway and Jefferson (2000) argue that people are not positioned in discourses just as a result of social forces (e.g., the ideological pressure to be a man); rather, they are invested in certain positions, implying some reward or satisfaction for the person. Thus, discourse psychology, in order to be a psychology, needs an account of the motivational processes involved in speaking and conversation. This has led to the adoption of psychoanalytic interpretive strategies within the discourse-oriented psychology. The sophisticated psychoanalytic ideas about emotional investment and fantasy can help to explain the conscious and unconscious 'reasons' behind a specific person's investment in any rhetorical or discursive position. Psychoanalysis is used by Hollway (2006) in two ways: first, to understand the way in which external events become incorporated 'into' the psyche or self (the outside-to-inside movement) and, second, to understand how the social is intersubjective as unconscious defences operate in relation to others with whom we are in communication (the inside-to-outside movement). She emphasizes the constant flow between inner and outer (and also within).

In one study trying to understand how the first-time mothers prepare themselves for the new situation of child-rearing, Hollway (2010) noted changing, emotional, conflicted and complex subjectivities. The expert advice available to them through doctors, senior mothers and child-rearing books was diverse and often contradictory. The stories of the first-time mothers were situated in the context of their particular dilemmas, prior life experiences, along with their anxieties, support or the lack of it. It was clear that it was not enough to understand the expert discourses and what they were trying to accomplish. These mothers were uniquely positioning themselves in relation to the expert advice, exercising choice and discrimination guided by their desires, anxieties and their gender, class and ethnic locations. Their position vis-à-vis the specific expert discourse was fluid and inconsistent, which was required in order to keep up with the baby's rapid transformations. It was concluded that mothers' positioning in expert discourses of child-rearing requires a complex account of subjectivity which in turn is made possible by a methodology that permits subjectivity to be expressed and noted in its situated, practical, life-historical, relational and dynamic as well as its discursive/conversational aspects. It is suggested by Hollway that discursive psychology has to embrace psycho-analytic methods to capture subjective experience.

The insertion of psychoanalysis into discursive social psychology is taking place under the aegis of 'psychosocial studies'. The term 'psychosocial' represents the attempt to study phenomena without reducing them to either social or psychological causes (Frosh, 2003; Hollway, 2004). In the above study, maternal subjectivity of the first-time mothers was understood as 'psychosocial' and not 'psycho-social' as it does not subscribe to individual–society dualism. Rather, subjectivity/experience/meaning is seen simultaneously as both psychological *and* social.

REVIEW QUESTIONS

1. 'Experimental social psychology is individualistic in nature'. Discuss.
2. In what way does the 'psychology of the social' reformulate the individual–social interface?

122 What Is 'Social' about Social Psychology?

How Is Attitude Understood in Competing Constructions of Social Psychology?

Given the striking differences in the experimental social psychology and social representations/discourse/critical social psychologies, how are the topics in social psychology addressed under both these paradigms? Let us try to understand this using the example of one of the most researched topics in social psychology: attitudes.

Attitudes in Experimental Social Psychology

Allport's (1935) classic definition of attitude is: 'a mental or neural state of readiness, organised through experience, exerting a directive or dynamic influence upon the individual's response to all objects and situations with which it is related'. According to this definition of attitudes, individuals are seen as responding to various 'attitudinal objects' (individuals such as Sachin Tendulkar and Indira Gandhi, social groups such as the elderly and women footballers, situations such as watching an advertisement and stone-pelting incidents in Kashmir, social issues such as gay rights and the demonetization of the Indian currency) and this response, it is supposed, is predetermined by their attitude towards that particular object. By denoting an attitude-holder's orientation to the attitudinal object, an attitude conveys that person's evaluation of that object. Attitudes are conveyed in the language of like/dislike, approach/avoid, good/bad; they are evaluative. Other influences on behaviour (such as situational factors, societal norms, past behaviour) are recognized in the 'theory of reasoned action' (Fishbein & Ajzen, 1975), but they are social factors tacked onto an essentially individualistic perspective. There is an assumption that there is an underlying attitude towards the object which will be expressed in a 'neutral' context. There are two general conceptions of attitude in mainstream social psychology: (1) that they are more or less consistent responses with a degree of organization and predictability; and (2) that attitudes are inner processes that give direction and consistency to a person's responses (Wicker, 1969).

Fraser and Gaskell (1990) have looked at what they call 'the individualization of the attitude concept'. For example, the basic deficiency of the period of attitude scaling (the 1920s–the 1930s) was the measurement of 'individual variables in isolation without appreciating the need for simultaneous scaling of several variables and the relationship between them' (McGuire, 1986, p. 92). An examination of the measurement procedures used (the galvanic skin response and the facial electromyogram, for instance) illustrates how exclusively individualistic the focus was. The 'social' is thus reduced to the 'individual'. Attitudes became reified as cognitive and emotional predisposition with a life of their own inside people's heads. More recently, attitude models have been refashioned to sit within the dominant social cognition paradigm with research focusing on how information is processed, how attitudes are structured and how memory works in relation to attitude formation and attitude change. For example, current research focuses on intra-attitudinal consistency, attitude accessibility, individual differences in attitude structure and the role of affective and cognitive information in guiding attitudes. The individual is conceived of as a 'thinking machine' rather than a social being embedded in a historical and cultural context.

Attitudes in the Social Representations Perspective

The 'uniquely European approach' of social representations with its focus on community, collective practices and the institutionalization of social knowledge has often been contrasted with the 'Americanization of the attitude concept' tied to the discourses of individualism and subjective evaluation. The social representations perspective has criticized attitude theorists for their failure to conceptualize the inherently social nature of attitudes. Crucially, it faults the attitude theorists for precluding the exploration of the relation between attitudes and identities, and how particular attitudes may defend, develop or challenge social relations in society as a whole. Attitude theories, then, offer little idea as to how and why the 'objects' about which attitudes are made have come into being and how our attitudes towards these 'objects' may support or further their social construction. Hence, they do not explore the history of attitudes or their relationship to ideology.

Rather than focusing on the individual's response to a particular object – whether cognitive, affective or behavioural – theories of social representations are concerned with social thinking. They focus on: (1) what the content of people's beliefs, values and knowledge is; (2) how the contents of our everyday thinking are created and generated through social interaction and communication by individuals and groups (through objectification and anchoring); and (3) what functions these representations serve. How representations differ from attitudes, however, is that they cannot be formed by the individual in isolation. The social representations take shape in interaction, in dialogue and in practice with others, and are anchored in our traditions and ideologies. Attitude is thus not seen as a property of an individual. Moscovici (1963) has stated: 'It is not enough to consider the content of an attitude, the broader structure which integrates this content must also be taken into account.' Also, social representation theory takes the view that the boundaries of the attitudinal object itself are drawn up through the process of social dialogue and debate. For example, what is implied by the attitudinal referents/objects 'refugee', 'anti-national' and 'terrorist' depends on the institutional cultures (e.g., of the army establishment and a human rights group), their social history and ideology. The very constitution of the attitudinal object is predicated on the social knowledge available within a group at any given point of time. By this logic, even the concepts of 'attitude' and 'social psychology' are social representations shared by the scientific community within psychology and have come into being through a historical process of evolution of knowledge and have been shaped in relation to other social representations related to 'individual', 'science', 'modernity', and so on.

124 What Is 'Social' about Social Psychology?

The theory of social representation has focused on the contents of social shared knowledge (ideas, thoughts and images) and the social process of communication and interaction by individuals and groups through which the subjective (individual) categorizations are formed. So, is there no individual in social representation? There is, but it is not an individual separate and influencing/influenced by the social but an individual and the social interpenetrating each other. Also, there is an acknowledgement that some representations may be less social in terms of less consensual, less socially agreed upon, but the process of generation, contestation and transformation of representations/thinking is fundamentally a social one.

Attitude in the Discourse Analytic Framework

Like social representations, discourse analysis too stresses the social origins and ideological consequences of representations/discourse and moves away from individualized accounts of attitudes. It provides a root and a branch re-specification of attitudes.

1. Potter and Wetherell (1987) challenge the epistemological status of the 'attitude' concept itself. The theoretical notion of an attitude and the assumption that it can be encapsulated by how a person responds to a questionnaire assume the existence of internal cognitive entities which are relatively enduring. In the discursive approach, such cognitive assumptions are considered problematic. Attitudes are conceptualized as evaluations of practices in everyday settings rather than underlying mental constructs. The stress is on what is done with evaluations – their practical use, explicit or indirect, in specific contexts instead of as an index of individual differences or as a predictor of later actions. This becomes clear from the following example. Wetherell, Hilda and Potter (1987) focused on men's talk about women's career opportunities in open-ended interviews. They did not attempt to ask these participants what their attitudes were to women's career advancement. Rather, the interview gave them the opportunity to provide descriptions, explanations and judgements as they dealt with a range of questions and comments from the interviewer. Close analysis of the interviews found a regular pattern. On the one hand, men supported the principle of women's career opportunity and attacked discrimination based on gender. On the other, the men offered a wide range of practical reasons, such as childcare responsibilities, for the failure of the women to reach full employment equality. These men have the ability to affirm both support for women's employment equality (in principle) and support for continued inequality (because of important practical concerns). The implications of this study are manifold. First, the attitude scale-driven research with its notion of unitary individual preferences is inadequate to explain how these people construct such split evaluations about gender and employment. Second, unlike the attitude researchers, the discursive

psychologists do not see this as a mismatch between 'attitudes' and 'behaviour' due to situational factors. Instead, they see it as the way talk is oriented to action. In presenting their views as egalitarian and practice as restrained, the men can deflect potential criticisms of themselves and maintain the status quo in which inequality is perpetuated. Traditional attitude measurement and theory pay no attention to what is done by attitude talk. Third, discourse analysis does not see ambivalence and contradictions manifested in questionnaire responses and in people's talk as located within the 'emotional and cognitive domain of the individual'. Such conflicts are not seen as between a feeling and a value, emotions and politics. Rather, it locates the dilemmas and conflicts within the argumentative and rhetorical resources available in 'liberal' and 'egalitarian' societies. The conflict is between competing frameworks to articulate social, political and ethical concerns.

2. One of the main lines of criticism of traditional work on attitudes revolved around the identification of 'variability in the use of evaluative expressions'. It is not uncommon for a participant to feel exasperated with the attitudinal rating scale and say, 'My attitude depends on the context.' The same individual may express different opinions in different situations or even during different parts of the conversation. Generally, such variability is missed or suppressed or ignored when more traditional attitudinal measurement is used. It cannot be explained by theories of impression management and the response tendency of social desirability. Traditional attitudinal research measure variability by items such as 'I sometimes agree and sometimes disagree with government's policies on taxation'. Here, the assumption is that there is an inner position reflected by the attitude, but it varies over time. This does not quite capture what discursive social psychology understands by variability. There is no assumption in this framework that people have consistent personally held evaluations that are carried from one context to another which change with time like weather. Variability is expected within discursive social psychology as people perform different actions with their talk, such as differentiating themselves from enemies, aligning with friends, and so on. In discursive social psychology, attitudes are performed rather than preformed. Potter and Wetherell (1987) summarize:

We do not intend to use the discourse as a pathway to entities or phenomena lying beyond the text. Discourse analysis does not take for granted that accounts reflect underlying attitudes or dispositions and therefore we do not expect that an individual's discourse will be consistent and coherent. Rather the focus is on discourse itself: how it is organized and what it is doing.

(p. 4)

3. The focus in discourse analytic research is on what is done with evaluations by people in their natural environment rather than in the artificial

environment of filling in questionnaires. Traditional attitudinal research treats as irrelevant the fact that 'responding' to an attitude scale is an activity. What people may be doing with their words in these settings is not made a topic of study; instead, the words are treated as a pathway to the speaker's inner world.

4. The traditional social psychological research on attitude is an etic approach in which the psychologist attempts to fine-tune the definitions of attitude objects and response categories offered to the participants to create precision and consistency. For example, in attitudinal research, response categories such as 'extremely good' and 'extremely bad' can overlap considerably with response categories such as 'like extremely' and 'dislike extremely' as has been found by Berger (1992) with respect to a new chocolate bar. However, we know that good and like are not interchangeable in ordinary discourses. A film may be rated as good but may not be liked by someone and vice versa. 'Good' points to the intrinsic merit of the film and 'like' indexes the preference of the person. Traditional attitude measurement blurs such potentially consequential distinctions. Because psychometric measurement relies on fixed response categories, it fails to explicate evaluations as they are constructed and understood by the participants in their contradictions and ambiguities.

In place of the attitude concept, Potter and Wetherell (1987) put forward the notion of 'interpretive repertoires' defined as a set of metaphors, arguments and terms which are used recurrently to describe and evaluate events and actions.

How Are Stereotypes and Prejudice Understood in Competing Constructions of Social Psychology?

Yet another topic of social psychology that has been reconceptualized within the traditions of social representations and discourse analysis is stereotypes and prejudice. Prejudice is a negative attitude held towards the members of a group based on their membership. At the heart of prejudice is a stereotype. A stereotype is a mental representation of a social group and its members. Both stereotypes and prejudice make discrimination against an out-group and its members more likely. Stereotypes are social schemas which are structures of knowledge in people's minds used to make sense of the social world. They are theory-driven, stable knowledge structures in memory; they have internal organizational properties and are learnt by individuals through experience. This has been the dominant conceptualization of stereotypes within the social cognition literature.

Social Schemas and Social Representations

There are a number of problems associated with the above conceptualization raised by social representation:

1. Schema models have treated the processes of classification and categorization of social reality involved in the formation of schemas as elements of individual cognitive functioning. Schemas are seen as cognitive structures originating and existing inside individuals' heads. There is little theoretical and empirical work that has been carried out to ascertain the degree to which various schematic structures may be shared or how they may arise from social interaction and communication. The social representation perspective opposes the individualistic notion of social knowledge and sees both the process of origination and content of mental representations as social. It asks the following questions: Why are certain schemas more prevalent than others? Are any of these knowledge structures shared and, if so, by whom and how many? Are there group variations in the content of these structures? The theory's clear imperative is to look for group differences in the content and structure of social knowledge.

2. Processes of schema development are assumed to be universal across different content domains and across different groups of people in social cognition research. Cognitive development theory has assumed that the acquisition of social knowledge proceeds via logical, sequential and universal developmental stages which are internally controlled by the cognitive capacities of the individual (e.g., Piaget's theory of cognitive development). However, the processes of anchoring and objectification, specified by Moscovici as central to the formation of social representation, are collective processes taking place within social communication and interaction.

3. Because schema theory is so theory-driven, it does not pay attention to data-driven processing, that is, how people are influenced by the nature of the stimulus information. To what extent are schematic structures and representations challenged by the introduction of information which does not fit easily with the usual categories of comparison and classification?

Social Categorization and Discourse Analysis

The underlying mechanism of stereotyping is social categorization. It involves categorizing people into groups, such as 'Indians', 'Americans', 'men', 'women', and so on, on the basis of the perception of common attributes. Basically, stereotyping suggests that, in much the same way as we categorize the material world into living and non-living, so too, we categorize our social worlds. We are naturally oriented to perceiving our physical and social world categorically, and racial stereotyping is understood as an extension of this hard-wired cognitive tendency to categorize. Categories such as man–woman, black–white, young–old, rich–poor are treated as uncontested and non-problematic social objects which are perceived directly through identifiable physical and social features. This categorization is understood by most social psychologists who study prejudice to be the processes that underlie the formation of in-groups and out-groups – groups we perceive to be 'like us' and those 'not like us'. Social

128 What Is 'Social' about Social Psychology?

cognitive researchers regard stereotypes as the reason for the distorted and biased descriptions of social groups.

The discourse analytic approach of Potter and Wetherell (1987) introduces an entirely different perspective to the study of categorization. Their discursive approach does not regard categories as cognitive phenomena located in people's heads – preformed static structures which are organized around prototypical representations of the category. Rather, they are more interested in understanding, first, how people discursively constitute categories and, second, which varied and flexible functions that categorization serves within ordinary accounts of group behaviour. This perspective will look for the category labels such as 'suicide bombers', 'army personnel', 'terrorists', 'Naxalites', 'politicians', 'republicans', 'man on the street' and so on in talk and text which draw out the boundary between them and us. It will then invite us to think critically about the politics of category construction (Reicher & Hopkins, 2001) and to recognize how our ways of classifying others often serve collective interests. For example, in a politician's account, the aggressive reactions of 'the army' may be selectively emphasized and constructed as a necessary 'reaction' to the violence of the 'local people', an essentially defensive step that has directly saved many lives. In terms of the global function, one might argue that these kinds of accounts are designed to legitimize some forms of collective violence and delegitimize others. At the very least, they establish a moral hierarchy in which violence by the army and local people becomes graded in terms of its level of acceptability. It is not difficult to see how these kinds of accounts may help to sustain fundamentally incompatible constructions of the political realities of, say, the Kashmir situation, maintaining the kind of context in which the potential for ongoing conflict is heightened. Variations of the arguments are constantly being relayed and circulated in everyday conversations, mass media reports, political or religious speeches, acting as an interpretive framework through which emerging events are evaluated. Potter and Wetherell (1987) argue that it is through the dynamic process of discursive interaction that a particular individual's subjectivity is defined and constructed.

PAUSE AND THINK

Try to think of the social categories that you use in everyday life, such as student, girl/boy, Indian. Pay attention to how you use these categories in your everyday talk. What function do these categories serve?

BOX 3.3 THE CONTACT HYPOTHESIS: CRITICAL REFLECTIONS

The contact hypothesis, which posits that positive interaction between members of different groups tends to reduce inter-group prejudice, is hailed as one of the most successful ideas in social psychology. Since its inception, it has served both an academic and a policy agenda. Theoretically speaking, it postulated prejudice as a product of fear, ignorance, hierarchy or lack of shared life patterns and goals. In the service of policy, it is used as a rationale for desegregation policies and as a guide for designing peace-building interventions. The palliative effect of inter-group contact is a central theme of Gordon Allport's landmark book *The Nature of Prejudice* (1956) where a set of situational conditions of contact leading to conflict reduction have been laid out. Allport conjectured:

> Prejudice may be reduced by equal status contact between majority and minority groups in the pursuit of the common goals. The effect is greatly enhanced if this contact is sanctioned by institutional supports (i.e. by law, custom, or local atmosphere), and provided it is of a sort that leads to the perception of common interests and common humanity between members of the two groups.
>
> *(1956, p. 281)*

The contact hypothesis is widely accepted as one of the most effective psychological interventions for social change that is based on the rehabilitation of prejudiced individuals. However, it is also subject to several searching critiques (McKeown & Dixon, 2017):

1. *Limitations of research design and methodology:* The list of situational conditions for 'good' interaction among the members of different groups seldom exists in pure form in the real world. Thus, much research has focused either on laboratory conditions or on specialized situations in which optimal contact can be easily manufactured, at least, for a short period of time. This masks the starker realities of everyday interactions among members of different communities. The Likert scale used to indicate participants' level of pre- and post-contact attitudes is also not a sensitive tool to assess the true change in prejudicial attitudes. Most studies use younger children or college students and very little is known about the effects of contacts on adults' ethnic or racial prejudice over 25 years of age.

2. *Inconsistencies and lack of generalization of contact effects:* Studies have shown that contact seems to work especially well as a strategy for reducing prejudice towards people with mental or physical disabilities. The effects are not as impressive for reducing ethnic/racial prejudice. There are also inconsistencies with regard to the level of analysis. Much research attention has focused on addressing whether the effects of contact on interpersonal perceptions (how a person of a group perceive another person of the out-group) generalize to alter inter-group perceptions. Contact, for example, often leads people to regard particular individuals as 'exceptions to the rule' rather than leading them to abandon their wider stereotype systems. There is also a dearth of good quality longitudinal

research on prejudice or prejudice reduction (Abrams, 2010). Another critique is that, in experimental studies, focus is on measuring outcomes immediately after an intervention. It is not well established whether the effects of contact endure for days, weeks, months or years.

3. *Disregard of everyday experiences of inter-group relations*: There is a disconnection between the kinds of short-term benign contact that psychologists have routinely investigated and the kinds of contact that participants experience in everyday life. In many historically divided societies, inter-group relations are marked by fear, suspicion, anger, disgust; routine dehumanization and exploitation of others; deep resentments felt by those who are targets of abuses of power and privilege and apprehensions about loss of power, wealth and status among those who are in dominant positions. In such societies, the possibility of contact leading to a celebration of differences or the creation of superordinate identities (we versus us/them) remains bleak. There is always a lurking danger of struggles over the comparative value of groups (which group identity is superior) or a resurgence of sub-group identities and their associated prejudices. Another related and fundamental issue is what if the processes that govern conflict between groups are relatively autonomous from interactions between individuals? Often, the conflictual processes, grounded in members' collectively constructed sense of their group's positioning in relation to the other groups, are shaped by a shared historical and political sense of relationship between 'us' and 'them'. This is relatively impervious to the day-to-day contacts experienced by individual members. Thus, it is important to consider the political and historical nature of inter-group conflict, especially in the context of ethnic/racial/religious contexts.

4. *Resegregation in desegregated environments*: Psychological research using methods other than self-reports and experimentation, such as observational methods, have mapped basic patterns of contact and their effects in everyday life spaces, such as classrooms. Such research is showing growing evidence for the tenacity of segregation in contexts where opportunities of contact were amply available, for example, US colleges and post-apartheid beaches. Seating among college students and spatial arrangements among holidaymakers showed racial segregation in colleges and on beaches.

5. *Ironic effects of contact on the political attitudes of the disadvantaged*: Cross-sectional surveys conducted in South Africa, for example, have suggested that contact between whites and blacks tends to improve the racial attitudes of both groups, but it also diminishes the black South Africans' readiness to recognize the persistence of racial discrimination in the post-apartheid era (Dixon et al., 2010). This has led some researchers to argue that prejudice reduction interventions may exert a 'sedative effect' (Cakal et al., 2011) on the collective resistance of historically disadvantaged groups to social inequality, even to the point of encouraging them to acquiesce in their own exploitation.

Final Comments

Contemporary social psychology is a fragmented and deeply divided discipline. Its history is marked by several junctures and turns. One of the turns is the cognitive turn aimed originally at establishing 'meaning' as the central concept in psychology. It resulted in the emergence of 'social cognition' as the dominant framework within social psychology. Over time, it led to increasing 'cognitivism' and 'individualism', thereby abandoning its original search for meaning. The second turn is the linguistic turn in social psychology, which saw cognitive processes as not located within individual minds but as something to be observed in common practices. The third turn is the historical turn which argued for both psychological objects and results shaped by, or dependent on, the culture in which they occur.

The two main disputes between the various forms of social psychology are with regard to (1) the meaning of science, and (2) the nature of the social world. The psychological/experimental social psychology largely subscribes to the use of a scientific (that is hypothetico-deductive) method to construct and test theories. On the other hand, the social representations/discursive/critical forms of social psychology do not see science as an exclusively hypothetico-deductive enterprise, rather as 'an effort to make accurate observations and valid causal inferences and to assemble these observations and inferences in a compact and coherent way' (Brickman, 1980, p. 10, as cited in Willig & Stainton Rogers, 2008). This enlarged sense of science has led to a critique of the variables-based approach, quantification and the lack of social relevance present in experimental and social psychometric approaches. Consequently, social psychological research has expanded to study 'everyday life' through investigations of conversations, media reports, speeches, social practices, and so on. The binaries of individual–social and agency–structure are of unique importance to social psychology because the discipline has come to be defined in terms of this dualism (the study of individuals in social contexts). The psychological tradition of social psychology has weighed more on the individual and constructs the 'social' in limited terms. The social representations/discursive/critical traditions of social psychology focus more on the social and invite critique about erasing the 'experiential' and 'agentic' dimensions of individuality. The way ahead for social psychologists is to go beyond the individual–social and agency–structure dualism and to carry out genuine 'psychosocial' enquiry. Such an enquiry will focus on how the individual and social aspects work together within and between people in particular settings.

Another important agenda for social psychology is not to limit its scope to a set of topics that we usually find in a social psychology text. Human subjectivity is inherently social psychological in nature. Thus, starting from body and self to emotions and memory to psychopathology and mental health to childhood and families, an understanding of their social nature is a must. Thus, a mature social psychology must emerge from the shadows of being a subset of general psychology. It should attempt to unravel the simultaneous private and contextual nature of human life.

4

WHERE IS 'CULTURE' IN PSYCHOLOGY?

Traditionally culturally focused psychology has not been a priority area within psychology. There are two chief ways in which culture figures in the logic of psychological science (Gergen, et al., 1996). First, as a field of difference where culture serves as a moderator or qualifier for universal theoretical propositions. Second, as a proving ground for the universality of the general theory. In the first case, cultural variations are either de-emphasized or simply bracketed for 'later study'. In the second case, culture itself is of secondary interest. However, in the past four or five decades, the relationship between psychology and culture has begun to attract a lot of critical attention. Discontent and doubts have been raised by a plethora of scholars in non-American, non-Western and/or Third World locales about the implicit presumption that there is a universally acceptable conception of psychological science. Misra and Gergen (1993) have explored important limitations of North American theories and research practices when imported into the Indian cultural context. Sinha (1990) has questioned the relevance of 'vertical collaboration', that is, psychologists from developing countries working on research initiated by investigators in the developed nations. He proposes 'horizontal collaboration' among researchers working on practical problems across various regions of a country or with those in other developing nations.

The relationship between psychology and culture is predicated on two challenging questions: First, how does psychology study culture? And, second, an even more radical one, whether psychology itself is a cultural manifestation. The latter question leads us to understand that mainstream psychology is largely an American ethnopsychology shaped by the research concerns, samples and methods of the white, middle-class, male-dominated science. Once this is recognized, psychology's treatment of culture can be placed in context.

DOI: 10.4324/9781003471851-5

What Is Culture?

Culture derives its original meaning from the Latin word, *cultura*, which referred to the 'cultivation of the soil'. Meanings of culture abound in the Western history of idea so much so that any attempt to encompass all its meanings in words 'is like trying to seize the air in the hand, when one finds that it is everywhere except within one's grasp' (Lowell, 1934, p. 115). In a classic review of the concept, anthropologists Kroeber and Kluckhohn (1952) brought more than 160 definitions to light. In order to grasp the meaning of this elusive concept, numerous issues pertaining to its definition have developed. Let us review a few salient ones:

- *Culture as the outer layer*: A vast literature, popular and technical, has dealt with the relative importance of biological and cultural components in a variety of domains of human behaviour, such as aggression, territoriality, sex role, sexuality. and so on. Poortinga, Van de Vijver, Joe and Van de Koppel (1987) suggested the metaphor of peeling an onion to suggest layers of culture can be peeled off to ultimately find primal man and raw human nature underneath. This idea also ties in with the widespread notion that culture is an influencing agent on the 'basic', 'universal' human nature, defined biologically or psychologically. This notion is untenable. Biological templates are transformed and elaborated into cultural patterns. What is needed is a complex interactional model, not a simple stratigraphic one.
- *Culture as material or ideational*: Often, a distinction is drawn between material (culture as the 'lived-in' world) and ideational (culture as the 'thought-of' world) dimensions of cultures. The term 'material' in material culture refers to objects made by man or modified by man. It includes categories of artefacts from more aesthetic to more utilitarian, such as art (paintings, sculpture, photography), diversions (books, toys, meals, games, theatrical performances), adornment (clothing, jewellery, hairstyles, tattooing), modification of the landscape (architecture, settlement patterns, mining, agriculture), applied arts (furniture, utensils, furnishings), or devices (machines, vehicles, scientific instruments) (Prown, 1982). Strategies of food production, methods by which people exchange goods and services and technology fall under the ambit of material culture. They enable adaptation to the particular ecological setting.

  A contrasting view of culture sees it as an ideational system of knowledge. Understood in this way, culture consists of widely held beliefs, values and shared behavioural scripts. Sometimes, also referred to as 'subjective culture' (Triandis, 1972), it provides individuals in the group with a shared way of thinking about the self and the world, or a common frame of reference for making sense of reality. Lévi-Strauss (1963) views culture as a shared symbolic system manifested in myth, art, kinship and language. Goodenough said:

134 Where Is 'Culture' in Psychology?

- Culture ... consists of standards for deciding what is ... for deciding what can be ... for deciding what one feels about it ... for deciding what to do about it, and ... for deciding how to go about doing it.

(1961, p. 522)

There is a tendency to view material aspects of culture as primary and the ideational systems as secondary and derived. Cultural change is believed to be driven by the technological– economic–environmental conditions. However, this misses the point that all the sectors of cultural complex are functionally related to each other. Knowledge about making tools, forming work groups, the environment and ways of extracting subsistence from it are as much a part of the ideational realm as patterns of religious beliefs and rituals. Processes of change and adaptation can be understood fully if we understand the total culture. For example, how are changes in ideas about subsistence strategy related to changes in ideas about kinship or changes in ideas about religious rituals? Or, how are ideas about choosing post-marital residence related to increased population or increased agricultural production?

- *Culture in 'mind' or culture as 'public'*: This debate parallels the debate that is present in social psychology about whether 'social' is defined in terms of cognitive constructs such as schemas, attributions and attitudes, or whether it is to be understood in terms of external context, such as the presence of a person or group membership. The debate is aptly put by Goodenough: 'People learn as individuals. Therefore, if a culture is learned, its ultimate locus must be in the individuals rather than in groups ...' (1971, p. 20).

  The view of 'culture in mind' takes the position that culture resides in the mind in the form of a loose network of knowledge structures, mental constructs and representations that are widely shared within a given context. In particular social situations, the relevant implicit cultural theories or shared assumptions become available, accessible, salient and applicable in the situation.

- There is no denying the fact that the cultural systems are created, shaped and constrained by individual minds and brains. Forms of culture depend on what individual humans can think, imagine and learn as well as on what collective behaviours shape and sustain viable patterns of life in ecosystems. Also, there is a range of diversity in individual versions of the 'shared' culture. It is not a social imperfection but an adaptive necessity, a crucial resource that can be drawn on and selected from in cultural change. Matsumoto (1996) p. 18) stated:

Individual differences in culture can be observed among people in the degree to which they adopt and engage in the attitudes, values, beliefs, and behaviors that, by consensus, constitute their culture. If you act in accordance with those values or behaviors, then that culture resides in you; if you do not share those values or behaviors, then you do not share that culture. While the norms of any culture should be relevant to all the people within that culture, it is also true that those norms will be relevant in different degrees for different people.

The other side of the conceptual dilemma is:
when individuals engaging in social relations—even if there are only two of them—share common meanings, common understandings of one another's acts then these shared meanings are greater than the sum of their "parts", their realizations in individual mind.

(Keesing, 1974, p. 84)

Thus, culture is a collective phenomenon. Geertz (1973) said that meanings are not in people's heads; cultural symbols, practices and meanings are shared by social actors – between, not in them; they are public, not private.

Yet another way in which culture is held as external is what Shore (1996) emphasizes, that culture exists not only as cognitive constructs in the mind of members of a community but also as public artefacts and institutions in the world. Hence, culture is represented at the public, external, social and material level.

- *Culture as integrated, homogeneous and bounded or culture as internally contradictory, heterogeneous and transnational*: There is a view that connects a singular, coherent and integrated culture to a demarcated population, usually defined by national boundaries. For example, the Japanese are often described in psychological research as being interdependent or collectivist. The assumption is that there is a world that is neatly divided into nations and countries, each representing its own culture. The expectation is that as we step into these unitary, disjointed, self-contained and territorially bounded spaces, we will see a variety of cultures, customs and social practices that are unique to that place. However, treating culture synonymously with a demarcated population presents various problems. First, it reinforces the tendency to stereotype by attributing cultural traits and essences to demarcated populations. The second important problem is, how to explain cultural differences and cultural variation within a given locale? The movement of multiculturalism and the idea of subcultures attempt to incorporate notions of cultural variation within their frameworks. Another idea that makes an attempt to acknowledge cultural differences is the notion of 'distribution of cultural meanings'. For example, ideas that constitute collectivism are more widely shared among Japanese people and institutions as compared to Euro-American people and institutions. However, within Japan, some are less collectivist than others, and collectivism is more widely distributed in some domains than in others (Oyserman et al., 2002). These frameworks are noteworthy in accepting 'plurality' as essential to an understanding of cultures, but they suffer the limitation of describing the plural cultures as existing in relation to a dominant or majority culture within the same space (Gupta & Ferguson, 1992). A similar problem arises when the traditional notions of ethnicity are used to describe the experience of immigrants within a given locale. For instance, the Indians living in America are perceived as having natural links to their Indian identity as 'found' within the geographical boundaries of India. This simplistic understanding of an Indian identity does not quite capture the experience of this diaspora community:The "Indianness" of the members of this community, i.e., what it means to "be" from a particular culture, may not be based upon their physical relation to their respective national space but on their "imagined", "re-invented" notion of Indianness in their new world. (Bhatia, 2007). Thus, to consider nations and cultures as isomorphic is untenable. Understanding of culture and self has to be reterritorialized and transnationalized.

Geertz (1966) suggests that cultural analysis is as much an exercise of mapping internal consistency and integration as of disconnectedness and internal contradiction. He provides a vivid metaphor of cultural organization:

The appropriate image, if one must have images, of cultural organization, is neither the spider web nor the pile of sand. It is rather more the octopus, whose tentacles are in large part separately integrated, neutrally quite poorly connected with one another and with what in the octopus passes for a brain, and yet who nonetheless manages to get around and to preserve himself, for a while anyway, as a viable, if somewhat ungainly entity.

(Geertz, 1966, pp. 66–67)

- *Culture and social as distinct or a mere reflection of each other*: It is an accepted fact that the psychological is affected by the context. The context is variously understood in 'ecological', 'social' and 'cultural' terms. Ecological environments refer to natural resources such as fertility of soil, availability of water bodies, flora and fauna and climatic conditions such as humidity level, heat and cold. The ways in which communities adapt to their ecological niches give rise to technologies, modes of economic organization, settlement patterns, modes of social groupings and various other behavioural and ideological patterns. These patterns of life of communities are called sociocultural systems.

  There is some conceptual confusion between what constitutes 'cultural' and what constitutes 'social'. Are 'culture' and 'social' the same? Is the cultural derived from the forms of social organization? Or, is social organization the behavioural embodiment of cultural patterns? Social is usually understood in terms of categories, such as sex, race, class, caste, and so on, which are associated with status and roles. A social structure refers to patterned interrelationships among statuses and roles. Status is a position occupied by an actor in a social structure. It may be ranked hierarchically in terms of prestige, power, access to resources. Role refers to behaviours, rights, obligations, beliefs and norms attached to a particular status position. It is a here-and-now concept. On the other hand, culture is a historically determined set of denotative (what is), normative (what should be) and pragmatic (how to do) knowledge shared by a group of individuals who participate in a form of social structure (Triandis, 1995). It is not only an ideational-shared meaning but also a part of collective routines and practices. For instance, collectivistic cultures emphasize interdependence and modesty not only in verbal statements but also in social customs and events.

Chapter 3 highlighted the importance of the social situation for an individual's actions. But what happens when the same situation is interpreted differently by two communities? For example, when two people are talking to each other and they are standing about 3–4 feet apart, the Americans see this as an appropriate distance while Arabs find it odd and a sign of a 'don't care' attitude (Hall, 1966). This highlights that there are certain assumptions, rules, norms and beliefs that are held in common by people which guide their behaviour and understandings in various situations. This 'shared' aspect is called culture, and it accounts for human diversity. Within psychology, the study of culture, thus, becomes important in understanding how shared meanings and practices give direction and form to our lives. Here, culture is conceptualized as a contextual factor beyond the social. The study of culture and psychology sheds light on whether and how social psychological phenomena such as self, categorizations, schemas, attributions and attitudes differ among human groupings.

It is important to tease apart the two levels of explanations: cultural and social. Cultural scripts are used to make meaning of social situations by people. However, not all typical situations found in a culture are related to a core of values. For instance, if parents sleep with their children, even though houses are large enough to have separate rooms, because sleeping with one's children is considered normative, then we have a satisfactory cultural explanation. It is a desirable institutional arrangement. However, if co-sleeping is the result of limited space or because of physical danger to the child if he/she sleeps alone, it is not a cultural explanation.

A cultural explanation is different from a socio-structural explanation because the former sees persisting patterns of behaviours as emanating from shared beliefs and values, while the latter sees patterns of behaviours as emanating from contemporary situational contingencies and constraints, such as the socio-economic structure. Cultural explanations are normative, relatively independent of a contemporary situation. The socio-structural explanation is a situational explanation more or less independent of

138 Where Is 'Culture' in Psychology?

normative processes. For example, to explain why the Indian subjects are more likely to distribute rewards on the basis of what people need rather than merit, both cultural and socio-structural explanations are possible. The cultural explanation will be that because Indians are collectivist, they use the need norm more than the merit norm. The socio-structural explanation will be that since resources are scarce, they distribute as per need rather than merit.

The main idea in a contextual culturalist explanation is that the values and beliefs characteristic of a culture or a subculture have a life apart from the situations and can endure well beyond the demise of the original situations (Ross & Nisbett, 1991). Let us take the example of honour cultures. Mediterranean and South American countries have been described as 'honour cultures'. In these cultures, the focal value of honour is anchored in a concern with one's extended identity in public behaviour. Scholars have identified socio-economic factors (shepherding, noble status and medieval-style army roles, and the weakness of the state) for the rise of cultures of honour. But, even when these social situations changed due to social evolution, the culture of honour persisted in these societies because the functional values (masculine pride, public violence in response to provocations) had crystallized in a 'way of life' that endured well beyond the demise of the original situations.

In summary, culture can be defined as:

patterns, explicit and implicit, of and for behaviour acquired and transmitted by symbols, constituting the distinctive achievements of human groups, including their embodiment in artifacts; the essential core of culture consists of traditional (i.e., historically derived and selected) ideas and especially their attached values; culture systems may, on the one hand, be considered as products of action, on the other, as conditional elements of future action.

(Kroeber & Kluckhohn, 1952, p. 181)

PAUSE AND THINK

Which cultural group do you identify with? Try to identify examples of the shared meanings, practices and artefacts of your cultural group.

Is Psychology a Universal Science?

The history of culture in psychology is a chequered one. There has always been a tension between a natural science and a human science model in psychology (Dilthey, 1883). The natural science model regards physics as the ideal of scientific enquiry and tries to establish a universal law-like causal explanation of a phenomenon. In contrast, the human science model emphasizes cultural and historical specificity, and interpretive understanding rather than experimentation as a method of knowing. Wilhelm Wundt, the father of modern experimental psychology, devoted much of his scholarly attention to *Völkerpsychologie* in his later life. This division in his body of work was underwritten by the assumption that culture and language affect higher-order mental functions, whereas more basic ones are unaffected by culture. As psychology emerged and grew into an academic discipline, the natural science model gained a strong hold. Behaviourism and even the cognitive revolution isolated enquiries around the cultural origins of the mind. Psychology became a hypothetico-deductive and experimental endeavour in search of universal laws of human behaviour. With this, culture and the emphasis on understanding human peculiarities were largely lost from the academic discourse in psychology.

Mainstream psychology believes in the 'psychic unity' of humankind. Its aim is to describe the fixed and universal properties of the human psyche. The processes which enable the human beings to think (classify, infer, remember, imagine, etc.), experience (emote, feel, desire, need, etc.), act (strive, prefer, choose, evaluate, etc.) and learn are believed to be inherent and are explained in terms of abstract phrases such as 'long-term memory store', 'fundamental attribution bias', 'cognitive assimilation', 'formal operational thinking', 'appraisal of stressor and coping resources', 'self-actualization' and 'life and death drives', which are universal. Stimuli, contexts, meanings, knowledge, religion, rituals, language, technologies and institutions are conceived to be external to or outside the 'deep-down' processing mechanism. Knowledge-seeking in mainstream psychology is the attempt to see the psychological processes untainted by content and context. Thus, it is culture-blind. The experimental lab is the privileged space where the effects of context, content and meaning can be eliminated, standardized or kept under control, and the inherent psychological mechanism can be observed in the raw. However, it has been found that many descriptions of mental functioning emerging out of laboratory research with educated Western population do not apply very well to subject populations in other cultures. For example, almost all adults in the Western world display the concrete operational thinking on Piaget's conservation tasks; many adults in the Third World do not. The study of diverse concepts such as self, cognitive style, emotions, attachment, or depression has revealed a great deal of cultural diversity, which has gone unnoticed in psychology. Thus, mainstream psychology is culture-bound.

Moghaddam (1987) has identified a tendency of mainstream psychology to gather and publish a disproportionate segment of data from selected geographical and cultural locations, mostly concentrated in North America (known as psychology's First World), and to generalize these data worldwide. Even if differences are found between Western cultures and other cultural groups, they are viewed as deficiencies. This is the ethnocentric bias in psychology. The term was coined by Sumner (1906), who noted that there exists a strong tendency to

140 Where Is 'Culture' in Psychology?

use one's own group's standards as the standard when viewing other groups, to place one's group at the top of a hierarchy and to rank all others as lower.

The cultural critics of mainstream psychology can be divided into those who questioned its external validity and those who questioned its internal validity. In terms of external validity, it has been suggested that Western psychological research tends to be Anglo-American centric at the levels of (1) selection of items and stimuli in a test; (2) choice of instruments, procedures and samples of study; (3) definition of theoretical concepts; and (4) choice of topics for research (Berry et al., 1992). The psychological theories that are derived on the basis of such practices reflect the goals, values and issues of the Western world and are not generalizable to other societies. In particular, much criticism has been directed towards the values of individualism inherent in the Western psychology that seriously limits the generalization of psychological knowledge in the non-Western world. The question of the 'internal validity' of mainstream psychology raises the issue that it excludes the subjective aspects of human functioning (i.e., consciousness, agency, meaning-in-context) in order to develop objective, abstract and universal theories.

How Did the Study of Culture Emerge in Psychology?

Intercultural contacts made possible by advances in transportation and necessitated by trade and colonial expansion sparked an interest in the systematic study of other cultures. Outside of psychology, the 1889 Cambridge Anthropological Expedition to the Torres Straits (between New Guinea and Australia) was seminal for the overall emergence of research across cultures. It sought knowledge on the language, society, folklore and cognitive abilities of the Torres Straits Islanders, who at the time were threatened by colonial expansionism. One of the members of the expedition was W. H. R. Rivers, an experimental psychologist at Cambridge University. He combined the empirical method of psychological experimentation with anthropological methods. In the Torres Straits, Rivers set out to test the theory, popular at the time, that non-Europeans possessed extraordinary visual acuity and perceptual abilities, at the expense of higher cognitive functioning. Although his claims about extraordinary visual acuity of non-Europeans were exaggerated and his methodology of performing controlled experimentation in 'exotic' locations was critiqued, his approach to study cultures decisively influenced the future direction of study of culture and psychology.

Since the 1930s, attempts have been made to systematize the body of knowledge available on the culture–behaviour link. They culminated in establishing the Human Relations Area Files (HRAF) under the auspices of Yale University in 1949. The HRAF has provided an ever-swelling knowledge resource based on two themes.

1. *The Outline of World Cultures* (Murdock, 1975, which is as comprehensive as possible a list of the world's cultural groups organized by regions

(e.g., North America), sub-regions (e.g., Southwest region of the United States) and subsistence types (e.g., hunting–gathering, agropastoral).

2. *The Outline of Cultural Materials* (Murdock & Douglas, 1975), which is a classification of topics that are considered eligible for studying world-wide, due to their universal applicability. It is organized into eight sections, including food and clothing, economy and transport, welfare, religion and science.

Beginnings of Cross-Cultural Psychology

In psychology, the 1950s and 1960s witnessed many seminal studies on perception (Segall et al., 1966), motivation (McClelland, 1961), cognition (Witkin & Berry, 1975) and mental abilities (Cronbach & Drenth, 1972), among others. They later became the bedrock of much of modern-day cross-cultural psychology. The motivation behind such studies was to test the premise of 'psychic unity' (i.e., basic psychological processes are the same across cultures) and see which aspects of behaviour and experience are common to all human cultures and which are not.

One of the most prominent lines of research was the 'culture and personality' school (Whiting & Child, 1953; Whiting & Whiting, 1975), which was dominated for many years by psychoanalytically oriented anthropologists. It was the forerunner of psychological anthropology, a new specialization that was born when Hsu edited a book with the title *Psychological Anthropology* in 1961. This perspective was concerned with particular cultures and how cultural organization gives rise to particular kinds of personalities. Works of one such anthropologist, Kardiner, were based on the premise that primary institutions (such as kinship and socialization) form the basic personality structure of a society, which in turn leads to secondary institutions, such as religion, art and folklore (Piker, 1994). The Six Cultures Project, developed by cultural anthropologists John and Beatrice Whiting, Irving Child and many of their colleagues and students, sought to uncover causal connections between cultural phenomena and the behaviour of members of cultures they studied. The Whitings (e.g., Whiting & Whiting, 1975) believed that any culture, with its specific environment and historical background, can be understood as a 'maintenance system' that is antecedent to child-training practices that match the specific needs of each culture. These practices, in turn, lead to the development of certain personality 'types' reflected in a culture's art, music, recreation, play behaviour, crime and suicide rates, and so on. The model has been influential in generating hypotheses about connections between the individual and the society in which he/she has been socialized. It has also influenced the development of more recent models of cross-cultural psychology, for example, the ecocultural model. Extending the work of culture and personality school, David McClelland's approach in studying achievement motivation took a host of background factors – high achievement standards infused by the family (especially the mother), low dominance by the father, particular kinds of religious values and a temperate climate – to be involved in shaping a child's level of motivation. Treated as 'causative' variables, they were believed to be causing children to compete for internalized standards of excellence, which in turn influenced a culture's rate of economic growth.

The institutionalization of cross-cultural psychology took place during the 1960s. The *Journal of Cross-Cultural Psychology* first appeared in 1970 and the International Association for Cross-Cultural Psychology was established in 1972, with Jerome Bruner as the president. In terms of publication outlets and an institutional basis, cross-cultural psychology had arrived by the mid-1970s. Harry Triandis co-edited a seminal six-volume *Handbook of Cross-Cultural Psychology* which reviewed much of the work done in the field up to the mid-1970s. The handbook was extensive in its coverage with volumes devoted to perspectives, methodology, basic processes, developmental psychology, social psychology and psychopathology. A separate volume on culture and human development (Munroe et al., 1972) was also published and attests to the vast amount of cross-cultural research conducted at the time.

Culture in Social Psychology

Social psychology, as a sub-discipline of psychology, evinced an early interest in the role of culture. The possibility of considering culture within a social psychological framework was opened up by the work of gestalt-influenced psychologists – Kurt Lewin, Solomon Asch, Fritz Heider. They emphasized that the 'meaning of the situation' is more important than objective conditions of the situation. Culture shapes the meaning of the situation that each member of that culture has. For example, in-group/out-group distinction is a basic social psychological fact. Research has well established the fact that self-in-group relationships are inherently different from self-out-group relationships. While the distinction between in-groups and out-groups is universal, cultures differ in the specific meanings of self-in-group and self-out-group relationships (Triandis et al., 1988). How cultural groups differ in this regard is characterized by the concept of individualism versus collectivism (Hofstede, 2001) or autonomy versus embeddedness (Schwartz, 2004), both of which are aspects of subjective culture. Individualistic, autonomous cultures may allow more in-groups to develop, and their members are not obliged as much to any single in-group as they are in collectivistic cultures. Collectivistic, embedded cultures, however, foster the development of fewer in-groups, but their commitment to in-groups is greater than in individualistic cultures. Thus, self-in-group and self-out-group relationships differ in individualistic and collectivistic cultures in the degree of harmony, cohesion, co-operation and conformity between the self and the group (Matsumoto, 2007). Thus, the theoretical integration of culture with social psychological phenomena became important.

One of the first psychologists attempting this integration was Harry Triandis, whose publication, 'Cultural Influences upon Cognitive Processes', appeared as the first chapter in the first volume of the celebrated series, *Advances in Experimental Social Psychology* (Triandis, 1964). The title of the chapter and that of the book provide us with an understanding of the way social psychology of culture has shaped. The title of the chapter suggests that culture acts on the psyche as a unidirectional force. There is little provision for the 'mutually constitutive' nature of culture and the psyche. Also, the method used to examine cultural sources of social behaviour was experimentation. Triandis' use of the experimental method broadly conceived and firmly established the understanding that there was no pragmatic impediment to the use of experimentation to examine cross-cultural variability. He authored one of the first clearly cross-cultural psychological books, titled *The Analysis of Subjective Culture* (Triandis, 1972), in which he incorporated a wide range of social psychological concepts in the study of culture. This work is widely credited as establishing the social psychology of culture with a comparative culture focus.

The paradigm of social cognition within social psychology has been closely aligned with cross-comparative research. Many social cognitive constructs such as schemas, attribution processes and the attitude–behaviour link have been tested for their universality. Social psychological research in the 1960s and 1970s, mainly conducted in North America, showed that people in the experiments have a strong tendency to explain someone else's behaviour (e.g., writing an essay about a political issue) in terms of the person's disposition (e.g., political opinion) while underestimating the importance of the context of the behaviour (e.g., someone with a legitimate power told him to write an essay taking a certain political stance). Although this tendency was taken to reflect a limitation of the human cognitive system, cultural research highlighted that this fundamental attribution error is often observed in North America, but not necessarily elsewhere. Miller's (1984) comparison between the USA and India as well as Morris and Peng's (1994) comparisons between the USA and Hong Kong showed that the error was not so fundamental, and that Indians and Chinese do not exhibit this tendency as strongly as their American counterparts.

The comparative cultural research within social cognition has led to the development of a dynamic constructivist approach which focuses on culture's situational influence. It proposes that culturally shaped internalized constructs do not continuously guide our information processing but rather do so only when activated (Hong et al., 2003). Culture, therefore, affects cognition when, in particular social situations, the relevant implicit theories or shared assumptions are available, accessible, salient or applicable in the situation. There is a specific emphasis on boundary conditions within which cultural differences will appear, disappear or reverse. Participants in an East Asian context, for example, did not differ from participants in an American context in their propensity to compromise in a decision-making task unless they were asked to provide reasons for making their decision (Briley et al., 2000). This is because 'reasons for choice depend on the cultural norms as to what is acceptable and persuasive' (Briley et al., 2000, p. 161). Hong and Chiu (2001) suggest that culture interacts with the psychological in a

144 Where Is 'Culture' in Psychology?

situational manner according to the basic social-cognitive principles of availability, accessibility, saliency and applicability.

Self-construal has emerged as a significant mechanism proposed to mediate and cause cultural effects. Many researchers have adopted social cognitive approaches geared towards delineating the causal role of self-construal as a cognitive mechanism in producing and/or mediating particular psychological effects. A priming technique has been used in an experimental framework to make salient aspects of either individualism/independent self-construal or collectivism/interdependent self-construal. The corresponding shifts in self-construal have been found, for example, to increase the retrieval of self-cognitions relating to the aspect of self that is primed (Trafimow et al., 1991), to mediate shifts in values and judgements of obligations (Gardner et al., 1999) and many other forms of social behaviour.

A Standard Theory of Cultural Comparisons

On the basis of the above trends, a standard theory of cultural comparisons has emerged. It has the following salient features:

- A view of culture as a quasi-independent variable and its effect on the behaviour.
- Dominance of experimental and psychometric (survey) approach.
- Selection of cultures using the HRAF or cultural dimensions suggested by Hofstede, Schwartz and Triandis.
- It samples nations as cultures. The most prominent comparisons have been made between North America and East Asia.
- Is more data-driven rather than theory-driven.
- Cultural differences have been investigated across a range of psychological processes: cognitive, social and developmental. Cultural differences are also shown to affect a wide range of interpersonal and organizational processes, including conflict, negotiation, justice, work motivation, leadership and team dynamics.

REVIEW QUESTIONS

1. Evaluate the limitations of psychology as a 'universal science'.
2. Why is a culture of interest to social psychologists?

What Is Cross-Cultural Psychology?

Cross-cultural psychology is a branch of mainstream psychology that tries to find out which aspects of behaviour and experiences are common to all human cultures, and which aspects are unique to certain places. It developed to provide answers to the interpretive dilemmas over population-based differences in performance on psychological tests and tasks. It has much in common with mainstream psychology. Both are interested in the study of individual differences and the sources of these differences; both use natural science methodologies and are typically guided by some current theory (or specific hypothesis derived from an extant theory); both take a linear view of causality; and both are interested in a psychology that includes broad topical coverage. Both are interested in the development of a psychology that will be much more 'universal' in its scope and application than is the case at present.

Some of the common questions asked in this tradition are as follows:

- Does thinking develop in children at the same rate in different cultures? (Piaget, 1966)
- Is the perception of three dimensions in drawings the same in different cultures? (Deregowski, 1972)
- Are secure parent-toddler attachments culturally universal? (Van Ijzendoorn & Kroonenberg, 1998)
- Is an autocratic leadership style among managers equally effective in different countries worldwide? (Van de Vliert, 2006)

It compares the behaviour and experience of people from different cultures in order to understand the extent of culture's influence on psychological functioning. Cross-cultural psychology assumes that culture is a major, if not the main, contextual factor contributing to individual differences in behaviour. It tries to understand the nature and scope of human diversity at the level of the individual by extending the range of variation of behaviour in the widest possible range of cultural settings.

A comprehensive definition of cross-cultural psychology is as follows: 'Cross-cultural psychology is the study of similarities and differences in individual psychological functioning in various cultural and ethnic groups; of the relationships between psychological variables and sociocultural, ecological and biological variables; and of current changes in these variables' (Berry et al., 1992, p. 2).

Goals of Cross-Cultural Psychology

Berry et al. (1992, p. 2) suggest the following as the major goals of cross-cultural psychology:

- *Transport and test*: The limits of psychological theory are tested by extending to other cultures a particular theory and/or the hypotheses that may be generated from it in order to determine how generalizable the theory might be. Thus, a theory is transported to other cultures and tested in those contexts.

- *Exploration and discovery*: Variations of behaviour not present in one's own culture are examined and explanations for such variations are sought. In other words, failure to generalize (the first goal) should be explored in an attempt to discover interesting variations of behaviour that may then be 'folded back' into the theory that guided the research in the first place.
- *Integration*: The findings generated in pursuit of the first two goals can be combined in attempts to help develop a more universal psychology.

The vast share of such research has attempted either (1) to demonstrate the cross-cultural universality of various psychological processes (research on universals in emotional expressions by Ekman and his colleagues is illustrative of this effort) or (2) to demonstrate cultural variation in some basic or universal psychological process (research on variations among cultural groups on universal dimensions such as individualism–collectivism by Kitayama and Markus, Triandis and many others).

Assumptions of Cross-Cultural Psychology

Cross-cultural investigations into cultural universality are underpinned by two key assumptions: theoretical and methodological.

Theoretical Assumption of Psychic Unity

Cross-cultural psychology, like mainstream psychology, assumes the psychic unity of mankind. In cross-cultural psychology, basic psychological characteristics are believed to be common to all members of the species and culture is seen as influencing the development and display of them. The metaphor is often of 'peeling the onion' (Poortinga et al., 1987) to reveal the universal, invariant psyche lying within. Thus, culture creates different variations on the underlying psychological givens (mind, memory capacity, perceptual processes). This is the universalist position.

Cross-cultural studies make a distinction between 'etic' or universal dimensions and 'emic' or culturally specific dimensions. Using a concept/measure from an alien culture leads to an 'imposed etic'. The researchers will scrutinize their concepts and methods for cultural appropriateness in a particular context. Insofar, as the search leads to similarities, 'derived etics' will be identified in terms of which valid comparisons can be made, at least across the cultures concerned. These derived etics are the psychological characteristics that are universally present. The pan-cultural dimensions identified by Triandis, Hofstede, Schwartz and Markus and Kitayama are examples of such dimensions.

Methodological Assumption of Cultural Equivalence

Cross-cultural research can be described as 'quasi-experimental' since it mimics the experimental method in psychology where an independent variable is varied to see its effect on a dependent variable of interest, keeping all other variables constant. In cross-cultural research, culture is the antecedent variable which can take the form of an independent mediator or a moderator variable affecting the dependent behaviour. Variation in the cultural variable is brought about by selecting participants from different cultural backgrounds (e.g., Indian and American adults) and they are compared on a selected psychological ability or capability (e.g., need for achievement, power distance, memory capacity, facial expressions, attachment patterns). Apart from the independent variable of cultural background, all other variables are held constant: This is the core of cultural equivalence. The most common way in which cultural equivalence is sought is by operationalizing culture in terms of social categories within which values (individualism–collectivism, high versus low power distance, etc.), practices and behavioural norms are shared, such as nationality, religious affiliation, social class, occupational group or region within a nation.

There are two kinds of equivalence involved here. First, participants are exposed to equivalent testing conditions (test material, instructions, timing and ethical considerations). Second, they are drawn from equivalent populations (in terms of factors such as social class, place of residence, etc.) within their own culture (defined as a group with distinct beliefs, opinions, customs and norms of behaviour). If equivalence is achieved in these two ways, the groups in the study differ only in terms of their cultural background. Therefore, any differences in the groups' performance can be confidently attributed to cultural differences. Equally, if little or no performance difference emerges (e.g., if participants score similarly on a test of need for achievement), the ability in question can be more confidently declared to be culturally universal.

Types of Comparative Studies

Van de Vijver (2009) identified four common types of comparative studies, each with its own assumptions about culture, methodological procedures and limitations with regard to the same:

1. *Generalizability studies*: Here, the focus is on verifying whether a theory, a correlational or causal relationship, or an instrument derived from a theory from a Western nation, holds true in another culture, usually a non-Western country. Examples of generalizability studies in the literature are a test of the universality of the structure of human values (Schwartz, 1992), the comparison of structure of intelligence across cultures (Irvine, 1979; Vernon, 1969), or the validation of the Big Five personality factors in a variety of cultures (McCrae & Costa, 1985). Here, a culture is defined vaguely in terms of a nation and the contextual factors relevant to the culture in which generalizability is sought are often not considered. Such studies are also referred to as replication studies as the design and procedure of the study usually follow the procedure of the original one.

148 Where Is 'Culture' in Psychology?

Replication of original results can be interpreted as a sign of generalizability when samples are equivalent. Lack of replicability of results can be due to cultural differences or a lack of equivalence of the samples.

2. *Theory-driven studies*: Such studies test a theory about a particular relationship between cultural variables and a psychological outcome. Here, cultures are often systematically sampled in order to maximize their contrast on some focal variable. For example, Berry et al. (1986) studied the cognitive style of two cultural groups – food gatherers and hunters – who are hypothesized to be different in their social organization and perceptual styles. Another example can be the study of Americans and Chinese subjects on social loafing (Earley, 1989). The two national groups were hypothesized to differ on the cultural dimension of individualism and collectivism which affects the extent of social loafing.

3. *Studies of psychological differences*: Such studies are similar to generalizability studies, except that the focus here is more exploratory rather than hypothesis testing. Most of these studies involve application of a measurement instrument, such as a test, an interview scheme or an observation scale, in a new cultural context to explore cross-cultural differences, either in the magnitude recorded by the instrument or in the structure underlying the instrument. A very common way of beginning cultural research of this sort is by stating, 'there are no non-Western studies (e.g., Indian studies) on this topic or using this tool'. Such research studies employ a non-Western sample (usually of one's own country), translate/adapt the Western tool and compare the results obtained with the results from Western studies.

4. *External validation studies*: These start from observed cross-cultural differences, usually in psychological factors, and aim to identify an appropriate interpretation of the differences. External validation is based on previous studies (either generalizability or psychological differences studies) and attempts to relate the differences to cultural-level measures.

Across these types of studies, two common types of questions are pursued:

1. Do two or more cultural groups (usually, operationalized in terms of nations/ecological contexts) differ in terms of psychological dimensions?
2. Is the structure behind human behaviour universal? For example, are there universal values? Is the structure of intelligence universal, that is, does the same kind of intellectual abilities account for intelligent behaviour across cultures?

In pursuit of the question, 'Do psychological processes vary as a function of cultural differences and how?', two levels of analysis are made in cross-cultural research. At the cultural level, culture is the unit of analysis, and the results obtained are characterizations of cultures, but not of individuals. The cultural syndromes identified by Triandis, the dimensions identified by Hofstede, the values identified by Schwartz, ecological factors and wealth and how different cultures vary are all cultural-level characterizations. These characteristics are believed to have relevance and the same meaning across cultures. However, with the exception of Schwartz's work (1992, 1994), there is no testing of the assumption whether the characterizations of cultures or similarities/differences found across cultures will hold true for each of the members of the cultures studied. For example, when a culture is known to be individualistic, its mean score on a scale of individualism will be higher than that of a collectivistic culture, but it does not mean that each person in that culture has a high score on individualism. Cultural-level analyses can lead to an ecological fallacy, the incorrect application of cultural-level characteristics to individuals.

The individual-level analysis depicts the characteristics of an average respondent within a culture/nation. It attempts to grasp the interrelationships among variables assessed on members of a single culture. An example of an individual-level finding is that a value such as openness to experience is found to be more frequent among younger and more highly educated respondents in a culture (Smith & Schwartz, 1997). When such results are repeatedly found among diverse cultures, we have a relatively well-established 'universal' relationship. The individual-level analysis is rooted within a culture/nation and is required to make predictions about individuals' behaviour, as a function of cultural factors, within that culture.

Schwartz argues that we cannot arrive at valid cultural-level measures until we have shown that the concepts used in constructing these measures have equivalent meanings in all parts of the world. For instance, many people may endorse a value such as 'freedom', but the ways in which this term is understood within different cultures could vary widely. The Schwartz Value Survey asks respondents to rate 56 briefly identified values as to their importance as a 'guiding principle in my life'. Data were collected from students and school teachers in more than 60 nations. Schwartz (1992) conducted a series of individual-level analyses within data from separate single nations. In this way, he was able to establish which values were in fact consistently related to one another in replicable ways, and therefore could be assumed to have equivalent meanings at all locations. Consequently, he could then compute country-level scores for his samples, using only those values with consistent meanings (Schwartz, 1994). Using these types of comparable individual- and cultural-level measures, Schwartz demonstrated further instances of the way in which variables relate quite differently at each level of analysis. For instance, he showed that, at the individual level, persons who see 'authority' as a guiding principle in their life are not the same persons as those who see 'humility' as their guiding principle. Indeed, endorsement of the two values is negatively correlated. However, at the cultural level, nations in which authority is strongly endorsed are the same nations as those in which humility is strongly endorsed. In other words, there are certain cultures that contain an interlocking set of role relationships built around authority and humility to a greater extent than is found in other cultures.

150 Where Is 'Culture' in Psychology?

The Culture–Psyche Relationship in Cross-Cultural Psychology

As mentioned earlier, while mainstream psychology is culture-bound and culture-blind, cross-cultural psychology treats culture as an important determinant of behaviour. Some of the important ways in which culture is understood in such research are as follows:

1. Culture is viewed as outside of and apart from the individual. Culture is external to the individual. The above makes it possible to conceptualize culture as an antecedent variable. It is assumed that culture regulates/shapes/determines/constrains human thought and behaviour.
2. As an antecedent variable, culture takes on the role of the independent variable (direct and proximal influence) or as a mediator variable (intervening variable accounting for the relation between the independent variable and the dependent variable) or as a moderator variable (control variable that affects the direction/strength of the relationship between the independent variable and the dependent variable). Culture as a mediator variable explains how or why certain behaviours occur in certain situations. As a moderator variable, culture specifies when certain kinds of behaviours will occur.
3. As a variable, culture is a package. It stands to represent a host of other complex aspects affecting human activity, such as philosophical ideals (individualism–collectivism), child-rearing values (economic and psychological value of children), parenting practices (authoritative and permissive parenting), subsistence economy (agrarian and industrial), location of residence (rural and urban), and so on. Quite often, when culture is understood in terms of shared social values, culture is described in psychological terms and is assessed psychometrically.
4. Culture is viewed as static and as unidirectionally shaping psyche. Less theoretical and research attention is given to the view that culture is a human product, that is, cultural contexts are dynamic and are reciprocally impacted by human thought and activity.

BOX 4.1 CROSS-CULTURAL RESEARCH ON KOHLBERG'S STAGES OF MORAL DEVELOPMENT

When Lawrence Kohlberg claimed that his stage theory of moral reasoning was universal, a storm of controversy greeted his theory. He then further intensified the controversy by claiming that pre-literate or semi-literate village peoples would generally fall behind other cultural groups in their rate and terminal point of development due to a relative lack of 'role-taking opportunities' in their daily life. The controversy stimulated much cross-cultural research to establish or discount the universality of the theory. One of the central questions

Where Is 'Culture' in Psychology? **151**

in establishing the universality of the theory is: Is the dilemma interview method a valid way of eliciting the moral judgements of people in other cultures? From a comparative culture perspective, the specific dilemmas used in research must be 'real' to the particular people involved, that is, they must raise issues and values important to the respondents. This requires thorough familiarity of the cultures being studied by the investigators. Benjamin Lee (1973), an American of Chinese descent, developed a completely new series of 'filiality' stories to study moral reasoning in Taiwan because filiality is a core Chinese value. He reported that subjects, especially of the older generation, scored higher on filiality than standard stories, because 'fairness' was not an important issue for them. Another important concern is whether the interview method is able to elicit the very best and most mature reasoning about moral problems in cultures other than the Western one. Findings from a wide range of studies have indicated that moral judgement Stages 5 and 6, and perhaps even full Stage 4, are not found in interviews of many groups. John Gibbs, a close associate of Kohlberg, has put forward the case that Stages 5 and 6 of the Kohlbergian system are different from Stages 1–4. While Stages 1–4 are genuine developmental stages, Stages 5 and 6, according to Gibbs, reflect 'second-order thinking' or 'meta-ethical reflections' about morality decisions. This kind of thinking is made possible primarily by higher education. Thus, many adults in all societies seem able to step into the 'moral elder' role (Stages 3 and 4), but they are not equally able to assume the 'moral theorist' role, as required by Stages 5 and 6. In response to criticism on the matter, Kohlberg revised his own earlier position (Kohlberg et al., 1983) as:

> We do not believe that the comparison of one culture to other in terms of moral development is a theoretically useful strategy for the growth of scientific knowledge … It is difficult to understand what a valid concept of 'comparative moral worth of culture' might be. But in any case, such a concept could not be established only on the basis of a comparison of means on our moral judgement assessment scale. There is no direct way in which group averages can be translated into statements of the relative moral worth of groups.
>
> *(p. 133)*

PAUSE AND THINK

Read the cultural research on personality and try to answer the following question: Is the five-factor model of personality cross-culturally valid? What evidence is used to examine this claim?

152 Where Is 'Culture' in Psychology?

What Are the Examples of Cross-Cultural Frameworks in Psychology?

Within cross-cultural psychology, there are many frameworks specifying the role of culture. A few salient perspectives are discussed in this section.

The Dimensional Approach: Culture as Societal Values

Several cross-cultural researchers such as Hofstede, Schwartz and Triandis conceptualize culture as a multidimensional structure that can be evaluated along a set of particular dimensions. Cultural differences can be best and most parsimoniously captured by identifying and describing cultures according to where they fall along a series of dimensions. The idea is that just as a country's geographical location on the map can be identified in terms of longitude and latitude, a cultural region's profile can be mapped by a specific combination of scores of its people on a series of dimensions.

In 1980, Geert Hofstede, an organizational psychologist working for a multinational corporation, provided a broad framework of cross-cultural comparison in his book, *Culture's Consequences*, based on his surveys about work values of IBM employees from more than 40 countries around the world (Hofstede, 1980). He identified four cultural dimensions – power distance, individualism and collectivism, masculinity and femininity, and uncertainty avoidance – on which each cultural group may be located. Cultures around the world – largely equated with nation-states as political units – could now be mapped within this multidimensional space. Despite its criticisms, the importance of Hofstede's (1980) study for cross-cultural research cannot be underestimated. Of Hofstede's four dimensions, individualism and collectivism became the focal point of empirical research in psychology by researchers like Triandis. Hofstede was the first to describe individualism as a cultural pattern that emphasizes the individual's goal pursuit and well-being, whereas collectivism places importance on the sustenance of a collective, such as an extended family or a kinship group. His research programme influenced another notable large-scale research programme by Schwartz and colleagues, which was a study of human values across over 44,000 teachers and students in 54 countries. In the Schwartz Value Survey, there are 10 value domains, including power, achievement, hedonism, stimulation, self-direction, universalism, benevolence, tradition, conformity and security. This instrument has been used in a large number of countries, thus providing a profile of values for each country, enabling an examination of relations among variables at the country level of analysis (e.g., GDP, GINI index, political and health indices). Some research programmes have also focused on intra-cultural variation – most notably work on the culture of honour in the US, North and South (Nisbett & Cohen, 1996).

Triandis terms these dimensions cultural syndromes. A cultural syndrome is a pattern of shared attitudes, beliefs, categorizations, self-definitions, norms, role definitions and values that is organized around a theme which can be identified amongst those who speak a particular language, during a specific historical period and in a definable geographical region (Triandis, 1993, 1994, 1995). Examples of these cultural syndromes are cultural complexity, tightness, individualism, collectivism, vertical and horizontal relationships. In this tradition of cross-cultural research, culture is defined and measured using psychological descriptions. Thus, culture is defined psychologically. The psychometric approach has been used to gather data that help researchers understand interactions between culture and behaviour. An example of how this framework functions is that although both the United States of America and Sweden are individualistic contexts (contexts privileging a notion of personhood as independent, autonomous and personally motivated), Sweden is a horizontally individualistic context emphasizing egalitarian social relations while the United States of America is a vertically individualistic context emphasizing a hierarchical conception of relations between people and groups (Triandis, 1995). Thus, the Swedish and American contexts and their psychological outcomes are more accurately characterized by utilizing both dimensions.

In this approach, what is the role of culture? Triandis (1990) clearly assigns primacy to culture in one of his analyses of individualism and collectivism. He writes, 'The effects of cultural complexity [one of the major determinants of individualism] are to create separation, distinction, and different lifestyles. Then the individual is confronted with conflicting norms and worldviews' (p. 44). This appears to be a classic example of 'culture-as-an-independent-variable' (see Figure 4.1). Culture is conceptualized as a major and immediate cause of individual dispositions. Being high or low on a syndrome results in differences in psychological phenomena.

However, it is silent on both how culture impacts the psyche, that is, how cultural processes constitute psychological functioning, and how psychological values and attitudes, in turn, shape social institutions and conventions. Furthermore, this approach has not attempted to address the dynamic, changing nature of culture and appears to view the culture–psyche relationship as rather static (Markus & Hamedani, 2007). Matsumoto (2007) posits that the IC (Individualism–Collectivism) construct needs to be refined with reference to its possible interactions with other cultural, social, demographic, institutional and political dimensions in its effect on psychological phenomenon.

Triandis, Leung, Villareal and Clack (1985) later developed another model in which psychological, rather than cultural, constructs were described as the immediate determinants of individual behaviour. 'Specifically, allocentrism and idiocentrism were conceptualized as stable personality dispositions that affect individual action and judgement.' This approach then rests upon a different

Culture $\longrightarrow$ Behaviour

FIGURE 4.1 Culture as an independent variable

assumption about the relationship between culture and behaviour. Culture acquires a secondary and distal status as a causal construct and internal, intra-individual determinants of behaviour (allocentrism–idiocentrism) are viewed as proximal causal mechanisms. This model treats culture as a mediator variable. As mentioned earlier, a mediator variable is one which explains the relationship between a psychological (predictor) and a performance (criterion) variable. It is a variable that is related to the predictor variable and affects the performance variable. Consider a theoretical model that attempts to explain why people in different cultures differ in their conformity to in-group expectations. The model proposed by Triandis et al. (1985) suggests that a personality trait such as allocentrism and idiocentrism predicts conformity quite well. Here, the personality trait becomes the predictor variable and conformity becomes a criterion variable. Culture, in this case, plays the role of a mediator variable which is related to the psychological variable of interest (idiocentrism/allocentrism) and, in turn, affects conformity. Culture, defined as normative beliefs about one's relationship with one's in-group (individualism or collectivism), affects the preponderance of specific traits (idiocentrism or allocentrism, respectively) and also affects the level of conformity expressed by the members. Individualism and collectivism as cultural constructs explain the relationship between the psychological trait and behaviour.

In collectivist cultures, people are likely to be higher on allocentrism, and this results in higher conformity behaviour in such cultures. As a mediator variable, the cultural dimension of individualism and collectivism may completely account for the observed individual difference in conformity without any need to rely on assumptions about an underlying personality trait (idiocentrism–allocentrism). Clearly, culture has an important explanatory power in such models (see Figure 4.2).

The reason for positing two levels of analysis (cultural and individual) is twofold. First is to create a causal chain of variables from culture to behaviour. Individualism–collectivism is a cultural-level variable and idiocentrism–allocentrism is an individual-level variable related to it. Both are defined psychologically. The

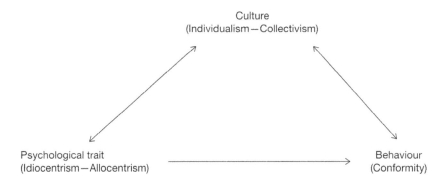

FIGURE 4.2 Culture as a mediator variable

individual-level trait variable helps in explaining how culture impacts dispositions and creates differences in the way we think, feel and act. Second, it underscores the point that while there are more allocentrics than idiocentrics in collectivist cultures and more idiocentrics than allocentrics in individualist cultures, it does not preclude the possibilities of having idiocentrics in collectivist cultures and allocentrics in individualistic cultures. Examples of items assessing individualism and collectivism are as follows (Triandis & Gelfland, 1998):

1. I often do 'my own thing' (item assessing horizontal individualism).
2. It is important that I do my job better than the others (item assessing vertical individualism).
3. To me, pleasure is spending time with others (item assessing horizontal collectivism).
4. It is my duty to take care of my family even when I have to sacrifice what I want (item assessing vertical collectivism).

Examples of items assessing idiocentrism and allocentrism are as follows (Alavi & McCormick, 2007):

1. I am a unique person, different from other group members (item assessing horizontal idiocentrism).
2. It is important to me that I do my job better than other group members (item assessing vertical idiocentrism).
3. It is important to me to maintain harmony within the group (item assessing horizontal allocentrism).
4. I should give priority to group rather than myself (item assessing vertical allocentrism).

The Ecocultural Approach: Culture as Context

This approach is often associated with John Berry and his colleagues. One of its most outstanding antecedent influences comes from the work of Segall et al. (1966) who found that Western people are more susceptible than non-Western people to the Müller–Lyer illusion and the Sander parallelogram illusion (see Figure 4.3). To explain these findings, they put forth the 'carpentered world' hypothesis and 'an experience with two-dimensional representations of reality'. The carpentered world hypothesis states that the non-Western tribal cultures do not have exposure to the built environments of the industrial societies that contain numerous artefacts constructed from straight lines and right angles. Also, they do not have much experience with two-dimensional representations of reality the way people in literate societies do. The researchers focused on ecological factors such as forms of houses, geographical surroundings, land vistas, and so on as factors influencing visual inference habits.

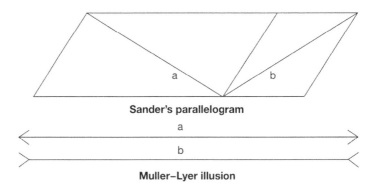

FIGURE 4.3 Visual illusions
Note: In both these illusions, the line a is perceived to be longer than line b, but physically a = b.

Unlike their interpretation of a direct effect of ecology on perceptual processes, later studies saw ecology as determining modes of subsistence, which in turn tended to shape culture or at least set certain constraints on it. A few related ecological perspectives on culture have been extended by Whiting and Whiting (1975) and Bronfenbrenner (1979).

The ecocultural framework by Berry et al. (1997) is rooted in two exogenous contexts: ecological and sociopolitical (see Figure 4.4). They influence the biological and cultural characteristics of the population through a process of long-term adaptation. These cultural and biological population variables are then transmitted to individuals through transmission variables (in the middle) such as cultural and genetic transmission, and acculturation. Behaviours (both overt and inferred, on the right) are considered to be the outcome of individual development in these contexts, as influenced proximally by these forms of transmission, and distally by the two exogenous inputs. The main flow of these linkages is from left to right (contexts to behaviours). However, the return arrow across the top portrays the influences from behaviours back to contexts and to population adaptations. That is, how we behave as individuals can screen, select, alter and even disrupt the features of the habitat in which we live.

The notion that ecological context influences culture is supported by several lines of evidence. Country-level affluence, for instance, is highly correlated with individualism (Hofstede, 1980, 2001; Kashima & Kashima, 2003). Kashima and Kashima reported country-level correlations between the latitude of capital cities and Hofstede's index of individualism, while Van de Vliert and his colleagues have demonstrated that climate is related to leadership behaviour and volunteer work across countries (Van de Vliert, 2006). Similarly, population density is another factor influencing culture. Members of groups with high population density, especially if characterized by low resource availability (affluence), may need to co-operate more with each other in order for groups to function effectively. These groups may require greater rules, norms and rituals in order to prevent social chaos, thus encouraging greater conformity and

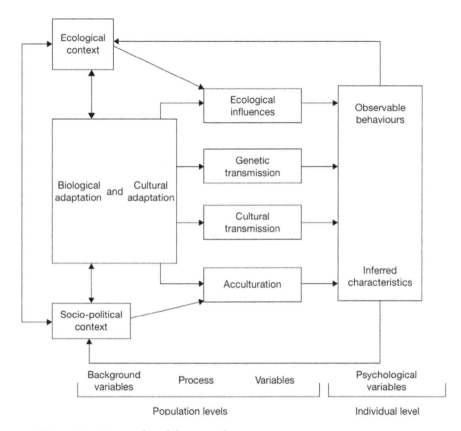

FIGURE 4.4 Berry's ecocultural framework
Source: Adapted from Lonner and Adamopoulus, cited in Berry et al. (1997).

homogeneity. Triandis (2001) likened these effects to a dimension known as tightness versus looseness of a society. Thus, ecological factors such as population density, climate and affluence most likely affect culture because different groups need to create different solutions for living in order to adapt to their specific ecological niche. Groups that live in conditions of low affluence, harsh climatic conditions and high population density will create a different pattern of life as a solution compared to groups that live in conditions of high affluence, mild climate and low population density. These different solutions create different cultural patterns.

How is culture understood in this perspective? 'Proponents of the ecocultural approach utilize the notion of context variables (e.g., ecological and socio-political factors) as a means to conceptualize culture as an independent variable.' Furthermore, it assumes that 'basic human characteristics are common to all members of the species (i.e., constituting a set of psychological givens), and that culture influences the development and display of them' (Berry, 2004, p. 4). Thus, culture is allowed to constitute some of the psychological system, but it

158   Where Is 'Culture' in Psychology?

does not go 'all the way down'. Bhatia (2007) provides an analysis of the challenges such a 'variable' approach poses for research on acculturation. The definition of acculturation by Berry and Sam (1997) basically assumes that all immigrating individuals and groups manifest the same kind of psychological operations during the acculturating process. This view suggests that while the population-level variables, such as history, ethnicity, gender and race, influence the different immigrant groups, the underlying psychological processes involved in acculturation are not mutually constituted with those properties of culture. Thus, for Berry and colleagues, culture and history are variables that enable the 'display' of the pre-given properties of the acculturating self, but these variables are not taken to be inextricably interwoven with the acculturating self.

Construal of the Self

In this model by Markus and Kitayama (1991), the basic premise is:

> For many cultures of the world, the Western notion of the self as an entity containing significant dispositional attributes, is simply not an adequate description of self-hood … In many Western cultures, there is a faith in the inherent separateness of the distinct persons … In contrast, many Non-western cultures insist … on the fundamental connectedness of human beings to each other.
>
> *(p. 224)*

According to their theory, people of Western, primarily individualistic, cultures have independent self-construals, where the person is

> [a] bounded, unique, more or less integrated motivational or cognitive universe, a dynamic centre of awareness, emotion, judgment and action organized into a distinctive whole and set contrastively both against other such wholes and against a social and natural background.
>
> *(p. 226)*

People of many non-Western, primarily Asian cultures, however, have interdependent self-construals, which feature the person not as separate from the social context 'but as more connected and less differentiated from others. People are motivated to find a way to fit in with relevant others to fulfil and create obligations, and in general to be a part of various interpersonal relationships.' The significant features of self are found in the 'interdependent and more public components of the self' (p. 227). Self-construals affect how people in cultures think, perceive themselves, feel and act. Thus, the psychological variable of self-construal is adequate in itself in explaining the individual differences in behaviour.

The implicit role of culture in this model is that the Western cultures' emphasis on individualistic cultural goals, such as uniqueness, autonomy, independence and self-assertion, provides the platform for the development of independent self-construals. Non-Western cultures' emphasis on collectivistic cultural goals, such as harmony, cohesion and co-operation, provides the platform for the development of interdependent self-construals. 'Culture is placed as a moderator variable in this framework. Unlike a mediator variable, it in itself cannot account for the individual differences in behaviour.' It can only have an indirect effect on the behaviour through its interaction with the variable of self-construal. Conceptualized in this way, the arguments of the mainstream psychology that challenge the necessity of including culture in psychological theory gain strength. After all, the essential theoretical variables remain the same, and culture simply adds refinement.

Matsumoto (1999) has pointed out several 'conceptual and methodological limitations' of the original framework proposed by Markus and Kitayama (1991):

1. A single cultural dimension of individualism–collectivism may not be able to explain cross-national differences in psychological phenomena. Thus, not only other subjective cultural elements need to be considered, such as Hofstede's (1980) power distance, uncertainty avoidance and masculinity, Hall's (1966) contextualization, and so on, but also other socio-structural factors, such as socioeconomic differences, religion and other demographic variables should also be considered in order to understand the interaction between culture, social factors and behaviour.
2. The presentation of independent and interdependent selves as mutually exclusive dichotomies is limiting as the conceptualization of self has increasingly incorporated the view that culturally bound cognitions related to the self are multifaceted – activated some of the time and dormant at others. Hermans and Kempen (1998) conclude that research and theories involving cultural dichotomies are based on the assumption that cultures are internally homogeneous, externally distinctive and geographically located. Instead they argue that due to increased cultural contacts and interpenetration of global and local, hybridity, intermixtures, contact zones and multiple identities have gained ground.

REVIEW QUESTIONS

1. How is the culture–psyche relationship conceptualized in cross-cultural research?
2. Compare and contrast the role of culture in the three main frameworks of cross-cultural research.

160 Where Is 'Culture' in Psychology?

What Are the Conceptual Challenges of Comparative Cultural Research?

1. Nandy (2004) notes that non-critical cultural relativism, which constitutes the core of conventional cross-cultural psychology, is not an antidote to universalism. He states:

> Such relativism was originally a response to the indiscriminate universalism that mirrored the parochial cultures in which the social sciences had grown. And it was supposed to correct the bias of the first generation of social scientists, often drawn from among Christian missionaries and colonial bureaucrats. But ... the idea of cultural relativism was soon co-opted by that particularism which the relativism was supposed to fight. Even in their more sophisticated versions, most cross-cultural and humanistic psychologies see modern psychology as a transcultural reservoir of knowledge and other psychologies as its handicapped cohorts waiting to be interpreted by and integrated with the world of modern psychology. The other psychologies thus become, definitionally, mixed bags of good and bad insights and good and bad data. The good in them are to be swallowed by modern psychology, the bad rejected. Neither cross-cultural nor humanistic psychology, despite the best of intentions, can grant alternative psychologies the right to integrate within the latter what they see as the best of modern psychology and to reject the bad.
>
> The implication of seeing the non-modern psychologies as sacks of isolated insights or data is that these insights and data can then be used to ornament, strengthen or alter the micro-theories of modern psychology.
>
> The basic paradigms and culture of modern psychology remain untouched and are, in fact, carefully adapted to new empirical facts. What changes over time are the microtheories, not the architectonics of modern psychology.
>
> *(pp. 324–338)*

Thus, comparative psychology stops short of thorough deconstruction and decolonization of Western psychology. It also does not pay sufficient attention to other cultures' understandings of psychological phenomena.

2. One big challenge facing comparative research is at what level culture should be defined. In cross-cultural research, culture is often defined by national boundaries. This slippage of culture with the nation is problematic. Bhatia (2007) notes the following:

> Anderson (1991, p. 3) has famously argued that nation, nationality and nationalism are notoriously difficult to define, let alone analyze. To posit that the 'nation' can be understood as a durable, ontological, material,

geopolitical concept ignores the counter narratives, the contested identities, and the historical inventions that continuously challenge any unified understanding of a nation. A nation is more than a geographically identified space; rather, it is what Anderson terms an 'imagined community', what Renan (1990, p. 19) calls a 'spiritual principle' constituted by memories that swallow up discordant details, and what Bhabha (1994, p. 297) refers to as a series of narrations constructed by 'scraps, patches and rags'.

(p. 316)

When the history of colonialism is considered, the national-level classifications of culture become even more problematic. Postcolonial writers like Spivak have demonstrated the indelible imprints of imperialist inscriptions on former colonies. Spivak (1993, p. 48) comments, the 'subject-position of the citizen of a recently decolonized "nation" is epistemically fractured' and can 'inhabit widely different epistemes, violently at odds with each other'. Additionally, the vast flow of migration of people and diffusion of ideas and practices across the world renders the idea that cultures can be circumscribed and defined by national boundaries as highly untenable.

It has been suggested that the definition of a culture, more properly named a 'culture-bearing unit' (or cultunit), has to coincide with the level at which a variable is operating. If political organization is of interest, the nation-state is the appropriate unit of selection. But if the study is on the psychological effects of tonality in language, the appropriate unit of selection should be the language group. Child-rearing practices usually will have to be defined on smaller culture-bearing units, as there can be large differences within a country, for example, between urban and rural groups. The underlying principles can be summarized in two points. First, the definition of a culture-bearing unit depends on the nature of the independent variable studied. Second, culture-bearing units have to be selected to cover adequately the range of variation on this variable (Berry et al., 2002).

3. In this tradition, culture is more often understood in terms of subjective meanings and knowledge that reside within the individuals. Self-report questionnaires are used to assess people's beliefs and values. In this way, cultures can be quantified on different dimensions and can be readily compared. Criticisms have been raised on the assumption of culture packed in the head of each individual member of the group. Cultural values and beliefs are externalized and materialized in the world and are inscribed into practices, institutions and ways of life. In this way of understanding, contemporary American society as a whole may be described as individualistic, not so much because many members of this society strongly endorse individualistic values (although this could also be true) but rather because this society is composed of interpersonal routines, situations, practices, social institutions and social systems that are fundamentally individualistic.

162 Where Is 'Culture' in Psychology?

4. The comparative view of culture takes a taxonomic approach in which culture is taken as a structure abstract enough to be shared with a high degree of consensus within a cultural group. A constructivist approach to culture takes it to be a fallacious assumption that knowledge structures at this level of abstraction (power distance, individualism–collectivism) are the determinants of these individual judgements and perceptions. Instead, it posits that a knowledge structure must be specific enough, that is, domain-specific, if it is to provide a useful heuristic in meaning construction (Bruner, 1990).

5. Culture is not a unidimensional variable. It is a package of variables. Groups of participants who differ according to cultural background may be different in a lot of respects such as family structure, economic activities, degree of social control or freedom, level of technology, dominant religion, cultural history and many more. So, when we study culture, which aspect of culture are we studying? This hampers the ability to set up equivalent testing conditions in diverse cultural locations.

6. Culture cannot be easily conceptualized as an independent variable. In classic experimentation, the researcher can 'control' the nature and magnitude of the independent variable. In cross-cultural research, such control can at best be approximated. In such research, culture as an independent variable does not usually exert its effects in a simple and direct manner of the stimulus–response type; rather, it is mediated in a complex and as yet inadequately understood manner by such processes as socialization and the experiences of interaction with others (Jahoda, 1993). Matsumoto (2007) argues that it is important to identify the potential effects of other sources, such as personality factors and situational contexts to demonstrate whether any observed differences are truly cultural or not. A research mindset to identify cultural differences can mask the effects of other potential sources. For example, Matsumoto (2007) conducted a study in which he demonstrated American-Japanese country differences on emotion regulation, with Americans demonstrating higher tendencies to reappraise emotion-eliciting events and Japanese demonstrating higher tendencies to suppress their emotional reactions. While many cultural theorists could take these findings and develop cultural theories to explain why Americans reappraise more and suppress less than the Japanese, such cultural theories would negate the possibility that individual differences in dispositional traits accounted for those country-level differences. Indeed, this study also included an assessment of the five-factor model of personality, and statistical analyses indicated that extraversion, neuroticism and conscientiousness fully accounted for the observed between-country differences in emotion regulation. These findings suggested that the source of the observed country differences was not cultural and instead lay in dispositional traits (Matsumoto, 2007).

7. Cross-cultural studies have as their prime aim identification of similarities and differences across cultural groups. They do not pay enough research attention to which and how cultural processes constitute psychological realities.

8. Comparative research also does not pay much attention to how culture is produced by the psyche. The subjective aspect of culture inscribed in the minds of people in the form of values and beliefs does not explicitly acknowledge the agency of human beings to shape their cultural contexts.

What Are the Methodological Challenges of Comparative Cultural Research?

1. The selection of cultures in cross-cultural study is often central to its scope for evaluating the hypotheses proposed. Usually cultures are selected because they represent different values on a theoretical continuum. For example, Japan and America are believed to be collectivist and individualist societies, respectively. However, often comparative researchers select cultures because of presumed differences on cultural dimensions rather than empirically demonstrable differences. Also, cultures are constantly evolving and there is huge heterogeneity within cultures, resulting in the invalidation of the research findings supporting such cultural differences. Cross-cultural research must constantly re-evaluate its theoretical assumptions in the light of cultural change and heterogeneity.
2. Culturally equivalent samples are hard to find. Undergraduate students in a university in an American town may not be equivalent to undergraduate students in a university in Varanasi, an Indian town, on the grounds such as social class, literacy penetration in family, and so on, which are over and above the cultural differences on which they are expected to vary.
3. Because of the involvement of several researchers in replicating studies and collecting data from various settings, the controls cannot be established stringently and they can vary.
4. Translating psychological tests and assessments along with the instructional materials into different languages results in the loss of meaning as terms do not translate with perfect equivalence. Japanese emotion *amae* and Indian emotion *lajja* have no equivalent words in English. The so-called matter-of-fact instruction 'Please be honest with your responses' may also have various meanings for people in different cultures. The translation of participant responses (if they are descriptive) faces just as many equivalence issues. Spivak (2000) says that translation is necessary and unavoidable, but impossible for generally 'no other word will do, and yet it does not really give you the literal meaning in the history of language, upon which a correct use will be based'.
5. Social research is not a familiar feature of everyday life across cultures. In such cultures, situations such as filling in a questionnaire or answering questions from an unfamiliar researcher will be experienced as strange and novel. Extraordinary behaviour will, effectively, be compared with that which is wholly ordinary. This will have an impact on the results.

164 Where Is 'Culture' in Psychology?

6. There are few cross-culturally agreed definitions of constructs and assessment methods that can be used reliably and validly across settings. Western psychological concepts such as personality, stress, need for achievement and intelligence often lose their meaning once they are taken into other cultural settings (Enriquez, 1993). A central component of personality in China is known as *ren qin*. This refers to the degree to which individuals choose to participate in a series of social exchanges and reciprocal favour rituals. Considering that this is an important aspect of personality in China, it will not be useful to compare personality characteristics of Australian and Chinese participants solely by using Eysenck's Personality Questionnaire which does not measure *ren qin* (Cheung & Leung, 1998). Therefore, many psychological concepts gain their meaning from the cultural context (Nsamenang, 2000). The cultural construction of such key variables presents considerable theoretical difficulties to the cross-cultural researcher who seeks to compare behaviour relating to those variables across cultures.

7. In comparative research, culture has come to be understood only at the level of individual representations and self-construals in the way in which questionnaires can assess them. Thus, data become encapsulated, pigeon-holed approximations of the more complex psychological phenomena we are trying to capture from real life. There is an urgent need to have cross-domain measures and multiple methods to capture the complexity of culture and psychological phenomena. Given that individuals bring to any context a wide range of psychological constructs – attitudes, opinions, values, self-perceptions and the like – there is a possibility that self-representations may differ in each of these areas and these differences may not be the same in various contexts. While this level of complexity is overwhelming for those who wish to deal with single score assessments of culture or self from a questionnaire, it is becoming obvious that such approaches are increasingly limited.

Broadly speaking, comparative culture research has left cross-cultural psychologists with more ambiguity and inconclusive findings than clarity. Repeating original studies in diverse cultural settings has not always highlighted the existence of psychic unity. So, where do we go from here? Cross-cultural psychologists are unlikely to call off the search for cultural universals altogether. Nor would they favour abandoning cross-cultural replication research. Instead, they have worked out several strategies for achieving better cultural equivalence in replication research, such as selecting comparable, heterogeneous samples, issuing standardized yet meaningful instructions to research participants, using the back translation method, using meaningful data collection methods and employing widely accepted dimensions of cultural variability. They are making some headway. Among the advantages of cross-cultural psychology are the use of cultural contexts as natural experimental settings; the study of culture change and the effects it has on people; the reduction in ethnocentrism; and use of knowledge of cross-cultural research for culture training programmes. However, other lines of enquiry regarding the relationship between culture and the psyche are branching out from replication-based research in order to pursue additional, alternative truths about the diverse cultural contexts of human beings. Sociocultural psychology and Indigenous psychology are two such alternative paradigms.

PAUSE AND THINK

Imagine you are planning to conduct research across cultures into the proposed relationship between subjective well-being and freedom. Outline the steps you will take to avoid ecological fallacy.

How Does One Move Towards a Differentiated and a Complex View of Culture in Psychology?

As evidence grew regarding the culture variability of human behaviour, not only in terms of frequencies and magnitude but also in terms of substantive aspects, a need to move beyond the reductionist understanding of culture as an antecedent variable emerged. Broadly speaking, it led to the development of two widely recognized approaches to the study of culture and psychology: cultural psychology and Indigenous psychology (besides many others, such as psychological anthropology and intercultural psychology).

Cultural Psychology

Perspectives identified as cultural psychology are diverse. It includes the ideas of Vygotsky (1978), Shweder (1990), Shweder and Sullivan (1993), Bruner (1990) and those who expanded on Vygotsky's ideas, such as Cole (1988, 1990), Rogoff (1990, 1995), Wertsch (1979, 1991) and many others. The investigators within the tradition share most but not all of their theoretical and methodological commitments.

The distinguishing characteristics between cultural psychology and cross-cultural psychology are not whether single or multicultural analysis is involved or whether a quantitative or a qualitative methodological stance is assumed. An approach may involve cross-cultural comparisons and empirical methods and still be in the tradition of cultural psychology (e.g., Markus & Kitayama, 1991), or it may involve analysis of a single culture through interpretive ethnographic techniques and be in the tradition of cross-cultural psychology. The most important differentiating element is the conception of culture held.

In the most general terms, cultural approaches represent a revival of phenomenology in reaction to the positivist paradigm of the mid-twentieth century.

According to Bruner (1990), cultural psychology has revived the original intention of the cognitive revolution in which psychologists aimed to bring meaning to the study of the mind. Behaviour tends to be described, not in terms of objective assessments by experts but in terms of the meaning that behaviour has for the behaving person and the intentions the person has with an act of behaviour, reflecting a 'phenomenological' and a 'meaning-centred approach'.

Rather than seeing culture as a static, independent variable exerting an influence over behaviour, it is understood as a psychological and inter-psychological process of creation, acquisition, transmission and use of shared activities and meaning (Greenfield, 1997). Culture is viewed as a socially interactive process, among beings biologically primed for culture, of creating shared activity (cultural practices) and the creation of shared meaning (cultural interpretation). Both shared meanings and shared activities are embodiments of shared cultural knowledge. The focus on the importance of cultural context on behaviour is highlighted in the works of Michael Cole and his colleagues, who published the influential book, *The Cultural Context of Learning and Thinking* (Cole et al., 1971), which spawned an approach quite at variance to cross-cultural psychology. Instead of cross-cultural testing and comparison, this approach emphasized exploring and understanding the specific context in which learning and thinking take place. Behaviour was conceived as integrally intertwined in specific sociocultural contexts. This approach was influenced by the works of Vygotsky, a Russian thinker, who argued that because thought is made possible through internalized language, and language comes from society, the mind is fundamentally a product of society. Human learning, he argued, 'presupposes a specific social nature and a process by which children grow into the intellectual life of those around them' (Vygotsky, 1978, p. 88).

Shweder articulated the basic premise of cultural psychology as that the human psyche cannot exist independent of its sociocultural contexts, and, therefore, the study of human actions must consider the contexts in which these actions take place (Shweder, 1995). Shweder's insistence on the mutual constitution of culture and mind focused researchers' attention on how culture shapes the human mind, and, in turn, how the mind makes culture (Shweder, 1990). His early criticism gave a strong injection of cultural anthropological thinking into the field of culture and psychology.

The cumulative and temporal characteristic of culture creates the necessity for developmental methods for studying the intergenerational transmission of culture. It also creates the necessity for historical methods for studying culture as a psychological process. The socio-historical specificity of each group's cultural meanings and activities defines the need for the use of culture-specific procedures (Greenfield, 1997).

Indigenous Psychology

Shweder (2000 suggested that cultural psychology and Indigenous psychology are kindred approaches. Various researchers have endeavoured to define the term 'Indigenous psychology'. One of these definitions is that of Kim and Berry, who define Indigenous psychology as 'the scientific study of human behaviour or mind that is native, that is not transported from other regions, and that is designed for its people' (1993, p. 145). A pioneer of the Chinese psychology movement, Yang (2000) reviewed the various definitions of Indigenous psychology and concluded:

> No matter how these psychologists define indigenous psychology, the definitions all express the same basic goal of developing scientific knowledge system that effectively reflects, describes, explains, or understands the psychological and behavioural activities in their native contexts in terms of culturally relevant frame of reference and culturally derived categories and theories.
>
> *(pp. 245–246)*

Here, it is emphasized that both content (traditions, practices, symbols, meanings) and context (familial, religious, historical, political, philosophical) should be relevant to the people being studied.

The motivations behind the rise of Indigenous psychology are both political and intellectual. Politically speaking, the concern for the indigenization of knowledge is an outcome of the need to decolonize knowledge among the former colonies of the Euro-American countries, to have 'Swaraj' or 'self-rule' in ideas (Bhattacharya, 1954). The intellectual thrust came from growing dissatisfaction with the universalism and decontextualized methodology of psychology in general and cross-cultural psychology in particular. Building on the understanding that the concepts and categories of science and its tools for the perception of reality are mediated by social forces, culture and tradition, a worldwide concern for making knowledge culturally appropriate grew. Indigenous psychology is the root of 'appropriate' psychology (Azuma, 1984), that is, a psychology that reflects the sociocultural reality of its society. Psychologists from different parts of the world, including those from the dominant ones, are now engaged in 'indigenous reconstructions', or the reconstructions of local psychologies vis-à-vis 'American psychology's dominance' (Teo, 2013).

In psychology, calls for a socially and culturally valid discipline have emerged at several locales – Africa (Durojaiye, 1993; Cameroon, Nsamenang, 1995; Zambia, Serpell, 1984), the Americas (Canada, Berry, 1974; Latin America, Ardila, 1982; Mexico, Diaz-Guerrero, 1977; the United States, Cronbach, 1975, Smith, 1973; Venezuela, Salazar, 1984), Asia (China, Ching, 1984; Hong Kong, Ho, 1982; India, Sinha, 1986; Japan, Azuma, 1984; Korea, Kwon, 1979; The Philippines, Enriquez, 1977; Taiwan, Yang, 1986), Europe (France, Moscovici, 1972; Germany, Graumann, 1972; Scandinavia, Smedsland, 1984), the Middle East (Iran, Moghaddam, 1987; Turkey, Kağitçibaşi, 1984) and Oceania (Fiji, Samy, 1978). Several native concepts have been analysed as examples of Indigenous psychologies. The concepts of *philotimo* in Greece (a person who is

168 Where Is 'Culture' in Psychology?

'polite, virtuous, reliable, proud', Triandis, 1972), *anasakti* in India (non attachment) Pande & Naidu, 1992), *amae* in Japan ('indulgent dependence', Doi, 1973), *kapwa* in The Philippines ('shared identity with other', Enriquez, 1993) and *jung* in Korea ('deep attachment and affection', Choi et al., 1993) have been analysed and various culture-bound syndromes have been introduced (Yap, 1974; cited in Kim et al., 2006).

In the context of India, Misra and Gergen (1993) have contrasted the main features of the Western view of psychological functioning with the Indian view (see Table 4.1).

Indigenous psychology is a part of the scientific tradition where an important aspect of the scientific endeavour is the discovery of appropriate methods for the phenomenon under investigation. Thus, it advocates the use of various methodologies: qualitative, quantitative, experimental, ethnographic, historical analysis. Indigenous psychology also makes use of comparative methodology.

TABLE 4.1 Comparison between Indian and Western views of psychological functioning

Indian view	Western view
Holistic-organic worldview	Anthropocentric and individual-centred worldview
Coherence and natural order across all life forms	Belief in control over nature and humanly created order
A socially constituted/embedded and relational concept of person	Autonomous and bounded self with fixed and strong boundaries
Non-linear growth in life	Belief in progress and growth
Continuity across various life forms	Belief in dualism and acceptance of a dichotomy between subject and object
Social individualism	Liberal ontological individualism and belief in freedom
The temporal and atemporal existence of the human being	Linear perspective on time
Contextualized relationships depending upon time, place and person	Decontextualized, contractual and open-ended nature of relationships
Emphasis on self-discipline	Self-interest, pursuit of wants and preferences, and consumerism as important values
Shared and relational notion of control	Personalized nature of control
Knowledge as moral and sacred	Knowledge (science) as amoral (value-free) and secular
Functional belief in multiple worlds (material-transitory and spiritual-eternal)	Functional belief in materialism and a utilitarian view in the service of possessive and self-contained individualism
Dharma-centred (duty) moral code	A moral code organized around the idea of right to self-fulfilment and the social contract

Source: Mishra and Gergen (1993).

Yang (1981) had contrasted the social orientation of the Chinese culture with the individual orientation of modernism, while Ho (1993) integrated Indigenous concepts across three Asian countries into a parallel psychological complex called relational orientation (Greenfield, 2000).

Since the impulse of Indigenous psychology is similar to that of the cultural psychology approach, the question that arises is: 'Is there a difference between the two?' There is a viewpoint that suggests that at a meta-theoretical level, cross-cultural, cultural and Indigenous psychologies all aim to tackle the same subject matter. Whereas cross-cultural psychology has supported universalism in a very traditional and positivistic sense (Lonner & Adamopoulos, 1997), both cultural psychology and Indigenous psychology have contributed to universal psychology by deconstructing it, highlighting its limits and enunciating the boundaries of a range of dissonant, even dissident cultural voices. Often in the past, a contrast was drawn between universal theory and Indigenous theories. With the aid of cultural and Indigenous psychologies, however, the so-called universal psychological theory can be seen as just another Indigenous theory that must be put in a higher-order conceptual framework, on the same footing with other Indigenous theories (Greenfield, 2000). Shweder (2000) alleges that the logic of filial piety or benevolence in Chinese psychology or the logic of *abhimaan* in Indian psychology or, for that matter, the concept of self-interest or personal control in Western Indigenous psychology are all helpful in understanding aspects of each other's culture. This implies the global relevance of all local knowledge and cultures.

However, a key to understanding the difference between the cultural psychological and Indigenous psychology approach lies in the distinction made by Enriquez (1993) between indigenization from without and indigenization from within. Indigenization from without involves taking existing psychological theories, concepts and methods and transforming them to make them appropriate to the particular sociocultural setting. The derived etic approach in cross-cultural psychology (e.g., Berry et al., 2002), research in cultural psychology (e.g., Greenfield, 2000; Shweder, 1991) and indigenization (Sinha, 1997) are examples of indigenization from without. In this approach, rather than assuming that a particular theory is universal *a priori*, researchers modify and adapt psychological theories to integrate them with the local cultural knowledge. The aspects that can be verified across cultures are retained as possible cultural universals. Existing theories in cognitive, developmental, social and organizational psychology have been modified and extended by Indigenous research (Sinha, 1997). In indigenization from within, theories, concepts and methods are developed internally, and Indigenous information is considered a primary source of knowledge (Enriquez, 1993). In Japan, the concept of *amae* that helps to define and maintain close interpersonal relationships is an Indigenous concept that questions the Western world's emphasis on individualism.

170 Where Is 'Culture' in Psychology?

BOX 4.2 THE INDIGENIZATION OF PSYCHOLOGY IN INDIA

Academic psychology began in India during the first decade of the twentieth century. The first Department of Experimental Psychology was inaugurated in Calcutta University in 1916. Since then, the bulk of research produced by psychologists in India has been replicative and imitative of Western psychological epistemology and methodology (Nandy, 1974) with few exceptions, such as that of Girindrasekhar Bose. He was India's first psychoanalyst and developed a technique and theory of psychoanalysis, especially the concept of Oedipality, which was different from the one that emerged in Freudian psychoanalysis, based on his understanding of Indian patients.

Dalal and Misra (2010) outline three streams of research in psychology in India: problem-oriented research, cross-cultural psychology, and Indian psychology. The concern of studying Indian problems is visible in a number of studies such as the work on political behaviour (Mehta, 1973), developmental norms for pre-school children (Muralidharan, 1971), the change in the level of aspiration and motivation of farmers (Sinha, 1969), prolonged deprivation (Misra & Tripathi, 1980), and health modernity (Singh, 1981). Pareek and Rao (1974) reviewed research in the field of family planning and presented a conceptual model of fertility-regulating behaviour. However, these studies did not yield any real insight or solutions to the Indian social problems as they were based on Western theories and methods. The parallel development of cross-cultural testing of psychological concepts and theories also led only to the testing of Western theories on Indian samples. Very rarely studies have originated from the needs of the Indian society or tested Indian concepts in other cultures. To a large extent, cross-cultural psychology remained a methodological enterprise and culture remained a peripheral concern (Misra & Gergen, 1993). The third trend involved using Indian concepts and theories to build culturally relevant psychology. Neki (1973), for example, suggested a guru–pupil model in clinical counselling to break the cultural and social barriers between the client and the counsellor. Sinha (1980) proposed a new leadership style – nurturant taskmaster – which is more likely to succeed in Indian work organizations. Kakar (1978, 1982) studied the role of traditional healers in maintaining mental health in traditional societies. Ramchandra Rao (1983) developed a concept of stress, based on ancient scriptures. Pande and Naidu (1992) developed a research programme to study the concept of detachment and its mental health consequences. Through the process of endogenous indigenization, an 'Indian psychology' is emerging which is based on spiritual–philosophical knowledge derived from Indian scriptures and philosophical texts of the last two or three millennia. Indian psychology has developed around the existential quest to overcome human suffering and in the process to raise the person to higher levels of awareness and mental state. The beginning of Indian psychology in present times can be traced to the writings of many eminent thinkers, such as Vivekananda and Sri Aurobindo in the early part of the last century. The monumental work of Jadunath Sinha (1958, 1962) on

Indian psychology can be considered a landmark in formally establishing it as an independent discipline.

What can the psycho-spiritual tradition of Indian psychology offer the world of psychology? Will it remain an interesting variant of the universal theory of psychology? Is India providing to Western psychology case material about this part of the world? Or, can the Indian theory give us an interpretation about the Western psyche? Can it offer to the world the Indian logic of the psyche (and not just the logic of the Indian psyche) (Dhar & Siddiqui, 2013)?

What Is Cultural Psychology?

The cultural psychology movement is more accurately depicted as a renewed field (Jahoda, 1990), approaching the study of the mind from historical antecedents in the work of eighteenth- and nineteenth-century scholars, such as Johann Gottfried von Herder, Giovanni Vico, Wilhelm Dilthey and Wilhelm Wundt.

The crucial difference between cross-cultural and cultural psychological enquiries is the question that they start from. The cross-cultural perspective begins by asking: 'Do intelligence, personality, depression, need for achievement, self–other relationship and self-construal vary across cultures?'. If yes, what forms do they take and what can be the cultural factors accounting for the differences in their manifestation and development? Such enquiries begin with an *a priori* assumption about the universality of psychological processes and view human diversity due to cultural factors as superficial layers. The metaphor of 'peeling the onion' (Poortinga et al., 1987) suggests that one can peel off the cultural layers until the 'basic', 'essential' and 'uniform' psychic structure is revealed. The interest of cross-cultural psychology is not so much in understanding the plurality of psychic forms as in arriving at a universal theory of psychic functioning. Thus, culture is not seen as inextricably interlinked with human potential. It is this kind of thinking in which culture does not go all the way 'deep down' that gives rise to the chief methodological problem in comparative research – the problem of non-equivalence of tools, constructs, research interactions, and so on, among cultures. This incommensurability in stimulus situations is due to the diversity of human goals, knowledge, wants, motives, feelings, daily routines, social, economic and political practices, something that cultural psychologists are primarily interested in.

Cultural psychology is founded on the following principle:

The abstract potentialities and specific heterogenous inclinations of the human mind are universal but only gain character, substance, definition and motivational force (i.e., assume the shape of a functioning mentality) as they are translated and transformed into and through the concrete actualities of some particular practice, activity setting, or way of life.

(Shweder et al., 2006, p. 13)

172 Where Is 'Culture' in Psychology?

The main tenets of cultural psychology are as follows:

1. Cultural psychology started out as a critique of general psychology and the 'variable approach' in cross-cultural psychology. Richard Shweder (1990) and Jerome Bruner (1990) attribute the revival of cultural psychology to the failures of the cognitive revolution of the 1950s and 1960s in the discipline of psychology. According to Bruner, the failure of the cognitive revolution consisted in the abandonment of meaning for information as the central organizing concept and in the shift from the construction of meaning to the processing of the information. Shweder construes the failure of the cognitive revolution as the inability 'to develop an adequate theory of the person because of the prevailing Platonism implicit in its scientific agenda' (1991, p. 1). Shweder identified Platonism as:

    > A claim to be able to isolate a universal internal abstract transcendent central processor from external concrete here-and-now environmental conditions, to procedurally abstract and withdraw the knower from what he or she knows, and to insist on a fundamental division between the processing mechanism of the person versus his or her personal or group history, context, stimulus and task environment, institutional setting, resources, beliefs, values, and knowledge.
    >
    > *(1991 p. 51)*

    Against the negative image of Platonism, Shweder declares the basic notions of cultural psychology:

    > [N]o sociocultural environment exists or has identity independent of the way human beings seize meanings and resources from it, while every human being has her or his subjectivity and mental life altered through the process of seizing meanings and resources from some sociocultural environment and using them.
    >
    > *(1990, p. 21)*

2. One of the central notions of cultural psychology is that individuals are biological as well as ineluctably cultural and social beings. The option of being asocial and acultural, that is, living as a neutral being not bound to particular practices and socioculturally structured ways of behaving, is not available. Many theoretical and empirical studies have made clear that people think, feel and act in culture-specific ways, ways that are shaped by the particular meanings and practices of their lived experience. It is in this vein that many cultural psychologists take the work of Lev Vygotsky as a pre-eminent starting point. As Vygotsky (1978) proposed that every process in the development of higher mental functioning occurs twice, 'first on the social level, and later, on the individual level; first between people (interpsychological) and then inside the child (intrapsychological)' (p. 57).

3. The psychological side of cultural psychology is the study of how individual persons think and act in the light of their particular goals, values and pictures of the world. The cultural side of cultural psychology is the examination of the socially assisted processes of learning and schema activation associated with becoming a member of a particular group. Cultural psychology, thus, is the study of the particular wants, feelings, knowledge, reasoning and values required for normative or competent participation in the local customary practices of some historically identifiable community. It is, thus, a simultaneous study of the psychological foundation of the cultural community and the cultural foundations of the mind.

4. The term 'cultural' expands the scope of analysis to include within itself both the conceptual and the material. It includes both meanings (ideas, images, representations, attitudes, values, prototypes and stereotypes, both implicit and explicit, about persons, society, nature, and the metaphysical world of the divine) and socio-structural elements (social practices, material artefacts and institutions which embody, animate and realize these meanings). Common to many approaches classified as sociocultural psychology is a belief that sources of mind and behaviour cannot be all located within the person. They are distributed, existing both internally in the mind and externally in the world. This commitment to 'thinking beyond the person' and the ways in which psychological processes are made up of, or made by, the social elements of one's contexts is revealed in some of psychology's early theorizing. Lewin (1948) wrote:

The perception of the social space and the experimental and conceptual investigation of the dynamics and laws of the processes in social space are of fundamental and theoretical and practical importance ... The social climate in which a child lives is for the child as important as the air it breathes. The group to which the child belongs is the ground on which he stands.

(p. 82)

5. Another important premise of sociocultural psychology is that the person is not simply a passive recipient of what the culture has to offer, but is instead an active, intentional (purposeful) being. People engage with and respond to the ideas and practices of a given context in somewhat variable ways, with variable intents (goals) and purposes. These varieties of engagement depend on the person's own particular set of interpretive frameworks, which themselves are a result of a host of other individual and situational differences. From a sociocultural–psychological perspective, the essential element of a behaviour is the encounter of a person making sense of the world replete with meanings, practices and objects. Thus, 'cultural psychology is the study of intentional worlds. It is a study of personal functioning in particular intentional worlds' (Shweder, 1990, p. 3).

174 Where Is 'Culture' in Psychology?

The thread that runs through the diverse perspectives within cultural psychology is the mutual constitution of culture and mind. Implicit in this theme is the non-essentialist understanding of both culture and mind. One direction of this dynamic process refers to the cultural constitution of mind. Mind is not just an expression of genetic make-up; instead, it emerges through active participation in and ongoing engagement with the possibilities and constraints present in the everyday world. The other direction of this dynamic process refers to the psychological constitution of cultural worlds. Cultural worlds do not exist apart and distant from human activity; rather, they persist (or not) because people in the ongoing flow of everyday life actively select and (re)produce features and deny/modify others in accordance with their own desires and beliefs. Thus, both culture and mind are understood as fluid and changeable rather than static and timeless. Shweder (1991) defines cultural psychology as:

> The way cultural traditions and social practices regulate, express, transform, and permute the human psyche, resulting less in psychic unity for humankind than in ethnic divergences in mind, self and emotion. Cultural psychology is the study of the ways subject and object, self and other, psyche and culture, person and context, figure and ground, practitioner and practice live together, require each other, and dynamically, dialectically, and jointly make each other up.
>
> *(p. 73)*

This mutually constitutive process is different from a simple interactional process. In the latter case, the psychological system is separated from its non-psychological context and then some type of external situational effect is invoked. In the former case, the contexts are theoretically presented as part of the psychological system and not simply as influences, factors or conditions external to the psychological system. The contexts are the necessary means for transforming a universal mind into a distinctively functioning mentality, a distinctive way that 'people think and act in the light of particular goals, values and pictures of the world' (Berlin, 1976, p. 169). The relevant contexts identified by cultural psychology are the customs, traditions, practices and shared meanings and perspectives of some self-monitoring and self-perpetuating group.

Mutual Constitution of Culture and the Psyche: Example of a 'Culture Complex'

Suppose we want to understand why mothers do/do not nurse their babies on demand or why children do/do not co-sleep with their parents or why/why not there is a time out and seclusion of females during their menstrual periods. None of these questions can be answered without taking the cultural context into consideration. Women, parents and children do not exist in a vacuum. What they know, think, feel, want, value and hence do/do not do (i.e., nursing, co-sleeping, assertiveness training) is infused with cultural beliefs, doctrines and practices.

Let us take the example of co-sleeping patterns in families. Co-sleeping patterns, 'who sleeps by whom in a family' is a customary practice invested with socially acquired meaning (Shweder et al., 2006). Research on family life customs in different communities has confirmed the existence of several divergent cultural complexes, each consisting of a network of interwoven and mutually supportive practices, beliefs, values, sanctions, motives and satisfactions. Since culture is understood in terms of both symbolic meanings and practices, let us first try to understand the aspect of behavioural practices. In the middle-class European–American scenario, the institutionalized practices related to the sleeping patterns in family involve the following:

1. The ritualized isolation of children during the night.
2. The institution of bedtime.
3. Exclusive co-sleeping of the husband and wife.

The distinctive beliefs, values and attitudes (symbolic meanings) attached to the practice shared in common by the members of European-American society (including parents, media, medical fraternity and such) are as follows:

1. Valuing autonomy and independence.
2. Promoting such values in children by having them sleep alone.
3. Valuing sexual intimacy with partner.
4. Co-sleeping with partner as the way of fulfilling sexual needs.
5. Privacy of spousal sexual space for self and children.
6. Not wanting children to witness parents' sexuality for their own mental health.

As can be noted in the above example, there is a close connection or partial fusion between the symbolic and practice aspects of the culture. This association forms the unit of analysis for cultural psychology, which Whiting and Child (1953) referred to as the 'custom complex'. Defined in this way, cultural psychology can be called the study of the custom complex. The principle of the mutual constitution of culture and the psyche underlies the culture complex. The culture-infested values, norms and practices form the basis on which people think, feel and act. The cultural complex is valued, considered right, reasonable and normal by the members of the cultural community and is internalized, that is, becomes habitual and automatic. Members use it to guide their own behaviour and also protect, promote and transmit such practices and values to their children.

A major challenge that faces the discipline today is how to arrive at a psychologically relevant theory and assessment of culture. When culture is understood as a historically situated, collective product, constituted by the values, beliefs, symbols and other human-created artefacts that are transmitted across generations, it is inescapably psychological in its composition.

Another major challenge is how to make psychology culturally focused. Shweder et al. (2006) suggest that culturally relevant psychology should study and assess both the practices (such as symbolic forms, communicative exchanges, rituals, mores, folkways and institutions) and the mental states (what the subjects of a particular group know, think, feel, want, value, and so on). There is an intimate relationship between mentality and practices in a cultural group. What people think, want, feel, value and hence choose to do is primed by or derivable from their participation in the symbolic forms, mores, rituals, institutions and folkways of some consensus-sensitive or norm-referencing group. Also, eating, health, sexual, religious and other such practices gain their credibility and motivational force from the psychological states that they have activated and given birth to. Shweder sees inter-dependency/sociocentrism/collectivism or independence/autonomy/individualism as mentalities that arise from and maintain a whole array of practices in and across domains (family, work, religion, politics) for large sections of people in diverse cultures, such as the Japanese and the American. Both practices and mentalities show significant differences across group and differential patterning of within-group variations, resulting in psychological pluralism.

Culture–Behaviour Interface in Cultural Psychology

The understanding of culture is fundamentally different in cultural psychology:

1. Culture is not seen as outside and apart from the individual. Culture and behaviour, culture and mind, are viewed as inextricable, yet not reducible to each other (Jahoda, 1992b). Culture is 'a way of knowing, of constructing the world and others' (Bruner, 1993, p. 516). Culture 'constitutes', as in creates, makes up or establishes the psychological tendencies and does not just interact with the psyche. It debunks many familiar binaries, such as individual–environment, self–society, that consider people as separate from their 'surrounding' contexts.
2. Culture is conceptualized as an interpretive concept and not as an independent variable (Geertz, 1973). To study culture is to study the codes of meanings shared by social actors. Shweder states that culture consisting of events such as 'stealing' and 'taking communion', processes as 'harm' or 'sin', roles as 'in-laws' and 'exorcist', visible entities as 'weeds' and invisible entities as 'natural rights' and crafted objects as 'abacus' and 'psychoanalytic couch' exist because there exists a community of persons who are involved with them and react to them as per the meanings they have of these. For example, weed cannot be understood as an impersonal, objective, botanical definition of plants that can be specified in a general or abstract way. A thorny rose in a vegetable patch is a weed as it is an unwanted plant and is plucked out. However, the same weed, if it is wanted, is cultivated with great care. Thus, culture is replete with meanings of objects, practices and institutions shared by people.

Where Is 'Culture' in Psychology?   **177**

3. The direction of influence is not only from culture to behaviour but reverse as well. Culture and the psyche are believed to be mutually constitutive: 'Culture and psyche make each other up' (Shweder, 1990, p. 71). Thus, mental processes and behavioural tendencies that are the subject of study in psychology are not separate from but are fundamentally realized through cultural ideas and practices. Also, culture is viewed as a product of human activity. They are the repositories of previous psychological activity and they afford psychological activity.
4. Sociocultural patterns of ideas, practices and products are not fixed; rather, they are open and dynamic. They are constantly in flux and undergoing transformation as they are engaged – appropriated, incorporated and contested – by selves acting or being in the world.

Cultural psychology transcends the universalism of both cross-cultural psychology and general psychology and gives a dynamic, situated and practice-based notion of culture. Where cross-cultural psychology has generally presumed a universal psychological process, viewing culture simply as a site of variation, cultural psychology tends to hold culture as the birthplace of psychological processes. The universal in psychology is replaced with the Indigenous. Thus, for example, Bruner (1990) argues:

> Scientific psychology ... will achieve a more effective stance toward the culture at large when it comes to recognize that the folk psychology of ordinary people is not just a set of self-assuaging illusions, but the culture's beliefs and working hypotheses about what makes it possible and fulfilling for people to live together ... It is where psychology starts and wherein it is inseparable from anthropology.
>
> *(p. 32)*

Cultural psychology focuses on the creation of symbolic meanings as grounded in everyday life and seeks to explain the constructed, mediated and relational nature of all human activity.

PAUSE AND THINK

Reflect on why a situation like 'a widow eating fish' is considered a moral breach in the traditional sectors of Indian society. What moral value does this action flout?

REVIEW QUESTIONS

1. What is the difference between cultural and Indigenous psychology?
2. How is the indigenization movement helping in decolonizing psychology?

What Are the Selected Frameworks in Sociocultural Psychology Telling Us?

Out of the many theoretical frameworks in cultural psychology, a few are discussed here.

Dynamic Constructivism

This perspective grows out of the work of Hong, Morris, Chiu and Benet-Martinez (2000) on the experience of multicultural individuals, in particular, the experience of constructing interpretations of ambiguous social events with the benefit (and burden) of cognitive tools received from differing cultures. The experience of multicultural individuals has not received much attention in the cross-cultural psychology paradigm. This is for several reasons. First, the multiple cultures within an individual are not picked up by cultural group variables such as country which often serves as the independent variable in cross-cultural studies. Second, the conceptualization of cultural knowledge in dynamic constructivism is quite at variance with the one in cross-cultural research. In the latter, culture is viewed in terms of domain-general, abstract tendencies, highly static and monolithic. In dynamic constructivism, culture is conceptualized as a system of specific knowledge structures that move in and out of activation. It uses 'frame switching' to understand the experience of biculturals who often report that the two internalized cultures take turns in guiding their thoughts and behaviour. Classical scholarship on African-Americans, for instance, describes a duality in social experience; according to DuBois (1903, p. 5), 'two souls, two thoughts, two unreconciled strivings, two warring ideals'. This suggests that more than one system of culturally bound social knowledge can remain 'alive' inside an individual. Also, learning a new culture does not mean losing one's first culture. Contradictory and conflicting cultural meaning systems can be simultaneously possessed by an individual; they simply cannot simultaneously guide cognition. A key idea here, drawn from the theory and method of social cognition research, is that in a particular interpretive situation, a particular subset of cultural knowledge becomes operative. This depends on the accessibility of the piece of cultural knowledge. The more accessible a construct, the more likely it is to come to the fore in the individual's mind and guide interpretation. But what determines whether a piece of knowledge is highly accessible? Cognitive and social psychological research has shown that a construct, such as a category, is accessible to the extent that it has been activated by recent use (Bruner, 1957). A widely used experimental technique to activate situation-relevant psychological constructs is priming. Researchers manipulate whether participants are exposed to a word or image related to a construct (a prime) and then measure the extent to which the participants' subsequent interpretations of a stimulus are influenced by the primed construct.

Where Is 'Culture' in Psychology? **179**

In the research on frame switching, researchers have used the concept of accessibility and the technique of priming to model the phenomena experimentally. The theory suggests that bicultural individuals who have been socialized into two cultures, A and B, have, as a result, two cultural meaning systems which can be referred to as A' and B'. Accordingly, priming biculturals with the images of culture A would spread activation through Network A', increasing the probability of accessing the categories and implicit theories of that network. Likewise, priming biculturals with images of culture B would spread activation through Network B', increasing the accessibility of the constructs that network comprises. The primes used are the cultural icons that activate constructs central to specific cultural networks yet not so directly related to the interpretive task. Examples of such national icons are national flags, landmark buildings, distinguished leaders. When participants were exposed to Chinese scenes, such as dragons and the Great Wall, bicultural Hong Kong Chinese showed more prototypical interdependent behaviours, but when exposed to American scenes, such as the Statue of Liberty or the Liberty Bell, they showed prototypical independent behaviours. Because the pertinent cultural knowledge is considered to construct psychological experience in dynamic interaction with certain personality characteristics of the actor, such as the need for cognitive closure, this approach is called the dynamic social constructivist approach.

Here, culture is understood in terms of internalized knowledge structures existing at the level of domain-specific categories. Rather than understanding individual response as a function of 'possessing' cultural knowledge, this framework sees it as a function of 'accessing' cultural knowledge. It suggests that findings in cross-cultural research that have been interpreted in terms of whether participants possess a construct (i.e., a performance difference reflects which self-concepts individuals possess in culture A versus culture B) can be more fruitfully reframed in terms of chronic accessibility (i.e., a performance difference reflects which self-concepts are made chronically accessible in culture A versus culture B). It sees factors outside the individual, such as institutions, discourses or relationships, as priming implicit cultural constructs in our daily life.

Another approach using the priming method is based on the assumption that the schemas of independence and interdependence are, in large part, universal and shared across cultures (Oyserman & Lee, 2007). According to this assumption, it is supposed that cultures are different in terms of availability of cues that call out one or the other schema. Within this theoretical framework, a number of researchers have investigated the potential effects of a variety of priming manipulations designed to call out either independence or interdependence. For example, participants may be presented with a paragraph describing the behaviours of a single individual who was referred to as 'I' or a paragraph in which the same set of behaviours was attributed to a group described as 'we' (Brewer & Gardner, 1996). Frequent reference to the personal self (I) may be assumed to call out independence, whereas frequent reference to the relational self (we) may be assumed to call out interdependence. Because

180 Where Is 'Culture' in Psychology?

this approach implies that the generic schemas of independence and inter-dependence are embedded in specific social situations that carry different sets of cues that call out the generic schemas, it is called the situated cognition approach.

These priming methods have been highly instrumental in advancing the understanding of the mechanism by which culture affects behaviour. Priming studies build on assumptions made in cross-national comparative research that provides information about average cross-national differences. However, com-parative research cannot address the question of which aspects of culture matter in accounting for these cross-national differences. The priming approaches have shown that once culturally relevant knowledge is activated, this knowledge mediates the effect of culture on behaviour. They will be enriched substantially when supplemented with an in-depth analysis of the nature of cultural knowl-edge that is called out by specific priming stimuli.

There are some important questions that must be answered in the context of this model of culture as knowledge structures: Does it capture all the manifes-tations of culture that matter? Is knowledge always a mediating element in all forms of cultural influence? Can culture's influences be most fully understood in terms of the ability of cultural contexts to activate key psychological constructs, such as independence and interdependence? The answer is 'no'. In this model, cultural practices are ignored.

An alternative perspective described below is that the sociocultural contexts afford cultural practices that become incorporated into the behavioural routines of daily life. These practices often reflect and foster values of independence and interdependence. From the very beginning of one's life, individuals are encour-aged to be engaged in such practices, initially only passively but gradually more and more actively. Repeated and continuous engagement in some select set of practices or situations involving certain features, such as self-expression in an independent cultural context or adjustment or conformity in an interdependent cultural context, may lead to some characteristic patterns of psychological responses. These responses may be initially deliberate and effortful, but they will eventually be highly practised and thus automatized. In fact, recent neuroscience evidences suggest that repeated engagement in certain tasks, including cultural tasks such as self-expression or conformity, is likely to cause corresponding changes in brain pathways (for reviews, see Han & Northoff, 2008; Kitayama & Park, 2010). It is evident, then, that culture may influence psychological processes not only by providing priming stimuli that bias one's responses in one way or another but also by affording a systematic context for development in general and the establishment of systematic response tendencies in particular.

Collective Constructionist Theory

Proposed by Kitayama, Markus, Matsumoto and Norasakkunkit (1997), the theory posits that the co-creation processes between culture and minds occur via everyday situations that are collectively experienced in specific cultural contexts. This theory provides an understanding about the mechanism of the mutual constitution of culture and the psyche – a fundamental principle of sociocultural psychology.

It assumes, first, that the cultural views of the self, such as independent and interdependent, are embodied in each culture's philosophical and ontological assumptions and, as a consequence, are reflected in patterns of social situations, social acts, practices and public meanings that are associated with such ontological assumptions of the culture. These cultural notions are historically constructed. For example, the independent view of self, which is common in the European-American cultural context, is rooted in the emphasis on rational thought and the value put on the expression of the 'natural self', both of which are legacies of the Enlightenment (Morris, 1991). Likewise, the interdependent view, as reflected in the contemporary Japanese culture, can be traced back to both the Buddhist ideal of compassion and the Confucian teaching of role obligation (Kitayama & Rarasawa, 1997). These ideas give rise gradually, over generations, to divergent patterns of social situations, practices and public meanings. Interpersonal communications play a pivotal role in the construction of social situations. Thus, in any given social setting (e.g., home, school and work), communication among members (agreement, challenge, modification) gives rise to a shared definition of the situation. Each person's communicative acts (whether verbal or non-verbal, deliberate or spontaneous) will take place within this common frame and, together, will afford or constrain the future actions of all the people involved. These acts of meaning (Bruner, 1990) then define the social reality. From this perspective, how a situation is defined and construed is not a matter of an interpretive frame applied after the situation occurs but an active and critical element of the situation itself (Miller & Goodnow, 1995). Therefore, definitions or construals of a situation may be taken as a reasonable proxy for the situation itself, although the latter obviously involves much more (such as non-verbal behaviours, interpersonal communications and subtle styles of language use in conversation) than the former.

Second, individuals necessarily enter a culture at a particular historical point prepared with a set of capacities to be engaged in relevant social units. In order to become a meaningful cultural participant, a person requires tuning and co-ordinating of one's responses with the prevalent pattern of public meanings and situations, or cultural practices. For example, contemporary North American culture, in contrast with the contemporary Japanese culture, involves a wide variety of practices, and attendant construals of social acts and situations, that highlight the importance and necessity of making personal choices, forming judgements and having opinions. In order to become a well-functioning member of this cultural context, one needs to possess a set of psychological processes – cognitive, emotional, motivational and behavioural – that can help each participating individual to perform these tasks, enabling the person to live naturally, flexibly and adaptively therein. Thus, cultural processes help develop psychological processes that are attuned to cultural system and which, in turn, help to support and reproduce the prevalent patterns of the cultural system.

182 Where Is 'Culture' in Psychology?

One important implication of this analysis is that the acquisition and maintenance of many psychological processes, such as a self-enhancing tendency in the United States and a self-criticizing tendency in Japan or a greater tendency to attribute behaviours to traits than to situations among the Euro-Americans as compared to the Eastern peoples, are mediated by a culturally shaped interactional process through which social acts and situations are socially defined, constructed, held in place and experienced within each culture.

To illustrate the mutually constitutive nature of culture and self, Kitayama et al. (1997) give an example of how a fairly common social event such as 'playing volleyball with friends' is collectively defined, maintained and held in place in very different ways across cultures. In the US, playing volleyball with friends is a fun activity which people enjoy. In Japan, on the other hand, volleyball is a more serious affair; it is organized as a win or lose affair. People are sober and competitive and, most of all, they 'ganburu' (effortfully persevere and hang in) until the end. Thus, an apparently identical social situation (e.g., playing volleyball) can carry dramatically different meanings and attendant 'atmospheres' and that anyone who participates in the situation cannot help but be influenced by these situational atmospheres. In this sense, psychological tendencies do not just unfold as a maturational process but are constituted by the cultural context through the historically and collectively constructed definitions of daily situations in which the members of a culture participate. This aids in the development of psychological systems which are attuned to cultural systems and which help in maintaining as well as transforming cultural systems. Thus, cultural psychology is constructed, realized and reproduced through the psychological. The psyche, then, is not a separate, autonomous set of processes; instead, it exists and functions only in close interdependence and attunement with the collective surrounding. Here lies a clear case in which culture and the psyche (i. e., psychological tendencies including thinking, feeling and acting) constitute each other (Shweder, 1991).

The specific methodology developed to substantiate the collective constructionist theory is the 'situational sampling method' (e.g., Kitayama et al., 1997; Morling et al., 2002). In this research method, by asking participants from different cultural backgrounds to describe certain situations (e.g., situations affecting self-esteem), researchers can analyse how certain situations are defined and constructed in different cultures and how individuals respond to those situations. Researchers typically find that situations produced by different cultural groups have subtle characteristics that reflect dominant psychological tendencies in their respective cultural contexts, even though participants are given an identical prompt. In two studies conducted by Kitayama et al. (1997), the researchers randomly sampled situational definitions relevant to self-evaluation from both Japanese and American cultures. They then examined the responses of Japanese and American people to situational definitions sampled from both Japan and America. They found a strong self-enhancing effect for Americans: American respondents chose a greater number of success than failure situations as relevant to their self-esteem. Further, these individuals judged that their self-esteem would increase more in success situations than it would decrease in failure situations. On the other hand, Japanese respondents chose a greater number of failure over success situations as relevant to their self-esteem and, further, judged that their self-esteem would be influenced more in the failure situations than in the success situations. This study then provides evidence for the collective constructionist theory of the self, which holds that the everyday social realities that are constructed in the middle-class US culture and the Japanese culture historically and collectively give rise to, reinforce and sustain the psychological tendencies for self-enhancement and self-criticism.

Culture, in this perspective, is understood in terms of the historical process of generating symbolic definitions and meanings reflected in everyday social situations and practices as well as interwoven with the developmental process that gives rise to adaptive psychological tendencies.

Cultural–Historical Activity Theory (CHAT)

CHAT refers to an interdisciplinary approach to studying mind and culture associated with the Soviet Russian psychologists, L. S. Vygotsky, A. R. Luria and A. N. Leontiev. The main goal of the Vygotsky–Luria project was the establishment of a 'new psychology' that brought in the notions of history and culture to the understanding of human activity, thereby transcending the Cartesian dualism between subject and object, internal and external, between people and society, between individual inner consciousness and the outer world of society. There are three principal 'stages' or 'generations' of activity theory, or 'cultural–historical activity theory' (CHAT). While the first generation built on Vygotsky's notion of mediated action, from the individual's perspective, and the second generation built on Leontiev's notion of an activity system, with emphasis on the collective, the third generation, which appeared in the mid-1990s, builds on the idea of multiple interacting activity systems focused on a partially shared object, and boundary-crossings between them. CHAT was introduced to the Western academia by Michael Cole, both through his writings (e.g., Cole, 1988) and through his Laboratory for Comparative Human Cognition (LCHC) at the University of California, San Diego. Other important researchers in the field are Yrjö Engeström, Jean Lave, Barbara Rogoff, Sylvia Scribner and James Wertsch.

Each word in the acronym CHAT is significant. C for 'cultural' points to the premise that humans are encultured, and everything people do is shaped by, and draws upon, their cultural values and resources. H for 'historical' is used together with cultural to indicate that since cultures are grounded in histories, and evolve over time, therefore analyses of what people do at any point in time must be viewed in light of the historical trajectories in which their actions take place. A for 'activity' refers to what people do together, and is modified by both cultural and historical processes to convey its situatedness. T for 'theory' is

184 Where Is 'Culture' in Psychology?

used in this label to denote a conceptual framework for understanding and explaining human activity (Foot, 2014).

Basic Principles of CHAT

1. Human beings interact with each other and the non-human world through culture.
2. Culture is embodied in artefacts. Artefacts are aspects of the environment that have been transformed by human beings through their participation in goal-directed activities over time. Thus, culture is our social inheritance. A wooden branch or a stone is a natural object but a hammer is an artefact because it is a modified object.
3. Artefacts, the constituents of culture, are simultaneously material and ideal/symbolic. They are materialized in the form of objects, words, rituals and other cultural practices. They are symbolic in that they have evolved to become prescribed means to prescribed goals in the minds of the people, 'partial solutions to previously encountered problems' (Cole, 1996, p. 294). Culture is exteriorized mind; mind is interiorized culture.
4. Artefacts incorporated into human action not only 'radically change his conditions of existence, they even react on him in that they effect a change in him and his psychic condition' (Luria, 1928, p. 493). Vygotsky referred to this kind of mediated action as the 'cultural habit of behaviour' which enables human beings to begin to regulate themselves 'from the outside'. Human psychological functions develop through participation in culturally organized activities. As Gallimore and Goldenberg (1993, p. 320) put it, 'Through participation in cultural activities that require cognitive and communicative functions, children are drawn into the use of these functions in ways that nurture and develop them.'
5. The psychological functioning of members of each generation is viewed as modified by existing cultural artefacts and practices while at the same time members of the successive generations contribute to the modifications of these artefacts and practices (Cole & Engeström, 1993).
6. Human psychological processes are acquired in the process of interacting with others and the physical world through culture and its central medium, language. Consequently, it is by analysing what people do in culturally organized activity that one comes to understand the process of being human. Studies focusing on the cognitive processing strategies of people who use cultural tools, such as an abacus, the arithmetic competencies of children engaged in selling sweets, see mind as neither internal nor external but as an emergent quality in the continuous interaction between subjects and the world of artefacts and practices.
7. Because cultural mediation is a process occurring over time, a CHAT perspective emphasizes that it must be studied over time. Time itself is conceived of with respect to four embedded domains: (a) phylogenesis, the

history of our species; (b) cultural history, the history of the cultural group into which we are born; (c) ontogeny, the history of an individual human being; and (d) microgenesis, moment-to-moment interactions that are the proximal locus of experience. One implication of this view is that all human beings are fundamentally hybrids of the phylogenetic and the cultural.

8. In addition to focusing researchers on time and change, a CHAT perspective requires them to focus on the social/spatial ecology of the activities they study – the relation of activities to their institutional arrangements, such as school, organization, bureaucracy, social class, ethnicity, religion, language, and so on.

9. A CHAT perspective places a special emphasis on the principle of multi-voicedness, the principle that every form of human interaction contains within it many different selves, arranged in multiple, overlapping and often contradictory ways. The contradictions, experienced by us as conflicts, are a major source of change. It is diversity all the way down.

While the dynamic constructivist view takes on the representational view of culture (culture as shared knowledge), the collective constructionist view of culture focuses on its regulatory aspect of culture, that is, the way it defines the daily situations and practices. CHAT places importance on cultural artefacts and human engagement with them.

BOX 4.3 CROSS-CULTURAL EQUIVALENCE VERSUS CULTURAL CONSTITUTION OF EMOTIONS

There is a substantial body of cross-cultural research pursuing universalities in emotional life. Triandis and Vassiliou (1972) showed that they could communicate the meaning of the Greek concept *philotimo* to their (mainly) American and West European readers even though there is no direct English equivalent of this term. They summarize by stating that a person who is philotimous 'behaves towards members of his ingroup the way they expect him to behave' (pp. 308–309). While this generic definition makes it looks plausible that non-Greeks can understand the implications of the emphasis by Greeks on *philotimo* for their actual behaviour, it is not certain whether such a definition captures all the essential elements of the meaning. Another set of studies to probe the cross-cultural invariance of facial expressions has been conducted by Ekman. Seven universal, basic emotions were identified: happiness, sadness, anger, fear, surprise, disgust and contempt (Ekman & Friesen, 1986). Ekman introduced the notion of display rules to suggest that while underlying emotions are universal but the manifestation of emotions, for example, the frequency and intensity with which emotions are expressed, show cross-cultural differences.

The cultural psychology of emotion, on the other hand, allows the inference of general principles of emotion through careful descriptive study of the

186 Where Is 'Culture' in Psychology?

emotional phenomena as they actually occur in their culturally particular forms. The question here is not whether it is possible to describe behaviour without reference to culturally rich meanings, but whether such description is relevant, given the question of interest. Cultural psychology contends that, in most cases, highly abstract descriptions of people's behaviour would capture neither the precise intentions of the behaviour nor their subjective experience. If one is to predict or understand what people will do, or want to do, in actual emotional contexts, one has to take into account the meaning that these behaviours have in these contexts, beyond just moving in a certain direction. Cultural research has focused on culturally embedded meanings in multiple emotional components such as antecedent events (conditions or situations that elicit an emotion), appraisal (evaluation of a situation in terms of a respondent's well-being or the satisfaction of goals), subjective feelings, physiological reaction patterns, action readiness (behaviour impulses for certain kinds of action), behavioural expression (such as facial expressions) and regulation (inhibition and control over expression). For example, cross-cultural differences in antecedents mainly have been related to different interpretations of situations and culture-specific beliefs leading to differences in subsequent emotional responses. This explains why, in response to insults, people belonging to honour cultures in the southern states of United States of America show more anger and aggressive responses than those in the North who do not belong to an honour culture. Insults are conceived of as honour violations in honour cultures. This interpretation also explains why Southerners are likely to bear less resentment than Northerners after they have expressed their anger (the score is evened; strength is being exhibited; Cohen et al., 1999). Similarly, among Americans, blaming someone else for an offence tends to result in assertion and anger towards the other. Whereas, among the Japanese, assuming that the other person had a good reason to offend leads to decreased emotionality and, in many cases, to doing nothing at all (Mesquita et al., 2005).

PAUSE AND THINK

Imagine that you are conducting field research in a cultural group quite different from your own. What kind of preparation will you make in order to ensure that you and your participants share the same perspective and communication goals?

What of History, Power and Hybridity in Culture?

While the move away from cross-cultural psychology towards cultural psychology represents a significant advance towards building culturally sensitive psychology, certain problems with the cultural psychology movement still remain. The cultural constructionist movement faults the reticence of cultural psychology in questioning the basic elements of the empiricist tradition of inquiry. The latter pays scant attention to the ways in which concepts and modes of representation enter culture and shape the future of cultural life for better or for ill.

While historical analysis and methods to study cultural history have been mentioned as important aspects of cultural and Indigenous psychological perspectives, they are not emphasized enough. The focus remains on developing the emic description of the practices, meanings, beliefs and values of the cultural group. The world of everyday life needs to be described through the meaning systems of the participants. But there is a likelihood that the participants' descriptions will be immediate and ahistorical. For this reason, emic descriptions must always be placed within the historical knowledge brought by the researcher. An infusion of historical analysis into the study of culture helps in locating it historically and structurally. History is to be understood as an active force in the present. The human events that have helped shape and constrain cultural processes continually affect the process of life in cultural groups. For example, the colonial experience of many Asian and African countries has continued to affect its processes. It is not enough to place history and class structure as a kind of backdrop to a drama, but we must look at these elements as constitutive aspect of culture formation.

Understanding culture like this also alerts us to the fact that culture is not so much the area of social life where people share understandings, but that area of social life where people struggle over understandings. Culture is a contested terrain with multiple visions embedded in power struggles. As Henry Giroux (2005) has suggested in the critical tradition:

> Culture is analyzed ... not simply as a way of life, but also as a form of production that always involves asymmetrical relations of power, and through which different groups in their dominant and subordinate positions struggle to both define and realize their aspirations.
>
> *(p. 2)*

Such analysis takes culture to be multi-voiced. Rather than understanding culture traditionally as a unified set of patterns and symbols shared by the group, it is better understood to be the expressions of the multiplicity of voices found in a group's membership, given the political, social and material power relations. Rather than seeking the commonalities (and therefore confusing consensus with domination), and uniform inter-subjectivities, one should be seeking the tensions and conflicts of a group. It is by giving expression to the silenced and legitimacy to their struggles that we advance the possibility for social transformation.

Bhabha (1994) makes a persuasive appeal to locate culture in the 'in-between space' as the third space which disrupts the politics of polarity – East–West, North–South, First World–Third World. This way of conceiving the location of culture as hybrid requires that scholars think dialectically, that is, that they, while addressing cultural differences, do not homogenize or absorb 'others' either in one or the other pole but recognize that our cultural and political identities constantly come to be through the co-influential processes that emerge out of these geopolitical divisions. Culture in the postcolonial condition is inextricably linked with the history of migrations and experiences of migration, exile, diaspora, displacement and dislocation. This leads to the redefinition of traditional homogeneous understandings of nation, culture, community, national identity and citizenship.

Final Comments

The relationship between psychology and culture is vexed. From treating it as irrelevant to considering it a source of variability in psychological phenomena to understanding it as constitutive of the psyche, psychology has engaged with culture in diverse ways. Methodologies to map culture have also differed accordingly. A variety of questions and understandings regarding culture and behaviour have been pursued within psychology; some of them are as follows:

1. What is culture?
2. Do cultures vary?
3. How do cultures vary?
4. Do psychological characteristics, such as self-concepts, perceptual abilities, motives and emotion display rules, vary as a function of cultural differences?
5. Through what processes, does culture impact behaviour?
6. How does the psyche influence culture?
7. What is the relationship between culture and the psyche? Is it interactionist or constitutive?

A central concern in the study of culture and psychology is the issue of psychic unity versus relativism. Raising the question of culture is in itself a critique of the assumption of universalism in psychology which resulted in making it culture-blind and culture-bound. However, the specific way in which culture difference is marked out in psychology needs to be attended to. Dhar and Siddiqui (2013) point out that the cultural difference argument can emerge in four forms: (1) where the Western idea is the universal or the universal is that which is Western; (2) there are cultural variants of the universal which result, due to differing forms of life, meaning-making practices and theorizations of their experience; (3) abandon the Western idea because the West and East have no meeting ground; and (4) to debate and dialogue with the West and arrive at an understanding of how the Western idea is native and local to the West. These four arguments move from a single standard of truth, that is, the universal Western original to the culturally relative, that is, the 'culturalized copies of the original' (p. 515) to the aboriginalization of the West. Much of cultural theorization and research in psychology is located between the first two. This raises several tricky questions. First, what is the Western-ness of an idea: Is the West the 'geographical' west? Did other cultures contribute to the idea of the 'West', historically? Is it an idea marked by the descriptor 'Christian', 'modern', 'secular', 'scientific'? Is the West or Western an undivided perspective? Second, what are the other cultures 'relative' to the Western original? Are the other cultures relatives/the underside of the One culture? Is the West, here, the donor/culture of origin of ideas and the rest recipients? Is the East/West, Orient/Occident, traditional/modern model not actually collapsing 'culture difference' once again to 'difference from the One culture'? Does the notion of cultural relativity then also not slide into the One culture argument? The aboriginalization of the West is a radical position where the mainstream psychology is seen as a cultural manifestation, more specifically an American ethnopsychology.

What is required for a truly liberatory study of culture is to let different cultural identities know/speak for themselves, to have an imagination of plurality of cultures, different from each other and not just 'other of the same' (Irigaray, 1977). The indigenization project in psychology is a step in this direction. It has the twin aims of resisting a dominating Western psychology (decolonization) and engendering a locally based and relevant psychology (indigenization).

5

HOW IS 'GENDER' TREATED IN PSYCHOLOGY?

We live in a two-sexed, two-gendered world. Take the example of any survey form asking personal details that we have to complete, whether for school admission or to book a train. Chances are that one is expected to mark either 'male' or 'female'. While many among us may have ticked one box without much thought, some others would have agonized over it as neither option captures their experience of their self. This either/or categorization does not fit many. Gender shapes our daily lives. Ideas about gender-appropriate behaviour structure people's most mundane practices, such as whether we use public toilets with urinals or not and whether we buy perfume or aftershave. It is a critical issue because it is associated with various social inequalities, exclusions and experiences of abuse. For example, women's work at home or even in public is valued and paid less, compared to that of men. Violence against men is much less reported compared to violence against women. People who transgress gender norms, such as people who are transgender, or those who transgress heteronormativity, such as lesbians or gay men, are also likely to experience a wide range of victimization, from harassment to abuse to violence, as well as exclusion from privileges.

Mainstream psychology's track record of dealing with gender as an evolving analytic concept has been quite poor. It mainly conceptualizes it as a social-contextual variable impacting human behaviour. Numerous reviews have revealed that much of psychological knowledge is male-centric, ignores the contribution of female psychologists, excludes feminine experience and pathologizes women's subjectivity. It understands sex, gender and sexuality in binary terms rather than as a continuum. It takes heterosexuality as the normative experience and treats deviations from it as abnormal. Mainstream psychology also does not quite engage with the thesis that sex, gender and sexuality are joined together in complex constellations.

DOI: 10.4324/9781003471851-6

How Does Psychology Understand Sex, Gender and Sexuality?

Gender emerged as a new concept, in the early 1970s, clearly distinct from sex. Within mainstream psychology, 'sex' refers to the biological categories of female and male, categories distinguished by genes, chromosomes and hormones. 'Sex category' refers to the placement of other individuals into the category of male or female. Individuals place others into sex categories based on observable displays and cues such as body size and shape. Sex category is generally treated as a proxy for sex. That is, if someone walks in wearing lipstick, heels and a skirt, we tend to assume that person is anatomically female (West & Zimmerman, 1987). 'Gender' refers to the social categories of woman and man. Gender categories are distinguished from each other by a set of psychological features and role attributes that society has assigned to the biological category of sex. For example, usually emotionality is considered a feminine trait and competitiveness is considered a trait of males. These traits are characteristics of gender (masculinity and femininity) rather than sex. Thus, gender is a cultural overlay of sex – what culture adds to the biology. While sex is defined in the same way across cultures, gender differs because each society has its own prescriptions for how women and men ought to behave. A feature of the male sex category is the Y chromosome: regardless of whether a male wears shorts or skirts or is competitive or nurturant, he is of the male sex because he possesses the Y chromosome.

The understanding that sex and gender are binary terms is deep-seated in psychology. Males and females and men and women are the two sexes/genders possible. The assumption underlying this binary model is that biological males are socialized to become masculine and biological females are socialized to become feminine, and both will think, feel and act as per their respective socioculturally sanctioned gender roles. Such individuals are referred to as sex-typed or cisgender individuals. With respect to sex and gender, such thinking reflects the processes of polarization (male/masculinity and female/femininity are opposites of each other), essentialism (male/masculinity and female/femininity are what we are or have) and differentiation (all men are alike and different from women).

Gender and sexuality are considered to be interrelated categories. Sexuality is usually understood in terms of sexual orientation, that is, the romantic or sexual interests and attractions to men, women or both. Heterosexual men are interested in women, and heterosexual women are interested in men. Gay men are interested in men while lesbians are interested in women. Bisexual men and women are interested in both men and women. Asexuals report no sexual interest in either men or women. Psychology is permeated by heteronormative discourse that inscribes a linear relationship between sex, gender and sexuality. This discourse prescribes that normal men will be masculine and will desire women and normal women will be feminine and will desire men. The normative structure of heterosexuality designates lesbians, gay men, bisexuals, transgender, queer and asexuals as anomalies.

Conceptual Challenges

The pervasive ideas about sex, gender and sexuality as outlined above have been heavily critiqued by feminism. Several challenging questions have been raised; we will discuss some of them here.

- Can sex and gender be clearly separated as belonging to realms of biology and culture, respectively?

Many scholars argue that the conceptual distinction between the two is not sustainable beyond a point, and 'sex' and 'gender' are dialectically and inseparably related. 'Sex', in this view, is not an unchanging base upon which society constructs 'gender' meanings; but rather, the sex/body itself has been affected by various factors external to it – there is no clear and unchanging line separating nature and culture. For instance, the rapid improvements in women's athletic records over the past two decades are an indication that social norms have shaped the capacities of their bodies. That is, the 'body' has been formed as much by 'culture' as by 'nature'. The body is not a simple physical object but rather is constructed by and takes its meaning from its positioning within specific social, cultural and economic practices (Menon, 2012). The ways in which the categories, such as male, female, intersex and other, are parsed are not inherently biological but relative to place and time. Butler's (1990) startling argument is that 'gender' is not the cultural inscription of meaning onto a 'pregiven' sex. Rather, gender as a way of thinking and as a concept pre-exists the body. It is gender that produces the category of biological sex. And gender produces sex through a series of performances, that is, the way people live the day-to-day moments of life. In this way, the focus of research is also dislocated from individual/group traits to the interpretation of the ways through which people make gender in their everyday life.

- Is a two-sexed/two-gendered world an adequate conceptualization of human bodies and experience?

'Sex' polarized as 'females' and 'males', 'sexuality' polarized as 'homosexuals' and 'heterosexuals', and 'gender' polarized as 'women' and 'men' cannot accommodate the experiences of hermaphrodites, pseudohermaphrodites, transsexuals, transvestites, bisexuals, third genders and gender rebels such as sports participants.

According to the hegemonic understanding of the human body, each and every body is clearly and unambiguously male or female. For example, conceptions of sex assume chromosomal arrangements XX and XY as the typical make-up for women and men, respectively. However, chromosomal configurations XXX, XXY, XYY and XO exist and indicate the need to expand the narrow conceptualizations of sex to include this diversity. A large number of bodies that do not fit the dichotomous description are designated as diseased or disordered in some way. Infants born with no clear determining sexual characteristics and eunuchs have to be disciplined into normalcy through medical and surgical intervention, or they must be declared to be abnormal or illegal. Feminine men and masculine women are likewise treated as gender non-conformists and experience social exclusion and abuse. Transsexuals/transgender people, whose gender identification is with the opposite of their 'genetic' sex, are treated as anomalies. The medical treatment of this is sex reassignment surgery through which alignment between sex and gender is brought about for the said person. However, such medical understanding plays into the binary conceptualizations of two sexes/two genders. The experiences of such people are diverse which often do not find a space in the medical models that reinforce the binary tropes of 'woman trapped in a man's body' (transwoman) or 'man trapped in a woman's body' (transman). What about people who do not identify themselves in binary terms, that is, non-binary transsexuals? Despite the research that suggests that genderqueer is the most commonly endorsed gender identity among an online and non-clinical sample of transgender individuals (Kuper et al., 2012), gender research has not provided clarity on how non-binary transgender individuals conceptualize their gender identity.

Classification of sexual orientation runs into similar issues. It is based on three dimensions: identity (what individuals identify as the most representative category for them), attraction (towards whom do they feel sexually attracted, men or women?) and behaviour (how does an individual act on one's desires and attractions?). Complete consistency among these three dimensions of sexual orientation seems to be the exception rather than the rule. A sexual identity does not necessitate behaviour in line with that. Also, feeling attraction and desires towards men or women does not necessitate them identifying in line with their attractions or acting on their attractions. This mismatch does not necessarily indicate individuals are 'confused' or experimenting with their sexual orientation, instead it reflects the lived realities of sexual orientation. Consider a woman who has dated men most of her life and feels attracted to men but is also attracted to women and fell in love and now lives with a woman. This woman would be classified as a bisexual, based on her behaviour and attractions, but she might choose to identify herself as a lesbian because it represents her current relationship.

The limited use of the term 'sexuality' as connoting just 'sexual orientation' (i.e., with whom one has sex) has also been objected to. It ignores the fact that a gendered ideology of passivity and activity pervades Western societies' notions of sex and sexuality: Men, masculinity and male sexuality embody activity; women, femininity and female sexuality embody passivity.

Butler (1990) uses the term 'heterosexual' matrix to refer to a constellation produced by institutions, practices and discourses – from biomedical sciences to religion and culture – looking through which, it appears to be 'a fact of nature' that all human bodies possess one of the two fixed gendered identities, with each experiencing sexual desire only for the 'opposite sex'. It renders invisible the multiplicity of bodies, gender experiences and sexual desires. The removal of this heterosexual matrix will reveal that human bodies and desires are fluid and have no necessary fixed gender identity or sexual orientation. It opens the space for a variety of gender experiences beyond the binary, such as genderqueer, gender nonconforming, gender fluid or agender individuals. Among the numerous examples scattered across societies, literature and other realms, the life of Bhakti saints is one such illustration of how the lines between male and female are continuously crossed and re-crossed. The restrictive sex, gender and sexuality binaries do not capture experiences such as the following stated by a transsexual: 'I slosh about between male, female, neither, and both' (Galupo et al., 2017). It is indeed the limitation of our language where only two words for gender are available to tag our experiences with. Sandra Bem (1995) opined that we should have 1,000 categories for sex instead of only two. She suggests starting with a modest 18 categories, derived from all possible combinations of sex (male, female), gender role (masculine, feminine, androgynous) and sexual orientation (heterosexual, homosexual, bisexual). By having so many categories, it would be difficult to have clear-cut boundaries between any two categories. The categories would become fluid and, ultimately, the distinctions among them less important, if not meaningless.

A new 'genderqueer' politics has emerged since the 1980s, which has challenged all gender binaries. It promotes new categories, such as non-op transsexual, TG butch, femme queen, crossdresser, third gender, drag queen or queen and transboi. It also promotes the use of postgender attitudes, such as promoting the use of gender-neutral pronouns such as 'ze', 'per' and 'zir', or the terms pansexual or omnisexual rather than binary 'bisexual'.

The deep-seated assumptions, such as the idea that the body is a passive inert set of resources to be put to human use; that bodies are naturally entirely one sex or another; that hermaphroditism (bodies possessing both male and female sexual characteristics) is a disease; and that desire naturally flows only between 'opposite' sexes, were absent in Europe prior to the late sixteenth century, and in South Asia and Africa until the early nineteenth century, when European modernity was universalized through colonialism. Thus, it is often forgotten that what seems like a natural fact is in fact only about 400 years old and has specific cultural moorings in the experience of the West.

- Is gender something that we have or is it something that we do?

The essentialist position on gender construes it as residing within the individual. It portrays gender in terms of fundamental attributes such as personality traits (e.g., relationality) or cognitive process (e.g., 'justice'-based moral judgement) that are conceived as internal, persistent and generally separate from the ongoing experience of interaction with the daily sociopolitical contexts of one's life. The social constructionist position is not to be confused with the socialization of gender which argues for the environmental origins of gender traits. Rather, the social constructionist argument is that gender is not a trait of individuals at all, but simply a construct that identifies particular transactions that are understood to be appropriate to one's sex. Gender so defined is not found in the individual but exists in those interactions that are socially construed as gendered. Gender is manifested in the way the individuals style their bodies, carry themselves and how they speak and move. During a romantic date, when the man pays the bill, he is 'doing gender', as this is the socially appropriate behaviour for him in such a gendered interaction. Its meaning is agreed upon by the participants, and it is reaffirmed by the process of engaging in this interaction. Gender as a social construct is particular to a specific sociocultural historical period, a result of shared cultural knowledge and language use. Categories of masculinity and femininity are not seen as naturally resulting from biological differences between 'male' and 'female' bodies, but as social products. Some social constructionists consider the idea that there are two types of sexed bodies and two types of gendered people who are different from each other as a powerful ideology that shapes reality rather than one that simply reflects reality. In this sense, we believe there are two sexes because the world around us continually reflects this idea and tells us it is so (and we, in turn, participate in reproducing this idea).

Not only gender, people 'perform' their sexuality too. An increasing number of people are changing sex or performing their 'sex' in different ways with different partners; and their partners, whether same or different, also learn to perform different kinds of sex in return. Thus, the central preoccupations of psychology with a stable, simple self or identity are being subverted.

PAUSE AND THINK

Try adopting some behaviour that does not fit your gender role and see how people respond, verbally and non-verbally. For example, if you are a male, try wearing make-up. If you are a female, try changing your car's tyre with a man standing close by.

REVIEW QUESTION

What are the various critiques of sex-gender binarism?

What Is the Psychology of Gender?

Despite the use of the word gender since at least the fifteenth century (according to the *Oxford English Dictionary*), the term came into use in psychology only after John Money's introduction of the phrase 'gender roles' in 1955 (Money et al.,

196 How Is 'Gender' Treated in Psychology?

1955). In the context of research on transsexuals, Stoller made it clear that sex and gender 'are not inevitably bound in anything like a one-to-one relationship, but each may go into quite independent ways' (1968, p. viii). The psychology of gender subsumes a diverse collection of topics, questions, methods and political underpinnings.

Is the Psychology of Gender the Same as the Psychology of Women?

Gender is something that all people experience. However, women are most frequently seen to have or embody gender, men just 'are'. That is the reason why the term 'gender' is often used as a more acceptable shorthand for 'women' (e.g., 'gender issues' studied within a university are typically 'women's issues').

Looking at the history of research in psychology, one can say that, on one hand, interest in the study of gender came about with the question of how men and women are different. On the other hand, interest in the study of women came about due to a concern with how, in this kind of research, women and women's experience were routinely made invisible, seen as inferior or pathologized in psychology. In the research on differences, men are presented as normal and women as 'different' from men and thus deficient, and their difference and deficiency are in need of explanation (Tavris, 1993). Psychological explanations of behaviours have routinely emphasized biological and other internal causes, as opposed to social or external causes. It reinforces the impression that the sex differences and thereby women's deficiency are unchangeable. This not only validates the widely held stereotypes about men and women but also contributes to women's oppression.

There is no denying the fact that a substantial amount of literature in the field of psychology of gender has been devoted to the study of female subjectivity. Specifically, the focus is on the works of women psychologists, studies using women subjects and theorizations to explain women's psychology. This has given rise to a psychology of women as the study of women, by women and for women. This preoccupation with women, as agents in shaping the discipline and as subjects whose psychology is important enough to be studied, is not without a reason. Although the issues of sex and gender were inconsequential for most male founders of the newly emerging science of psychology, this was not the case for the early women psychologists. Women's sex categorization and the prevailing constructions of masculinity and femininity directly influenced whether they could gain access to university training in psychology and, if so, where and with what possible outcomes. Furthermore, societal beliefs about the unsuitability of women for higher education and intellectual work, especially in the sciences, made their status as 'women scientists' exceptional, even an oxymoron. Until 1929, women were explicitly banned from an influential group of psychologists known as the experimentalists formed by Titchener in 1904. Boring (1951), in an article, explained the continuing low status of women as due to their lack of productivity and unwillingness to work long hours in the laboratory. He did not consider it to be sexism but realism. He had this to say about the impact of marriage on women professionals: 'If married, they have more divided allegiance than the man. If unmarried, they have conflict about being unmarried' (Boring, 1951, p. 681). Thus, much effort has gone into bringing to light the rather invisible contribution of women psychologists. Some of these women made the empirical investigation of supposedly natural male–female differences the focus of their scientific work (e.g., Hollingworth, 1914a; Nevers & Calkins, 1895; Thompson, 1903). Also rampant in psychology is the trend of using male samples and male experiences to construct theories, deemed to be applicable to both men and women, leading to a neglect of female experience in psychological research and theorization. Therefore, works like that of Gilligan and Josselson have taken women samples to research female subjectivities and tried to redress the androcentrism in psychology. Topics that centre on the aspects of women's lives, such as motherhood, violence against women, gender-based discrimination, need for achievement in women and so on, became important.

The psychology of women coalesced as a distinct field during the 1970s. Besides, there was a proliferation of publications that explicitly identified with this area, such as *Sex Roles* (1975), *Psychology of Women Quarterly* (1976) and *Women and Therapy* (1982). The Association of Women in Psychology and the Psychology of Women (APA Division 35) were formed in 1969 and 1973, respectively. Erica Burman (1998, p. 2) stated that the 'psychology of women is a call for a woman-centred psychology … aimed to speak of and for the specificity of women's experience of psychology'.

Mainstream psychology is critiqued as being sexist (women are regarded as inferior to men and are discriminated against because they are women) and heterosexist (anyone who is not a heterosexual is discriminated against). Also, while psychology claims to be a 'neutral', 'value-free' and 'objective' science, it is actually value-laden, taking men as the 'universal standard', around which everything else revolves. So, along with being sexist and heterosexist, psychology is also androcentric (male-centric). Mainstream psychology has been referred to as 'malestream' psychology because it ignored women and failed to address topics of relevance to women's lives. The focus on women is, hence, the result of efforts to rectify the male bias, the invisibility of female subjectivity and the notions of female inferiority. One trend led to seeing 'woman as a problem' which documented the ways women appeared to be deficient compared to men. Martina Horner's work on 'fear of success' falls into this category. The other trend led to seeing 'women as special', and Gilligan's work on feminine morality of care falls into this category. Regardless of how women were seen in relation to men, the common thread was an emphasis on sex comparisons.

However, the psychology of gender is not, and cannot be, only a study of women by women. It also studies the interrelationship between masculinity and femininity, gender role ideology, stereotypes, gender socialization and sexual orientation.

Is the Psychology of Gender and Woman Dominated by Feminist Politics?

The paradigm of sex differences, which has been one of the major research programmes in the psychology of gender, is not a feminist project. Here, the terms 'sex' and 'gender' are taken as subject variables used to identify people as belonging to one or the other category or as independent variables believed to be impacting the behaviour of people. It is not used as an analytic concept. As discussed later in the chapter, it has served to reinforce the popular stereotypical notions of masculinity and femininity, rather than break them down.

However, with regard to the psychology of women, Beall and Sternberg (1993, p. xix) observed, 'few fields of study have such political overtones as the study of woman'. One might even argue that the psychology of women would not exist if it were not for feminism. The field began by challenging the notion that women are inherently inferior. However, Erica Burman (1998) has mourned its depoliticized stance. Unger (1998) opines that the study of gender in psychology has remained more empirical and less theoretical than feminist scholarship in most other disciplines. It remained within the purview of the strong positivist and empiricist orientation of psychology. Feminist empiricism is the most common approach used in psychology to counter gender biases in experiments. It tries to remove the methodological 'errors' such as experimental biases, poorly representative samples, faulty measurement techniques and misrepresentation of data, to achieve a kind of science that will be applicable universally. This kind of positivist empiricist stance has been critiqued for trying to 'beat the master with his own tools'. Researchers have countered feminist empiricism with the charge that 'methods' can never reveal reality and empiricism does not pay sufficient attention to other ways of knowing.

The psychology of women has also not consistently paid attention to the social context. An investigation of the early US textbooks on the psychology of women reveals a focus on intrapersonal forces. For example, the content of the first two textbooks on the psychology of women, authored by Judith Bardwick (1971) and Julia Sherman (1971), reflected the individualistic thrust of mainstream psychology. They showed the important early influence of theories stressing intrapsychic differences between the sexes. Consistent with the individualistic focus of psychology in the US, research within the field focused on sexism in interpersonal attitudes and behaviours. There was little research on societal sexism. Many of these studies were atheoretical in nature. They were designed to show that discrimination against women existed in a variety of circumstances, in minor as well as major arenas. The theme of achievement has been an important focus of research in the psychology of women to understand why women were not as successful as men. Martina Horner's classic work on 'fear of success' focused more on internal variables such as attitudes and motives than on external barriers to success. Thus, not all of the psychology of women is feminist in nature. Crawford (1995) questions the extent to which the

How Is 'Gender' Treated in Psychology? **199**

fields of psychology of gender and women have a political commitment to challenge and transform relations of power which maintain the myriad inequalities experienced by women.

Feminist psychology, which has been defined as 'psychological theory and practice which is explicitly informed by the political goals of the feminist movement' (Wilkinson, 1997, p. 247), swept a radical new agenda into the discipline. It pointed out the historical absence of women as participants in psychological research. It highlighted that psychological knowledge discriminates against women's ways of knowing and reasoning. It was not until feminists started researching topics such as rape and sexual assault that these topics were taken seriously as an important focus for research. There is still relatively little non-feminist psychological research on topics such as emotion, marriage and motherhood because these are seen as 'women's issues' (Dryden, 1999). Feminist critics have also argued that Western psychological epistemology is based on individualism and on the Cartesian dualism (mind–body split). Similarly, feminist researchers were instrumental in developing the use of qualitative methods in (and beyond) psychology, methods that some mainstream psychologists still devalue as unscientific and subjective.

Worell (2000) lists the major influences of feminist psychologists in the discipline. These are as follows:

1. *Asking new questions.* By asking new questions and reframing old questions, feminist psychologists have illuminated the hidden experiences and gender asymmetries that remained submerged and unexplored. For example, instead of asking, Why doesn't a woman move out of an abusive marriage?, feminists ask, What are the barriers that prevent her from leaving? Such a question redirects the focus from a woman's internal pathology to the pathology of the system that keeps women imprisoned by fear and lack of resources.

2. *Naming and renaming the problem.* By naming several experiences of women, such as 'mother work', 'date rape', 'marital rape', 'sexual harassment' and 'domestic violence', feminist researchers have opened up these topics for research attention. Violence against women has become visible now, due to the feminist efforts. They have documented its prevalence and launched public action to demand prevention and legislation.

3. *Challenging research priorities.* Feminists in psychology challenged the positivist science notion that all research is objective and value-free. Rather, they make a strong case that all research is underwritten by personal and political values. Research is used to redress the injustices of the existing power structures of knowledge, to empower the research participants and to bring about social change. Feminist research pays special attention to experiential realities shaped by the context of the participants. Feminist standpoint theory posits that knowledge claims on women's life situations can be made in the best way by asking women to think, reflect

and report on their own lives. Their accounts have to be understood through the predominant social structures (cultural history, social status) in which the women are located. This makes qualitative research methodology a favoured way of doing research for them. A collaborative research relationship is forged between the researcher and participants and the voice/narrative of the participants is foregrounded. Within psychology, Gergen (1988, pp. 90–91) has suggested that a feminist method should include the following principles:

a   Recognizing the interdependence of experimenter and participant.
b   Avoiding the decontextualizing of participants or experimenters from their social and historical contexts.
c   Recognizing and revealing the nature of one's values within the research context.
d   Accepting that the facts do not exist independent of their producers' linguistic codes.
e   Demystifying the role of the scientist to establish an egalitarian relationship between researcher and participant.
f   Acknowledging the interdependent relationship between science and its consumers.

4. *Revising therapeutic practice.* Feminist psychologists protested against the inclusion of homosexuality as an official diagnosis in the APA's *Diagnostic and Statistical Manual of Mental Disorders* during the 1970s. They also protested the inclusion of categories that pathologized women's behaviour and experience such as late luteal phase dysphoric disorder. The introduction of a new sub-field of feminist therapy and counselling was a direct response to the sexism and bias that characterized both Freudian psychoanalysis and other more traditional therapies. It redirected attention to the structural sources from the intrapsychic sources of women's problems. Power imbalances between the male therapist and female patient are acknowledged and egalitarian relationships are encouraged both within and outside of therapy. Intersecting identities of women, that is, their gender, class, caste/race/ethnicity, religion, nationality, sexuality and ableism, are honoured and explored. Feminist therapists validate women's lived experiences, identify personal strength and encourage women to value themselves and others.

BOX 5.1 DISCOURSES BLAMING THE MEDIA FOR BODY IMAGE-RELATED DISTURBANCES

Feminism refuses to treat women as 'encapsulated individuals, separate from society and its structures'. In this vein, a substantial body of work has investigated the relation between media influence and body image and the confluence of eating disturbances, body image distress, mediated images and highly susceptible female audience (Orbach, 1986). While recognizing the significance of

How Is 'Gender' Treated in Psychology? **201**

the media in propagating a slender ideal, later feminist work is also wary of overemphasizing the 'inscriptive power of culturally mediated images of thinness'. It suggests that sociocultural factors in body image dissatisfaction cannot be restricted to the effects of media images. The feminist argument is that body distress and/or disordered eating may not be motivated solely by the drive for pursuit of thinness or any distortion of body image, but rather by wider experiences of 'restricted agency' faced by women. Research suggests that women may resort to food refusal/denial as an instrumental means of negotiating the transition, disconnection and oppression that they uniformly endure as they move between the worlds of work and home, tradition and modernity. Historically, women are called upon to exert greater regulation of 'appetite', in relation to food intake, sexual desire and ambition. There are cultural messages with regard to how women are 'small eaters'. Later feminist approaches have sought to situate body image and eating disorders in relation to the wider social expectations surrounding Western femininity, ranging from gendered discourses on appetite, sexuality and economic power to social roles.

The power of the discursive frame which reduces sociocultural factors in body distress/eating disorders to questions of media effects is immense and that is the reason why it is often voiced by those who suffer from such problems. However, it is inadequate in capturing personal conceptions of aetiology and experience of such problems. This is clear from what a participant in a feminist therapy group had to say:

> So [it is] less, like, well, there's a model, a skinny model in a magazine, looking at that, you have been looking at that too much and so you just wanna' be like them ... I don't agree with that at all. I think that completely trivializes it.
>
> *(Holmes et al., 2017)*

Such experiences suggest that conceptions of body distress and disordered eating as induced by the media (and other related industries, such as the film and the fashion industry) are perceived to foster a trivializing and stigmatizing attitude towards the problem. Sociocultural factors such as media effects are somehow perceived as more controllable, fostering a kind of volitional stigma in which body disturbances are trivialized as a behavioural choice of the sufferer. The blame thus shifts from the 'media' to the vulnerable 'women'. Wendy Spettigue and Katherine A. Henderson (2004, pp. 3–4) outline how

> females who have already internalized the thin beauty ideal and/or who already have high levels of body dissatisfaction are the most vulnerable ... [Further], women with anorexia engage in heavy media use and describe their consumption of fashion magazines as an 'addiction', with many saying that the greatest media dependency occurred after their eating disorders had taken control of their lives.

> In this passage, the females who have 'internalized the thin beauty ideal' and who have 'high levels of body dissatisfaction' are represented as pathological. They are seen as 'addicted' to fashion media. They are viewed as passive consumers of media images and as being 'suggestively vulnerable' (Levitt, 1997) to its influence. Media and cultural studies approaches to audiences have challenged the hegemony of media 'effects' on passive consumers and have instead brought to light how media audiences actively engage in the process of meaning making within broader operations of social power (Gillespie, 2005). In addition, the media cannot be held responsible for body disturbances in a linear causal fashion.

There are numerous paradigms in psychology – biopsychology, trait theory, behaviourism, psychoanalysis and social cognition – that have theorized gender. While some lean towards internal factors, such as biochemical processes, anatomical structures, genetics, trait dispositions, unconscious fantasies and cognitive schemas, others focus on external factors such as role models, social reinforcements, gender norms, or social context.

Biology

Since its inception, psychology has taken many of its ideas and theories directly from natural science, biology in particular. As Burr has argued in relation to the nature–nurture debate:

> There is a common sense assumption (which may have no factual basis) that biological factors exert a powerful 'push' in particular directions, and that (weaker) environmental influences have a merely moderating effect. Biological influences are assumed to be deeper and stronger than societal forces, which are seen as more superficial. It is significant that the study of the biological sciences has often seemed more relevant to the education of psychologists than has sociology.
>
> *(1998, p. 32)*

The biological foundation of human behaviour and experience rests on genetics and neurochemical processes. The specific differences between men and women are determined by the following:

1. Genetic, that is, the XX female and XY male chromosomal pattern.
2. Hormonal, that is, oestrogen (female) and androgen/testosterone (male).
3. Genital, that is, the visible physical characteristics of penis/vagina.

A biological male is one who has all three characteristics pertaining to the male sex and a biological female is one who has all three characteristics pertaining to the female sex. The hormonal differences between males and females lead to different development at puberty. Sex hormones clearly have a different influence on physiology and, through this, on morphology too. This means that male and female bodies are differently shaped (although there is a wide variation in both male and female body forms) and work somewhat differently at a biological level. The physiological and morphological differences can have an impact on behaviour. The research evidence suggests that there are small differences in the way men's and women's brains are organized, leading to small average differences in their mental function. At least some of this may well be a result of biological differences, particularly as they affect the development of the brain in infancy and early childhood. The process of lateralization seems to progress slightly differently in men and women. The reproductive system and the hormones in the woman's body are often used to explain women's maternal behaviour, pre-menstrual syndrome, and so on.

While the biological perspective suggests a binary view of the sexes, medical research has shown that variation exists with respect to metabolic rate, bone size, brain function, stress response and lung capacity, within and across sex categories. This variation cannot be captured by simple 'male' or 'female' designations, which is why it is important to think about sex in more than binary terms. Also, bodies are not the products of biology alone, but are also socially constructed. For example, the way intersex bodies are now treated has changed due to the awareness created by the intersex movement. Now sex assignment surgery at birth (where genitals and secondary sex characteristics are made to look male or female) is no longer widespread due to the controversy over the physical, emotional and sexual harm it can cause (Fausto-Sterling, 2000). Technological changes are radically transforming the situational context in which biology operates. Thus, the human organism can actually be liberated from what had earlier seemed to be its intrinsic biological limitations. For instance, as a biological species, human beings are susceptible to infections from various bacteria and viruses which meant that it was part of the human condition to routinely die from such infections. But now human beings have invented antibiotics to fight infections which has changed the human reality of death due to infections.

Evolutionary Psychology and Sociobiology

From the perspective of evolutionary theory, sex differences among humans reflect adaptations to the differing social and physical environments that have operated upon females and males since primeval times. In the course of their evolution, males and females faced different adaptive problems and thus developed different adaptive strategies to ensure their survival and maximize their reproductive success, that is, maximizing the number of genes that one passes onto the next generation. This idea has been neatly encapsulated in the term 'selfish genes' (Dawkins, 1976), within a form of evolutionary theory called sociobiology. It proposes that organisms are predisposed, because of the force of evolution, to behave in ways that increase the probability of producing offspring and maximizing the number of offspring produced. The resolutions to the adaptive problems evolved psychological mechanisms that are specific to each problem domain and that differ between women and men. Buss and Kenrick (1998) described evolutionary psychology's approach to understanding sex differences as a 'meta-theory' and summarized it as '[m]en and women differ in domains where they faced different adaptive problems over human evolutionary history' (p. 994).

In the hunter–gatherer socioeconomic system, men hunted while women gathered. This division of labour suggests sex-differentiated pressures linked to survival and reproduction. It could have affected the cognitive skills of men and women with men acquiring the superior spatial skills that followed from ancestral hunting and women acquiring the superior spatial location memory skills that followed from ancestral gathering (e.g., Geary, 1995). The effective adaptations are retained in human design and perpetuated over time through genetic and hormonal processes. Sex-typed evolved mechanisms are translated into behavioural sex differences by various cognitive and affective processes.

This perspective helps to explain various kinds of social behaviour such as sex differences in mate selection, sex differences in preference for casual sex, male promiscuity and female fidelity, male aggression and female nurturance, sexual jealousy among men, and so on. Men, according to this argument, are pre-programmed for promiscuity. They maximize their genes' chances of surviving by having sex at every opportunity and with as many women as possible. Women, on the other hand, are, according to this theory, pre-programmed for selectivity and settling down. Women will maximize their genes' chances of surviving by carefully selecting a mate who will produce the strongest, most-able-to-survive children, and who will stay around to protect and feed her and the children until they reach sexual maturity. So men ostensibly look out for signs of 'female fertility' like youth and sexual attractiveness when selecting a potential sexual mate, while women look out for signs of 'masculine strength and stability'. The difference, it is proposed, comes about because, relatively speaking, women can produce only a limited number of children in their child-bearing years, whereas men can inseminate large numbers of women and hence have many children. Because of larger parental investment of females in child-bearing and child-rearing, short-term mating (casual sex) is not a large component of a female's sexual strategy.

According to evolutionary psychologists (e.g., Buss), sex differences in numerous psychological dispositions arose from the contrasting sexual strategies of men and women. Because men competed with other men for sexual access to women, men's evolved dispositions favour violence, competition, jealousy, risk-taking, territoriality, and so on. Women, in turn, developed a proclivity to nurture and a preference for long-term mates who could support a family.

Psychoanalytic Theory

Psychoanalysis has played a decisive role in the shaping of social scientific understanding of gender and sexual difference. The Freudian perspective sees issues of gender development and sexual difference as centrally concerned with psychical reality rather than material reality, with the realm of fantasy rather than nature or culture. While the Freudian version is the most popular one, the contribution of other psychoanalytic theorists, especially the psychoanalytic feminists, is crucial to understanding the full import of this framework. The Oedipal narrative of Freud has been subject to multiple and divergent interpretations by feminist scholars. The Oedipal story is the story of psychic development, how we become subjects and, in becoming subjects, how we become sexually differentiated. The psychoanalytic theory is discussed in detail later in the chapter.

Social Learning Theory

The social learning theory (Bandura & Walters, 1963; Mischel, 1966) states that we learn behaviour in two ways. First, we learn behaviour that is modelled; second, we learn behaviour that is reinforced. These are the primary principles of social learning theory, and they apply to the acquisition of gender role behaviour as they do to any other domain of behaviour (Mischel, 1966).

According to observational learning theory, children develop gender roles by patterning their behaviour after models in the social environment. If others reward the behaviour, it is likely to be repeated. Thus, modelling and reinforcement interact with each other to influence behaviour. One sex-related behaviour that has been examined extensively in terms of social learning theory and reinforcement is aggression. Why do examples of aggressive behaviour lead people to imitate them? Witnessing another's behaviour not only teaches us how to perform the behaviour but also suggests that the behaviour is appropriate. It also makes aggressive behaviour a cognitively available response to provocation. Thus, when faced with a conflict, aggressive behaviour may be more likely because it is a learned and cognitively accessible response. There are more physically aggressive role models for boys than for girls. Also aggression is a behaviour that is more likely to be reinforced in males than females, by parents, teachers and peers (Feshbach, 1989).

Girls and boys are rewarded for different behaviours, and the consequences of a behaviour determine whether the child performs it again. When a girl plays with a doll, a parent may smile, play with her or buy her another doll. While if a boy plays with a doll, a parent may ignore the behaviour, take the doll away, frown or even scold the boy and say, 'only girls play with dolls!' Society is less tolerant of and more likely to punish cross-sex behaviour among boys than among girls. It does not mind if women wear ties or suits, but it minds if men wear dresses; athletic women are accepted, but graceful men are frowned upon.

206 How Is 'Gender' Treated in Psychology?

Same-sex attraction is tolerated to a much greater level among women as compared to in men. Homosexuality is viewed as a greater violation of the male gender role than the female gender role, that is, men are more likely than women to be punished for being homosexual.

The application of social learning theory to sex-related differences suggests that as the norms change and the role models of a culture (e.g., in the media) change, gender differences will also change. As non-traditional roles for women and men have gained increased acceptance, the models for female and male roles have become more varied.

Gender Role Socialization

Social learning theory is believed to be the basis for gender role socialization theory. According to social learning theory, behaviour is a function of rewards and observational learning. According to gender role socialization, different people and objects in a child's environment provide rewards and models that shape behaviour to fit the gender role. Gender roles can be described as social norms or rules and standards that dictate different interests, responsibilities, opportunities, limitations and behaviours for men and women. Gender roles influence the various 'parts' that individuals play throughout their lives, from choice of clothing to occupation to leisure time activities. Men, women and other genders are treated differently and have diverse life trajectories as a result of their ascribed role and the degree to which they conform.

Boys are taught to be assertive and to control their expression of feelings, whereas girls are taught to express concern for others and to control their assertiveness. This encouragement may take the direct form of reinforcement or the indirect form of modelling. Gender role socialization may not only contribute to actual sex differences in behaviour but could also contribute to the appearance of sex differences. Women and men may distort their behaviour in ways to make them appear more consistent with traditional gender roles. This may explain why sex differences in empathy are greater for self-report measures than measures that are more objective. Studies suggest ways in which parents may treat girls and boys differently. For example, boys are more likely to be physically punished than girls (Zahn-Waxler & Polanichka, 2004). Other behaviours may be more subtle. One observational study showed that mothers spent more time watching boys and more time actively involved with girls (Clearfield & Nelson, 2006). Clearfield and Nelson concluded that parents could be sending the message that it is okay for boys to be independent whereas girls require assistance. One area in which parents may treat children differently is emotion. To the extent children model same-sex parent behaviour, girls learn to be more comfortable expressing emotion than boys do. In general, females are socialized to express their emotions, whereas males are socialized to conceal their emotions. The one exception is anger. Parents are more accepting of boys' than girls' expressions of anger (Zahn-Waxler & Polanichka, 2004). Aside from parents, siblings may influence gender role behaviour. One study showed that boys with older brothers and girls with older sisters were more sex-typed than only children (Rust et al., 2000). In addition, boys with older sisters and girls with older brothers were the least sex-typed and most androgynous of all. Peers too play an important role in socialization. Harris (1998) argues that the source of influence on children comes from outside the home, in particular, from the peer group. Toys, books and the media are other sources of information about gender roles. This theory promotes a conventional dualistic understanding of gender roles. This is problematic because they are not representative of the diversity that exists within and across populations. It also contributes to the discrimination of individuals who do not conform to these prescribed roles. Furthermore, the notion of gender as a role obfuscates the performative and distinctive nature of gender, instead suggesting a situated and static function (West & Zimmerman, 1987). It is criticized for its overemphasis on the developmental decisiveness of early childhood as the moment that gender socialization occurs. It also does not explicitly question the differential opportunities and constraints that are built into gendered socialization practices creating gendered individuals.

Social Role Theory

According to social role theory, differences in women's and men's behaviour are a function of the different roles women and men hold in our society (Eagly et al., 2000; Wood & Eagly, 2002). This is a variant of the gender role socialization theory. Whereas gender role socialization theory focuses on the individual and the environmental forces that shape the individual, social role theory focuses on society and how societal role structures shape behaviour across groups of people. That is, social role theory focuses on the more abstract social conditions of society rather than on the concrete ways that specific individuals (parents and teachers) behave with women and men. The gender role socialization theory is faulted for not taking into consideration the questions of power and privilege; for not asking why female socialization disadvantages women; and why male roles are associated with power while female roles are devalued.

The reasons why men and women occupy certain social roles are many, biological endowment being one. Men's greater size and strength give them priority in jobs requiring strength, especially upper body strength. Women's child-bearing and nursing obligations give them priority in roles involving the care of very young children and cause conflict with activities requiring absence from home for long periods of time. Thus, the particular activities that each sex performs, based on a combination of biological, social and ecological factors, determines its placement in the social structure. Men specialized in activities (e.g., warfare and herding) that yielded greater status, wealth and power, especially as society became more complex. Thus, when sex differences in status emerged, they tended to favour men. This feature of social structure is called the gender hierarchy or what feminists call patriarchy. Men's accommodation to roles with greater power and status tends to be associated with more dominant behaviour, and women's accommodation to roles with less power and status produces more subordinate behaviour. Dominant behaviour is controlling, assertive, directive and autocratic, and may involve sexual control. Subordinate behaviour is more compliant to social influence, less overtly aggressive, more co-operative and conciliatory and may involve a lack of sexual autonomy. Women and men also seek to acquire specific skills and resources linked to successful role performances by adapting their social behaviour to role requirements. Women's accommodation to the domestic role and to female-dominated occupations favours a form of behaviour termed as communal (Bakan, 1966) involving superior interpersonal skills and the ability to communicate non-verbally. In contrast, men's accommodation to the employment role, especially to male-dominated occupations, favours a pattern of assertive and independent behaviours termed as agentic.

Social role theory does not specify that women must be communal and men must be agentic. It simply states that the roles women and men hold in society are responsible for such sex differences in behaviour. However, most societies have organized women's and men's roles in a way so that women develop communal characteristics and men develop agentic characteristics. As men's and women's roles have become more similar in Western cultures, sex differences have decreased (Larson & Wilson, 2004). When males and females are provided with equal access to education, males and females take on more similar roles in society, such as females delay marriage and parenthood and take on the work role. Similar levels of education in females and males, however, do not always mean equality, especially if women are educated and oriented towards domestic roles and men are educated for paid employment roles.

The language of gender role presumes a stability of behaviour expected of women (or men) across their social contexts, their life cycles and whatever cultures and subcultures they might enter. This view of gender role has come under serious review by the more sociologically oriented perspectives.

Gender Schema Theory

A schema is a construct that contains information about the features of a category as well as its associations with other categories. We all have schemas for situations (e.g., marriages, funerals), for people (e.g., the Americans, the nerds) and for objects (e.g., animals, vegetables). The content of a schema varies among people. Those of us who are psychology students have more elaborate schemas for psychology than those of us who are not psychology majors. A gender schema includes our knowledge of what being female and male means and which behaviours, cognitions and emotions are associated with these categories. It is likely that all of us have gender schema, to some extent. Bem (1981) argues that gender is a pervasive dichotomy in society that guides our thinking about which clothes to wear, which toys to play with and which occupations to pursue. But there is variability among us in how readily we think of gender when processing information. The person who does not rely on male/female categories as a way of organizing the world is gender aschematic. This person is less likely to be concerned with the gender category both for one's own behaviour and for that of the other. It does not occur to them that it is not acceptable for a male to wear a skirt or girls to play with trucks.

Gender schema theory is a theory about the process by which we acquire gender roles; it is not a theory that describes the content of those roles. The theory simply states that we divide the world into masculine and feminine categories. The culture defines those categories. Gender schema theory combines elements of both social learning theory and cognitive development theory in describing how we acquire gender roles. Social learning theory explains how we acquire the features of the male and female gender categories and what we associate with those categories. Cognitive development theory describes how we begin to encode new information into these cognitive categories to maintain consistency. A child learns to invoke a gender role category or schema when processing new information.

Considering the Context: Deaux and Major's Model

Instead of focusing on how gender-related behaviour is acquired, like the other theories reviewed above, Deaux and Major (1987) focused on the conditions that create the display of gender-related behaviour. Thus, they incorporated the situation into their model of gender. Deaux and Major's model emphasizes three determinants of gender-based behaviour: (1) the perceiver's expectancies; (2) the target's (i.e., person who may or may not display the sex difference) self-concept; and (3) the situation (see Figure 5.1 for more details).

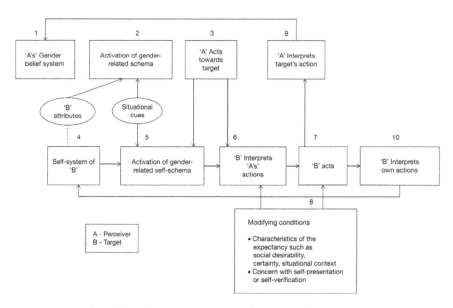

FIGURE 5.1 Models of social interaction in gender-related behaviour
Source: Adapted from Deaux and Major (1987).

The perceiver is the person observing the behaviour. The perceiver has an expectation about whether a person, the target, will display a behaviour. This expectation is likely to be confirmed by either cognitive confirmation or behavioural confirmation. Cognitive confirmation is the idea that we see what we want to see; it explains how two people can see the same behaviour and interpret it differently. Thus, the person who believes baby boys are more active than baby girls will probably maintain this belief despite numerous counter-examples because he or she is free to interpret a wide range of behaviour as active or inactive. Behavioural confirmation is the process by which a perceiver's expectation actually alters the target's behaviour. The target then confirms the perceiver's expectancy. For instance, a mother who believes that girls are more capable than boys of taking care of small children is likely to give her daughter more opportunities to take care of the new baby in the family. Thus, it will not be surprising if the daughter becomes more skilled than the son at feeding and entertaining the baby. The target in an interaction is the person whose behaviour is of interest. The target of an interaction influences whether she or he displays behaviour consistent with stereotypes about sex differences by two processes: self-verification and self-presentation. Self-verification is one's concern with behaving in ways consistent with one's self-concept. For a traditional male, it may be important to marry a woman less educated than him. Self-presentation is one's concern with how one's behaviour appears to others. A traditional male may show respect for women.

There are individual differences in concerns with self-presentation and self-verification. Self-monitoring is an individual difference variable that describes the extent to which one is more concerned with self-presentation or self-verification (Snyder, 1979). A high self-monitor is someone who changes his or her behaviour to fit the situation. A woman is ambitious and aggressive in the workplace while docile and submissive at home. This person is very much concerned with self-presentation. A low self-monitor typically behaves the same from one situation to the next. So that woman may act in the same way in both the workplace and at home. The low self-monitor is most concerned with self-verification.

The situation, however, will also influence whether we are more concerned with self-verification or self-presentation. If one's values are very strong, then one may be more concerned with adhering to one's principles and values and want to behave in a way that is consistent with them. If the issue is something one cares about strongly, one will stand firm in one's beliefs, no matter what the situation is. In some other situations, specifically the ones where one wants something from others, a person is highly likely to be concerned with how one appears to others. In such a situation, sometimes, even a low self-monitor may behave differently according to the situations.

Situations also differ in terms of behavioural constraints with respect to gender. For example, a patrilocal living arrangement, where the couple lives in the husband's house, has high behavioural constraints. The division of labour is highly gender-determined. Neolocal residence has comparatively low behavioural constraints and there is a greater ease in partners sharing household and childcare responsibilities.

REVIEW QUESTIONS

1. Why is a psychology of women needed?
2. What is the agenda of feminist politics in psychology?
3. What are the problems with biological theorizing of gender in psychology?

How Is Gender Understood in Psychology?

There are various understandings of gender in psychology. On one hand, it is treated as a variable of individual difference influenced by biology, intrapsychic processes and social context. On the other, it is understood as a social practice embedded in social institutions.

Gender as Difference

One of the first forms of empirical investigation of gender focused almost exclusively on behavioural sex differences between males and females. Debates about gender differences research continue to the present. At one level, the debate revolves around whether difference or similarity should be emphasized. For example, comparing women and men glosses over within-group differences, accentuates the importance of difference between groups over similarities, and reifies the categories of woman/man as having some explanatory standing on their own. Hyde (2005) has proposed an alternative approach, that is, gender similarities, not differences, are more scientifically appropriate to study. At another level, arguing difference/similarity masks the more pressing issues. In a cogent critique of differences research, Fine and Gordon (1989, p. 151) assert: 'This almost exclusive construction of gender-as-difference functions inside psychology as a political and scientific diversion away from the questions of power, social context, meaning, and braided subjectivities.' Indeed, gender as difference is the principal way gender is discussed and explained in popular culture discourse which, in turn, is absorbed into scientific discourse (Shields & Bhatia, 2009).

Differences between men and women have been largely explained in terms of internal factors, such as biological characteristics or traits. Gradually, with feminist thinking, a view emerged that socialization and societal expectations, not simply biology, were important in understanding why and how gender differences are produced. An excellent example of this theme is Eccles' works (1987, 1994), which exemplify how theory is made stronger when the question shifts from a gender differences perspective to one that examines gender in a social context. Instead of asking why women do not make the same career choices as men, Eccles (2011) asked, both then and now, why men and women make the choices they do. Her expectancy-value model (Eccles et al., 1983) complicated the idea that the reasons for making achievement-related decisions reside solely within the individual. She demonstrated how the social environment affects individuals' expectations of success, ideas about the importance of a task, and the perception of available options. Her model is different from Horner's work that has largely made internal attributions to explain gender differences in achievement and has significantly impacted the way social psychologists think about gender differences in achievement.

Gender as Personality

In an article published in 1979 in *American Psychologist*, Rhoda Unger described in detail the theoretical construct 'gender', which she defined as 'those characteristics and traits socio-culturally considered appropriate to males and females'. Like other feminist scholars of that time, Unger wanted to set aside social aspects of maleness and femaleness from biological mechanisms so that the former would become the focus of scientific scrutiny (Unger, 1979). In this sense, psychological gender is understood as stable traits (characteristics, interests, strengths, weaknesses) or roles (functions, tasks, activities) that men and women come to possess. Such research led to an extensive study and assessment of masculinity and femininity and androgyny (i.e., males and females who identified themselves as both masculine and feminine).

The Freudian version of gender psychology is also located in this framework. In it, gender is understood in terms of intrapsychic developments taking place from infancy to adolescence. The core idea was that male–female psychological differences were natural, deep-seated and of profound personal and social consequence. Furthermore, biological sex, gender identity, adherence to gender roles and sexual orientation were considered monolithic, that is, completely consistent with one another in 'normal' individuals. For example, the healthy and normal girl or woman identified herself as female, conformed to cultural expectations for appropriate feminine personality and demeanour, and was heterosexual. The same applied for the boy/man. These ideas, of course, built on already prevailing beliefs and had long-term effects for how gender was studied by psychologists.

This history of conceptualizing 'gender' as exclusively or primarily an aspect of personality masked the influence of situation in making gender salient. Social situations are saturated with differentiated role beliefs and expectations for how men and women should behave. For example, there are role expectations from a woman leader in an organization which are different from the male leader in the same organization. Women not wanting to have children and men wanting to pursue dance are seen as violating gender role beliefs. The power of beliefs about gender influences people's perception of, and expectations regarding, the behaviour of themselves and others.

Deaux and Major (1987) emphasized that the individual's gender repertoire was only one ingredient in any social situation. Other individuals with whom the person was interacting had their own expectations about the other person's behaviour and their own repertoire of gender-related attitudes, beliefs and behaviour. The situation, too, could be described as one that varied in how 'gendered' it was and in what ways it was gendered. For example, in both situations of a board meeting with only one token woman present or a heterosexual date, gender is salient, but observers and targets carry different gender-related expectations for each situation. Thus, whether gender-typed behaviour is observed depends on the interaction among person, observer and social context.

Gender Roles and Stereotypes

Within psychology, traits-based understanding of gender shifted towards the study of socially constructed gender roles and their stereotypical understanding. Research on androgyny showed that masculinity and femininity were differentially valued and the evaluations varied with the contexts in which they took place. Thus, researchers began to concentrate on how psychological gender is perceived and enacted. Here, gender precedes sex and gives meaning to our and other people's behaviours, feelings and thoughts as well as objects, social settings and contexts. An abundance of research has demonstrated the structural complexity of gender stereotypes and their power to influence others' perceptions (e.g., Eagly & Kite, 1987; Kite et al., 2008) and, in some circumstances, even recall of one's own behaviour (Robinson et al., 1998). Weisstein (1993) argues that the gendered attributes characterizing women – 'inconsistent, emotionally unstable, lacking in a strong conscience and superego, weaker, nurturant rather than productive, intuitive rather than intelligent, and if they are at all "normal", suited to the home and family' – add up to the description of a typical minority group stereotype of inferiority (Hacker, 1951).

Work in this domain has studied attitudes towards men's and women's roles which are referred to as 'gender ideologies' (Hochschild, 1989). Questions investigated in this regard are as follows: Do you think it is acceptable for women to work outside the home? Should men stay at home and look after children? A traditional gender ideology maintains that the proper sphere for women is the home and for men is work. An egalitarian gender ideology maintains that power is distributed equally between men and women and both identify equally with both spheres. A transitional attitude towards gender roles is that it is acceptable for women to devote energy to family and work domains, but women should hold proportionately more responsibility for the home, and men should focus more of their energy on work. Cultural and ethnic differences in gender role attitudes towards men and women are also investigated.

Sexism is also a much-researched topic in psychology. Traditional sexism includes endorsement of traditional roles for women and men, differential treatment of women and men, and the belief that women are less competent than men. Modern sexism, by contrast, includes the denial of any existing discrimination towards women, an antagonism to women's demands, and a resentment of any preferential treatment for women.

Psychologists hold that socialization and gender learning are the key mechanisms responsible for shaping the experience of having culturally defined, gender-specific behaviour, beliefs and attitudes. Feminist politics led to the understanding within psychology that gender ideologies are embedded in socio-structural systems. Earlier feminist psychologists had connected women's roles and socially sanctioned limits on women's behaviour to a broader system of patriarchal domination. Later, the intersections of gender with other socio-structural systems, such as class and race, also became important in the feminist enquiry. It also requires acknowledging what feminist psychologists have long asserted: There is always a political dimension to the study of behaviour, especially when that behaviour is overtly connected to the systems of power and status.

Mainstream psychology largely focuses on gender at the individual level. Its focus is on how gender identities are constructed through early childhood development, explicit socialization, modelling and adult experiences and internalization of social mores. It also studies how gender organizes the interactional expectations that every human being meets often in every moment of life. Women are expected to be more empathetic and nurturing, men to be more efficacious and agentic. Status expectations create a cognitive bias towards privileging men with agency and women with nurturance (Ridgeway, 2011). Cognitive bias of this sort helps to explain the reproduction of gender inequality in everyday life. It is less cognizant of the way gender structures social life not only by creating gendered selves and cultural expectations that shape interactions but also by organizing social institutions and organizations. As Acker (1990) and Martin (2004) have shown, work organizations embed gender meanings in the definition of jobs and positions. Women are often paid less than men for similar work (as in the Hindi film industry) and workplaces are often gendered, with certain departments and even entire occupations (e.g., school teaching or nursing) dominated by a particular gender. The conception of a valued worker – who is available 50 weeks a year, at least 40 hours a week, for decades on end – presumes that such a worker has no practical or moral responsibility for taking care of anyone but their own self.

PAUSE AND THINK

Design a small research study to examine gender stereotypes reflected in TV commercials. Take a sample of ten commercials and record for each of the characters his/her sex, appearance, role, personality traits and behaviour.

BOX 5.2 MOVING GENDER BEYOND INDIVIDUAL TRAITS

In psychology, there is a growing awareness of understanding gender beyond individuals, beyond socialization of gender roles and beyond gendered stereotypes that are expressed in action creating confirming evidence for those beliefs. This awareness is shaped by the following trends in the sociology of gender:

1. *The new structuralist framework in gender.* Kanter (1977) focused on the question of gender inequality rather than gender difference, as is typical in the case of psychology. She showed that organizational structures in the form of unequal opportunity, power and tokenism were at the core of gender inequality, not the differences in the patterns or personalities of women and men as individuals. Her research found that when women/men of colour and white majority men held organizational positions with little upward mobility and low organizational power, they all acted alike – low ambition and motivation at work, more controlling autocratic leadership style. This case study revealed that apparent sex and racial differences in leadership styles represent inequalities of power and status differentials, rather than their gendered/racial personalities. Similarly, women's choice of domestic- or work-focused lives depends more on structural factors related to marital stability and probability of their success in the workforce rather than their feminine selves. Epstein (1988) argued that if men and women were given the same opportunities and constraints, the differences between them would vanish.

2. *Doing gender framework.* West and Zimmerman (1987) argued that gender is something that we are held morally accountable to perform, something we do more than something we are. They opined that there is a performative link between bodies and gender. The sex category that one occupies does not always coincide with one's biological sex. Rather, it is established through 'required identificatory displays', which include but not limited to sex-specific clothing, hairstyles and appropriate behaviour. That is, to claim a sex category, men and women have to do gender. By conceptualizing gender as something that we do, they were able to draw attention to the ways in which behaviours are enforced, constrained and policed during social interaction. This perspective and Butler's (1990, 2004) conceptualization of gender performativity share the focus on the creation of gender by the activity of the actor. However, they differ on the ontological reality of the possibility of a self, outside the discursive realm. The social scientific perspective as advanced by West and Zimmerman (1987) sees the self as constructed; it presumes the existence of a self, even if temporarily. On the other hand, Butler, a philosopher and queer theorist, sees the self as an imaginary figment and deconstructs the possibility of even a temporary self outside of discourse. Qualitative research has provided a great deal of evidence that women and men do gender, but do so dramatically differently across time, space, ethnicity and social institutions.

3. *Intersectional framework.* During the 1980s and 1990s, feminists of colour were also theorizing about gender as something beyond a personality characteristic, with a focus on how masculinity, femininity and gender relations varied across ethnic communities and national boundaries. For example, Patricia Hill Collins (1990), Kimberlé Crenshaw (1989), Deborah King (1988) and Audre Lorde (1984) conceptualized gender as an axis of oppression intersecting with other axes of oppression, including race, sexuality, nationality, ability, and religion. They shared a goal of highlighting how social location within gender, race, sexuality, class, nationality and age must be understood interactively as opposed to studied as distinct domains of life. Ingraham specifically critiques feminist sociology for ignoring sexuality in studies of gender, resulting in concealment of 'the operation of heterosexuality in structuring gender (by closing off) any critical analysis of heterosexuality as an organizing institution' (1994, pp. 203–204).

An Integrative Approach: Gender as a Social Structure

Just as every society has a political and economic structure, so, too, every society has a gender structure (Risman, 1998, 2004). The gender structure differentiates opportunities and constraints based on sex category and has consequences on three dimensions: (1) at the individual level for the development of gendered selves; (2) during interaction as men and women face different cultural expectations even when they fill identical structural positions; and (3) in institutional domains where power and status differentials are gender-specific.

What Does the Sex Differences Paradigm Tell Us?

Are men and women different? Many sex comparisons have been made in cognitive abilities: Who has better spatial abilities? Who has greater aptitude in mathematics? Are women or men better with language? Sex comparisons have also been made in social–emotional–moral domains: Is one sex more empathic? Who helps more? Are men really more aggressive than women?

Psychological interest in sex differences was stimulated by the emergence of the functionalist movement in the United States in the late 1800s, which began to converge with a focus on intelligence (Shields, 1975). Ellis published a book, *Man and Woman: A Study of Human Secondary Sexual Characters* (1894), which called for a scientific approach to the study of the similarities and differences between men and women.

Popular ideas from phrenology and neuroanatomy were used to explain sex differences in the gross differences in size, structure and appearance of the brain. The advances in biological sciences led to an increased understanding of genetic and neurochemical factors responsible for physiological differences between the sexes which were, in turn, used to explain differences in psychological traits. For example, testosterone levels have been shown to play an active role in aggressive behaviour. Evolutionary and sociobiology theories have also been extensively used to support the conclusions drawn from such research.

The field is dominated by the gender difference model (GDM), which is shaped by and, in turn, reinforces the popular belief that men and women differ on several counts, biological as well as psychological. This model has been countered since the beginning of formal psychology by academics such as Helen Thompson Woolley (1910) and Leta Stetter Hollingworth (1914a). Building on such works, Jane Hyde (2005) formally presented what is known as the gender similarities hypothesis (GSH), which states that men and women are more similar than they are different in most respects. Maccoby and Jacklin's (1974) seminal work, *The Psychology of Sex Differences*, straddled both positions. Using a methodology that was an early precursor to meta-analysis, they looked at over 1,600 articles that examined gender differences across a number of domains. They wanted to document which of our beliefs about gender differences were supported by empirical evidence and which were not. In the end, they concluded that only four variables repeatedly showed significant gender differences: aggression, verbal ability, visual–spatial ability and mathematical ability. The remaining variables, which ranged from suggestibility and self-esteem to achievement motivation and learning styles, showed no significant differences. Interestingly, proponents of both GSH and GDM have used this landmark work to justify their theories (Hyde, 2005).

Lacunae in the Conceptualization of Gender in Psychology

An analysis of the body of work in sex differences paradigm reveals many lacunae in the conceptualization of gender.

- *Conflating gender and sex*: Psychology makes a clear distinction between gender and sex (even though this distinction is being challenged by feminists of late). But, in spite of the well-established distinction, the terms sex and gender are often used interchangeably in psychological research. Williams and Best (1986, p. 259) stated, 'While this (the distinction between sex and gender) appears to be a useful distinction, we use the terms interchangeably in this chapter.' Pryzgoda and Chrisler (2000), in their research on the ambivalence of these terms for the general public, concluded that people might feel more comfortable using 'gender' while thinking about sex. Gender is often used as a stand-in for 'sex' to refer to the biological body. Even the American Psychological Association is not consistent in its employment of these terms. For example, when submitting an article to be published in a scientific journal, the editor often replaces the phrase sex differences with gender differences. There is a good chance that the author is simply referring to differences between people who are biologically male versus biologically female without any thought to their psychological attributes (Helgeson, 2012). Thus, gender is reduced to a mere classifier that elicits comparisons between women and men. Wigginton (2017) provides an illustration of this conflation by reviewing studies of 'gender differences in tobacco use/cessation' on questions such as:

a   Has a working definition of gender been provided?
b   If 'gender' and 'sex' have been successfully differentiated?
c   Are there any major theories or ideas contributing to the major conceptual underpinnings of the study and do they support or undermine gender within the study?
d   Has gender been used as a category of analysis or is it simply one variable that has been analysed?
e   Have multilevel models been employed to see whether societal forces have an important role in causing the differences?
f   Has gender been categorized as a social construct?

These questions are a subset of the Feminist Quality Appraisal Tool (Morgan et al., 2016) designed to assess gender biases and inequities in research. It was found that none of the reviewed articles effectively differentiated sex and gender or defined gender, despite 'gender differences' being central to the research. Instead, authors frequently substituted information about a participant's sex (female/male as the dichotomous variable) with extrapolations made about men/ women as gendered subjects. Morgan observed that gender appeared to be a taken-for-granted category through which biological and social terminologies are conflated. She cited instances such as that of Ernster, Kaufman, Nichter, Samet and Yoon (2000), who in summarizing their findings state: 'While men and women differed on several key variables, the pattern of associations between psychological determinants of smoking was similar in the two sexes' (p. 97). Nakajima and al'Absi (2012) similarly conflate terminology: 'female and male smokers were comparable in demographic information, smoking history and biochemical measures except that men had higher BMI than women' (p. 634).

- *Individualism in gender research*: The persistence of the idea of individualism that characterizes modern American psychology may explain why gender became merely another word for sex in psychological research. As stressed by Morawski (1994) in her critique of the research on sex/gender categories, '[a sex] difference thus implies individualism through the equation of subjectivity with individual traits' (p. 156). Gender, like sex, has largely remained a variable of individual difference, a categorical independent variable positioned as an explanation for behaviour. Carolyn Sherif (1998) noted that the discipline of psychology did not seem ready to question the position of sex as an explanatory variable. It goes without saying that a person's sex is considered an independent variable, not a dependent one, despite the fact that everyone and no one knows what that means (Sherif, 1998, p. 65).

- *Sex and gender are seen as binaries*: The dichotomous view of sex and gender (male/female, men/women) implies that men and women are opposites. Thus, it disregards the fact that there is a great deal of overlap between these categories. For example, what of masculine females and feminine males? It overlooks the lived reality and identities of people occupying identity(ies) beyond the binaries, such as the intersex and transgendered people for whom sex and gender identities are not simply 'interchangeable'. The linear progression from biological sex to 'appropriate' gender identities (formation of cisgender identities) does not take place for many individuals. By not measuring gender appropriately and indeed not even reporting on the measurement of this variable, the sex/gender difference studies operate in discriminatory ways by privileging cisgender identities and making identities beyond the binary invisible. A tenth-century devotee of Shiva, Devara Dasimayya, wrote, 'If they see breasts and long hair coming, they call it woman; if beard and whiskers, they call it man. But look, the self that hovers in between is neither man nor woman.'
- *Essentialist understanding of gender*: When sex and gender are conflated, it promotes an essentialist view of gender where, like sex, gender is seen as a fixed and stable feature of the person and does not change depending on situation or context. In this conceptualization, gender is what you are. Even when gender is conceptualized as a social role in which people are socialized on the basis of their biological sex, it is seen as something relatively static and directly related to one's sex. Also, here gender is what you have – an internalized part of the individual due to social learning of cultural norms. It de-emphasizes the importance of social context in determining the way gender roles are lived out. Essentialism also implies that these sex/gender categories are real and natural and thus historically and universally invariant.
- *Biological differences in gender*: When the phrase 'sex differences' is used, it suggests that the difference is biological in nature. However, if a study of males and females is conducted (with no independent assessment of their gender roles) and results indicate that the females have better finger dexterity than males and males outperform females on video game score, can we conclude that such differences are due to biological factors alone? The answer is 'no'. Males and females come into the laboratory with their own values, histories and experiences, and their social status, gender roles and many other aspects will affect their behaviour. It makes for 'bad science' if psychological research fails to examine whether the difference is due to biological sex or gender roles or the circumstances in which people are located. Even aggression, for which there is a substantial agreement about the existence of sex difference, is partly due to biological sex and partly due to gender roles, that is, society's acceptance and encouragement of

aggression among males. Situational factors like fear of retaliation play a more important role in deterring aggression for women than for men.

When sex and gender are seen as inextricably interlinked with each other and gender is not just a cultural 'overlay' over biological sex (as discussed above), then the biological difference thesis does not hold water. Even sociobiologists cannot overlook the fact that the impact of any biological feature depends in every instance on how that biological feature interacts with the environment in which it is situated.

Since early times, biological essentialism within sex differences has been criticized. Mary Whiton Calkins (1896), Helen Bradford Thompson (1903) and Leta Stretter Hollingworth (1914b) all called for the investigation of the relationship between social environment and sex differences. However, this was largely ignored, and research drawing conclusions that are centred on women's innate inabilities in comparison to men continued.

- *Gender as a participant variable*: Due to the conceptualization of gender as a property of the individual, something that one 'is' or 'has', gender is treated merely as a participant variable in sex difference research (Wigginton, 2017). Those who observationally appear as belonging to the cisgender category are chosen to be studied in such researches. There is a little exploration of what gender means to a particular individual or how it intersects with certain expressions of oneself. For example, a girl may be chosen for the sample of girls as she 'appears' to belong to the gender of woman. However, when she is questioned about her level of body satisfaction as a woman, she counters that she does not feel feminine and her identity as an individual is more important to her than her gender (observation based on actual experience of conducting a qualitative study using interviews). Thus, an appearance-based atheoretical understanding of gender does not enable a consideration of how gender may be more or less salient for some participants.

Nigerian scholar Oyeronke Oyewumi (1997) asks the question: Did all societies at all times and in all places make male/female distinctions that sustained themselves over stable bodies? She argues that Western anthropologists, even feminists, failed to understand African society in its own terms, because they assumed that gender identities and hierarchies were universal: 'If the investigator assumes gender, then gender categories will be found whether they exist or not.' She makes a radical suggestion that gender as a category did not operate in any significant way in pre-colonial Yoruba and many other African cultures. She argues through her own work that among the Yoruba, seniority is the defining axis of hierarchy not gender. Yoruba language is gender-neutral.

When gender is conceptualized as a variable, we also lose out on acknowledging and analysing how gender intersects with other sociostructural factors such as race, class, (dis)ability(ies) and sexuality(ies).

- *Quantification of gender differences*: Carolyn Sherif (1998) argued that the 'orthodox methods of studying and interpreting sex differences were capable of delivering only mischievous and misleading trivia' (p. 58). Gender differences are usually measured in terms of their expressions in individual-level variables (e.g., coping mechanisms, self-concept, mathematical aptitude, etc.). Relationships between various 'variables' and gender as a dichotomous variable (often on the basis of sex data, i.e., male/female) are explored. According to Marecek (2001), quantifying gender or expressions of gender is based on the notion that gender is a 'locus of agency' that compels people to behave in gender-specific and gender-differentiated way. She points to the term 'gender effects' as an illustration of this (deterministic) conceptualization of gender as the cause of actions and ways of being. The quantitative study of gender differences has attracted feminist critiques. Fine and Gordon (1989) argued that focusing on gender differences produced through quantitative assessment and analysis diverts attention from questions of power, context, meaning and subjectivity. Quantification of gender serves to reify the 'aspects of personal experience which are ideologically constructed and born of inequality' (Fine & Gordon, 1989, p. 152). By partialling out the effects of gender, it also negates the intersectionality of gender with race, ethnicity, social class and other social realities. Feminists have also asked, How much difference is enough difference?
- *Overemphasis on gender differences rather than similarities*: The paradigm emphasizes sex differences rather than similarities, the likely consequence of this being strengthening of sex stereotypes and gender division in the society. Early work undertaken by women researchers failed to confirm the dominant theories of the time. For example, Leta Hollingworth and Helen Montagu examined the hospital length and weight records of 2,000 newborn boys and girls to test the Darwinian hypothesis that males were innately more vulnerable than females. They did not confirm this hypothesis. Helen Wooley Thompson (1903) examined the mental abilities of adult males and females in her first doctoral research on sex differences titled 'The Mental Traits of Sex' and repeatedly found more similarities than differences between them. However, these works were forgotten and rendered invisible in the history of psychology. Even modern work demonstrating sex similarities rather than sex differences tends to be altered, as it becomes part of psychology's official record. For example, Maccoby and Jacklin (1974) found few confirmed sex differences and more sex similarities in their landmark survey of sex differences studies. However, when discussed in introductory psychology textbooks, the few sex differences are much more apt to be mentioned and detailed than the sex similarities (Unger, 1979). Hyde and McKinley (1997) referred to the file drawer problem that prevails in the meta-analytic studies designed to seek out sex differences. Studies that do not find sex differences are not published and end up in investigator's file drawers.

222   How Is 'Gender' Treated in Psychology?

Another problem of the focus on differences between men and women is that it takes the attention away from the wide variation that exists within men and women categories. Researchers who believe that two sexes are more similar than different are known as the minimalists. The minimalists believe that any differences in behaviour observed between men and women might be due to the roles they hold or the situations in which they find themselves.

- *Female inferiority*: The sex differences are situated within a power discourse. In modern societies, as well as societies in the past, women are subordinate to men. Therefore, traits attributed to the category 'female' tend to be viewed as inferior as compared to male. Galton concluded, 'women tend in their capacities to be inferior to men' (cited in Lewin & Wild, 1991, p. 582). The conclusions highlighting women's inferiority in relation to men and claims to male superiority have been historically grounded in explanations provided by evolutionary theory. Within evolutionary theory, the focus on variability – deviations from the average or norm – which was argued to be greater in men than women, was taken as support for the variability hypothesis that men were naturally more progressive than women.
- *Androcentric bias*: The concept of androcentrism was first articulated in the early twentieth century by Charlotte Perkins Gilman, who wrote in *The Man-Made World; Or, Our Androcentric Culture* (1911):

[A]ll our human scheme of things rests on the same tacit assumption; man being held the human type; woman a sort of accompaniment and subordinate assistant, merely essential to the making of people. She has held always the place of a preposition in relation to man. She has always been considered above him or below him, before him, behind him, beside him, a wholly relative existence – 'Sydney's sister', 'Pembroke's mother' – but never by any chance Sydney or Pembroke herself ... It is no easy matter to deny or reverse a universal assumption ... What we see immediately around us, what we are born into and grow up with ... we assume to be the order of nature ... Nevertheless ... what we have all this time called 'human nature' ... was in great part only male nature ... Our androcentric culture is so shown to have been, and still to be, a masculine culture in excess, and therefore undesirable.

(pp. 20–22)

Androcentrism is the privileging of males, male experience and the male perspective. On the one hand, it is about:

[T]reating males as the main characters in the drama of human life around whom all action revolves and through whose eyes all reality is to be interpreted, and the treating of females as the peripheral or marginal characters in the drama of human life whose purpose for being is defined only in relation to the main – or male – character. Alternatively, one could also say that androcentrism is the treating of the male as if he were some kind of universal, objective, or neutral representative of the human species, in contrast to the female who is some kind of a special case – something different, deviant, extra, or other.

(Bem, 2008)

According to Tavris (1993, p. 149):

In any domain of life in which men set the standard of normalcy, women will be considered abnormal … Many women experience tremendous conflict in trying to decide whether to be like men or opposite from them, and this conflict in itself is evidence of the implicit male standard against which they are measuring themselves. This is why it is normal for women to feel abnormal. Because of such understanding, much of the research in psychology is designed to find out why women are not like men, as intelligent, as moral, as rational. It is also the view underlying the enormous self-help industry advising women to be more beautiful, more competent, more independent/ dependent. Men, being normal, feel no need to fix themselves in corresponding ways.

Tavris (1993) uses the example of self-esteem research to highlight the androcentric norm in sex difference research. In the study asking women and men to predict their scores on a creativity test (Olson, 1988), women were found to be estimating at a lower level than men. Keeping the men's results as the standard of performance, the question posed in the research was why women do not behave like men. It was concluded that women do not value their efforts, have self-esteem problems and are not as confident as men. However, if women's performance was kept as the standard of evaluation, then there would be a different question: Why do men make higher estimations of their scores? Then the notion of the problem would change. Then men will be seen as conceited, overvaluing their work and as over-confident. Further analysis of these results have also indicated that women's predicted score shows lower discrepancy from the actual score received by them, while men's predicted score shows greater discrepancy, usually in the direction of over-estimation, from the actual score. This again indicates that men are less realistic in their assessments of their performance. Thus, it leads to another associated limitation of such studies that the findings of sex differences are interpreted in the light of the kinds of questions posed.

Tavris (1993) argues that most people will see at once that this way of talking about men is derogatory and biased. But the point is why such a derogatory tone while discussing men is considered a problem. It is because while it is acceptable to compare women against men, constructing the difference as weakness or deficiency, it is not acceptable to compare men against women and see men as lacking.

- *Futility of the sex difference question*: Crawford and Marecek (1989) question the very relevance of asking the literal and limited question: Do men and women differ? They support the agenda of asking a different set of questions: Why is everyone so interested in differences? Which differences are people interested in? What functions do the beliefs in these differences serve? For example, we might ask what is the result of the belief that women's professional performance is affected by their hormones, which is not the case for men? What is the result of the belief that men are less emotionally expressive than women? This view asks us to consider where our theories come from, who benefits from them and where do they lead us? Feminists support shifting the focus from sexual difference to sexual inequality and asking what kinds of social institutions support the subordination and inferiority of women.

In a nutshell, gender in psychology is primarily understood as a binary and a fixed attribute of an individual. It renders invisible the fluidity of gender identities and heterogeneous forms of sexuality. Although there is an awareness of the social context impacting gender, biological explanations are often invoked to rationalize differences between women and men. From the twentieth century onwards, the hormonal conception of the body has become one of the dominant modes of thinking about the root of sex differences. As Oudshoorn (1994) points out, the hormonal conception of the body in fact allows for the possibility of breaking out of the tyranny of the binary sex difference model. That is, if bodies can have both female and male hormones, then maleness and femaleness are not restricted to one kind of body alone. However, the biomedical sciences prefer to treat the presence of androgen in female bodies and oestrogen in male bodies as abnormal. Further, the female, but not the male, is portrayed as a body completely at the mercy of hormones. The political and scientific implications of research beset with such limitations are huge. This focus on biological differences takes attention away from androcentric institutionalism. It stalls the possibility of social change. It also transforms male–female difference into female inferiority. Naomi Weisstein (1993, p. 197) opines:

> [T]he idea of the nature of human possibility that rests on the accidents of individual development or genitalia, or what is possible today because of what happened yesterday, on the fundamental myth of sex organ causality, has strangled or deflected psychology so that it is relatively useless in describing, explaining or predicting humans and their behaviours. It then goes without saying that present psychology is less than worthless in contributing to a vision that can truly liberate – men as well as women.

BOX 5.3 GENDER BINARISM IN PSYCHOLOGY

Psychological research is replete with stagnant notions of gender and sex that contrast masculine males with feminine females. It focuses on studying the cisgender individuals. An example of how gender binarism operates in psychology is transsexualism. A transsexual person is one whose external genitalia and secondary sex characteristics are of one sex but whose personal identification is that of the opposite sex. S(he) desires medical assistance to transition from one gender to another. The first male-to-female and female-to-male surgical and hormonal experiments began after the Second World War. Christine Jorgensen, a former US soldier, made headline news in 1952 after receiving a sex change operation and breast implants in Denmark.

The first wave of male-to-female and female-to-male pioneers often adopted extreme versions of gender stereotypes in order to legitimize their transition. The criterion for eligibility for sex reassignment has been based on binary gender and heterosexism. The assumption of binary gender implies that transgender people are transitioning from one end to the other end of the gender binary (male-to-female; female-to-male). The assumption of heterosexism implies that one had to be either a woman who desired men or a man who desired women. In such a model, intermediate and novel sex/gender performances and bodies, such as biological males cross-dressing and living as women with breast implants, but not seeking genital implants, are not possible.

Queer activists have been arguing that as long as gender surgeries and therapies remain within a therapeutic model, however, instead of part of a body modification or self-expression model, it will be very difficult for transgendered people to pursue non-normatively postgender bodies (Oudshoorn, 1994). Dean Spade (2006), a female-to-male transgender attorney, wrote that the medical model of 'gender identity model' inherent in psychology has its drawbacks:

> First, the medical approach to gender variance, and the creation of transsexuality, have resulted in a governance of trans bodies that restricts our ability to make gender transitions which do not yield membership in a normative gender role. The self determination of trans people in crafting our gender expression is compromised by the rigidity of the diagnostic and treatment criteria. At the same time, these criteria and the version of transsexuality that it posits produce and reify a fiction of normal, healthy gender that works as a regulatory measure for the gender expression of all people. To adopt the medical understanding of transsexuality is to agree that SRS [sex reassignment surgery] is the unfortunate treatment of an unfortunate condition, to accept that gender norm adherence is fortunate and healthy, and to undermine the threat to a dichotomous gender system which trans experience can pose. The reification of the violence of compulsory gender norm adherence, and the submission of trans bodies to a norm-producing medical discipline, is too high a price for a small hope of conditional tolerance.

226 How Is 'Gender' Treated in Psychology?

In light of this, the postgender movement argues that gender is an arbitrary and unnecessary limitation on human potential and foresees the elimination of involuntary biological and psychological gendering in the human species through the application of neurotechnology, biotechnology and reproductive technologies. They do not call for the end of all gender traits, or universal androgyny, but rather that those traits become a matter of choice. For example, assisted reproduction will make it possible for individuals of any sex to reproduce in any combinations they choose, with or without 'mothers' and 'fathers'. Thus, bodies and personalities in a postgender future will no longer be constrained and circumscribed by gendered traits, but enriched by their use in the palette of diverse self-expression.

REVIEW QUESTION

What conceptual challenges does the sex differences paradigm throw up?

In What Way Do Sex Differences Operate in Moral and Social Development?

In a Different Voice: Differences in Moral Reasoning

Carol Gilligan's influential book *In a Different Voice* (1982) delves into the repeated exclusion of women from the critical theory-building studies of psychological research. In particular, she points to a disparity between women's experience and the existing models of human growth and thereby construing it as a 'riddle' or as 'inferior', most notably in the works of Sigmund Freud, Jean Piaget and Kohlberg. In doing so, it points to and remedies 'a problem in the representation, a limitation in the conception of human condition, an omission of certain truths about life' (Gilligan, 1982, p. 2).

Freud concluded that women 'show less sense of justice than men, that they are less ready to submit to the great exigencies of life, that they are more often influenced in their judgments by feelings of affection or hostility' (1925, pp. 257–258). Piaget (1932) notes that girls are more tolerant in their attitudes towards rules, more willing to make exceptions and more easily reconciled to innovations. As a result, the legal sense, which Piaget considers essential to moral development 'is far less developed in little girls than in boys' (p. 77). Lawrence Kohlberg's (1958, 1981) six-stage theory (see stages 1–3 in Table 5.1), describing the development of moral judgement from childhood to adulthood is based empirically on a study of 84 boys whose development Kohlberg followed for a period of over 20 years. The exclusion of women's experience in the building of the theory resulted in the devaluation of their moral abilities in the

TABLE 5.1 Kohlberg's stages of moral development

	Stage	Behaviour
1	Pre-conventional stage	Concern for consequences; fear of punishment, obedience
		Concern for consequences; motivated for rewards
2	Conventional stage	Conformity to others' expectations to; concern with disapproval
		Adherence to legitimate authority; emphasize rules and justice
3	Post-conventional stage	Concern with community respect; focus on law
		Developing internal standards; moral principles

Source: Helgeson (2012, p. 129).

Kohlbergian scheme of morality. When measured by his scale, women's judgement seems to exemplify the third stage of his six-stage sequence, thereby marking them as deficient. At the third stage, morality is conceived in interpersonal terms and goodness is equated with helping and pleasing others. Kohlberg and Kramer (1969) consider this conception of goodness to be functional in the lives of mature women insofar as their lives revolve around household. The implication of this is that only if women enter the traditional arena of male activity will they recognize the limitations of this form of moral reasoning and move towards more advanced stages where relationships are subordinated to rules (stage 4) and rules to universal principles of justice (stages 5 and 6).

Gilligan highlights the paradox that the markers of 'goodness' of women, that is, the very qualities of care and sensitivity to others also mark them as deficient in moral development. Thus, the relational bias in women's thinking has been seen to compromise their moral judgement and impede their development. In this version of moral development, however, the conception of maturity is derived from the study of men's lives, and it reflects the importance of individuation in their development. She argues that as long as the categories by which the development is assessed are derived within a male perspective from male research data, divergence from the masculine standard can only be seen as a failure of development.

Her project is to recover a different voice located in the feminine experience and construction of self and morality. She argues that a different outline of moral conception begins to emerge when one studies women's experience and produces developmental constructs from their lives. She argues that it is important to go beyond the question: How capable are women of engaging in the abstract and hypothetical construction of reality? It is important to identify the frequently occurring real-life moral dilemmas that encompass women's life and their characteristic forms of thinking. These will be the issues where women have the power to choose and thus are willing to speak in their own voice. Gilligan made use of the issue of birth control and abortion, as this is a personally relevant issue in which the woman has a right to choose for herself

228 How Is 'Gender' Treated in Psychology?

but such a choice also brings her into conflict with the conventions of femininity, particularly the equation of goodness with self-sacrifice. This conception of morality is concerned with the activity of care and centres on the understanding of relationships and responsibility. It differs from the Kohlbergian conception of morality as fairness tied to the understanding of rights and rules. This different construction of the moral problem by women may be seen as the critical reason for their failure to develop within the constraints of Kolhberg's system. The morality of rights differs from the morality of responsibility in its emphasis on separation rather than connection and consideration of the individual rather than relationship. By taking the example of two respondents, a 25-year-old male from Kohlberg's study and 25-year-old woman from her own study, Gilligan showed the gender differences in the construction of moral dilemma. Men focus on how to exercise one's rights without interfering with the rights of others, while women construct the moral dilemma as how to lead a moral life that includes obligations to herself and her family and people in general. She asserts, 'The psychology of women that has consistently been described as distinctive in its greater orientation toward relationships and interdependence implies a more contextual mode of judgment and a different moral understanding' (Gilligan, 1982, p. 22).

The abortion dilemma, in particular, has revealed the existence of a distinctive moral language of women, the language of selfishness and responsibility which defines the moral problem as one of obligation to exercise care and avoid hurt. Infliction of hurt is considered selfish and immoral in its reflection of unconcern while the expression of care is seen as the fulfilment of moral responsibility. In the development sequence that follows, women's moral judgement proceeds from an initial focus on self at the first level to the discovery of responsibility and caring for others at the second level. However, when goodness is construed solely in terms of care for others, the logical inequality between the self and other and the psychological violence that it engenders create the disequilibrium that initiates the transition to the next level. The transition is marked by the woman separating the voice of the self from those of others and asking if it is possible to be responsible to herself as well as to others and thus to reconcile the disparity between hurt and care. This leads to the establishment of a new equilibrium that dissipates the tension between selfishness and responsibility. By elevating non-violence – the injunction against hurting – to a principle governing all moral judgement and action, she is able to assert a moral equality between self and other. Care then becomes a universal obligation, the self-chosen ethic of a post-conventional judgement that reconstructs the dilemma in a way that allows the assumption of responsibility for choice.

Gilligan's postulation of a different voice, while celebrated, has also been critiqued for its implication that women might be a naturally existing homogeneous category comprised of those who speak with the same voice in spite of numerous markers of difference such as age, class, (dis)ability, ethnicity and sexuality.

Who Am I? Differences in Social Development

Erik H. Erikson proposed a timetable of identity development in his stage theory of psychosocial development. According to this theory, one must have established a firm identity before one can establish a truly intimate relationship. People who study gender disagree with the sequence proposed by Erikson in which the stage of identity precedes the stage of intimacy. Some researchers have argued that Erikson's sequence may describe men's social development better than women's social development (Gilligan, 1982; Marcia, 1993) because women are more likely to experience identity and intimacy simultaneously. That is, part of women's identity is their relationship with others. Thus, women's and men's social development may follow different courses. Studies have shown a stronger relation between identity and intimacy development in men than in women because intimacy is as likely to precede as to follow identity development in women (Orlofsky, 1993). A study of high school students showed that identity issues were more salient than intimacy issues in both male and female decision-making (Lacombe & Gay, 1998). However, female students were more likely than male students to merge the two concerns.

PAUSE AND THINK

Design an experiment to see the effect of situational expectations in creating gender differences in task performance. Take two equivalent forms of spatial and verbal tests. In the control condition, let the boys and girls perform on one spatial and one verbal test with no instructions. In the experimental condition, speak about how girls usually perform well on verbal tests and boys perform well on spatial tests and then allow participants to work. Use the same sample of girls and boys or take equivalent groups. Compare the scores of the girls and boys in the two conditions. Assess whether the scores differ significantly between the two conditions.

How Does Freudian Psychoanalysis Conceptualize Sexual Difference?

> [All] human individuals, as a result of their bisexual disposition and of cross-inheritance, combine in themselves both masculine and feminine characteristics, so that pure masculinity and femininity remain theoretical constructions of uncertain content.
>
> *(Freud, 1925)*

Freudian psychoanalysis is one of the most influential accounts of gender. However, as is clear from the quote above, Freud saw the impossibility of conceptualizing masculinity and femininity as stable, coherent and reified entities. In spite of this disclaimer, Freud developed an elaborate edifice of theorization regarding the development of a gendered self among men and women and the subsequent emergence of heterosexuality. The theory is said to be born out of the womb of hysteric women as its premises were developed out of Freud and Breuer's clinical work with women patients suffering from hysteria. However, he acknowledged that he was baffled by the 'riddle' of femininity and regarded feminine sexuality as the 'dark continent' of psychoanalysis. Nonetheless, his ideas on the matter formed the foundation on which subsequent generations of thinkers have built their perspectives on sexual difference.

For Freud, all children are bisexual to begin with. In the beginning of child development, there are few psychical differences between boys and girls. Both little girls and boys begin their lives as sexual beings, where sexuality is primarily autoerotic, polymorphous and is primarily incestuous. They enter the phallic stage with their mother as the first love object. Phallic here implies active sexuality discovered by both boys and girls through masturbation. The boy's phallic sexuality is centred on his penis and will always be his penis after the Oedipus complex. However, for the girl, it is her clitoris that is considered her phallic organ during this phase. According to Freud, phallic sexuality in children during this phase does not relate to reproduction, which is why the clitoris and not the vagina is the central organ for girls at this moment. Although children understand that there are differences between men and women, boys and girls, they do not yet attribute these differences to genitalia.

Around the age of 5, both boys and girls enter their Oedipus complex and the lives of both sexes begin to diverge from a seeming sameness into something quite different. Sexual differentiation begins to take place. The Oedipus complex is a family complex, involving mother, father and child. Although both boys and girls endure an Oedipus complex, they do not experience it similarly. The end result is entirely different for each sex.

Development of Masculinity

During the phallic stage, the penis is the focused erotogenic zone, thus increasing the likelihood of the boy being caught masturbating, which is a frowned-upon act. Quite frequently, no heed is taken to the castration threats since they seem unbelievable. This threat, however, gains strength by the presence of the father, who appears on the scene of the mother–child dyad as a rival (third figure) in the fantasized sexual union with the mother. The boy realizes that he cannot compete with the superior phallic authority of the father for exclusive love of the mother, and that, were he to continue desiring his mother, he may face castration as a form of punishment at the hands of the father. Also, sighting that his sister/girl playmates do not have a penis like him leads him to the realization that the potential loss of the penis is possible. In *The Dissolution of the Oedipus Complex*, Freud (1924) writes, 'More or less plainly, more or less brutally, a threat is pronounced that this part of him which he values so highly will be taken away from him.' Threats of taking away something valued are quite familiar to the child since the child remembers having to give up the mother's breast as well as one's own faeces at one point. The boy sees that the girl does not have a penis and he believes that she was castrated as a form of punishment and, in fact, all women, including his mother, are castrated beings.

The fear of losing his penis, an organ with heavy narcissistic investment, is what brings the boy to give up his Oedipal position – the desire to possess the mother and supplant the father, his rival. For 'normal' masculinity to occur, the little boy learns to give up the mother as a sexual object due to the fear of castration. He also begins to perceive the body of the mother as inferior to the male body, since it lacks the male genital organ. He learns to accept the superiority of the father and tries to identify with him, in order to find his own future place in the triad, and in the larger social structure. Normal development of masculinity entails that the son hopes to find someone like the mother if he becomes a man like his father. The Oedipus complex, or the incestuous desire of the little boy for the mother, is thus repressed, if not completely abolished by the threat of castration. The superego, the guardian of social, moral, cultural and religious values, is formed. Any remaining Oedipal desire will find its place in the id, where it will persist in the form of an unconscious desire whose manifestation will usually only be made visible through dreams.

The other two pathways that Freud spoke of for the little boys to the castration threat are fetishism and homosexuality.

Development of Femininity

Freud seems genuinely puzzled by how femininity comes about: Given the girl's prehistory of love and attachment to the mother, why would she switch allegiances to the father as the sexual object? And since, prior to genital organization, she too goes through a phallic (masturbatory) stage, why would she switch the site of bodily pleasure from the clitoris to the vagina? These are among the mysteries he designates as the riddle of femininity. In Freud's later writings on femininity, including *Femininity* (1933), *Female Sexuality* (1931) and 'Some Psychological Consequences of the Anatomical Distinction between the Sexes' (1925), Freud postulates that the little girl's Oedipal complex runs a different course than the little boy's and holds a different relation to castration anxiety.

Upon sighting a boy's genitals, the girl experiences a feeling of inadequacy and inferiority on her part, since she does not possess a penis. She understands that her own small clitoris, which she thought was a valuable organ, is unworthy of the comparison to the boy's sex organ. She reluctantly accepts her 'castrated' status. Freud writes:

> When the little girl discovers her own deficiency, from seeing a male genital, it is only with hesitation and reluctance that she accepts the unwelcome knowledge … When she comes to understand the general nature of this characteristic, it follows that femaleness – and with it, of course, her mother – suffers a great depreciation in her eyes.
>
> *(Freud, 1931, p. 233)*

232 How Is 'Gender' Treated in Psychology?

This knowledge represents an irreducible narcissistic wound to which the girl child cannot easily resign. She envies the penis and wishes to possess it. Indeed, the girl child continues for a long time to hope that one day she will find herself endowed with a 'true' penis, that is, her own tiny organ will develop and will be able to hold its own in a comparison with the one which the male child (brother or other male playmates) has. While waiting for such hopes to be confirmed, she turns her desires towards her father, wanting to obtain from him what she lacks – the very precious male organ. This envy leads her to turn away from her mother, whom she blames for not giving her a penis. The little girl also realizes that all women, including her mother, share the same fate of being castrated. Furious with and contemptuous of her mother, her first 'sexual' object, she abandons her to enter into the Oedipus complex, or the desire for her father. Thus, the girl's Oedipus complex – her incestuous desire for the father – follows the castration complex, inverting the sequence observed for the boy. Castration complex for the boy is a threat of loss, the fear of a not-yet-accomplished act, whereas, for the girl, it is a *fait accompli*: an amputation already done. For the boy, the threat of the loss of the penis brings the Oedipus complex to a resolution. The resolution of the Oedipal complex in the woman is a long-drawn-out process requiring transformations that are much more complicated and difficult than the linear process in the boy. The repeated refusals of the father and the repeated frustrations that she experiences vis-à-vis the father lead her to deflect her desire away from him. The girl realizes that she can never have a penis but can have a male child which will be the penis equivalent. The woman learns to privilege the reproductive function and sees the male child as the bearer of the longed-for penis substitute. This marks the transformation of the active desire to have a penis to the passive receptivity that is expected of women's sexuality. For this transformation to take place, the girl has to change her erogenous zone as well. The 'penile' clitoral erogenous zone has to relinquish its importance in favour of the vagina, which 'is now valued as the place of shelter for the penis; it enters into the heritage of the womb' (Freud, 1923, p. 145). Of course, it is not by her father that the little girl will in reality have a child. She will have to wait until much later for this infantile desire to be achieved. And it is this refusal that the father opposes to all her desires that underlies the motif of the transfer of her drives onto another man, who will finally be a paternal substitute.

Freud believed that such psychological manoeuvres were difficult to achieve and likely to fail. Woman's masculine claims would never be entirely resolved and penis envy would continue to play a role in her psychic drama. Also, penis envy would account for many peculiarities of otherwise 'normal' femininity, for example, 'a larger amount of narcissism' than the man, 'physical vanity', 'little sense of justice' and even 'shame'. Among the pathological trends of femininity, Freud mentions female homosexuality, frigidity, masochism and hysteria.

How Is 'Gender' Treated in Psychology? **233**

After all that Freud said about femininity, he insists that he has not got beyond the 'prehistory of women'. Whatever he may have said or written on the sexual development of women, that development remains quite enigmatic to him, and he makes no claim to have got to the bottom of it.

Feminist Objections to the Freudian Theory of Gender Development

Freudian psychoanalysis has come in for serious review by a range of theorists, a large number of them being feminists, who have worked on its limits, impasses and possibilities.

The pivotal thesis around which Freud elaborates sexual difference is the 'idea of castration': the realization that women do not have a penis. This affects each sex differently and thereby accounts for the difference between them: Boys wish to protect their narcissistic possession and so give up their Oedipal wish for the mother; girls recognize their lack and turn away from the mother and towards the father who can give them the penis in the familiar equation (penis = baby). This thesis grounds masculinity and femininity within the bipolar structure of activity–passivity, subject–object, whereby femininity usually occupies the subordinate pole of passivity and object. Many feminist objections flow from such an understanding:

- The 'normal' resolution of the Oedipus complex for both the little boy and little girl hinges on viewing the mother as a 'castrated' and lesser being. This is supposed to turn the boy and the girl towards the father and into the reproduction of patriarchy generation after generation. The mother is completely denigrated in the resolution of the Oedipus complex. The mother, who carried and gave birth to these children, and was the first love object for the nurturing she provided, must be abandoned by children of both sexes in order for the patriarchal pact to be made.
- Freud postulates that it is the realization that the beloved mother is castrated that prompts the little girl to turn her love towards her father. Feminists question, why is the discovery that she does not have a penis such a trauma to a girl in the first place? It appears that Freud was remarkably incurious about the background of this reaction.
- Since castration does not resolve the Oedipal complex but leads the girl to enter it, Freud claims that it is never wholly brought to a conclusion or demolished, thus accounting, in his view, for girls' weaker superegos and lesser capacity for sublimation:

The fact that women must be regarded as having little sense of justice is no doubt related to the predominance of envy in their mental life; for the demand for justice is a modification of envy and lays down the condition subject to which one can put envy aside ... There are no paths open to further development; it is as though the whole process had already run its

234 How Is 'Gender' Treated in Psychology?

course and remains thenceforward insusceptible to influence – as though, indeed, the difficult development of femininity had exhausted the possibilities of the person concerned.

(Freud, 1933, pp. 134–135)

Freudian narrative is that of female inferiority. Although he recognized that activity and passivity could not simply be equated with masculinity and femininity, respectively, nor could passive aims be equated with passivity, Freud did not consistently avoid this pitfall as is evident from his observation that, for the girl, abandonment of the clitoris 'clears the phallic activity out of the way, smooths the ground for femininity' (Freud, 1933, p. 128).

- The boy's Oedipal story is more seamless and continuous since he retains his organ of phallic pleasure (the penis), and, although he must displace the immediate object of his desire (the mother), he can look forward to substitute objects (someone like her). But the girl's Oedipal complex is necessarily more complicated. The girl turns from her mother not in fear but in contempt and because of envy for what the mother does not possess. The father represents for her neither a threat (she finds herself already castrated) nor the prospect of a fulfilled desire in the future (the only replacement for the missing penis is a child of her own), as he does for the boy who can identify with him and hope to eventually have what he has. In the trajectory of the girl's Oedipal complex, femininity is realized as the passive desire to be the object of masculine desire so as to gain the desired child as the penis substitute. This is the reason for the shift of the site of sexuality for mature, heterosexual women from the clitoris to the vagina.
- Freud's androcentrism is clear from the way he referred to libido as masculine; recognized 'the little girl is a little man'; equated masculinity with active aims and femininity with passive aims. He stated:

With their entry into the phallic phase ... We are now obliged to recognize that the little girl is a little man. In boys, as we know, this phase is marked by the fact that they have learnt how to derive pleasurable sensations from their small penis and connect its excited state with their ideas of sexual intercourse. Little girls do the same thing with their still smaller clitoris.

(Freud, 1933, pp. 117–118)

- In fact, the story of Oedipality for the little girl cannot be told in Freudian theory except in comparison and contrast to the story of the little boy.
- Feminists also question whether in the classical theory, masculinity and femininity are defined by object choice, whom we love. Normal development of masculinity and femininity rests on the little boy retaining the original love object (mother) and the little girl shifting her allegiance to the father. In this sense, normality is equated with heterosexuality where desire

flows towards a person of the opposite sex while all other outcomes are treated as pathological.

- Freud (1924, p. 178) pronounced, 'anatomy is destiny' – a view that has been vehemently critiqued by most feminists. Simone de Beauvoir (1949) claimed that Freud slighted women in his theory and falsely credited anatomy for male supremacy in culture and public life. She argued, instead, that social factors explained the observable characteristics and relationships of the sexes.

What Do Feminist Thinkers Have to Say About Freudian Psychoanalysis?

There is a parallel body of work of feminist thinkers who have critiqued and reformulated the Freudian theory on gender in order to address the objections mentioned above.

Karen Horney

Karen Horney was the first to refuse to subscribe to Freud's point of view on female sexuality. She suggested various refutations and reversals to Freud's claim on the subject. Horney (1967) objected to the essential elements of Freud's formulations that were biased and unacceptable such as the idea that the vagina was unknown to both sexes, 'primary penis envy' as a motive and the 'secondary' derivation of the Oedipus complex, that is, of heterosexuality.

- *Discovery of the vagina*: Freud maintains that the feminine vagina is undiscovered by children of both sexes until the phallic stage. Karen Horney refutes this and suggests that the girl has already discovered her vagina. The relationship of the little girl to her vagina cannot be described in terms of ignorance but in terms of 'denegation', that is, the girl may appear not to know consciously what she knows. This 'denegation' of the vagina by the little girl would be justified by the fact that knowledge of that part of her sex has not been sanctioned at this stage and also by the fact that this knowledge is dreaded. Her belief was that the boy too 'instinctively divines the existence' of the vagina (Horney, 1967, p. 66).
- *Innate heterosexuality*: Horney disputes that it is 'penis envy' which turns the girl away from her mother, who does not have one, and leads her to father, who might give her one. She rejects the idea that the girl desires to be a man and to have a penis in order to be (like) a man. In fact, she argues that no explanation for a girl's turning to her father is needed. It is simply 'the manifestation of so elementary a principle of nature as that of mutual attraction of the sexes' (Horney, 1967, p. 68), that is, an expression of an innate heterosexuality which develops spontaneously in a girl.

236 How Is 'Gender' Treated in Psychology?

- *Disputing the primary role of penis envy in feminine sexuality*: In Horney's opinion, the spontaneously occurring 'womanly and maternal developments' take a different route. She argues for the presence of a specifically feminine desire for incestuous relations with the father. But because the girl child is frustrated in her feminine desire that she reaches the point of penis envy and secondarily of coveting the penis/baby as a substitute for the father. The feminine desire for incestuous relations with the father presupposes that the girl has already discovered her vagina and she wishes as much as fears the penetration by the father. She is an active agent in her desire. Using her clinical observations of female patients, Horney interprets the symptom of penis envy or penis wish as a manoeuvre to compensate for their disappointment at having been deprived of the penis object and/or to defend themselves against the guilt accruing to incestuous desires. Horney added that the important role assigned to penis envy in the psychoanalytic formulations of female sexuality was itself an affront to feminine narcissism, an opinion widely echoed in recent feminist critiques of psychoanalysis.

- *Cultural basis of neurosis*: In contrast to the emphasis in Freudian psychoanalysis on biological and intrapsychic factors, her understanding of personality emphasized cultural and interpersonal ones, Horney (1939) wrote that she had arrived at the conviction 'that psychoanalysis should outgrow the limitations set by it being an instinctivistic and a genetic psychology' (p. 8). She opined:Cultural factors exert a powerful influence on women; such, in fact, that it is hard to see how any woman may escape becoming masochistic to some extent ... There may appear certain fixed ideologies concerning the 'nature' of women; that she is innately weak, emotional, enjoys dependence, is limited in capacity for independent work and autonomous thinking. It is obvious that these ideologies function not only to reconcile women to their subordinate role, but also to plant the belief that it represents a fulfillment they crave, or an ideal for which it is desirable to strive.

(Horney, 1936, p. 224)

- *Reformulation of the phallic stage for boy*: Horney posits that the little boy has incestuous desire for the mother. But he knows that his penis is much too small for his mother's vagina. He 'reacts (to it) with the dread of his own inadequacy' (Horney, 1967, p. 142). In consequence, genital anxiety (with respect to the father's large penis) is primary in the girl and genital inadequacy (with respect to mother's large vagina) is primary in the boy, the reverse of Freud's views of feminine lack and castration anxiety among men. His perceived sense of inadequacy is a 'wound to his self-regard'. The boy is left with a 'narcissistic scar' and a denial of the vagina which is often expressed in a man's fear of being rejected and derided by a woman. According to Horney, it leads to various kinds of psychic unfolding in the boy. At one level, it may lead to the boy's disgust with the male role and a repressed wish to be female. In another psychic move, the boy withdraws

How Is 'Gender' Treated in Psychology? **237**

his libido from his mother and 'concentrates it on himself and his genital'. This is, then, Horney's derivation of the phallic phase, an intensification of phallic narcissism. Horney sees castration anxiety of the boy as secondary to his anger at being frustrated, the wound to his self-regard and his compensatory wish to be a woman. Once an intensification of phallic narcissism takes place, the penis becomes an overvalued organ for the little boy which sets the stage for castration threats to become effective.

- *Dread of women:* Freud 'explains' the development of boys' contempt for their mothers as coming from their perception of genital differences, particularly their mother's 'castration'. He takes this perception to be unmediated by social experience. According to Horney, these phenomena are manifestations of a deeper 'dread of women' – a masculine fear and terror of maternal omnipotence that arises as one major consequence of their early caretaking and socialization by women. Psychoanalysts previously had stressed boys' fears of their fathers. Horney argues that these fears are less severe and therefore less in need of being repressed. Unlike their fears of a mother, boys do not react to a father's total and incomprehensible control over his child's life at the time when the child has no reflective capacities for understanding: 'Dread of the father is more actual and tangible, less uncanny in quality.' Moreover, since their father is male like them, boys' fears of men do not entail admission of feminine weakness or dependency on women: 'Masculine self-regard suffers less in this way.' Boys and men develop psychological and cultural/ideological mechanisms to cope with their fears without giving up women altogether. They create folk legends, beliefs and poems that ward off the dread by externalizing and objectifying women.

Horney's critique has pointed to the need for a more comprehensive formulation of the way gender development is viewed in orthodox Freudian theory. However, her views on innate heterosexuality from the outset have been opposed.

Nancy Chodorow

Nancy Chodorow is well known for her book, *The Reproduction of Mothering: Psychoanalysis and the Sociology of Gender* (1978) and other essays in which she reformulated the orthodox psychoanalytic views on gender from a feminist perspective. Chodorow's reformulation of Freudian theory lies in her use of object relational perspective which 'incorporates a view of the place of both drives and social relations in development' (Chodorow, 1978, p. 47) and focuses on the pre-Oedipal stage and maternal identification in gender development. For those who follow Freud, the father/phallus is the starting point, masculinity is presumed and femininity is defined as the other. For those like Chodorow, the mother is the starting point, maternal identification is primary and masculinity comes into being as not mother. Such reformulations have permitted the development of a conception of the psychic experience of gender that is contingent upon configurations other than Oedipal and the castration complex, such as the pre-Oedipal dynamics of attachment, separation and loss.

- *Relational complexities in the female Oedipus situation*: Chodorow (1978) states that the development of a girl's child identity does not involve a rejection of the girl's early identification with mother. Rather, her later identification with her mother is embedded in and influenced by both her primary identification and pre-Oedipal attachment with her. Chodorow reviews several reasons given by different analysts for the 'change of object' from mother to father in the girl:It may be partly a broadening of innate sexual drives, and it is probably in part a reaction to her heterosexual father's behavior and feelings toward her and his preoccupation with her (hetero-)sexuality. The turn to the father, however, is embedded in a girl's external relationship to her mother and in her relation to her mother as an internal object. It expresses hostility to her mother; it results from an attempt to win her mother's love; it is a reaction to powerlessness vis-à-vis maternal omnipotence and to primary identification. Every step of the way, as the analysts describe it, a girl develops her relationship to her father while looking back at her mother – to see if her mother is envious, to make sure she is in fact separate, to see if she can in this way win her mother, to see if she is really independent. Her turn to her father is both 'an attack on her mother and an expression of love for her'.

  (Chodorow, 1978, p. 126)

  Her own thesis is that because mother is an earthy figure and she has a genuine relationship to the daughter as a person (as they both share the 'feminine space' in the household), the daughter develops a 'personal' identification with mother's general traits of character and values. Even when the father becomes an important primary person, he takes his place in the context of a bisexual relationship triangle. The girl's libidinal turning to her father does not substitute for her intense attachment to the mother. She internalizes these other relationships in addition to and not as replacements for it. She oscillates emotionally between her mother and father. Mothers experience daughters as one with themselves. The girl's love for the mother, then, contains both a threat to selfhood and a promise of psychic unity which love for the father (father substitutes) never does. Thus, a daughter looks to the father for a sense of separateness and for the same confirmation of her specialness that her brother receives from her mother. The implications for this is that most women emerge from their Oedipal complex orientated towards the father and men as erotic objects but men are clearly emotionally secondary to primacy and exclusivity of the girl's emotional tie to her mother and women.

  Chodorow's line of thinking establishes two crucial departures from Freudian thinking. First, the question of separation becomes more central to understanding the psychic reality of women, and the feminine sense of self appears less as lack and more as continuity with the maternal object. Second, the turn to the father, then, whatever its sexual meaning, is embedded in emotional–relational issues of self and other. These issues tend to be resolved by persons in roles that are systematically gender-linked, not because of qualities inherent in persons of either gender but because of the family organization.

- *Why do women mother?*: Chodorow argues that given the triangular situation and the emotional asymmetry of her own parenting, a woman's relation to a man requires, on the level of psychic structure, a third person, since it was originally established in a triangle. It is the child that completes the relational triangle for a woman on the level of psychic structure. Chodorow (1997) states that having a child and experiencing the relationship to a man in this context completes the intrapsychic triangle for her. It also makes her take a new place in the triangle – a maternal place in relation to her own child from where she recreates the symbiotic mother–child relationship of her own infancy. For this reason, it seems psychologically logical to a woman to turn her marriage into a family.

  She argues that specific features of the female Oedipus experience facilitate the reproduction of mothering, through both the mother and the daughter:

  Women develop capacities for mothering from their object–relational stance. This stance grows out of the special nature and length of their preoedipal relationship to their mother; the non absolute repression of oedipal relationships; and their general ongoing mother–daughter pre-occupation as they are growing up. (Chodorow, 1978, p. 204)

- *Emphasis on social ideology*: Most psychoanalytic and social theorists claim that the mother inevitably represents to her daughter (and son) passivity, regression, dependence and lack of orientation to reality, whereas the father represents activity, progression, independence and reality orientation. However, Chodorow (1974) counters this by saying that the specific sociopolitical context, in which the mother–child duo is situated, plays an important role. On the basis of the ethnographic accounts of working-class mothers and daughters in three cultural groups, she noted that women's kin role and, in particular, the mother role were positively valued in all these groups. They had control over real economic resources and gained in status and prestige as they grew older. Also strong relationships existed between women in these societies. In these societies, mother–daughter ties were close, composed of companionship and mutual co-operation, positively valued by both mother and daughter. A daughter's identification with her mother in this kind of setting is with a strong woman with choice and control over important spheres of life whose self-esteem reflects this. Thus,

240   How Is 'Gender' Treated in Psychology?

acceptance of her gender identity involves positive valuation of herself and not an admission of inferiority. Thus, cultural devaluation of femininity is not a given social fact.

- *Psychic developments in the boy*: A boy's relationship with the mother is different. The mother positions the boy as the complementary other as compared to positioning the daughter as self-same. Thus, the boy expresses his separateness and masculine oppositeness to her. This masculine identification is usually based on identifications with a boy's father or other salient adult males. But, since the father is more remote than the mother, performing his male role activities away from where the son spends most of his life, a boy's male gender identification often becomes a 'positional' identification. He identifies with an unclear male role or what he fantasizes to be the male role. Additionally, his attempts to gain an elusive masculine identification often come to define it in negative terms, not feminine. Internally the boy tries to reject his mother and deny his attachment. He also tries to deny the deep personal identification with her by repressing whatever he takes to be feminine inside himself and importantly by denigrating and devaluing whatever he considers to be feminine in the outside world. Chodorow suggests that the boy first defines himself as not-mother before, in the Oedipal power move, he defines her as not-male, not the generic universal human 'he' first thought her to be. His training for masculinity and repression of affective relational needs and his primarily non-emotional and interpersonal relationships in the public world make him look for deep love bonds with women (mother substitutes), thereby establishing heterosexuality.

Critics have argued that Chodorow's thesis of reproduction of mothering reproduces the problematic social stereotype of woman being 'good' at relationships, whereas man being 'bad' at them. By treating this as a psychological truth, she sanctifies it as a natural fact. Also, the binary opposition and complementarity between men and women, that is, X is not Y and Y is not X is maintained in this theory.

Luce Irigaray

Irigaray is known for her radical scholarship on sexual differences. She critiques what she sees as the deep-seated notion of sexual indifference in the Freudian perspective while apparently trying to explain the differences between men and women. She also departs from the likes of Carol Gilligan and Nancy Chodorow who keep the duality between sexes intact and argue for a positive evaluation of feminine capacities. According to Irigaray ([1977] 1985), in all these perspectives, femininity has always been formulated on the basis of a specific difference from masculinity. As long as masculinity remains the standard, there can only be complementarity and opposition. There is no actual other subject with its own path of development. So Irigaray, like other French feminists, wonders about feminine subjectivity, asks if women can be subjects or citizens without adapting to masculine norms and impeaches Freud's and Lacan's phallocentrism.

- *Sexual difference*: Irigaray ([1977] 1985) argues that the relationship between women and men takes one of these three forms: (1) women are less than men; (2) women are equal to men; and (3) women are complementary to men. In Freudian psychoanalysis, these dynamics are demonstrated during different phases of development of the little girl and little boy. During the pre-Oedipal phases, girls and boys are the 'same' ('little girls are little men', as Freud says); during the Oedipus complex, women are 'inferior' versions of men (because Oedipality is never completely resolved in women, according to Freud); and after the normal resolution of Oedipality, women are opposite yet 'complements' to men. Complementarity is present in Freud's assumption that 'normal' women will desire men and be desired by them and thus each sex can fulfil the longings of the other. With regard to sexual identity, Freud models the feminine Oedipal complex on a masculine paradigm and origin, with the feminine as its distorted copy. In both sexual desire and identity, Freud contrives to understand women as the complementary other to men, an other modelled on the same.

  Therefore, the relationship between men and women is set up in binary structure, in which man is the standard to which women have to measure up in order to become 'same'. The Oedipus complex, in its normalcy, demands that the little girl give up her phallic sexuality for a passive/vaginal sexuality. Sexuality is regulated to specific erogenous zones with the end purpose of reproduction, recreating the nuclear family and Oedipal dynamics. She objects to the Oedipal theory that thrives on reproducing sameness. Irigaray ([1977] 1985) writes:

It seems that two possible roles are available to her [the woman], roles that are occasionally or frequently contradictory. Women could be man's equal. In this case she would enjoy, in a more or less near future, the same economic, social, political rights as men. She would be a potential man. But on the exchange market – especially, or exemplarily, the market of sexual exchange – woman would also have to preserve and maintain what is called femininity.

(p. 84)

In patriarchy, equality is equality and sameness to men. Irigaray is stating that even if women achieve this equality, they are still expected to enact a femininity that is prescribed by phallocentrism, therefore eliminating any sexual difference. As long as women strive to be equal to men, and men remain in the dominant position, only male representations and institutions that benefit masculinity will exist. She advocates the theorization and politics of sexual difference as a tactic to go beyond sameness and equality.

- *Phallocentric notion of desire*: Irigaray critiques the psychoanalytic concept of desire which is supposedly a lack that needs to be filled, and, particularly for women, they are forever 'lacking' the phallus. Accordingly, women as castrated, lacking beings will strive to 'possess' the phallus through the birth of a baby boy, which is its equivalent. In this negative understanding of desire, women's desire is for what they lack – the phallus, therefore psychoanalysis does not offer an account that thinks of women's desire outside of phallocentrism. Irigaray sees in this account a masculine desire for women's desire to be directed towards men. Also, in a patriarchy, as little girls cease to be little men, post-Oedipal, they are expected to be appealing visual objects, in the position of the object of masculine desire.

  Her critique of desire goes hand in hand with her critique of the primacy of the phallus and the commodification of woman. Only in a patriarchal society can the penis, represented as the phallus, retain power and be an object of envy for those who do not 'have' it. In addition, Irigaray argues that within this patriarchal society, women have become commodities of exchange between men (father and husband). Women are consistently relegated to an inferior position in society.

  Psychoanalytic discourse views woman's desire as limited in this phallocentric framework, their organs are looked upon as lack in themselves, and the vagina offers nothing to be seen. What Irigaray makes clear in her critiques is that women's desire is unknown in a phallocentric society since women have been subsumed to 'sameness' in the interest of the phallus. Irigaray has a creative response to the assumption of woman's bodies and desires. She writes that woman has 'two lips', an image she plays on woman's genital lips and that these lips are always touching, engaging with one another (Irigaray, [1977] 1985). Therefore, women's sexuality cannot be reduced to one or to nothing, but rather their sexuality is multiple. Furthermore, their desires 'would not be expected to speak the same language as man's'. She speaks of a desire that incorporates sexual difference and is not solely reduced to genitality.

- *Matricide and the suppression of maternal genealogies*: Another issue that Irigaray takes up with Freud is the way he characterizes the girl's relation to the maternal figure as an 'especially inexorable repression' (Freud, 1931, p. 226). She argues that Freudian psychoanalysis denies that a pre-Oedipal mother–daughter relationship ever existed, since a daughter becomes a daughter properly, becomes feminized or sexually differentiated (as a girl or woman) only post-Oedipally. Not only is the maternal connection lost or repressed, but the ability to name or identify the loss as a loss is also barred. Banished from memory, the loss of the mother cannot be mourned. Irigaray claims that it is this genealogical asymmetry, in which the father's name is memorialized and the mother's connection is lost, that sustains the legitimacy of patriarchy and propels the conviction that the sexes are reciprocal and complementary in their identities and desires.

- *Being two and between two*: Irigaray moves away from a certain position of knowing what a woman is or what femininity is. She says that the phallocentric system has denied femininity its own images and language, fashioning women through men's language, images and desires. Against this homogeny, with its same and its other, Irigaray ([1977] 1985) develops her theory of sexual difference: Sexual difference as being two and a relation between two. Being two is a challenge to being one, that is, having a single (masculine) standard, and many, that is, empty relativism. It is also not about affirming the feminine traits that have been ascribed to women, since these are actually, in her view, the traits of sexual indifference, defined only with reference to men. Being two is the path towards liberating both femininity and masculinity from their metaphysical and political constraints by allowing them each to cultivate their own unique and interdependent natures. The idea of a between two does not mean a singular path that is shared by both; rather, it indicates, in addition to the value of a specifically feminine sexual identity and a specifically masculine sexual identity, the ethical path of an intersubjective relationality that allows them to appreciate and value one another. Since the between two is premised on being two, it is in the cultivation of this sexual difference that the possibility of an ethical sexual relation, what Irigaray (1984) calls an ethics of sexual difference, lies.

Jessica Benjamin

Benjamin (1995) reconstructs the Oedipal standpoints by offering an alternative analysis in her formulation of sexual difference. She maintains that separation occurs equally for boys and girls and that children of both sexes continue to identify with both parents. Therefore, the loving yet limiting father is as important for girls as for boys. Masculinity and femininity are reconfigured and are no longer polar opposites. In contrast to Chodorow, she suggests masculine and feminine identifications are located internally within each subject (Benjamin, 1998). This creates the possibility for multiple subject positions rather than oscillating between the polar opposites of male and female. The subject experiences the difference as exciting and pleasurable instead of threatening and diametrically opposed to their sense of self. Benjamin perceives the construction of the self to contain multiple subject positions in which the variances reflect an attraction to difference and to the ongoing process of identification. Instead of binary opposition – subject–object, male–female, active–passive – the mutual recognition of commonalities and difference is recommended.

The maternal function of holding, containing and the activity of giving back have been traditionally perceived by Freud as passive. In contrast, Benjamin (1998) perceives the process of understanding another subject experience, recognition and the process of digesting and giving back, expression, as active. Benjamin considers this process to be intersubjective, essential for the

244 How Is 'Gender' Treated in Psychology?

emergence of the somatic self. Autonomy requires the child to be recognized by a person who is different and separate from the child. Also, the child needs to perceive the mother out of her omnipotent control, thereby, transcending the subject–object complementarity and the positioning of the woman as the other.

The feminist critiques of psychoanalysis have been very influential in shaping the gender discourse.

REVIEW QUESTION

What are the core challenges to the Freudian psychoanalytic theory?

Is the Study of Gender Roles Adequate?

Lewis Terman and Catherine Cox Miles (1936) concluded in their seminal work *Sex and Personality: Studies in Masculinity and Femininity* that there are no sex differences in intellect and the real differences between men and women can be captured by measuring masculinity and femininity. Terman and Miles (1936) developed the first masculinity/femininity scale (M/F scale) called the Attitude Interest Analysis Survey. The items chosen were based on statistical sex differences observed in elementary, junior high and high school children. This meant that items on which the average female scored higher than the average male were labelled feminine, and items on which the average male scored higher than the average female were labelled masculine, regardless of the content of those items. The M/F scale was also bipolar, which meant that masculinity and femininity were viewed as opposite ends of a single continuum.

A few years later, Hathaway and McKinley (1940) developed the Minnesota Multiphasic Personality Inventory. It eventually included an M/F scale consisting of items reflecting altruism, emotional sensitivity, sexual preference, preference for certain occupations and gender identity questions. The most notable feature of the scale was that the femininity items were validated on 13 homosexual men. These men were compared to heterosexual male soldiers as, at that time, heterosexual male soldiers epitomized masculinity and homosexual men were considered feminine. In fact, feminine traits were considered to be a predisposing factor to homosexuality in men (Terman & Miles, 1936). This led to two major objections. One, women were not even involved in the research on femininity. Two, it reveals a confusion between sexual orientation and gender roles. Femininity in men was a gender non-conforming behaviour and was perceived as a valid description of homosexual men.

Constantinople (1973) critiqued the use of sex differences as the basis for defining masculinity and femininity in such instruments. She also questioned whether M/F was really a unidimensional construct that could be captured by a single bipolar scale. This early work was followed by the pioneering work of Sandra Bem (1974) that conceptualizes psychological gender, rather than biological sex, as responsible for individual differences in human behaviour. Psychological gender refers to the traits, behaviours and interests ascribed to males and females by the society. Masculinity and femininity are the gender roles that go along with being male versus females. This has bolstered the study of gender within social psychology with a focus on gender roles.

Bem's Sex Role Inventory

Sandra Bem tried to displace the question of sex difference by arguing that masculinity and femininity were not a unidimensional construct in which masculinity and feminine are opposites and based on a negation of other. Rather, they were empirically and conceptually independent variables (Bem, 1974). Thus, the respondent could be placed in any one of the four categories – masculine individual (high on masculinity and low on femininity), feminine individual (high on femininity and low on masculinity), androgynous (high on masculinity and femininity), and undifferentiated (low on masculinity and femininity). It was a constructive step away from the binary division of gender. Rather than two, there were now four possibilities of gender identity. It also undercuts the strict association of masculinity and femininity with particular bodies (i.e., men and women, respectively). Also, the final items for the Bem's Sex Role inventory (BSRI) were selected for the two scales if they were judged to be more desirable in American society for one sex as compared to the other (Bem, 1974). Thus, the psychological gender was not conflated with biological sex, and the role of society in deciding the definitions of gender roles was foregrounded in the test construction. Those scoring high on masculinity and femininity were considered to be sex-typed persons, that is, persons who have internalized society's sex-typed standards of desirable behaviours for men and women. Another advance in this work was that an androgynous person rather than a sex-typed individual was seen as the ideal. Androgyny is 'a term that denotes the integration of both masculinity and femininity within a single individual' (Bem, 1976, p. 196). That is, androgynous individuals, according to situational demand, may be both masculine and feminine, agentic and communal (Bakan, 1966), instrumental and expressive (Parson & Bales, 1955). This further disentangles sex and gender, as no longer are masculinity for males and femininity for females perceived to be essential for mental health.

Evaluation of the BSRI

1. Though BSRI has tried not to conflate sex and gender, defining masculinity and femininity in terms of what is stereotypically understood as desirable male and female qualities, it is posing a conflation of another kind – between psychological gender and sex stereotypes (beliefs about the features of biological males and females). BSRI assesses such masculine personality traits as acts as a leader, aggressive, ambitious, analytical,

246 How Is 'Gender' Treated in Psychology?

competitive, dominant, independent, and so on. The feminine characteristics assessed include affectionate, cheerful, childlike, flatterable, gullible,
loves children, loyal, and so on. Critics have argued that when subjects
rate themselves on a seven-point scale of how well each of these characteristics defines him/her, what is being assessed by BSRI is not really
psychological gender but the extent of endorsement of sex-appropriate
stereotypes for self by an individual. Although the Bem scale is an advance
on sex differences measures (in that it does not assume sex differences *a
priori*), it tests conformity to stereotypes generated in one particular
situation.

2. Clifton, McGrath and Wick (1976) demonstrated that Bem's 'femininity' is
a particularly 'narrow stereotype'. When Clifton asked people to generate
descriptions of various types of women (e.g., 'career woman', 'bunny',
'woman athlete', 'housewife'), he found that only description of 'housewife' corresponded to Bem's 'femininity' construct. It ignores the fact that
masculinity and femininity are not singular concepts. Multiple and conflicting masculinities and femininities have been identified that have varying degrees of power and are born from varying social contexts.

3. Another important criticism of this work is the non-inclusion of negative
characteristics of stereotypes of masculinity and femininity.

4. At no stage of the procedure, be it the initial (400) item selection, final (60)
item selection or the subsequent use of the completed scale on other subjects, do situational influences on the subjects play a significant part in
Bem's analysis. As a value-laden attribute, gender has considerable social
salience; therefore, one would anticipate that an important part of impression management would be the emphasis or de-emphasis of masculinity and
femininity. Perceived situational factors (e.g., the sex of the experimenter,
the authority of the experimental situation, etc.) may well be factors that
influence one's BSRI score. One might thus well expect the BSRI score
(obtained in a laboratory situation) to differ substantially from that which
might be expected on the basis of subjects' actions in specific normal,
everyday situations. The ideals which one endorses in the laboratory have
no necessary link to one's normal range of response (Locksley & Colten,
1979). Bem does claim that the BSRI has a predictive value for behaviour:

because the BSRI was founded on the conception of the sex-typed person as
someone who has internalised society's sex-typed standards of desirable
behavior for men and women, these personality characteristics were selected as masculine or feminine on the basis of sex-typed desirability.

(Bem, 1974, p. 155)

However, this assertion is based largely on laboratory experiments.
Outwith the experimental situation, the range of responses that individuals
produce may be very different.

How Is 'Gender' Treated in Psychology? **247**

5. BSRI sees stereotypical traits as fixed. There is no enquiry into the history and process of social change responsible for fixing the facts of gendered understandings.
6. Towards the later part of her career, Bem (1981) began to acknowledge that androgyny could be restrictive in the sense that the person has two ideals to meet: a masculine one and a feminine one. Androgyny also does not rid society of the two culturally defined gender categories.

Bem's Sex Role Inventory has some lethal social implications. The masculinity and femininity scales perpetuate stereotypical thinking about psychological gender. It legitimizes and normalizes a certain ideology of femininity, masculinity and androgyny, and reinforces this ideology as a taken-for-granted orthodoxy. While Bem followed the historically derived tradition in categorizing the traits, the feminine traits are less socially desirable than those that are defined as masculine. This perpetuates gender discrimination and perpetuation of the idea of female inferiority.

Later, she came to the realization that because androgyny focused on masculinity and femininity, and not the culture that created the concepts, it reproduced 'the gender polarization that it [sought] to undercut' (Bem, 1993, p. viii). Her later book, *The Lenses of Gender: Transforming the Debate on Sexual Inequality* (Bem, 1993), built upon her earlier ideas, explained how a society's gender schemas or lenses (gender polarization, androcentrism and biological essentialism) work to maintain the oppression of women and sexual minorities. It was through these works that Sandra Bem gained the reputation she has today as a feminist icon.

Gender Schema Theory

Bem advanced her gender schema theory (Bem, 1981) to explain (in part) sex typing. Gender schema is a general readiness in people to see the world in gender stereotypical ways. As the self-concept gets assimilated in the gender schema, that is, the ways in which one perceives oneself becomes gendered due to socialization, sex typing results. Since gender schema vary in strength, the BSRI assesses the extent to which the individual is sex-typed. Bem developed gender schema theory in order to investigate and place greater focus on the ways in which society creates and enforces the categories of gender. In her own words, 'by shifting the focus of my research from androgyny to gender schematicity, I wanted to establish that masculinity and femininity were, in my view, cultural constructions' (Bem, 1993, p. 126). She further explained gender schema theory as follows:

> Specifically, gender schema theory argues that because American culture is so gender polarizing in its discourse and its social institutions, children come to be gender schematic (or gender polarizing) themselves without

even realizing it. Gender schematicity, in turn, helps lead children to become conventionally sex-typed. That is, in imposing a gender-based classification on reality, children evaluate different ways of behaving in terms of the cultural definitions of gender appropriateness and reject any way of behaving that does not match their sex. In contrast to Kohlberg's cognitive-developmental account of why children become sex-typed, this alternative account situates the source of the child's motivation for a match between sex and behavior, not in the mind of the child, but in the gender polarization of the culture.

(Bem, 1993, pp. 125–126)

Gender Role Stereotypes

A whole field of work is devoted to understanding people's beliefs and attitude towards gender roles, referred to as gender role stereotypes. Gender role stereotypes are strongly affected by our strong expectancies about the differences between men and women. A landmark study to assess people's beliefs about masculine and feminine behaviour was conducted by Broverman, Vogel, Broverman, Clarkson and Rosenkrantz (1972). They found a prevalence of strong sexism in the highly consensual responses in the sample about the characteristics of women and men across age, sex, religion, marital status and education. The male characteristics focused on competence, rationality and assertion. The female characteristics focused on warmth and expressiveness. Broverman et al. (1972) also found that the male characteristics were more highly valued than the female characteristics. When the investigators asked women and men to indicate which of these traits are most desirable in an adult, without specifying the adult's sex, more masculine than feminine items were endorsed. Mental health professionals also rated the masculine items as healthier than the feminine items for an adult to possess. That is, the stereotype of the healthy adult more closely approximated the stereotype of an adult male than an adult female.

These findings showed that mental health professionals equated 'men' with 'adults'. Effectively, they saw them as one and the same – to be a mentally healthy man is to be a mentally healthy adult. But this was not true of their ideas about women – to be a mentally healthy woman was not seen as the same as being a mentally healthy adult. Rather, for a woman to be viewed as mentally healthy, she needed to be 'feminine'. If she failed to conform to accepted feminine qualities, then she could not be a mature, healthy and socially competent woman. The danger of stereotyping is that it influences our perceptions of and behaviour towards others. Stereotyping can influence our behaviour towards others in such a way that others confirm the stereotype. This is known as a self-fulfilling prophecy.

Research has identified three key types of stereotypes: descriptive, prescriptive and proscriptive. 'Descriptive stereotypes' refer to how a group is perceived as being. Descriptive stereotypes can have damaging effects when an

How Is 'Gender' Treated in Psychology? **249**

individual is assumed not to be qualified or capable or competent. For example, women face disadvantages in attaining leadership positions partially because they are stereotyped as nice, warm and caring – a description that does not fit with leadership responsibilities of being assertive, competitive and unemotional (Koenig et al., 2011). Men are not capable of nurturing children, as they are aggressive, task-oriented and individualistic. Because individuals hold descriptive stereotypes of men as masculine and women as feminine, gay men and women are regarded as gender non-conforming: Gay men are assumed to be feminine while lesbians are assumed to be masculine. Such stereotypes are partially responsible for the unfavourable treatment of sexual minorities.

Stereotypes can carry more weight than a simple description of a group. 'Prescriptive stereotypes' describe ways that individuals should act (Prentice & Carranza, 2002). For example, women are not only described as being nice and warm but are prescribed to be nice and warm. In contrast, men are prescribed to be assertive and independent (Rudman et al., 2012). While prescriptive stereotypes describe how individuals should act, 'proscriptive stereotypes' describe ways in which individuals should not act (Rudman et al., 2012). Many of the proscriptions around gender represent prescriptions for the other category. For example, men are proscribed from being emotional, weak or insecure. Women are proscribed from being aggressive, dominating or self-centred (Rudman et al., 2012). Violations of prescriptive and proscriptive stereotypes carry serious consequences. Women who violate prescriptions to be nice and warm are disliked and are thus less likely to be hired in job contexts and offered lower salaries (Heilman et al., 2004; Rudman & Glick, 2001). Men also face a backlash when behaving in ways that violate masculine prescriptions for behaviour. Men who violate prescriptions to be assertive and aggressive by showing more modest traits earn lower salaries and are viewed negatively (Moss-Racusin et al., 2010). In the workplace, those who behave in ways that are perceived as feminine, such as taking parental leave, also face a backlash and are seen as worse workers than men who behave in more traditionally masculine ways (Rudman & Mescher, 2013).

BOX 5.4 WHY SHOULD THERE BE A PSYCHOLOGY OF MEN?

The psychological study of men and masculinity has grown substantially from the early 1970s to the present. Why do we need such a study? Is not all of psychology the psychology of men, anyway? Well, yes. Psychological research has taken men as the focal point, but it has viewed men as representatives of the whole. The study of men and masculinity is no longer approaching masculinity as a normative referent but as a complex construct, much like femininity. Psychologists are questioning the traditional norms of the male roles (e.g., independence, toughness, control over feelings, etc.) and the problems associated with adherence to such norms (e.g., violence against women, substance abuse, detached fathering, etc.). A new psychology of men and masculinity is contributing to understanding and solving some of these long-standing problems that have long affected women, men, children and society in negative ways. It is also addressing the 'masculinity crisis' which is resulting due to the pressures on men to behave in ways that conflict with the traditional masculinity ideology. These pressures include pressures to be expressive in feelings, to share housework, to nurture children, to integrate sexuality and love, to curb aggression and violence. No longer is masculine essence seen as something historically invariant. Rather, notions of masculinity and femininity are socially constructed from bits and pieces of biological, psychological and social experience to serve a particular purpose (Pleck, 1981). Another direction, in which intensive efforts have been directed by the researchers studying the psychology of men and masculinity, has been to define, measure and refine the various forms of masculinities related to racial, ethnic, sexual, socioeconomic groups and other important demographic and cultural distinctions. Much research has focused on the negative impact of the traditional masculine gender role on men's and women's health and psychological adjustment. Future research can also make efforts to explicate some positive aspects of the psychology of men and masculinity.

Final Comments

Gender operates in psychological research by pushing for certain kinds of research foci, methods and epistemologies. The scientific process is itself gendered, privileging the 'hard' research approaches over 'soft' ones. Thus, research designs and methodologies are themselves gendered. Psychological research must move beyond the gender binary. This involves two important elements: (1) reconsidering the conceptual distinctions between masculine/ feminine and male/female, and (2) rethinking conceptualizations of gender as strictly social and of sex as strictly biological. The psychological study of gender routinely makes dangerous and static associations between women and femininity and men and masculinity, eroding much of the diversity that exists within and among these categories. Also, understanding gender requires going beyond the sex difference paradigm. As Addis and Cohane (2005, p. 635) attest, 'Gender is about much more than sex differences between men and women on interesting dependent variables.' The human body, such as intersex and trans bodies, disrupts strict and static categories of sex and gender. It is the site where ideas of sex, sexuality and gender collide. Researchers need to move towards increased conceptual clarity on sex and gender. Both are multidimensional and fluid concepts, but research often does not specify which aspect is being studied. With respect to gender, conceptualizations vary from micro to macro: institutionalized gender, gender roles, gender identities and gender as performance. Identifying the relevant aspects of sex and gender for a study is important, as this will shape the measures and means of data collection as well as the types of analytic approaches used. For example, in considering sex and gender and health outcomes related to smoking, one might ask if the different symptoms reported by men and women are related to biological factors (e.g., hormones) or social factors (e.g., the forms of masculinities and femininities that influence the risk factor of addiction) or biases inherent in our measures of smoking (e.g., a form of institutionalized gender).

6

WHAT IS 'ABNORMAL' IN CLINICAL PSYCHOLOGY?

Clinical psychology is one of the most recognizable faces of psychology in the world. Most people associate psychology with the study of mental disorders, such as schizophrenia, depression and anxiety. Psychiatry and psychology are the linchpins of the discourse on psychopathology and abnormality. Psychopathology is the core object of study for both psychiatry and psychology and they provide authoritative knowledge about its definition, classification, causation and treatment.

Scientific discourses of psychology and psychiatry treat psychological abnormality as a disorder present in an individual, akin to a physical illness, in need of some treatment. What should be treated?: The neurotransmitters, the hormones, the genetic make-up or the dysfunctional schemas, unconscious conflicts, maladaptive behaviour or social inequalities and violence? While the fields of psychology and psychiatry acknowledge all three sources of psychopathology, the biological and psychological treatments receive the most attention. Crucial to the notions of abnormality and normality in psychology is the idea of adaption, adjustment and functionality. Psychological abnormality is seen exclusively as an individual problem that needs to be fixed. These fields pay scant regard to the fact that madness, insanity, lunacy and abnormality have historically been contested terrains. There are unanswered questions such as the following: Is madness a medical disease, a problem in living, or a social labelling of disapproved behaviour? Abnormality is a complex signifier and this complexity is negated in the medicalized discourse.

What Is the Relationship of Abnormality to Normality?

Abnormality is usually understood as a movement away from normality. In physical health, the indicators of normality are well established and can be assessed reasonably objectively with the help of medical procedures, such as

DOI: 10.4324/9781003471851-7

physical examination, pathological tests and neurological scans. Examples include the normal range of blood pressure, blood glucose, red blood cells, cholesterol, number of chromosomes, hormone levels and other signs of normal anatomical and physiological functioning of internal body organs and systems. In the case of psychology, there is no defined understanding of normal functioning. The evidence-based practice approach in psychology necessitates the use of a psychometric approach in assessing abnormality in which the 'norm' of the psychological tests and rating scales determine 'normalcy'. When a psychological test is standardized, norms are constructed, which are the distribution of scores on a particular construct (e.g., personality trait, anxiety levels, depressive mood) of a representative sample of people. The range of scores which are frequently occurring are earmarked as indicating average/normal functioning while those which are obtained by fewer people in the standardization sample are indicative of psychopathology. In this conceptualization, abnormality is considered to be an infrequent form of behaviour, that is, behaviour which is not demonstrated by most people in a group. This is often referred to as the 'statistical deviance' criterion of abnormality in the mental health language.

The criterion of deviance suggests that abnormality is 'away from the norm'. The norm can be statistical and/or cultural in nature. In terms of statistical deviance, abnormality is too low or too high levels of certain thoughts (e.g., perception of danger), feelings (e.g., sadness) and behaviours (e.g., activity levels) when compared with standardized norms. Common examples include low and high scores on tests of anxiety and intelligence as indicative of abnormality. In terms of cultural deviance, abnormality refers to behavioural patterns that are not considered appropriate or sanctioned according to cultural norms. For example, the act of dressing as the opposite gender (cross-dressing) is considered an inappropriate form of behaviour in most cultures.

The categorical classification system of mental disorders as laid out in psychiatric frameworks like the *Diagnostic and Statistical Manual of Mental Disorders (DSM)*, published by the American Psychiatric Association (APA), and the *International Classification of Diseases* (ICD), published by the World Health Organization (WHO), view abnormality and normality as disjunctive, opposing categories. In this conceptualization, abnormality becomes an all-or-nothing entity denoting a complete absence of normalcy. The categorical form of classification of mental disorders, a legacy of Emil Kraepelin, is the end product of the series of historical events marking the rise of medicalization of insanity.

Is Psychopathology Psychological or Biological in Origin?

The age-old debate over psychopathology is: 'Are the mad mad because of faulty parenting, unbearable social pressures or because of genetic vulnerabilities?' There have been three dominant approaches to understand abnormality: the supernatural, the biological and the psychological. The 'supernatural approach' does not distinguish between mental and physical disorders but believes both to be inflicted on a person by some evil forces or God's wrath. Natural events such as monsoons, earthquakes and diseases are attributed to human motivations of invisible superhuman beings or the result of magical manipulations by one's enemies. The methods that are widely used for warding off illnesses are prayer, threats, submission, punishment, atonement, intimidation and also exorcism, magical rituals and trepanation (making holes in the skull for the evil spirit to escape). The 'biological approach' is usually traced to the ideas of the Greek philosopher Hippocrates. He is widely regarded as the father of medicine but actually he can be seen as the culmination rather than a beginning. Several important physicians before him had challenged practices based on magic and demonology. However, Hippocrates' great accomplishment was that he took the development of naturalistic medicine to new heights. He critiqued the vestiges of supernatural medicine that still existed in his time. He suggested the humour theory which remained influential among physicians until almost the eighteenth century. According to this, humans are made up of four natural elements – earth, air, water and fire. These elements were believed to be associated with four substances (humours) in the body – earth with black bile, air with yellow bile, fire with blood and water with phlegm. Individuals whose humours were properly balanced were healthy; an imbalance among the humours resulted in illness. No distinction was thus far made between physical and mental illness. The brain became the source of all forms of illness. Abnormalities developed when the brain was too hot, cold, dry or moist. Galen extended this theory into one of the first theories of personality in which different humours were linked with different kinds of temperamental characteristics. Psychological treatments such as catharsis, hypnosis, relaxation and offering support, reassurance and love to the sufferer have been employed throughout history.

There has been an ongoing tension between the supernatural, psychological and medical models of psychopathology. All of them have always existed in one form or another; what has changed throughout history is how one model has been emphasized over the others. The mainstream history of abnormality, as given in texts of abnormal psychology and psychiatry, has made a strong case for the superiority of the scientific understanding of mental illness (offered by psychiatry) over any other understanding, such as theological or metaphysical. It denounces the ancient and medieval periods of history for the superstitious and supernatural understanding of mental disorder in which abnormality was attributed to possession by God or a demon. The themes that recur throughout this history are that the mentally ill at all times were either neglected or harshly treated and their real condition was ignored, misunderstood or mistaken. It is with the advances in understanding of mental illness as akin to physical illness and biological treatments that the riddle of mental illness has been solved. In this respect, this history is Whiggish in the sense that it sees the change in the form of mental illness from mental illness as 'possession' to mental illness as 'sickness' as progress. It establishes the biomedical model of mental disorder as the foundational cornerstone of psychopathology.

The Biomedical Model of Mental Disorders

The biomedical model of psychiatry is a powerful discourse of mental illness in today's world. It is based on the assumption that abnormal behaviour is biological in nature. It is due to some biological malfunctioning (anatomical and/or physiological), and it should be treated medically (Deacon, 2013). It has many 'assumptions' as well:

1. Signs (objective indicators such as elevated thyroid levels) and symptoms (subjective feelings of low mood and loss of pleasure) are indicative of an underlying physical pathology within the individual.
2. Medical treatment should treat the underlying pathology in order to cure the disease.
3. Placing the patient's signs and symptoms in the correct disease category (the process called diagnosis) is the key to understanding and treating the disease. This grants the psychiatric classification and diagnosis of disorders a great deal of power.
4. The physician (psychiatrist) is the chief healthcare provider as he/she is the expert in diagnosis and treatment. Patients are expected to comply with his/her advice.
5. The disease condition of the patient is of the utmost importance. Other aspects of the patient, such as social, psychological and cultural factors, are considered external and less important. Thus, what is important is what illness the person has, rather than who the person is who has the illness.

This medical model enjoys the power to define what is normality and what is abnormality in human functioning, and separates the two as opposite categories, which is reinforced and reproduced in society through scientific institutions such as the APA (that publishes the *Diagnostic and Statistical Manual*), the WHO (that publishes the ICD), funding agencies that grant financial support for research advancements, scientific journals, certification agencies (e.g., the Rehabilitation Council of India) that provide registration only to such professionals who are trained in the medical model, the media, the educational system, the capitalist interests in the pharmacological industry and many more. The power-imbued discourses act on people as they learn to discipline themselves and behave in expected ways. They learn to avoid and fear signs and symptoms of abnormality and strive for what is acceptable and sanctioned forms of behaviour. This is what Foucault (1982) calls 'subjectification'.

An Expanded Framework of Mental Illness: The Biopsychosocial Model

George Engel (1977) advanced a new holistic model as an alternative to the prevailing biomedical model that had dominated science since the mid-twentieth century. His new model came to be known as the biopsychosocial model. Engel did not deny that the mainstream of biomedical research had fostered important advances in medicine, but he criticized its excessively narrow (biomedical) focus for leading clinicians to regard patients as objects and for ignoring the subjective experience of the patient. He understood psychological abnormality as resulting due to a combination of factors – biological, psychological and social. Engel championed his ideas not only as a scientific proposal but also as a fundamental ideology that tried to reverse the dehumanization of medicine and the disempowerment of patients. Engel's 'critique of biomedicine' was as follows (Borrell-Carrió et al., 2004):

1. A biochemical alteration does not translate directly into an illness. The appearance of illness results from the interaction of diverse causal factors, including those at the molecular, individual and social levels. Psychological factors, under certain circumstances, may also manifest as illnesses and health problems, including, at times, biochemical correlates.
2. The presence of a biological dysfunction does not shed light on the meaning of the symptoms to the patient.
3. Psychosocial variables are more important determinants of susceptibility, severity and course of illness than had been previously appreciated by those who maintain a biomedical view of illness.
4. Adopting a sick role is not necessarily associated with the presence of a biological dysfunction.
5. The success of most biological treatments is influenced by psychosocial factors, for example, the placebo effect.
6. The patient–clinician relationship influences medical outcomes. Compliance and adherence to a chosen treatment are a function of this relationship.
7. Unlike inanimate subjects of scientific scrutiny, patients are profoundly influenced by the way in which they are studied, and the scientists engaged in the study are influenced by their subjects.

In advancing the biopsychosocial model, Engel criticized the dualistic nature of the biomedical model, that is, the separation of body and mind. He rejected the view of encouraging physicians to maintain a strict separation between the body-as-machine and the narrative biography and emotions of the person – to focus on the disease to the exclusion of the person who was suffering – without building bridges between the two realms. His research in psychosomatics pointed towards a more integrative view, showing that fear, rage, neglect and attachment had physiological and developmental effects on the whole organism. Engel objected to a linear cause–effect model to describe clinical phenomena. Clinical reality is far more complex. For example, although genetics may have a role in causing schizophrenia, no clinician should ignore the sociological factors that might unleash or contain the manifestations of the illness. Engel's proposal also supported a relationship-centred view in which arriving at a correct

What Is 'Abnormal' in Clinical Psychology? **257**

biomedical diagnosis is only a part of the clinician's task. It is also important to interpret illness and health from an intersubjective perspective by giving the patient space to articulate his or her concerns, finding out about the patient's expectations and showing the patient a human face. This approach represents movement towards an egalitarian relationship in which the clinician is aware of and careful with his or her use of power. This model provides a much greater scope to psychological knowledge and social factors in shaping the understanding of the clinical dynamics and picture of mental disorders. However, researchers interested in sociocultural factors suggest that not everything is equal within the biopsychosocial framework, with the social aspects of the equation often relegated to secondary status within the treatment contexts.

More recent evaluations of biopsychiatry have raised serious doubts about its viability. One serious objection is: How can mental disorders be considered biologically-based brain diseases, or valid medical conditions, when researchers have not identified biological variables capable of reliably diagnosing any mental disorders, distinguishing between individuals with or without a mental disorder or distinguishing different mental disorders from each other? Another objection is: If psychiatric medications are safe and effective, why has the rate of mental health disability risen as the use of these medications has risen? Shouldn't the widespread use of safe and effective psychotropic medications lead to less severe, chronic and disabling mental disorders, which is clearly not the scenario as of now, worldwide (Deacon, 2013)?

In spite of such objections, biopsychiatry continues to dominate the field of psychopathology.

BOX 6.1 CLINICAL PSYCHOLOGY IN THE CONTEXT OF MEDICAL DISCOURSE

Lightner Witmer coined the term clinical psychology in the opening article of the first issue of his journal called *Psychological Clinic* in 1907. He described the new profession as follows:

> Although clinical psychology is clearly related to medicine, it is quite as closely related to sociology and to pedagogy ... The phraseology of 'clinical psychology' and 'psychology clinic' will doubtless strike many as an odd juxtaposition of terms relating to quite disparate subjects ... I have borrowed the term 'clinical' from medicine, because it is the best term that I can find to indicate the character of the method which I deem necessary for this work ... The methods of clinical psychology are necessarily involved wherever the status of an individual mind is determined by observation and experiment, and pedagogical treatment is applied to effect a change, i.e., the development of such individual mind.
>
> *(Witmer, 1907, p. 2)*

Since its inception until now, clinical psychology has largely operated within the ambit of biomedical discourse. It has shared primarily a compliant or an eclectic position vis-à-vis psychiatry. 'Compliance' is best summarized as taking care not to rock the medical boat. An example is the use of psychometric assessment procedures for a host of assumed illnesses. Clinical psychologists in the compliant position perform psychometric assessment, thereby giving the diagnostic system a scientific gloss. This can range from agreeing that someone 'has' post-traumatic stress to confirming that a person's IQ is less than 70. 'Eclecticism' has all the signs of a collaborative endeavour but with a hint of offering an alternative to the diagnostic and physical excesses of psychiatry. Psychotherapy and counselling as an adjunct to medication for a host of diagnosed individuals might be positioned as eclectic responses. In this arrangement, the clinical psychologist offering therapy neither directly challenges the diagnosis ('what does the term schizophrenia tell us?') nor the use of medication ('has anyone tested the brain-biochemical imbalance that is believed to produce this person's feelings of being overwhelmed?'). Instead, the clinical psychologist offers a variety of psychotherapy to the patient and reports progress to the referring physician or psychiatrist. The public stance of clinical psychology as a discipline has consistently failed to challenge the medical discourse. The academic journals in the field have a long history of supporting the psychiatric diagnostic nosologies and professional/patient dichotomies. Psychologists take a default position of utilizing medical terminology to position themselves as experts in the human condition. There is an ongoing attempt among the professionals of the field to align with the natural sciences, to position themselves as objective observers and recorders of human conduct. Such objectivity is supposedly achieved via a battery of psychometric tests and the use of 'evidence-based' therapeutic technologies.

In fact, Foucauldian analysis sees moral therapy, a psychological approach to the treatment of the mentally disordered, as making possible the emergence of modern psychiatry in the late nineteenth century. According to Foucault (1965), in the moral therapy establishments, mad people were placed in a regime of perpetual observation in which their behaviour was searched for any error or incongruity where madness might show itself. They were turned into objects of the keeper's (sane world) gaze, subjected to a system of rewards and punishments for every detail of their behaviour. The keeper was a moral authority and judge. The madman shared a non-reciprocal relation to the keeper. The mad person became the other and the split between reason and unreason was complete. This 'moral' system of power, which was based on an objectifying observation and denied validity to the voice of the mad, made possible the definition of madness in terms of its signs and symptoms triggering the development of psychiatric classification. It established madness as a biomedical condition.

PAUSE AND THINK

Compare the psychiatric classification of disorders with any other classification of diseases in another medical specialization. Reflect on the reasons why psychiatric classification is atheoretical with regard to the causation.

REVIEW QUESTIONS

1. How do value judgements enter the process of defining abnormality?
2. How does the biopsychosocial model improve upon the medical model of psychopathology?

How Did Biopsychiatry Rise to Power?

A discursive analysis of history can help answer the critical questions: How did biopsychiatry rise to power? What kind of web of cultural, intellectual and economic structures shaped the transitions and elaborations of meanings related to madness through history?

Michel Foucault, a French philosopher, a historian of ideas and social theorist, has produced one such history of madness in his text *Folie et déraison: Histoire de la folie à l'âge classique*, a French text translated into English as *Madness and Civilization: A History of Insanity in the Age of Reason* (Foucault, 1965). He critiqued Whiggish history and debunked notions of linear 'progress' and 'human nature'. He questioned the obviousness of basic categories of experience such as madness. He suggested that objects of study such as madness, psychology, psychiatry and crime do not just exist, rather they are constructed and produced. They have no inherent essence or fixed properties. How they are understood is contingent upon the factors present during a historical period. Thus, these objects of study change historically in terms of what they are and how they are understood. In the Foucauldian scheme of things, there is no 'The TRUTH'. He stated:

> Truth is a thing of this world ... And it induces regular effects of power. Each society has its regime of truth, its 'general politics' of truth: that is, the types of discourse which it accepts and makes function as true; the mechanisms and instances which enable one to distinguish true and false statements, the means by which each is sanctioned ... These 'general politics' and 'regimes of truth' are the result of scientific discourse and institutions, and are reinforced (and redefined) constantly through the education system, the media, and the flux of political and economic ideologies. In this sense, the 'battle for truth' is not for some absolute truth that can be

discovered and accepted, but is a battle about 'the rules according to which the true and false are separated and specific effects of power are attached to the true'... a battle about 'the status of truth and the economic and political role it plays'.

(Foucault, cited in Rabinow, 1984, p. 115)

In *Madness and Civilization*, Foucault tries to present the complex relationship that madness shares with normalcy and society through the three historical periods: the Renaissance; the Age of Confinement (roughly the seventeenth to the mid-eighteenth century) and the Age of Positivism (from the end of the eighteenth century until the nineteenth century).

Madness during the Renaissance

During the Renaissance, madness and unreason were still undifferentiated experiences. They shared borders with normalcy. Foucault (1965, p. 34) said: 'Madness circulates, was part of common decor and language, a daily experience that one seeks to exalt rather than master.' The Renaissance madness evoked both fascination and fear. In the world grappling with concerns of death and apocalypse, madness became a container for locating concerns about the darker side of life and fear about the end of the world. Repeatedly, in the texts of that time such as Erasmus's *In Praise of Folly* or Cervantez's *Don Quixote* or Shakespeare's *King Lear* or the mad soothsayer of *Julius Caesar*, the mad became a symbol of the truth of the world.

The chasm between madness and reason began to widen subsequently to reach a point today where, in the hands of science, abnormality is the polar opposite of normality. One does not include the other. Madness is now a worthless, nonsensical experience requiring riddance.

The Institutionalization of Insanity

According to Foucault, an enormous change in the meaning of madness took place during the classical age (the seventeenth century). Enormous houses of confinement were built which had absolute sovereignty over their inhabitants and jurisdiction without appeal. The year 1656 was the landmark date which represented the founding of the *Hôpital général* in Paris. About 1% of the population of Paris was confined there. Such houses of confinement emerged all over Europe – the Bridewell, Houses of Correction and Asylums in Britain; the *Zuchthausen* in Germany; the *Rasphuis* in Holland. In this institution of confinement congregated what is to modern eyes a scandalous medley of different types of persons: the mad along with the criminals, the diseased, the poor, the sexually depraved and corrupt. Here, the distinctions between madness and crime, the ill and the mad were not made. 'Madness took up multiple meanings of sin, disease and violation of social norms.' It was placed in this web of

What Is 'Abnormal' in Clinical Psychology?   **261**

relationships which the nineteenth-century psychiatry took over. Abnormality was still an amorphous experience, but now it did not have value. It was dangerous or undesirable. By confining it, it was torn away from the imaginary freedom it had in the Renaissance period. According to Foucault (1965), such large-scale confinement of madness was central to the genealogy of the modern asylums. 'Madness could not have become a specialized object of knowledge at the hands of psychiatry in the nineteenth century without having already been an object of internment.' These houses of confinement were not yet medical establishments offering care to the mad. This is evident due to several factors:

1. The admission to the *Hôpital général* in Paris was not contingent on medical diagnosis or jurisprudence. Its internees came to it through a variety of channels: heads of families, administrators, judicial tribunals and individuals who turned up themselves at its portal. These internment procedures were for the most part based on coarse divisions such as 'good or bad for internment' and 'dangerous or offensive'.
2. Confinement did not result due to any sense of sympathy for or understanding of the insane. It emerged out of economic–political situation that Europe was facing at that point in time. There was severe economic crisis – high inflation, harvest shortages – and this was matched by political crises in many countries. The emerging bourgeois ethic of that time championed work productivity in human beings to handle the economic crisis. To work and contribute to society attained high importance. Not only an economic, there was a moral dimension to work as well. Work was the very essence of what it was to be a rational human being. 'Idleness was not seen merely as an offence against the bourgeois normative order but as a violation of reason – a loss of humanity.' The institutions of confinement condemned idleness, made labour imperative for the inmates and, in doing so, expressed the emerging normative order of society. The real meaning of these institutions, Foucault argued, was not to provide medical attention or humanitarian concern, but to separate the unworthy from the society, to indoctrinate in those who could not or would not produce/work an 'ethical consciousness of labour'. The identification of the moral order with reason was sustained on the basis of excluding unreason. Madness became one of the forms of unreason.

Madness, Idleness and Animality

Confinement imposed secrecy on some forms of unreason, such as sexual depravity and the corruption of morals. They were hidden away out of shame and to protect society from scandals. 'But madness was chosen to be revealed on the stage of the world in these houses of confinement.' This created a split between madness and other forms of deviance. In Bethlem/Bedlam, London, people could pay to watch the animal-like madmen behind the bars, much like

262 What Is 'Abnormal' in Clinical Psychology?

the zoo. Mad people became a pure spectacle for the general delight and the antics and conditions of these lunatics provoked pity, laughter, repulsion and horror among the spectators. It was something to look at from a distance through the eyes of reason but not to mingle with, not to engage within oneself. As Foucault (1965, p. 198) puts it: 'The animal in man no longer has any value as the sign of a beyond; it has become madness without relation to anything but itself.'

The mad personified the association between idleness, unreason and animality. Nakedness, a dark and filthy living environment, little human contact, caged and chained, and used as beasts of burden were the brutal conditions which marked their existence. Their animality could be mastered only by discipline and brutalizing. Their bestiality was supposed to give them the strength to withstand the cold, hunger and pain. 'They were not, as yet, seen as mentally sick.'

Rise of a New Division

The course of madness changed again with a new division shaping up in the eighteenth century that led to the segregation of the criminals, political subversives and counter-revolutionaries from the mad. The former were incarcerated in prisons and the latter were put in the asylums to be treated. This segregation was based on a view that criminals and paupers merited a regime free of madness and not out of any concern for the mad. This new division rose in response to another historical situation. Confinement came to be seen as counter-productive as it confined those who could work and also proved to be a burden on economic resources. 'Physicians working in these asylums were referred to as "mad-doctors" or alienists and not psychiatrists.' The term psychiatry was coined by a German physician, Johann Christian Reil, much later in 1812. 'The mad-doctors had more of a custodial rather than a therapeutic approach towards the inmates.' They had a low social status in the hierarchy of the medical profession.

The Medicalization of Mental Illness

Until the middle of the eighteenth century, medical doctors showed little interest in securing public recognition as 'experts' in insanity. However, as the number of private madhouses increased significantly, offering a potential new source of status and profit, physicians changed their attitude (Scull, 1979). In England, the Vagrancy Act of 1774 delegated the inspection of the asylums to the Royal College of Physicians and mandated that confinement of the insane could be approved only by licensed medical doctors. The result was a growing public recognition of the medical jurisdiction over insanity. It was at this time that physicians began to describe insanity as 'a medical disease'. Physicians knew they had no convincing evidence that insanity was a disease or that it could be cured by medical means (Scull, 1979).

Towards the end of the eighteenth century, both psychiatry and moral management tussled to gain control over madness. Reformers such as physician Philippe Pinel in France and a religious Quaker, William Tuke in England, during the late eighteenth and early nineteenth centuries, developed a therapeutic approach which eventually came to be known as the moral therapy. The model of moral therapy was a model of psychosocial care based on the psychological principles of eliminating cruelty towards the mad and understanding the patient as an individual human being. The term 'moral' meant several things at that time: 'It carries within itself emotional connotations of the words zeal, hope, spirit and confidence. It also has to do with custom, conduct, way of life and inner meaning' (Bockoven, 1956, p. 173). Stresses of a psychological nature were referred to as 'moral causes'. The model saw good therapeutic success with patients. Cooter (1976, p. 5), another historian, wrote: 'The moral therapy threatened the status and very existence of physicians within asylums: if cures could be effected by nonmedical means, then the administrators of physic [mind] were reduced to mere custodians of the insane.'

A central concern was, how were doctors to demonstrate that madness was a medical condition for which they possessed special skills? Scull (1979), a historian of the lunacy trade, opines that physicians eventually got a foot in the door by suggesting that a combination of medical treatment and moral management would work best. When the moral management programme was instituted with caring and dedicated superintendents of hospitals and asylums, the programme flourished. Unfortunately, most of the hospitals that began to later incorporate the moral management programme did so superficially. Several factors eventually led to the fall of moral management, including the failure to train a second generation of practitioners, the overcrowding of the moral management facilities, and the fact that moral treatment did not appear as economical as other approaches. The moral management model was eventually replaced with a biological model in the latter part of the nineteenth century.

By the middle of the nineteenth century, the medical profession had assumed control of most public asylums in England and the United States. This was further accomplished by assigning physicians oriented to medical treatment to vacant superintendent posts instead of those skilled in moral management techniques. Concurrently, physicians were constructing their own theories of insanity. They were able to generate social acceptability of those theories by forming professional organizations and floating academic journals. During the second half of the nineteenth century, doctors increasingly acted as if inmates were biologically sick (Scull, 1979). Microscopes became a standard part of asylum equipment. Drugs were increasingly used to sedate the inmates, and postmortem studies were regularly performed in an attempt to locate brain lesions. It is important to understand that psychiatry, at this time, was able to establish itself as a medical profession but not because it identified any true diseases.

264 What Is 'Abnormal' in Clinical Psychology?

Towards the end of this period, organized psychiatry began work to categorize the behaviours associated with madness into 'disease' syndromes. Kraepelin, widely credited as being the father of modern psychiatry, provided the necessary credibility that psychiatry so badly needed via the grouping and labelling of certain behaviours. Psychiatry, it was claimed, had finally established madness as a medical disease. Following medical procedure, Kraepelin classified major mental disorders by describing their symptoms. As with other medical investigators of his time, he observed the patients carefully over time, noting common symptoms and patterns. One of the patterns he noticed was that mania or euphoria was commonly followed by depression. He labelled this condition as 'manic-depressive insanity'. He also noticed another syndrome consisting of teenage onset, hallucinations, delusions, general mental confusion and deterioration over time, resulting in complete incapacity. He labelled this group of symptoms as 'dementia praecox' (deterioration with early onset), which later became known as 'schizophrenia'. Once these syndromes were identified and published in Kraepelin's (1883) textbook, psychiatry simply assumed that they were brain diseases. Yet no brain pathology associated with any of these syndromes had been discovered. These syndromes were 'identified' and 'classified' by observation alone, with no substantiating biological testing (Kupfer et al., 2002).

The first official, largely Kraepelinian, classificatory system in the USA was produced by the American Medico-Psychological Association, the forerunner of the APA, in 1918. There were 22 principal groups of mental disorder in the first *Statistical Manual for the Use of Institutions for the Insane*. Of them, 20 represented forms of disorder assumed to have biological foundations. Between 1918 and 1942, the *Statistical Manual* went through 10 editions, the tenth making provision for psychoneuroses and behaviour disorders – almost certainly a response to the observation that soldiers could be returned to the battlefield of the Second World War within days of treatment, involving rest and companionship, an outcome that common sense suggested could not be achieved if their distress had an organic substrate. In 1952, the APA published the first *Diagnostic and Statistical Manual of Mental Disorders (DSM I)* – a step towards a unified and definitive diagnostic system for all of American psychiatry. The manual had 106 categories of disorders divided into two main sections, one for disorders with established organic brain disease and the other for disorders without evidence of organic brain findings. The latter disorders were labelled 'functional' and were subdivided into disorders of psychosis, psychoneurosis and personality. These psychiatric disorders were assumed to have psychodynamic causality. The third edition of the *DSM*, published in 1980, was a landmark revision which replaced psychodynamic formulations and related terminology with criteria that were atheoretical and agnostic with regard to the aetiology of psychiatric disorders. It emphasized an empirical and operationalized definition of mental disorders which added legitimization to the field as a medical specialty. These advances were part of a larger movement at the time in American psychiatry to re-medicalize psychiatry, grounding the field in empirical research. *DSM III* marked the complete conquest of biomedicine over the phenomenon of madness.

Implications of the Revisionist History of Madness

There are powerful implications of this revisionist history of madness for our contemporary understanding of abnormality. Many of the meanings that have come to be overlaid on the understanding of madness survive even today. Madness and sanity are seen as the converse of each another. The historical process of separation of the two was set in motion during the seventeenth century, and it gained scientific legitimacy with the development of the classification nosologies of mental disorders. The history of insanity in which confinement was seen as a legitimate response to it explains why psychiatry is perhaps the only branch of medicine in which involuntary confinement of the patient is not only lawful but also scientific. The association between idleness and insanity finds its remnants in the criterion of dysfunctionality in which the inability to work remains one of the most important indicators of defining abnormal behaviour. Treatment is then accordingly directed towards making people more adaptive and functional in their work and relational contexts. The modern mad person is not treated as inhumanly as they were in the seventeenth-century madhouses. However, the modern mad person in psychiatric case conferences is still put on display, under the medical gaze of all interns and senior doctors and asked perfunctory questions to confirm his/her diagnosis. He/she also still evokes similar reactions of repulsion, fear and laughter that the madmen at Bethlem/Bedlam evoked. Psychology and psychiatry have brought together morality and science and have masked the former with the power of the latter. Modern psychological talking cures are confessional (and the link to sin, guilt and morality is evident), aimed at making a person look at themself and their own irrationality. There is a culpability that the patient has in the creation of his/her symptoms ('it is your thoughts and emotional reactions that are irrational') and a responsibility to effect one's own cure. The system of reinforcement in behavioural therapy is centred on the principles of rewards and punishments for one's behaviour. The psychiatrist/psychologist remains a moral authority in the way he/she uses clinical judgement to assess deviance from social norms as a sign of abnormality. While psychiatric/psychological practice may take recourse behind scientific neutrality, the fact is that it is a value-laden enterprise, constantly dabbling with morality-imbued notions of normality and abnormality. In the light of the above, it becomes important to debate whether the rise of the medical model is a sign of progress in knowledge about psychopathology and a symbol of liberation for the mad.

The history of madness is often conflated with the history of psychiatry, implying that madness came into being with the emergence of psychiatry, which is a fallacious claim. Foucault analysed the history of madness rather than the history of psychiatry, thereby, liberating the various epistemes related to madness and relativizing the contemporary scientific/medical discourse of mental illness. He suggested that what we currently understand of an object of study like mental disorder is only a particular discourse about it.

How Is Abnormality Understood in Clinical Psychology?

As has been discussed earlier, clinical psychology has operated largely within the discourse of biopsychiatry. It makes use of its classification system and accepts the view that normalcy and abnormality are two discrete categories.

Abnormal behaviour is understood as unusual, erratic and deviant behaviour. The question 'When does a problem become a disorder?' is answered in abnormal psychology by referring to the 'four Ds' – deviance, dysfunction, distress and dangerousness. The criterion of 'deviance' (statistical or cultural), as mentioned before, suggests that abnormality is an infrequently occurring behaviour/socially unacceptable behaviour. It is 'away from the norm' (the norm can be statistical average or cultural norm). The statistical deviance criterion give an impression of value neutrality as it makes use of standardized tests and quantification procedures. But it doesn't ask the following questions: How is the cut-off point decided above which psychopathology begins? Why are very high levels of IQ scores not indicative of psychopathology while very low levels of IQ are? Aren't value judgements at play here? In the case of the cultural deviance criterion, the question is never asked: Who defines the social norms, what purposes do they serve and whether the norms and social roles can themselves be pathological rather than the individual who fails or refuses to adhere to them? In such a conceptualization, normality is equivalent to conformity and abnormality is conflated with individuality, rebellion, unorthodoxy. Thus, psychiatric diagnosis and treatment (including psychotherapy) can become a form of social control of deviance.

The next criterion of 'dysfunction' implies that abnormality is what impairs the person's ability to function effectively, including the ability to care for oneself, have good relationships with others, and manage academic or work responsibilities. An illustration of this is depression, which interferes with all these tasks of life and creates maladaptive behaviours such as trouble in getting out of bed, inability to enjoy life, difficulty in concentrating and thinking. This criterion runs into a controversy that impairment is not an absolute category but is relative to expectations, environments and the task demands typically imposed by the majority social groups. A particular mental condition would not give rise to dysfunctionality, it can be argued, if tasks and expectations were not incompatible with it. The controversy in the 1970s about whether homosexuality is a mental disorder was one expression of this general issue. Contemporary examples include the controversy about ADHD – if this is a real illness to be treated by medication or rather temperamentally-based high activity levels in (mainly) boys causing difficulty because of socially inappropriate expectations in, for example, school settings?

'Distress', as the third criterion, views abnormality as that which creates suffering and agony for the person. Somatic symptom disorder in which the person fears potential illnesses, thinks the worst about one's symptoms and continues to search for an explanation even when serious medical conditions

What Is 'Abnormal' in Clinical Psychology? **267**

are ruled out, exemplifies this criterion. Such a person experiences significant physical and emotional suffering due to health concerns. The problem with grounding the conceptualization of mental disorder in distress is that distress can arise due to many factors other than mental disorder, such as normal life transitions, challenges and losses in education, work and family life, social deprivation, migration, exclusion, and so on. How does one distinguish between disorder-related distress and non-pathological distress? Given psychiatry's tendency to regard distress as fundamental to its domain, there is the inevitable risk of its spreading into kinds of suffering that are apparently not a matter of mental disorder. For example, there is concern that normal life suffering is being pathologized as a depressive disorder and that typically higher rates of diagnosable mental disorders among the socially disadvantaged reflect social exclusion rather than disorder (Bolton, 2010).

The fourth criterion of danger understands abnormality as patterns of behaviour 'dangerous' to self and/or to others. Substance abuse disorder is one such instance which has dangerous physical effects through the health conditions related with it and dangerous mental health effects evidenced by the emotions and feelings that people exhibit when the substance is unavailable or when they are trying to quit. Alcohol abuse is also comorbid with domestic abuse and violence and thus poses a danger to others too. In the context of this criterion, mental health services become involved in the protection of the public from danger, in the matters of public safety, which is more obviously a function of state agencies. In its role in compulsory detention and treatment, mental health services look like an agency of social control, a medicalized police force.

Another 'D' criterion that becomes important is 'duration'. It helps to decide if an emotion, behaviour or cognition is a fleeting symptom without consequence or is persistent enough for diagnosis. Feeling anxious for a few weeks does not merit a diagnosis of a psychological abnormality. When anxiety persists for at least six months, then a diagnosis of generalized anxiety disorder can be considered.

Each of the above criteria of abnormality is a useful indicator of mental disorder but none specifies precise boundaries for the concept of mental disorder and different situations call for different definitions. It is important to recognize that such conceptualizations understand abnormality as residing within an individual. These indicators of abnormality are also reflected in the definitions of mental disorder provided by psychiatric classification frameworks such as the *DSM* and the *ICD*. The fifth edition of the *Diagnostic and Statistical Manual of Mental Disorders* defines mental disorder as:

> A mental disorder is a syndrome characterized by clinically significant disturbance in an individual's cognition, emotion regulation, or behavior that reflects a dysfunction in the psychological, biological, or developmental processes underlying mental functioning. Mental disorders are usually associated with significant distress in social, occupational, or other important activities. An expectable or culturally approved response to a common

268 What Is 'Abnormal' in Clinical Psychology?

stressor or loss, such as the death of a loved one, is not a mental disorder. Socially deviant behavior (e.g., political, religious, or sexual) and conflicts that are primarily between the individual and society are not mental disorders unless the deviance or conflict results from a dysfunction in the individual, as described above.

(APA, 2013)

In the definition above, it is important to note that the consequences of the condition (dysfunction and distress) and not its aetiology determine whether the condition should be considered as a disorder. This is the essence of the atheoretical stance of the *DSM* towards aetiology.

PAUSE AND THINK

Can you think of examples of social norms and regulations in your own social milieu which are unreasonable or contradictory and create distress and confusions within you and people you know?

REVIEW QUESTIONS

1. What are the various bases of defining abnormality? Critically review them.
2. Are all infrequently occurring behaviours abnormal?
3. According to the critical perspective, which factors have led to the rise of psychiatry and its control over the phenomenon of madness?

Is Classification a Boon or a Bane?

Most of us understand psychopathology in terms of the different forms it takes such as mental retardation, schizophrenia, depression, and so on. These disorders are categories of psychopathology defined by certain clinical features and indicators, on the basis of which they are diagnosed. Classification is the foundation of clinical practice and research in psychiatry. Classification in the *DSM* and the *ICD* is categorical in nature which means that mental disorders are divided into types based on prototypal criteria and descriptive features (signs and symptoms). It specifies rules for diagnosing a disorder (e.g., major depressive disorder, specific phobia, paranoid schizophrenia) differentiating one from another (e.g., differential diagnosis between major depressive episode and dysthymia, specific phobia and generalized anxiety disorder, paranoid schizophrenia and delusional disorder) and allows systematic communication and research in the field. Thus, the psychiatric nosology is based on phenomenological and behavioural descriptions of clinical features rather than aetiology. The various types of disorders in the most recent version of the *Diagnostic and Statistical Manual, DSM 5*, are neurodevelopmental disorders, schizophrenia spectrum and other psychotic disorders, bipolar and related disorders, depressive disorders, anxiety disorders, obsessive-compulsive and related disorders, trauma and stress-related disorders, dissociative disorders, somatic symptom and related disorders, feeding and eating disorders, elimination disorders, sleep–wake disorders, sexual dysfunctions, gender dysphoria, disruptive, impulse-control and conduct disorders, substance-related and addictive disorders, neurocognitive disorders, personality disorders, paraphilic disorders, and other mental disorders. The priorities for the *DSM 5* revision of the criteria were to incorporate aetiological and neurobiological research into the definitions of psychiatric disorders and to improve the clinical utility of the criteria. For example, because recent studies have shown that obsessive-compulsive disorder involves distinct neurocircuits, this and several related disorders constitute their own chapter instead of being addressed in the chapter on anxiety disorders. In *DSM 5*, the Roman numeral 'V' in its name has been replaced with the Arabic number '5' in a deliberate change of naming convention to create discontinuity from the previous *DSMs*.

Problematics of Classification

While exerting a significant influence on the way abnormality is understood, there are some fundamental scientific and philosophical aspects of psychiatric classification which are called into question:

- The dominance of nosology in psychiatric practice eclipses the debates on the nature of mental disorders. It hides the fact that answering a broad question, 'what is psychopathology/abnormality?' is more of a challenge than describing the characteristics of people suffering from a specific mental disorder. Karl Jaspers (1963) compared psychiatric nosology to botanical classification. He stated that it is much easier to describe a single plant than to describe what a plant is. This is because, as a linguistic label, 'psychopathology' or 'plant' does not directly specify the particular limiting attributes of these categorical terms.
- This classification largely uses behavioural signs and symptoms to describe syndromes. It assumes that overt signs of dysfunction and deviance in behaviour are sufficient in themselves to comprehend psychopathology. Clinical assessment tools like psychiatric rating scales provide a way to quantify aspects of a patient's psyche, behaviour and relationships with individuals and society aiding the diagnosis. Through the process of the operationalization of concepts, rating scales can measure both internally experienced variables (e.g., mood) and externally observable variables (e.g., frequency of handwashing behaviour). This reliance on observable descriptors is largely governed by the need to objectively diagnose abnormality and increase inter-clinician reliability vis-à-vis clinical diagnosis. However, the symptom-based language tells us a

lot less regarding the lived experience of the person. It tells us what the problems are that a person has but not about the person who has the problems and how these problems may be shaped and lived with. R. D. Laing (1960), an existential-phenomenological thinker, conducted research into schizophrenia and sought to go beyond the discrete symptom-based understanding of people afflicted by it. He carefully explored the actual experiential meanings of the words used by those involved, i.e., the patient and his/her friends, family and mental health professionals. This led to a totally different 'concept' of schizophrenia: instead of it being a disease that is primarily genetic and/or biological, with symptoms such as meaningless language and hallucinations, and only treatable by medication, it could be seen as an individual's rich, metaphoric and highly meaningful linguistic reactions and explorations of essentially dysfunctional and distorted relationships and as a desperate attempt to obtain a sense of self. This phenomenological account led to new forms of 'treatment', mainly drug-free and in therapeutic communities, where different 'relationships' can be formed. A possibility is opened up where the so-called 'undesirable' experience or behaviour can have an undisclosed 'meaning', or its 'content' (rather than form) becomes significant. Psychiatric classification, on the other hand, attempts to fit the patient's suffering into already available categories of disorderly behaviours and thus ignores or denies the patient's individual experience.

- Psychiatric classification texts, such as the *DSM*, since its third revision, have adopted the 'language of medicine' to describe and understand psychological suffering. This language includes terms such as disease, symptom, patient, syndrome, relapse, prognosis and diagnosis. Besides, research efforts have increasingly concentrated on searching for biological bases of suffering and pharmaceutical treatments. These biomedical frameworks disregard the sufferers' personal history, the interpersonal and relational contexts for their distress and the influences of the larger social, political and cultural systems. For example, attempts to find the genetic and neurological substrates of PTSD, the anatomical locus of post-traumatic stress in the brain and the possible childhood precursors of PTSD have shifted attention away from the impact of war, natural calamities, or unemployment on psychological suffering. Further, the medicalization of PTSD individualizes the suffering, that is, sees it as residing within an individual.

- There is a steady 'proliferation of disorders' in each subsequent edition of the *DSM* which brings increased scrutiny and regulation of the patients' personal life by the mental health professionals. PTSD and borderline personality disorder were not part of the American diagnostic criteria until the former was included in *DSM III* in 1980, and both of these diagnoses have persisted through the current edition of the criteria. Acute stress disorder, bipolar II disorder and Asperger's disorder did not exist until they were introduced into *DSM IV* in 1994. In addition, the criteria for many diagnoses have become less stringent, so that less severe difficulties are now seen as illnesses in need of professional remedy. For example, *DSM 5* has removed the bereavement exclusion criteria from the diagnosis of major depressive disorder. This implies that the subset of persons who meet the full symptom–duration–severity criteria for major depression within the first few weeks after bereavement (i.e., the death of a loved one) will no longer be excluded from the set of all persons with major depression – as many would have been – under *DSM IV*'s exclusion guidelines. Many critics feel that this puts people experiencing bereavement at risk of being diagnosed with major depression (Zisook et al., 2012). It contributes to what has been called 'the diffusion of deficit', that is, the tendency to label everyday unhappiness, ordinary shortcomings and personal eccentricities as pathological.

- Classification systems are usually categorical – all-or-nothing systems. This implies a dichotomy between normal and abnormal states. An individual is either mentally ill or not. This dichotomy is becoming increasingly difficult to sustain. There is increasing evidence that while the thought content and behaviour of people with and without mental health problems may differ from the norm, the processes underlying them are essentially the same. This had led to the emergence of the dimensional approach of classification that suggests that people who are diagnosed as having mental disorder may better be considered to be at the extreme end of the distribution of normality, not categorically different from others. Many of us have been anxious or depressed at one point or other, not felt like engaging with the world, or ate and slept poorly. These experiences are not unique to people with depressive disorders. Whether or not we consider them to be problematic is dependent on their frequency and the intensity with which they are experienced. Dimensional approaches are attempting to identify various kinds of psychological parameters (such as personality traits) and then assessing the degree to which problems are experienced vis-à-vis those dimensions. If individuals score above a threshold score, based on severity and frequency of their experiences, they may require some help in those aspects of their life. Thus, this approach avoids forcing the presenting problems into a diagnostic category into which they do not easily fit.

There are a few guidelines that can help us understand how some disorders might best be moved to a continuum classification system from a categorical one and how others can feel more secure in their current categorical one.

In Table 6.1 are some of the questions to be asked before deciding on a categorical or dimensional scale (Tyrer, 2010, p. 34).

Classification has been criticized for its circularity. Symptoms are used to define a disorder but they are also accounted for by the presence of the disorder, using the following logic:

272 What Is 'Abnormal' in Clinical Psychology?

TABLE 6.1 Deciding on a categorical or dimensional scale

Knowledge question	Answer	Choice of category or dimensional approach
Is there a truly independent measure of the diagnosis?	Yes	Use category
	No	Be inclined to use dimensions
Are there clear boundaries between the disorder and related ones?	Yes	Use category
	No	Use dimensional approach
Does the disorder have a different natural history and course from other (apparently related) disorders	Yes	Use category
	No	Use dimensional approach
Is there a specific treatment for the disorder that makes it useful to identify separately?	Yes	Use category
	No	Use dimensional approach

Q: How do you know this patient has schizophrenia?
A: Because she lacks insight into her strange beliefs and she experiences auditory hallucinations.
Q: Why does she have strange beliefs and experience auditory hallucinations?
A: Because she suffers from schizophrenia.

Classification also suffers from reliability and validity issues. Often, the same patient is diagnosed with different disorders over time, indicating poor reliability. In spite of attempts to provide precise behavioural descriptions for every disorder, there are still problems of inter-diagnostician reliability stemming from the lack of agreement among diagnosticians on the diagnosis of a disorder. For personality disorders, the inter-diagnostician reliability is quite problematic. There is also increasing dissatisfaction with the conceptual validity of the criteria becoming apparent with complaints that the criteria do not adequately distinguish disorders, leading to 'boundary confusions' (notable examples include people with depressive personality disorder and dysthymia, conversion and dissociative disorders, etc.) and high rates of 'diagnostic comorbidity' – instances in which two or more supposedly separate disorders (e.g., anti-social personality disorder and substance abuse disorder) are found to be occurring together in the same person on a regular basis. In addition, many observed syndromes do not fit any diagnostic classification or are assigned to 'residual categories', such as 'psychotic disorder not otherwise specified (NOS)'. Another important form of validity where *DSM* is lacking is predictive validity. A diagnostic category should predict the course, prognosis and treatment of the illness.

What Is 'Abnormal' in Clinical Psychology? **273**

While a valid diagnosis has to have good reliability, it is possible to consistently use a label which is still not valid. These doubts about the validity and reliability of psychiatric diagnoses have led some to argue that mental disorder is very difficult to measure and that the dividing line between the normal and abnormal is fuzzy.

BOX 6.2 THE SPLIT UNDERSTANDINGS OF SCHIZOPHRENIA

Since schizophrenia is regarded as the most-discussed psychiatric illness, it is reasonable to assume that it is a real, recognizable, unitary and stable psychiatric construct. A closer look at the history of the disorder shows that many of its proponents – Benedict Morel, Emil Kraepelin, Eugen Bleuler, Kurt Schneider – were actually providing quite distinct descriptions of what is believed to be the same construct. Early in the nineteenth century, John Haslam described a typical *ICD 10* case of a boy with schizophrenia but no one paid attention to it (Haslam, 1810). In the 1850s, Benedict Morel used the phrase '*démence précoce*' not as an official clinical category but as a description of a state of intellectual deficit. It had already sunk into oblivion by the time Kraepelin had decided to use the term '*dementia praecox*' (implying dementia with an early onset) in 1896. By 1919, Kraepelin's understanding of *dementia praecox* had expanded, and it was here that it was at its broadest and subsumed the following 'forms': simple, simple–stuporous, hebephrenia, delusional, depressive, circular, agitated, periodic, catatonia (both excited and stuporous), paranoid (mitis and gravis), and confusional speech (schizophasia). Dementia praecox was defined as:

> Their clinical relations are not yet clear but they all display two peculiarities, that they are in the first place, so far as can be seen, not occasioned from without but arise from internal causes, and that secondly, at least in the great majority of cases, they lead to a more or less well-marked mental enfeeblement.
>
> *(Kraepelin, [1896] 1971, p. 1)*

Dementia praecox became 'schizophrenia' in a book published by Bleuler in 1911. The reasons put forward by Bleuler to justify its coining are as follows: 'I call dementia praecox schizophrenia because, as I hope to show, the splitting of the different psychic functions is one of its most important features' (Bleuler, [1911] 1958, p. 5). He also stated that in schizophrenia, such splitting occurred vertically (i.e., it separated mental functions from each other). He powerfully influenced the first diagnostic manuals developed after the Second World War, *DSM I* and *DSM II*. At the time, psychiatry in the United States was strongly psychoanalytic and easily assimilated Bleuler's relatively broad and psychologically-based diagnostic category of schizophrenia, which did not emphasize psychotic symptoms.

However, by the 1970s, it had become apparent that the diagnostic criteria for schizophrenia had become so broad and diffuse that they could not be reliably applied. The third edition of *DSM* gravitated towards the 'Schneiderian criteria of schizophrenia' which were more easily delimited from the normal range of experiences. In 1959, Kurt Schneider gave the 'first-rank symptoms' as the core features of schizophrenia. These symptoms included hearing one's thoughts spoken aloud, auditory hallucinations commenting on one's own behaviour, thought withdrawal, insertion and broadcasting, somatic hallucinations, or the experience of one's thoughts as being controlled or influenced by outside forces. Manifestation of one first-rank symptom in the absence of organic disease, persistent affective disorder or drug intoxication was sufficient for the diagnosis of schizophrenia. Second-rank symptoms included other forms of hallucinations, depressive or euphoric mood changes, emotional blunting, perplexity and sudden delusional ideas. When first-rank symptoms were absent, schizophrenia might still be diagnosed if a sufficient number of second-rank symptoms were present. This move to emphasize specific psychotic symptoms in the diagnosis of schizophrenia continues to exercise its influence on the diagnosis of schizophrenia to the present day.

So, while Kraepelin defined *dementia praecox* as a collection of several states sharing the symptom of mental weakness, similar in terms of onset (early) and course (progressively deteriorating), Bleuler saw splitting as the chief manifestation of schizophrenia and Schneider made psychotic symptoms of hallucination and delusions as central to the diagnostic category. Are we describing the same disorder or different disorders? Will the real schizophrenic stand up, please?

Psychiatrists today face the issue that different people with the *DSM* diagnosis of schizophrenia can present with very different problems and experiences. This heterogeneity of symptomatology contradicts the notion of a disorder that has an underlying mechanism: If this were the case, all these people should have presented the same cluster of symptoms. A related point is that different people with schizophrenia respond to different medications, including neuroleptics, lithium and benzodiazepines. Others fail to respond to any of these medications. Accordingly, the course and treatment of the condition vary considerably across individuals. As Bentall, Jackson and Pilgrim (1988) noted: 'We are inevitably drawn to an important conclusion: schizophrenia appears to be a disease which has no particular symptoms, which has no particular course and which responds to no particular treatment' (p. 147). On this ground, they suggested that this diagnostic category has no validity and should be abandoned. Another attack on schizophrenia is its all-or-nothing nature. Schizophrenia-like symptoms are present in other syndromes as well, such as schizoaffective disorder, delusional disorder, schizotypal personality disorder, schizophreniform disorder, brief psychotic disorder, giving rise to the term schizophrenic spectrum disorders. A further issue of relevance is that the experiences of people diagnosed with schizophrenia, or even disorders of the schizophrenic spectrum, are not exclusive to them. Many people who do not

What Is 'Abnormal' in Clinical Psychology? **275**

> come to the attention of the psychiatric services also hear voices. What distinguishes between people who seek help for their problem and those who do not appears to be differences in their responses to the voices and their ability to cope with them.

How Sound Is the Practice of Psychiatric Diagnosis?

Psychiatric diagnosis is the sine qua non of biological psychiatry. It is the clinical practice of determining which condition or disease explains the patient's symptoms and signs by matching them with the classification system so that treatment can be prescribed. Clients' encounters with the mental health system typically begin with an assessment of their difficulties and a diagnosis. Although the formal diagnosis is not of central importance for psychotherapy, diagnostic classifications play an important role in prescribing medications. Moreover, in the USA, diagnosis has assumed importance because managed care systems use them to determine if clients are entitled to be reimbursed for mental health treatment and how much and what kind of treatment they can receive.

Diagnosis is supposed to be a scientific act of judging and naming a condition. But do clinical practitioners not make biased judgements? Indeed, many studies have found that clinicians evaluating identical case materials make different diagnostic judgements in response to information about gender, social class, racial identity or sexual orientation (Becker & Lamb, 1994; Robertson & Fitzgerald, 1990; Strakowski et al., 1995). Moreover, clinicians may make different treatment recommendations depending on the social status of a client, even when their symptom descriptions and diagnoses are identical. Fads in diagnoses also continually emerge and then recede. In the USA, for example, bipolar disorder has shifted from being an unusual diagnosis to an extremely common one. What explains this? Possibly clinicians have acquired a new acumen in recognizing a previously unrecognized problem or have they unwittingly shifted their judgements in response to the aggressive marketing efforts of drug companies?

There are many other documented shortcomings of psychiatric diagnosis, such as obscuring of personal, social and cultural contexts, the individualizing of problems, stigma and disempowerment, removal of responsibility, the omission of the client's viewpoint and loss of personal meaning (Johnstone & Dallos, 2013). A clinician working within a biological model of mental health would aim to provide a diagnostic label but the exact nature of the problems an individual faces or how they are expressed will be only of secondary interest. A person with schizophrenia who is hallucinating will be treated with drugs that stop hallucinations, the nature of the hallucinations will not influence the drug treatment given. It is perhaps important to be sensitive to the potential abuses of psychiatric labels. There is a grain of being human in all patients that resists diagnostic pigeonholing. It is the calling of the therapeutic profession to struggle to translate diagnostic categories into human terms so that neither the patient nor the professional is dehumanized.

One way of doing this is 'psychological formulation'. Formulation is a possible way of re-introducing personal meaning, personal and social contexts and mutual collaboration into mental health work. Psychological formulations attempt to identify the processes that led to and maintain the problems an individual is facing. They may be internal, external, familial and structural. These factors then become targets of intervention. A formulation is an explanatory hypothesis about the nature of the clinical problem and is theory-driven.

In a similar vein, medical anthropologist Arthur Kleinman advocates the practice of developing an 'illness narrative'. Each patient brings to the practitioner a story of his illness. Illness, here, refers to patient's perception, experience, expression and patterns of coping with symptoms. The person's experience of symptoms is mediated by language, illness beliefs, socially learnt ways of behaving when ill, personal significance of pain and suffering (Kleinman, 1988). Disease refers to the way doctors recast illness in terms of their theoretical models of pathology. Diagnosis is the semiotic act of reinterpreting the patient's illness (experienced symptoms) as signs of particular disease states. Kleinman suggests that doctors should rather listen to illness narratives of the sick. That story enmeshes the disease in a web of meanings that make sense only in the context of a particular life. Illness narratives are not merely accounts of symptoms but a mechanism through which people become aware of and make sense of their experience of suffering. A transformation takes place from something 'lived' (full of complexity but not given a single, crystallized meaning) into something 'interpreted' (given structure and meaning through the dialogue that takes place between the patient and the physician). 'Narrativization' therefore acts as a reflexive, therapeutic and even a transformative mechanism for people who have experienced illness. Kleinman (1988) suggests certain questions that can help clinicians relate to their patients in an empathic rather than a mechanical manner:

1. What do you think has caused your problem?
2. Why do you think it started when it did?
3. What do you think your problem does inside your body?
4. How severe is your problem? Will it have a short or long course?
5. What kind of treatment do you think you should receive?
6. What are the most important results you hope to receive from this treatment?
7. What are the chief problems your illness has caused you?
8. What do you fear the most about your illness/treatment?

PAUSE AND THINK

Nowadays, we hear about 'spectrum disorders', such as autism spectrum disorders, schizophrenia spectrum disorder, bipolar spectrum, trauma spectrum, and so on. Examine the reasons behind 'spectrum-based classification' in psychiatry.

> **REVIEW QUESTIONS**
>
> 1. How do psychiatric classification and diagnosis dehumanize patients?
> 2. How does the practice of psychiatric formulation and eliciting patient's illness narrative help?

How Is Culture Implicated in Psychopathology?

A critical issue facing psychiatry and the study of psychopathology is: should culture be considered as a factor impacting abnormal behaviour? This is part of the larger concern about the role of culture in influencing behaviour, in general (this issue is debated in detail in Chapter 4).

There is a 'tacit model of pathogenicity' in psychiatry which has become close to a professional orthodoxy that suggests that biology is presumed to determine the cause and structure of the forms of mental disease (pathogenesis), while cultural and social factors at most shape or influence the content/symptom of the disorder (pathoplasticity; Kirmayer, 1998). In the context of a disorder such as schizophrenia, this model explains that the biologically-based disease causes the structure of delusional thought processes – the system of cultural beliefs organizes the content of paranoid delusions. Another example that is explained with reference to this model is the predominance of somatic symptoms in depression in non-Western societies, among traditionally-oriented ethnic minorities and among the less-educated members of the lower socioeconomic classes. It is taken to mean that the biology of depression and anxiety disorders underwrites the inner form of these disorders, but cultural values and beliefs shape the experience and expression of the disease. In other words, this is also taken to mean that disorders such as depression, anxiety and schizophrenia are universal categories but their experience, expression, course and outcome can be culturally variable. The primacy given to the biological factors as aetiological determiners of psychopathology is clearly evidenced in the way most books on abnormal psychology first discuss the biological perspective and then move on to the psychological and sociocultural perspectives (according the latter much less space than the former) while discussing the causation of mental disorders.

Can Culture Be of Aetiological Significance for Mental Disorders?

Increasingly, sociocultural factors are seen as having a causative influence on mental disorders. The general systems theory suggests that specific socio-environmental stressors can act as aetiological determiners of mental disorders at an individual level. For example, specific variables, such as a culture's lack of coherence and integration, eventually influence the mental health and well-being of its members via intervening levels such as social stress, identity confusion and subsequent psychobiological changes and behavioural problems. This pathway is expressed in Figure 6.1.

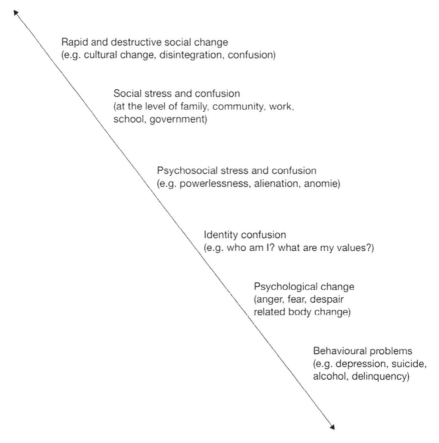

FIGURE 6.1 Sociocultural pathways to deviance, distress and disorder
Source: Marsella and Yamada (2007).

Among the numerous sociocultural variables which have been posited as the sources of psychopathology (and not merely factors affecting its manifestations/courses/outcomes), the major ones are acculturation, urbanization, migration and poverty. All of these variables exercise their effects via stressors and stress variables. But each is unique in the specific stressors it embodies and in the variations in the stress response that occurs (Marsella & Scheuer, 1993).

Marsella and Yamada (2007) suggest that cultural factors have an aetiological significance for mental disorders in the way culture determines the following:

1. The types and parameters of physical and psychosocial stressors.
2. The types and parameters of coping mechanisms and resources used to mediate stressors.
3. The basic personality patterns, such as self-structure and needs/motivational systems through the use of child-rearing practices.

How Does Culture Affect the Epidemiology, Manifestation and Course of Mental Disorders?

Epidemiology

Lower rates of schizophrenia have been reported in less-developed societies and the highest rates in North America and certain European countries (Sikanartey & Eaton, 1984). A chronic mode of onset of schizophrenia is more common in Western societies and an acute mode of onset is more common in developing societies. There is greater variability in the epidemiology of non-psychotic disorders such as depression. Clinicians in many non-Western societies have claimed increases in the prevalence of depression over the period of modernization of their societies. More personality disorders are detected in the West. There is also evidence that social change contributes to fluctuations in suicide rates. For examples, suicide rates in Sri Lanka among the Tamil ethnic minority had tripled between 1955 and 1974 (Kearney & Miller, 1985). This is attributed to the rapid population growth, increased competition for education and employment and the breakdown of a stable society, placing great pressure on Tamils.

Symptomatology

The manifestation of psychopathological responses also shows cross-cultural variation. A salient international finding is the marked predominance of somatic symptoms among depressed and anxious patients in non-Western societies, albeit these symptoms are common in the West too (Good & Kleinman, 1985). Kleinman, Anderson, Finkler, Frankenberg, and Young (1986) have shown that headaches, dizziness and lack of energy form a symptom cluster in neurasthenic illness behaviour associated with mixed depressive and anxiety disorders in ancient Chinese society and in contemporary Taiwan and China. The research literature also points out that feelings of guilt are much less commonly associated with depression in the non-Western world than in the West. How can we then equate the experience of depression in which chronic low back pain is a salient complaint with the experience of depression centred on guilt-ridden existential despair? On what basis can we also say that the underlying disease is the same when the illness experience is different?

Suicide has also been said to be less common among depressed patients in the Third World. In Argentina, as opposed to the USA, there is a penchant for passive, as opposed to active symptomatology. There is a tendency towards distortion and elaboration, as opposed to deficit in the sphere of ideational symptoms; there is greater concern with social relations in the symptomatology. Draguns (1973) suggested that when psychologically disturbed, Latinos feel less socially isolated and less ideationally active. Another provocative finding is that trance and possession states are ubiquitous in the non-Western societies and were so in the West prior to the modern age. The findings of the WHO's cross-cultural comparison of 'schizophrenia' discloses important cultural differences in the onset and symptoms of schizophrenia.

What explains these differences in the manifestation of mental illness? Obviously, culture! Anthropologists suggest that a more accurate mapping of the illness states such as somatized depression is provided by regarding such behaviours as 'idioms of distress' (Nichter, 1981). Distress can be personal, social or political and each culture offers unique ways of experiencing and expressing that distress as well as interpreting that experience.

Cultures where body and self can be experienced in non-dualistic forms make possible trance and possession in which different layers of experience are split off into gods, ghosts or ancestors. When these states occur in culturally authorized ritual and group settings, they are normative and normal. When they occur outside these settings, and are accompanied by floridly psychotic behaviour, the behaviour is labelled psychopathological. The erasure of trance and possessions from the modern, secular world can be attributed to the lost ability of modern man to access the otherwise pan-human dimensions of the self. The rationalizing powers of modern secular Western society have created a distance from participating emotionally in life and have instead intensified a meta-self – a critical observer who watches over and comments on experience. This kind of self-consciousness interferes with total absorption in lived experience which is the essence of a highly focused state of attention characteristic of trance.

Venkoba Rao (1973) points out several cultural factors in India that may protect against suicide. These include the emphasis on family obligations over individual rights, the legitimation of suicide, at least in historical periods, under ritual conditions (*sati*), and the concept of Karma (which would lead individuals to avoid suicide lest they be reborn in a less desirable state).

Barrett (2004) offers evidence that the sense of a split or divided self that is associated with both professional and lay discourses on schizophrenia in the West may emerge as salient because of the Western conception of the person as a bounded individual self. Patients in the West report feeling a split in personality while this aspect of the disorder is not central to the experience of the disorder in China and other non-Western countries where the discourse of self is different.

Course and Outcome

Research suggests a better outcome for schizophrenia in less-developed societies compared to Western societies. High competency requirements for normal living (literacy, tax forms, automobile maintenance, housing, etc.) from former patients, complex co-morbidities (alcohol abuse, trauma), isolation from family and community, and assumptions regarding personal control and responsibility are some of the salient potential reasons suggested to explain this finding. Societal and professional views about psychopathology also affect the course and outcomes. Waxler (1979) suggests that in cultures where schizophrenia is popularly viewed as an acute reaction and patients suffering from it are expected to recover from it like those suffering from other acute disorders, the family and community responses to the patient encourage normalization and discourage acceptance of a disabled role. Factors such as the economics of disability and the investment of certain mental health programmes in maintaining patients in long-term patient roles are further obstacles to a better outcome from schizophrenia. The medical profession may inadvertently abet these forces, since in North American and Western European societies, its members are trained to treat schizophrenic patients with low expectations of recovery. T. Y. Lin and M. C. Lin (1981) indicate that the stigma associated with madness in Chinese culture is more severe than that in the West, since the stigma attaches not just to the afflicted member but also to the family as a whole.

Which Psychometric Factors Must Be Considered When Conducting Epidemiological Research Across Cultures?

It is important to emphasize that cross-cultural research in psychopathology is beset with methodological problems of incomparability of samples, diagnostic criteria and assessment tools used. To assess cultural differences adequately, it is essential to translate local idioms of distress and add them to standard questionnaires, while deleting those that make no sense in the local culture. Colloquial terms such as 'feeling blue' or 'feeling down' used to evaluate depressive affect in North America may make little sense when translated to languages of other cultures. Leff et al. (1987) have found that negative expressed emotion (EE) measured solely in the verbal mode is lower in India than in British or Danish families. But an analysis of EE, based entirely on the direct expression of 'critical', 'hostile' or 'negative' verbal terms, cannot be an adequate method of assessment because it underestimates its occurrence. Anthropologists have shown that emotion in India is communicated non-verbally through posture, gait, facial movements as well as subtle, indirect verbal displays of etiquette and other salient social metaphors such as offering food and receiving gifts. Thus, EE can be measured in a valid manner by a culturally sensitive, ethnographic mode of study that explores what EE – negative and positive, high and low – means in the context of families of schizophrenic patients in Indian culture.

Are Cultural Syndromes of DSM 5 Variations of Universal Categories of Psychiatric Disorders?

The tendency in the biomedical model is to interpret the culture syndromes as exotic manifestations of universal mental disorders such as 'anxiety disorders', 'depressive disorder', 'hysterical disorder' and 'psychotic disorders'. For example, *susto* (prevalent in Mexico) is taken to be a cultural variant of depressive disorder; *dhat* syndrome (prevalent in the Indian sub-continent) is a version of anxiety disorders; *amok* (prevalent in Malaysia) is a homicidal version of brief psychotic disorder; *ataques de nervios* (prevalent among Hispanics) is a kind of panic disorder; and *taijin kyofusho* (among Japanese) can be seen as a type of social phobia. Here, again, we see the professional orthodoxy in psychiatry which makes a distinction between pathogenesis (causation and structure) and pathoplasticity (experience and expression), where the former has a biological basis and cultural factors can at best affect the latter.

Reality is much more complex than these simplistic equations. Do the apparent similarities or approximations indicate that the cultural syndrome has the same aetiology, course and outcome as disorders in the Western world? A strong emergent view suggests that it is not possible to separate a disorder from the actual psyche in which it is construed and the actual social context in which people respond to it. In fact, the following questions are being raised now: Is identifying a group of disorders as 'non-Western' not a testimony of ethnocentric bias? Are all disorders identified in psychiatric nosology not culture-bound? Littlewood and Lipsedge (1987) argue that 'anorexia nervosa', a universal mental disorder, should be regarded as a culture-specific illness behaviour of the West, as it is not highly prevalent outside the West and those sections of the population of the world which are strongly influenced by the Western aesthetic standards that value extreme slimness and which view strict dieting as an emblem of moral discipline.

PAUSE AND THINK

Try to find out how cultural syndromes such as *dhat* and *susto* represent particular idioms of distress in relation to personal and cultural meaning complexes. With what forms of psychiatric disorders do these syndromes coincide?

Is Psychopathology a Form of Social Suffering?

Kleinman, Das and Lock (1997, p. ix) state:

> The clustering of substance abuse, street violence, domestic violence, suicide, depression, post traumatic stress disorder … among people living in disintegrating communities runs against the professional medical idea that sufferers experience one … major problem at a time. That grouping of human problems also defeats categorization of such issues as principally psychological or medical and, therefore, individual.

This perspective considers mental disorder, in all its manifestations, to be a form of social suffering, a form of distress that is both a cause and consequence of interlinked social problems that may include poverty, social isolation, victimization and trauma. In this sense, the subjective experience of mental disorder

What Is 'Abnormal' in Clinical Psychology? **283**

(anxiety, sadness, hallucinations) is not simply one of intrapsychic conflict or existential angst; it is a consequence of troubling and traumatic social experiences – broken relationships, lost opportunities, social hostility, public failures, stigma, grinding poverty and chronic isolation. In short, mental disorder is not experienced as a discrete problem. It is part of an entangled set of circumstances. When people speak about their distress, they often focus on problems, such as the breakdown of relationships, stigma, lack of money, hunger, homelessness, and so on. 'Hearing voices', 'feeling sad' or 'experiencing anxiety' is an aspect of a series of interconnected difficulties that they face. The emphasis on suffering as a collective, socially embedded experience challenges the construction of mental disorders as an individual, as a set of discrete disorders requiring psychological or pharmacological responses.

The rationale for psychopathology as a socially caused form of human misery emerges from various sources. One supportive research trend is wide intracultural variation besides intercultural differences in psychopathology. The most important social variables in which disparity in mental disorders is found are social class, ethnicity and gender. Most mental disorders have their highest prevalence rate in the lowest socioeconomic classes. In North American society, members of Black and Hispanic minority ethnic groups, who are over-represented in the lowest socioeconomic class, are also at higher risk for such disorders. Some problems like anti-social personality are more common among inner-city Black youth in the United States. Worldwide, women in most studies are shown to be at a greater risk of depression than men, and research points to the importance of their relative powerlessness owing to their gender.

Another supportive trend is the increase in the rates of alcoholism, drug abuse and suicide during the periods of 'rapid modernization' of traditionally oriented populations such as North American Indians, Alaskan Natives and South Pacific, New Guinean and East Asian populations (Lin et al., 1981). Uprooting and forced acculturation among refugees, immigrants and migrants have repeatedly been shown to create increased rates of mental illnesses. Extreme conditions such as the Holocaust, the Cambodian genocide, the Vietnam War and the Cultural Revolution in China have been shown to increase the long-term burden of mental distress.

Studies on mental health and work argue for a significant role of unemployment, problematic work relationships and stressful work conditions in the development of mental health problems. Significant changes in the life events perceived as stressful – bereavement, divorce, other key losses and threats – have been repeatedly shown to precede the onset of mental illness, whereas adequate social support and coping resources have been found to protect individuals from these problems.

The findings reviewed above do not support the view that social factors are the sole determinants of mental disorder. However, they do underline the importance of social influences that place certain categories of people at greater risk of the onset of mental disorder or that contribute to the worsening of the

284 What Is 'Abnormal' in Clinical Psychology?

course of the disorder. Severe family, work or economic problems trigger syndromes of distress that have biological and psychological correlates which are labelled a psychiatric disorder. The social scientists reconceive these disorders as the psychobiological sequelae of social pathology and human misery. The social theory proposes that the psychological and biological vulnerability of the person combines with local social pressures to create syndromes of distress reflected in neuroendocrine, autonomic, cardiovascular, gastrointestinal and limbic system responses. Such responses constitute a spectrum of affective, anxiety and somatic complaints. A case in point is dysthymia which refers to chronic states of depression associated with feelings of demoralization and despair. This can be an instance of the medicalization of social problems where severe economic, political and health problems create endemic feelings of unhappiness, hopelessness and helplessness. Rethinking medicine from this vantage point leads to the proposition that much of ill health is one domain of human misery and a large part of this misery originates from sociopolitical, socioeconomic and social psychological affairs.

PAUSE AND THINK

A link between social class and various aspects of mental disorder has been accepted. Try to find out what are the actual mechanisms through which poverty affects everyday life and causes the onset or exacerbation of mental distress.

REVIEW QUESTION

What is meant by 'idioms of distress'?

BOX 6.3 WOMEN'S REPRODUCTIVE FUNCTIONS AND MENTAL HEALTH: DOES SOCIAL CONTEXT MATTER?

Mental health is dominated by gender-blind theories that assume and seek evidence to prove women's greater biologically-based vulnerability or proneness to mental disorder. Sex, a biological given, and gender, a social and cultural construct, are invariably conflated, leading to systematic bias. This confounding has led many researchers to narrow the scope of their investigations to a search for biological causes of disorders, such as depression, that by preordained understanding could only be found to be existing in women. Notions about women's reproductive organs and hormones being responsible for mental disorder are embedded in the long history of hysteria. Much research in the recent times has looked into the hypothesized relation between reproduction-related events, such as menstruation, pregnancy, miscarriage, childbirth, premature delivery, infertility, abortion and menopause, and women's higher rates of depression. This biological and individualizing emphasis on reproductive functions has long diverted attention and investigation of the social and structural determinants of women's mental health.

The important question – what are the health concerns and factors that women themselves believe impact their mental health? – is rarely asked. Avotri and Walters (1999) found that the importance and attention paid by researchers to reproductive functioning does not accord with women's own perspectives and health priorities. Nearly three-quarters of the women in their sample belonging to the Volta region of Ghana identified psychosocial health problems such as 'thinking too much' and 'worrying too much' as their main health concerns. The explanations women gave of their health problems stressed heavy workloads, the gendered division of labour, financial insecurity and responsibility for children. Research taking social and psychological factors into consideration often finds that biological factors are either mediated by such aspects or become irrelevant. For instance, research on postnatal depression has identified partner and social support, life events, the experience of maternity and infant temperament as critical risk factors for the development of depression in the postnatal year, rather than the hormonal status and bodily factors (Small et al., 1994).

While the contribution of women's reproductive functioning to their mental health has received intense scrutiny, the relation between men's reproductive functioning and their mental health has been ignored. Do men have no reproductive functions or are they unaffected by events and conditions such as infertility, attachment to and loss of foetus, extreme premature births, transition to parenthood? Such questions require urgent research attention.

Gender interacts with structural determinants, including income, education, workplace and social position and roles related to family, unpaid work and caring, and the experience of intimate, gender-based violence, to influence mental health. Explanatory models of emotional distress must move beyond biological theorization to focus on socio-structural factors that interact with bodily aspects. Gender, income inequality and poverty form a nexus as poverty and female gender are almost coterminous. Economic policies that cause sudden, disruptive and severe changes to the income, employment and living conditions of large numbers of people particularly affect those who are powerless to resist them, and poor, unskilled women in low-paid jobs constitute the large majority of such people. Such material and social disadvantages easily result in higher levels of vulnerability to depression, anxiety, somatic complaints among women and other similarly placed groups. Subjective experiences, such as exclusion and powerlessness, feelings of low self-regard, shame and humiliation, entrapment and devaluation, are linked to subordinate status and rank in society, increasing the likelihood of adverse mental health outcomes.

Final Comments

What do we understand as the meaning of abnormality on the basis of the preceding discussion? One important import is that, before anything else, madness is a word, a human artefact, put together to refer to something about human behaviour or one's perception of this behaviour. As a linguistic sign, its meaning is forever open to reinterpretation by those responding to it. Indeed, the history of madness suggests a plethora of possible meanings, often contradictory (e.g., devil possession versus pathological personality versus brain disease versus faulty learning versus recourse to one's essential truth versus socially disturbing/disruptive behaviour). When the referent itself is so fluid, then any attempt to fix its meaning is an untenable exercise. Rather, it is something like a linguistic black hole that sucks in all kinds of peculiar human behaviours that society cannot comprehend but is compelled to explain and control. However, the discipline of clinical psychology takes a rather reductionist position. It is heavily influenced by the biopsychiatric discourse that understands psychopathology as rooted in an individual's biology, expressed in the form of discrete signs and symptoms and treatable by technical responses, such as pharmacology and/or psychotherapy. A variety of critiques of this discourse reviewed in this chapter – the biopsychosocial model, the cultural perspective, the 'idioms of distress' view – and the 'social suffering' standpoint raise significant scientific, philosophical and ethical objections to the biomedical model. It becomes clear that mental disorders cannot be seen as akin to brain diseases because scientists have not yet identified a biological cause of, or even a reliable biomarker for, any mental disorder. Also, the claim that biological psychiatry has made great progress in reducing the societal burden of mental disorders is untenable because mental disorders are steadily becoming more common, severe and chronic. Additionally, mental distress is not just an individual experience stemming from within. It is also simultaneously a social experience in the sense that it is socially caused as well as socially shared by people who are threatened by interlinked problems, such as trauma, displacement, victimization, poverty, social isolation, and so on. Thus, the responses to it should not merely be technical but also structural (macro-level policies and programmes).

7

WHY SHOULD WE RETHINK 'CHILD' AND 'DEVELOPMENT' IN PSYCHOLOGY?

Developmental psychologists believe that their discipline is an academic sub-field within psychology that seeks to explain how and why most children (and now adults and old people) think, feel and behave at particular ages and stages, as well as evaluate both positive and negative environmental influences. It makes sense of behaviours such as: A 5-year-old claims that spreading out a row of toffees increases the number of toffees. A schoolchild uses a good strategy to successfully solve a problem and later uses a less reliable strategy for the same task. An adolescent girl vacillates between the life of an artist and a corporate career. Developmental research and theories shape and impact practices related to child care, parenting and education, as well as policies regarding the rights and needs of children, adolescents and old people. The attachment paradigm with its focus on the need for secure attachment in early childhood, the importance of maternal sensitivity and the impact of maternal rejection has had a profound influence on attitudes and practices in child care and beliefs about what constitutes 'good mothering'. The Piagetian account of cognitive development was hugely influential in shaping beliefs about primary education practice during the 1960s and 1970s. Thus, developmental psychology is not just a scientific discipline but it is also an ideology that becomes a part of common sense and defines what is and what is not growth and under what conditions, growth is possible.

Most textbooks of developmental psychology begin with an overview of the issues of development, such as nature vs nurture; stage vs continuous development; organismic vs mechanical view of development, structure vs process, etc. This foregrounds the fact that the idea of development is highly contested. The sub-field of human development has become quite diverse in response to critical questions about the plasticity, diversity, specificity, directionality, or sources of development. Inherent in them are certain assumptions related to presentism,

DOI: 10.4324/9781003471851-8

288 Why Should We Rethink 'Child' and 'Development' in Psychology?

ageism, universality, or directionality, among others. This calls for a critical reflection on what constitutes 'development' in developmental psychology and its ideological underpinnings.

Why and How Did the Infant and Child Become the Objects of Study of Psychological Development?

Study of human development emerged as an established subfield in North America and in European countries such as England around the 1900s. It was predated by the 'child study movement' which flourished around Europe in the mid-nineteenth century. It treated children's growth, development and learning as a specialized area for scientific study. Many accounts take Charles Darwin's *Biographical Sketch of an Infant*, published in 1857, as the first child study. Darwin's interest was in understanding the relative contribution of heredity and environment, identifying the characteristics that distinguished humans from non-humans. Thus, the child study movement was motivated by the questions drawn from evolutionary theory, that is, comparing humans with animals, and comparing different groups of human beings, to understand the role of heredity.

The Child Is the Father of the Man

The infant is depicted as a biological organism abstracted from its material and familial environment. The infant as being closer to nature with relatively less experience of learning has been perceived to be the route to knowledge. The study of infancy is seen as providing insights into the development and functioning of adult capacities which seem to be automatic because they are so skilled. Thus, biology and epistemology met in the study of infancy and children. As Burman (2017) notes, the study of infants converted the age-old epistemological questions into psychological concerns such as: What are we born with? What can we acquire? What are the age-related limits to learning? Research responding to these questions has been the backbone of early intervention programmes which develop remedial tools and therapeutic strategies to deal with deficits (undeveloped) or retardations (underdeveloped) at different ages. Whether the focus has been on epistemological concerns or on intervention imperatives to avoid stigmatized endpoints of development, such as deviance, pathology, criminality, teenage pregnancy etc., the concern to study infants and children did not emerge from an interest in knowing about their actual states and processes.

The evolutionary logic dictated the study of infancy and children. The child in psychological discourse has been equated with the 'savage' and considered 'undeveloped' since both were perceived as immature and primitive and were studied to illuminate the necessary steps for subsequent development. James Sully (1881) notes:

The modern psychologist, sharing in the spirit of positive science, feels that he must, being at the beginning, study mind in its simplest forms ... [H]e carries his eye far afield to the phenomena of savage life, with its simple ideas, crude sentiments and naive habits. Again he devotes special attention to the mental life of lower animals, seeking in its phenomena the dim foreshadowing of our own perceptions, emotions, etc. Finally, he directs his attention to the mental life of infancy, as fitted to throw most light on the later developments of the human mind,

(Sully, quoted in Riley, 1983, p. 47)

Comparison between the child, the primitive and the savage presupposed a conception of development, of individual and of evolutionary progress, as unilinear, directed steps up an ordered hierarchy.

The Child as an Artefact of Psychological Testing

The study of child psychology has been closely aligned with the rise of the psychological testing movement which too was gaining ground in late nineteenth and mid-twentieth century. But the technology of testing both requires and relies on the very institutions that permit its administration. Rose (1990) notes:

Developmental psychology was made possible by the clinic and the nursery school. Such institutions had a vital role, for they enabled the observation of numbers of children of the same age, and of children of a number of different ages, by skilled psychological experts under controlled experimental, almost laboratory, conditions. They thus simultaneously allowed for standardisation and normalisation – the collection of comparable information on a large number of subjects and its analysis in such a way as to construct norms. A developmental norm was a standard based upon the average abilities or performances of children of a certain age in a particular task or a specified activity. It thus not only presented a picture of what was normal for children of such an age, but also enabled the normality of any child to be assessed by comparison with this norm,

(p. 142)

North American psychologist Gesell (1971) claimed that his book, *The First Five Years of Life*, contributes 'more than any other book to the foundations of systematic developmental psychology'. He provided the descriptions of development as absolutely age-graded whereby, specific capacities emerged at specific points of months and years. It promoted a maturational view of development as a process of natural unfolding. The psychological testing paradigm created a standardized notion of the 'normal child' distilled from the comparative scores of age-graded populations. On closer examination, it was an abstraction as no real child lies at its base. It has led to the segregation of 'subnormal' or 'abnormal' from the normal. The developmental norms, widely used, are primarily derived from the White, Educated, Industrialized, Rich, and Democratic (WEIRD) samples reflecting the shared cultural experiences of children and researchers of Euro-American descent. Culturally-specific descriptions are too easily translated into universal prescriptions about child 'needs' and 'rights', the appropriateness of learning experiences, the effectiveness of parenting techniques, and the evaluations of early intervention studies are generalized beyond their context. Because developmental psychology studies the 'individual' mind bereft of its context using experimentation, observation and psychometric tests, the findings are believed to be generalizable. This has created an image of the 'child' as an asocial, situationally indifferent, naturally developing biological organism.

The Study of the Development of Rational Masculinity Through the 'Male' Child

Ideas of cultural masculinity have seeped into developmental models through notions of 'mastery', as noted by Walkerdine (1988), and the privileging of the cognitive over the affective, as highlighted by Broughton (1988). The preponderance of developmental theories describing cognitive processes and the inherent cognitivism in theories of social and emotional development testify that the cognitive has triumphed over the affective. Kofsky Scholnick (2000) has called out the seemingly innocuous arrow ($\rightarrow$) for its masculinist assumptions. He states:

> The arrow metaphor expresses three contemporary explanations of developmental change: (1) biology, which launches movements; (2) an ideal solution to a cognitive task, which serves as the target for development; and (3) linearity, which ensures continuity of travel. Arrows describe linear thought and linear development in a universal child. Arrows are also, of course, typically associated with aggression, domination, imposition of a view, and penetration of an influence. An arrow expresses development as a push towards change, not as a force that simultaneously transforms and is transformed,
>
> *(p. 34)*

The classic theories of development such as those developed by Freud, Piaget, Erikson and Kohlberg have been subjected to intense feminist critique for ignoring and, worse still, pathologizing female development. Perhaps no theorist has been as scrutinized and challenged by feminists as Sigmund Freud (for a thorough feminist critique of Freudian psychoanalytic theory, see the discussion in Chapter 5). Carol Gilligan (1982) exposed masculine biases in theories of psychosocial and moral development, focusing attention on Erikson, Piaget and Kohlberg. Gilligan's studies of girls and women, beginning with *In a Different Voice* in 1982, and extending through her study of 'at risk' adolescent girls (Taylor, Gilligan & Sullivan, 1995), have tried to ensure a better, more accurate

Why Should We Rethink 'Child' and 'Development' in Psychology? **291**

'story' by including the lives of women and girls in the databases upon which such theories or truths are built.

The Child in the Adult-Centric World

The model of development in developmental psychology is essentially an evolutionary model: the child growing into an adult represents a progression from simplicity to complexity of thought, from irrationality to rationality. Children's activities—their language, play and social interactions—are seen to pre-figure the child's future participation in the adult world. There is a clear directionality of change involved. Socialization is the process that turns the 'immature, irrational' child into a 'mature, rational' adult. Elkin (1960) shows how this model of socialization works: 'The socialising agents teach, serve as models, and invite participation. Through their ability to offer gratification and deprivations they induce cooperation and learning and prevent disrupting deviance' (p. 101).

The children in this model are by and large passive representatives of the future generations. They gradually interiorize cultural practices, language and skills in order to become more civilized. Their responsibility is to reproduce and maintain the stability of the social order. Lev Vygotsky, a Russian developmental psychologist, asserts that adults and children assist each other's learning as a form of adaptation that makes possible the transmission of culture from one generation to another. Summarizing traditional approaches to socialization theory, Shildkrout (1978) comments that:

> child culture is seen as a rehearsal for adult life and socialisation consists of the processes through which, by one method or another, children are made to conform, in cases of 'successful' socialisation or become deviants in cases of 'failed socialisation'.
>
> *(pp. 109–110)*

This explains the plan of most developmental psychology texts that include chapters on 'Family', 'School', 'Peers', 'Media', to make the point that they are the social agents responsible for socializing the children harmoniously into society's functioning.

In the developmental model, adaptation is a natural process guided by the evolutionary logic giving rise to regular patterns of change through infancy and childhood. It provides the theoretical link between the biological and the social. The social or the societal is seen as an evolutionary step above or beyond biology; the child moves from being a 'biological' organism to a 'social' citizen. This formulation encourages an emphasis on development as adaptation which is naturally regulated. The focus on adaptation rests on the dichotomy between the individual and society and either treats the individual as distinct from and prior to society or treat society as distinct from and prior to the individual. It treats the individual and society as distinct (as in, an individual adapts to the society).

292 Why Should We Rethink 'Child' and 'Development' in Psychology?

Summing up: Developmentalism in Developmental Psychology

The developmental explanations (termed as 'developmentalism') that characterize the psychological study of infant/child development are constituted by the following ideas:

1. The unit of analysis for describing, explaining and optimizing development is 'the child', conceptualized as a self-regulating and self-organized entity. There is ignorance of 'children' as a socially constituted group of people or 'childhood' as a specific structural and cultural variable.
2. Evolution and development are intricately involved with each other. There are many ways in which the evolutionary logic is expressed in prominent theories of human development:

    a   In equating infants/children with primitives, savages and animals, evolutionary ancestry is treated as somehow 'within' the human, manifesting itself in the characteristics of infants/children.
    b   Evolution is progressive and humans stand at the highest point of an ascending path. In much the same way, the infant/child is immature and moves towards greater differentiation and integration. Thus, development is goal-directed and directional.
    c   Just as evolution is in the service of helping the species survive, development is in the service of an individual's pragmatic adaptation to society. This enables the improvement of the capabilities of an individual so that the individual can serve the best interests of the society.
    d   The line of evolution from animals to humans is a single ascending path. Accordingly, there is one (or a limited few) developmental pathway. Thus, development is universal.
    e   Development is naturally regulated. Even when the role of social factors has been emphasized, it is the natural interdependence between children and adults which makes it natural for children to become engaged in processes of 'guided participation' in cultural activities.

What Ideas Constitute the Psychological Meta-narrative of Human Development?

Broughton (1987) has identified four perspectives on human development: (1) the traditional psychological development perspective; (2) the social-contextual perspective; (3) the social constructionist perspective; and (4) the post-structuralist/ critical psychological perspective. Within mainstream psychology, the narrative of truth about human development is primarily woven by the traditional perspective and the social-contextual perspective. It enables us to ask and respond to questions such as: What are the capacities of an infant? How much does a child of age X know? What can be done to improve a child's functioning? How does a child

Why Should We Rethink 'Child' and 'Development' in Psychology? **293**

transform into an adult? The mainstream development perspective tries to understand the development of 'the child' as systematic, sequential, successive changes in the organization which mark a progress from immaturity to maturity, irrationality to rationality, lesser to greater level of complexity.

The best-known classical developmental theories are the theories developed by Freud, Piaget, Kohlberg, Bowlby and Ainsworth. Vygotsky's socio-cultural theory Bronfenbrenner's bio-ecological systems theory and Bandura's social-cognitive theory are among the well-known perspectives in the socio-cultural paradigm. Erikson's theory of psychosocial development can be placed in the intermediary space between the two paradigms for its adherence to the epigenetic principle (development change occurs in steps) of the classic theories as well as its strong contextual approach in which every behaviour has to be understood as embedded in four interrelated domains (Erikson, 1968):

1. the present life-stage of the individual;
2. the life history of the individual;
3. the present state of the culture of the individual;
4. the history of the culture of the individual.

The similarity between the two mainstream approaches is that they both take the individual as an integrated, self-regulating, autonomous organism. Let us look at the important differences between them with regard to how development is conceptualized:

1. *Split vs. relational meta-theory*: In the classic stage theories of development, a split meta-theory is adopted in which the organism and the contextual environment are treated as separate, self-contained and static entities. They are not only analytically distinct but ontologically split, i.e., they do not need each other to exist or to be defined. The two split-off pure entities function independently in cooperative/competitive ways. The socio-contextual perspective is closer to the relational meta-theory in which the organism is embedded in the socio-cultural context and the environment, in turn, is selected, manipulated and created by the organism.

2. *Interaction vs. coaction*: In the split meta-theory, an interactionist view is subscribed to, expressed as: 'the organism influences the environment and the environment influences the organism'. This preserves the ontological split between the two entities. Development is the outcome of the additive 'interaction' of both. The relational meta-theory, on the other hand, sees the organism and the environment as co-actors in the process of psychological development. They interpenetrate each other; they are embedded in each other, thus, multidirectional influences result in development.

3. *More focus on nativist factors vs. more focus on contextual factors*: The classical stage theories of development assume that the inherent structures in the organism set the limit and/or predisposition for development and the socio-cultural determiners influence the pace/expression of development. They privilege the nativist factors while acknowledging the effects of the environment. The contextual perspectives focus more on the coaction between the multiple levels characterizing the organism and the environment and how development is the result of this.

4. *Systematic change vs. dispersive change*: In the stage theories, development is teleological, i.e., it moves towards end goals, such as formal operational thinking in Piagetian theory, genitality in Freudian psychoanalysis, or the balance of psychological states, such as basic trust and basic mistrust in the Eriksonian framework. In the contextual framework, the focus is less on understanding the direction of change. Rather, it emphasizes the multidirectional influences and coordination among various levels of organization in the organism and the environment. In pure contextualism there is simply no prediction possible from one point in life (or history) to the next. In other words, a purely contextual approach sees the components of life as completely dispersive (Pepper, 1942) – as lacking any necessary across-time organization, systemic connection, or successive patterning.

The above discussion highlights that the meta-narrative of human development as provided by mainstream psychology is not a coherent one in itself. Rather, it is characterized by differing positions on several important theoretical issues related to development. Developmental psychology, like the other sub-fields of psychology, has been caught in numerous split and dualistic conceptions, such as biology–culture, individual–social, active–passive, universal–particular, reason–emotion, etc. Unsurprisingly, the major theoretical issues about development in child/human development are framed in terms of antinomies. On the question of human nature, two contrasting worldviews are available: mechanistic (elementalism) vs. organismic (holism). The issue of causality of development set up an antinomy between antecedent–consequent relations vs. structure–function relations. What changes due to development is discussed in terms of split conceptions related to variational vs. transformational change and continuous vs. discontinuous change. The sources of development are debated in terms of nature vs. nurture. These antinomies set up a standard way of questioning: Which one is more true? This approach elevates one concept of the pair to a privileged position, builds a research programme on this concept, and then strives to demonstrate observationally that the non-privileged concept can be denied or marginalized. Even when the opposites are said to co-exist, as in the continuity–discontinuity debate and the nature–nurture controversy, the question often is: Which is more important?

REVIEW QUESTIONS

1. How is evolutionary logic embedded in developmental thinking in psychology?
2. What are the major differences between the organismic and contextual models of development?

What Are the Major Theoretical Debates About Development in Psychology?

An appreciation of conceptual debates in the field of human development is not merely a philosophical indulgence, rather, it is a necessity in order to make meaning of research. The starting point of all research is a theoretical worldview which enables certain questions to be raised, guides towards certain methodological strategies, shapes observations as data and permits making sense of the research findings. The two most important theoretical issues debated are: mechanical vs. organismic view of human nature and the nature–nurture controversy.

The Mechanist vs. Organismic View of Human Nature

In developmental terms, these worldviews translate into the question: Is the infant/child active or passive? Put in other words, the question is: Is the infant/child active or is the environment active? While the study of the infant/child had biological roots, the behaviourist ideas shifted the focus towards environmental history. Whether the emphasis is on biological roots or on environmental history, the metaphor remains of a 'passive infant/child' in the mechanist worldview. A machine is passive until it is activated. Similarly, the mechanist model takes the human as inherently passive; his or her activity results from the action of external forces, ones placed on the person through environmental stimulation or in the person through genetic inheritance. The mechanist model is an elementaristic one. A machine is understood as a composition of discrete parts which work together. Similarly, human functioning is reduced to its core, essential constituent elements (e.g., S-R connections, genes).

In the 1970s, with the rise of cognitivism, the image of the passive, incompetent infant changed to an active, perceiving, learning and information-organizing individual. The metaphor of the organism embedded in the organismic worldview takes the infant as spontaneously active and self-regulating. The child effects work (e.g. Bell & Harper, 1977) investigated what the child elicits from its caregivers. Thus, both child and parents learn from each other. Technologies such as ultrasound and measures of brain electrophysiology can reveal the capacities of a foetus, neonates and infants, which played a key role in the revision of the image of the infants. The organismic model is a holistic

296 Why Should We Rethink 'Child' and 'Development' in Psychology?

conception which sees the organism as an organized totality such that the whole is more than the sum of its parts. Organismic theories constitute a family of holistic psychological theories which tend to stress the organization, unity, and integration of human beings expressed through each individual's inherent growth or developmental tendency. Werner and Kaplan (1963) indicated:

> [The organismic perspective] maintains that any local organ or activity is dependent upon the context, field or whole of which it is a constitutive part: its properties and functional significance [meaning] are, in larger measure, determined by the larger whole or context.
>
> *(p. 3)*

The mechanist model stresses a passive organism in an active world; it emphasizes reductionism, the continuity of laws governing development, only quantitative behavioural change across life, potential multi-directionality of change, essentialism, and causality through antecedent–consequent relations; it also eschews the idea of stages as qualitatively distinct periods of life. The organismic model stresses an active organism in a relatively passive world, and it emphasizes emergence; qualitative change in structure–function relations across life; unidirectional, teleological, goal-directed change; holism; and the appropriateness of the idea of stages as qualitatively distinct levels of organization.

The mechanistic and organismic models differ from each other on several important issues related to development:

- *Antecedent-consequent and structure-functions relations*: The mechanist model sees the antecedent–consequent relations as central to development explanations. According to this model, development is a consequence of past reinforcement history and/or genetic endowment (antecedent). Behaviour is reduced, then, to an analysis of a qualitatively unchanging, continuous, and unbroken chain of cause–effect (e.g., stimulus-response (S-R), gene-behaviour) relations. The organismic model sees the active organism constructing or reconstructing its organization, giving rise to newer kinds of functions, as can be seen from progressive refinement and the hierarchization of conceptual understanding.
- *Variational and transformative change*: Within the mechanist model, development is a matter of quantitative constancy or change (variation), with elements being added to or subtracted from the organism's repertoire in accordance with, for instance, the laws of conditioning. In this exemplar of the mechanist model in human development, what changes in development is the number of S-R connections in the organism's repertoire, and there is no *a priori* necessary direction to such change. Such changes are variational in nature. The organismic model, on the other hand, emphasizes changes in structures and functions, and they stress that these changes are specified *a priori* to move towards a final goal or end state. That is,

development is teleological within this view; it is goal-directed. Indeed, Reese and Overton (1970) indicate that, within the organismic model, the definition of development is 'changes in the form, structure, or organization of a system, such changes being directed towards end states or goals' (p. 139). Such changes are transformational (Overton, 2015).

- *Continuity and discontinuity*: Gradual increments of behavioural change are more emphasized in the mechanist view of development. Thus, the discontinuity implied is of a quantitative nature. Whereas, in the organismic model, the active organism may construct – or, better, revise – its structure and, in so doing, a new (transformed) structure–function relation will be created. Thus, qualitative discontinuity is possible within organicism. Such a change constitutes not just more of a previously or already existing structure; rather, it constitutes something new or novel, something that cannot be reduced to a prior state or status of the organism. As noted earlier, such changes are said to be transformational in character and are emergent ones.

Nature vs Nurture

Most developmental psychology theories posit development as an outcome of the interaction between nature (heredity) and nurture (environment), in which they may give more importance to one account over the other. Nature's position within mechanistic and organismic worldviews of human nature privileges the hereditary factors as the source of development, ascribing weak effects to the environment. The sociobiological theory and instinct theory are examples of a mechanist, nature point of view whereas Piagetian and Freudian theories are an example of an organismic, nature point of view. The nurture position within mechanistic and organismic worldviews of human nature privileges the environmental/contextual factors as sources of development, granting heredity a secondary role. The conditioning theory of behaviourism is an example of the mechanist, nurture point of view, while Eriksonian theory and Vygotsky's sociocultural perspective are closer to the organismic, nurture point of view.

This is a central debate in the field of child/developmental psychology. Its terms have moved beyond 'which one?' and 'how much?' to 'how?'. The questions development psychologists are asking are: How do nature and nurture dynamically interrelate to produce behavioural development? How do the effects of each multiply to provide a source of development? In the view associated with these questions nature and nurture are both fully involved in providing a source of any feature of human development. Nature and nurture cannot, therefore, function in isolation from one another but must always be systemically fused in their contributions. This fusion (which cannot be appropriately construed to mean addition) can be conceptualized as an integrated coaction – that is, a type of relation in which the full presence of each source is completely intertwined with the other. Heredity and environment never

298 Why Should We Rethink 'Child' and 'Development' in Psychology?

function independently of each other. Nature (e.g., genes) never affects behaviour directly; it always acts in the context of internal and external environments. That is, genes are influenced by the inside-the-organism context (e.g., the cellular and the extra-cellular physiological environment within the body of the organism) and the outside-the-organism context, for example, social relationships and the conditions of the natural and designed physical ecology. In turn, the environment (e.g., social stimulation) never directly influences behaviour; it will show variation in its influence depending on the heredity-related attributes of the organism on which it acts. Riegel (1975) identifies the four levels: (1) environment-inner-biological; (2) individual-psychological; (3) physical-environmental; and (4) sociocultural-historical, which denote the types of nurture-related variables that may provide the context for coactions with nature.

Levels of Interactionism

The nature–nurture debate has extensively relied on the use of the term 'interaction' to conceptualize the additive effects of mutually exclusive factors of heredity and environment. Interactionism varies on a continuum from weak to strong. Weak interactionism highlights the role of a single factor as a contributor of development. Weak interactionism is posited in the notion of 'predetermined epigenesis'. It holds that there is a unidirectional relationship between structural maturation and function, whereby the former determines the latter (structural maturation → function) but not the reverse. Nature – not nurture – is the main force in this interaction. Although variables associated with both the organism and the context are said to be involved in the interactions associated with developmental (i.e., stage) progression, environmental (contextual) variables are only seen to facilitate or inhibit trajectories of primarily intrinsic (i.e., maturational) origin (Emmerich, 1968). According to predetermined epigenesis, contextual variables cannot alter the direction or sequence of developmental change.

Strong interactionism moves away from an additive notion to that of mutual embeddedness. Any attribute of the individual (e.g., a physical characteristic such as body build or a behavioural attribute, such as a rhythmic temperamental style) will have different implications for developmental outcomes under different contextual conditions (e.g., in regard to different cultural ideas of bodily attractiveness or in regard to the requirements placed by different parents on their children in regard to the regularity of their sleep-wake cycles; Lerner, 1976). The individual characteristic is given its functional meaning only by virtue of its relation to a specific context and, since contexts vary (among themselves and each across time), the same characteristic will have a different import for development. In turn, the same contextual condition will lead to alternative developments because different individuals co-act with it. Thus, a given characteristic of individuality only has meaning for human development by virtue of its timing of interaction; that is, its relation to a particular set of time-bound contextual conditions. In turn, the import of any set of contextual conditions for psychosocial behaviour and development can only be understood by specifying the context's relations to the specific developmental features of the individuals within it.

Strong interactionism is compatible with the probabilistic epigenetic position. According to Rose (2016):

1. Both experience and maturation are invariably involved in determining the qualitative changes that characterize development.
2. The timing of the co-actions between maturation and experience is a factor of importance in the determination of behavioural development.
3. Since these relations cannot be expected to occur at exactly the same time for every organism within a given species, one can only say that specific emergences will probably occur. Individuality, and not homogeneity across all members of a group, is the case in human development.

The model of probabilistic epigenesis suggested by Gottlieb (1997) assumes that human development implicates four levels of organization: (1) genetic activity; (2) neural activity; (3) behaviour; and (4) the environment (physical, social and cultural). These levels have reciprocal, bidirectional influences on each other. Thus, this supports a relational concept of causality: Development outcomes are a consequence of at least two specific components of co-action from the same or different levels of analysis. Since, the co-ordination of formative functional and structural influences within and between all levels of analysis is not perfect, a probabilistic element is introduced in all developing systems and their outcomes. This 'probabilistic' nature of development is explained by Gollin (1981):

> The determination of the successive qualities of living systems, given the web of relationships involved, is probabilistic. This is so because the number of factors operating conjointly in living systems is very great. Additionally, each factor and subsystem is capable of a greater or lesser degree of variability. Hence, the influence subsystems have upon each other, and upon the system as a whole, varies as a function of the varying states of the several concurrently operating subsystems.
>
> *(p. 232)*

A probabilistic epigenetic conceptualization of development allows far more variability in developmental trajectories. If intra-individual development is an outcome of the co-action of intra-organism and contextual variables, and if the context does and/or can be made to change, then the person's developmental trajectory can, at least in part, be altered. It follows that constraints on development – for example, those that might be imposed by genes or by early experience – are not fixed or immutable.

300 Why Should We Rethink 'Child' and 'Development' in Psychology?

PAUSE AND THINK

Identify any one organismic theory. Try to analyse how the issues of development hold up in that theory.

How Has the Role of Context Expanded in the Field of Child Development?

As is evident from the discussion above, purely mechanist and nativist positions are treated as reductionist in contemporary developmental psychology. Rather, it is the fusion of the organismic and contextual models of development that has emerged as the dominant paradigm in recent years.

Building on the insights of Bell (1968) about the potential presence of bidirectional influences between parents and children in correlational data about socialization, Lewis and his colleagues argued that, 'Not only is the infant or child influenced by its social, political, economic and biological world, but in fact the child itself influences its world in turn' (Lewis & Rosenblum, 1974, p. xv). One key instance of this influence arose in regard to the study of infant attachment. Lamb and his colleagues approached the study of infant attachment within the context of the assumptions that:

1. Children have an influence on their 'socializers' and are not simply the receptive foci for socializing forces.
2. Early social-emotional development occurs in the context of a complex family system rather than in the context of the mother–infant dyad.
3. Social and psychological development is not confined to infancy and childhood but is a process that continues from birth to death (Lamb, 1978, p. 137).

Stimulated by scholars of infancy such as Michael Lewis and Michael Lamb, the study of human development during the 1970s and 1980s became increasingly focused on developing models, and conducting research that enabled the understanding of interactions, reciprocal influences, or bidirectional relations between individuals and the complex contexts within which they developed.

Rise of Contextualism as a Model of Development

The above developments gave rise to contextualism as a worldview in developmental psychology. According to Pepper (1942), the main metaphor of contextualism is neither the machine nor the whole organism. It is the historic event. In contextualism, every behaviour and incident in the world is a historic event, and thus change and novelty are accepted as fundamental. A contextual model has the following assumptions:

1. *Constant change at all levels of analysis*: The assumption of constant change denotes that there is no complete uniformity or constancy. Rather than change being a phenomenon to be explained, a perturbation in a stable system, change is a given (Overton, 1978). Thus, the task of the developmental scientist is to describe, explain, and optimize the parameters and trajectories of processes that reflect the relations among the levels of the system and that show time-related changes in their quantity and/or quality.
2. *Embeddedness of each level with all others*: This stresses the interrelation of all levels of analysis and, thus, supports the view that changes in one area promote changes in all. Because phenomena are not seen as static but rather as change processes, and because any change process occurs within a similarly (i.e., constantly) changing world (of processes), any target change must be conceptualized in the context of the other changes within which it is embedded. Thus, change will constantly continue as a consequence of this embeddedness.
3. *The organism in relation to context*: There is an organism in the contextual perspective, but it is conceived of as an 'organism in relation' (Looft, 1973), or an 'organism in transaction' with its context (Dewey & Bentley, 1948; Sameroff, 2009). Baltes (1979, p. 2) states:

    As development unfolds, it becomes more and more apparent that individuals act on the environment and produce novel behaviour outcomes, thereby making the active and selective nature of human beings of paramount importance. The relations between an active organism and active environment are the focus of developmental analysis. They (relations) constitute the basic process of human development. Just as the context changes the individual, the individual changes the context. As such, by acting to change a source of their own development – by being both products and producers of their context – individuals affect their own development.

4. *Timing of the relation between organism and context*: Both the developmental time and the historical time are critical in contextualism. The tissue, organism, or person reacts differently to what appears to be the same environmental circumstance at different points in development. Individuals react differently because of their individual histories. As Freud is reported to have said: ;The human mind is from start to finish incapable of separating itself from its own experience but can only build upon that' (Rosen, 1989, p. 126). The organism (person) as developed to that point in time engages the environment in particular ways (selecting, 'interpreting', reacting to, and eliciting). This means that development builds on whatever has gone before. Acquired capacities are retained yet changed in meaning when new capacities are acquired and organized with them into more complex wholes through the co-actions of the organism and context.

At the same time, contextualism stresses the factors associated with the historical time within which people were born (i.e., with membership in particular birth cohorts) and/or with events occurring at particular historical times. Thus, historical events appeared to account for more of these changes, particularly with respect to adult intellectual development, than did age-associated influences. The recognition of the interplay between age-graded, history-graded, and non-normative life events suggests a contextualistic and dialectical conception of development. This dialectic is further accentuated by the fact that individual development is the reflection of multiple forces that are not always in synergism, or convergence, nor do they always permit the delineation of a specific set of end states.

Data were generated during this period that suggested that contextual variables exist which differentiate people born at given times in history (e.g., economic crises; Elder, 1974, 1999). As a consequence of this differentiation, these contextual variables might influence the particular direction of individuals' ontogenetic changes. In addition, there also may be contextual variables, present only at specific times of measurement, which may 'cut across' cohorts and influence the direction of change of people from different cohorts. Brim and Kagan (1980, p. 13) concluded that 'growth is more individualistic than was thought, and it is difficult to find general patterns'. Factors associated with the historical time within which people were born (i.e., with membership in particular birth cohorts) and/or with events occurring at particular historical times appeared to account for more of these changes, particularly with respect to adult intellectual development, than did age-associated influences (Baltes, 1983).

In sum, empirical findings emerging throughout the 1970s and 1980s indicated that organism-centred models of developmental change could not account for the multi-directionality of developmental change. Furthermore, the multiple levels of the context linked to the individual level over the course of the lifespan cannot be reduced to the molecular elements of any extant mechanistic-behaviouristic theory. Thus, the context of human development needed to be incorporated into any adequate analysis of the diversity of developmental trajectories which was seen to characterize the life course. Time and place, therefore, are matters of substance, not error; and to understand human development, scholars must appreciate how variables associated with person, place, and time coalesce to shape the structure and function of behaviour and its systematic and successive change.

Bronfenbrenner's bio-ecological system approach (1979, 1989; Bronfenbrenner & Morris, 1998), which conceptualizes the organism in multi-dimensional context, Bandura's social cognitive theory (1986, 1997), which emphasizes bi-directional interaction, and Vygotsky's sociocultural approach (1978, 1981), which understands development as a product of activity of persons in interaction, are the leading contextual models of child development. These theories converge on their focus on the social, i.e., a focus on situation and socio-structural institutions, such as family, school, religion, etc., as important determiners of development. However, these theories, especially the bio-ecological and social-cognitive theories provide limited discussion about the role of culture. (For the distinction between the social and the cultural, see Chapter 4.)

Where Is 'Culture' in Mainstream Development Psychology?

The discussion above primarily reflects the knowledge base of mainstream child/developmental psychology shaped by the coming together of organismic and contextual meta-theories. Both these frameworks are critiqued for their under-developed theorization of the role of culture in human development. (For a detailed discussion of the culture-behaviour interface in psychology, see Chapter 4.)

The Cultural Critique of the Organismic Perspective

The organismic theories, such as those proposed by Freud, Erikson, Piaget, Kohlberg, Bowlby and Ainsworth, suffer from many conceptual and methodological limitations from the cultural perspective:

1. The organism, i.e., the living organized structure, is the fundamental unit of analysis in this framework. Moghaddam (2010) discusses this assumption as the embryonic fallacy, i.e., the assumption that the independent individual is the source and centre of psychological experience. While lip service is paid to the 'relevance of context', it is often reduced to superficial extrinsic variables of influence. Looked at this way, the person and the environment are separate and mutually exclusive rather than mutually constitutive (Shweder, 1990).

2. Owing to the unbridgeable dualism of the individual and the context, the impetus of development is largely conceptualized as stemming from 'inherent' structures (drives, instincts, mental structures) which it 'brings to' and 'takes away' from the environment. The environment, on the other hand, is understood as offering opportunities for constraining or promoting growth. This reduces the importance of culture from a constitutive force in development to an 'additive' factor. This is in line with the pre-determined epigenetic position, according to which, though variables associated with both the organism and the context are involved in the interactions associated with stagewise progression, contextual variables cannot alter the direction or sequence of developmental change.

3. The role of the environment in early childhood development, including the phase of infancy, is considered to be highly restrictive. Piaget argued that the social world increasingly begins to penetrate the essential structures of the child's thinking only around the time of the concrete operational stage. The pre-operational child is essentially a solo thinker who adapts to the social constraints imposed by the environment without reaching 'genuine'

304 Why Should We Rethink 'Child' and 'Development' in Psychology?

intellectual equilibrium. Thus, early childhood development is construed as following a 'natural' (biological) course which intertwines with social development at a later time.

4. According to Jahoda (1992a), the study of child development is built on a fundamental belief in 'psychic unity' which implies 'that all humans are part of nature and as such are subject to general laws and can be encompassed within positivistic scientific principles' (p. 115). Developmental research adhering to the principle of psychic unity seeks to explain how and why most children think, feel and behave in particular ways at different ages and stages using general laws of development. Thus, the universality of development is assumed and cultural variation is ignored.

5. However, not all organismic theories are stage-based, many provide a timetable of development which is believed to be culturally invariant. Claims of the universality of development outcomes, such as the resolution of the Oedipus complex, identity formation in adolescence, formal operational reasoning, secure attachment, set them up as idealized end goals to be achieved for healthy development, everywhere. Any deviations from the universal, prescribed trajectory are construed as pathological and/or deficit in development. Rather than understanding 'development' as the acquisition of particular cultural skills and tools that are important in a particular socio-economic context and historical epoch, it is understood as a once-and-for-all universal process.

6. Cross-cultural research has used Western concepts and methodologies like Piagetian conservation tasks and the Strange Situation, etc., to test for evidence of universality in perception, memory, problem-solving, cognitive style, attachment and personality, to mention a few of the topics studied over the years. Variations of behaviours of the non- WEIRD sample are dubbed as evidence of abnormality or inferiority. It is largely assumed that both concepts and methodologies constructed in Western labs could be applied anywhere, and that the impact of culture and context would be revealed by the extent of differences. Equally, areas of commonality in children's psychological functioning were assumed to point to shared psychic make-up and shared maturational processes. The possibility that points of similarity might also be accounted for by cultural processes (shared cultural processes) appeared to elude them (Cole, 1992).

7. The idealized end points of development set up by the organismic perspectives are culturally derived. For example, psychological autonomy is a culturally valued goal of individualistic societies and, thus, is aspired to as a developmental end state. Similarly, the decontextualized, abstract, syllogistic logical thinking identified by Piaget as the penultimate form of reasoning constitutes the privileged form of 'scientific' thinking in the Western world (see Box 7.1). Children in this world develop this thinking and discover scientific practices through interactions with members of their sociocultural group. 'They have to learn to talk and write and reason in phrases, clauses,

Why Should We Rethink 'Child' and 'Development' in Psychology? **305**

sentences, and paragraphs of scientific languages' (Lemke, 1990, p. 12). Western children who have learned to say, for example, that liquid poured from one container to another container remains the same have learned something about how to talk about science in their particular cultural practices.

BOX 7.1 CULTURAL VARIATIONS IN CHILD-REARING PRACTICES AND ITS IMPLICATIONS FOR SOCIAL RELATIONSHIPS

The 'expert' understandings of and interventions in childcare in psychological and psychiatric research rely overwhelmingly on moral assumptions and ideas about family life of the Western middle class that do not represent the wide variety of ways that families are organized in various locales in the West or around the world. By far the most influential theory of children's socio-emotional development is attachment theory. In this theory, 'sensitive responsiveness' is a necessary precursor to 'secure attachment'. Focus is laid on the elicitation of psychic-emotional intimacy, which is defined in terms of a 'loving, responsive, and nurturing relationship' (Morris et al., 2018, p. 2), rather than physical care and nourishment that were foregrounded by theorists in earlier times (Burman, 2017).

However, the parenting style that is defined as optimal in attachment theory is simply not a global norm or valued way of interacting in all settings, as numerous cross-cultural and intracultural studies have pointed out. In many of the studied groups, caregiving practices that focus on children's physical needs such as feeding, washing, holding, and carrying are foregrounded, being variously described by these culturally grounded researchers as 'pediatric' (LeVine et al., 1994), 'proximal' (Keller, 2007), or 'body-centred' (Scheidecker, 2023).

Heidi Keller (2007) found urban middle-class mothers as typically engaging in a 'distal' parenting style that closely resembles 'sensitive responsiveness' as described in attachment theory. In rural, non-Western contexts, by contrast, Keller sees mothers tending to use a 'proximal' parenting style that focuses more on the physical needs of children through body contact and primary care such as feeding. Rather than leading to differences in attachment security, these two parenting styles highlight different dimensions in emerging social relationships: The distal style promotes an emphasis on psychological autonomy while the proximal style promotes hierarchical relatedness. Keller's research demonstrates that body-centred care practices like feeding may play a much more central role in caregiver–child relationships in some contexts than envisioned in attachment theory. Further, it could be argued that such body-centred care practices elicit physical-material warmth between mothers and children and hence, contribute to the development of an emotional bond between them.

Source: Funk et al. (2023).

306 Why Should We Rethink 'Child' and 'Development' in Psychology?

The Cultural Critique of the Bio-Ecological Model

The contextual frameworks of development emphasize environmental settings such as family, schooling, neighbourhood, religious institutions, the media and the prevalent ideologies and attitudes of culture as intertwined with development. This is most clearly represented in the bio-ecological theory of human development in which the growing individual is in a lifelong process of mutual accommodation with the immediate environment and larger social contexts, each embedded in the other (Bronfenbrenner, 1979, 1789, 1998). Such emphasis has resulted in intensified developmental research on the positive and negative effects of environmental aspects such as parenting practices, learning experiences in school, opportunities of play, interactions with peers and adult authority members, and so on. Many cultural critiques have been launched against the ecological model:

1. The majority of research within the framework resulted in 'conceptual confusion and inadequate testing of the theory' (Tudge et al., 2009, p. 198). Among the conceptual confusion, the notion of culture stands out as particularly problematic. The bio-ecological theory 'raises questions about treating individual and cultural processes as separate entities' implicitly (Rogoff, 2003, p. 44), where 'individual and "larger" contexts are conceived as existing separately, related in a hierarchical fashion as the larger contexts affect the smaller ones, which in turn affect the developing person' (p. 46). In its many transformations, in Bronfenbrenner's model, a proper in-depth definition of culture and an acknowledgement of its important role in human development have been lacking. Culture has been situated 'out there' in the distal environment (macrosystem) and said to play a role because of the interdependence of the systems. But how these transactions operate and how culture is operationalized and measured remain invisible in these models.
2. Environmentally-oriented contextual research and practice de-emphasize the relation of culture to the environmental settings. It assumes uniformity of social contexts such as school, family, parenting practices, neighbourhoods, etc. across the world. However, all environments are culturally constructed, shaped by generations of human activity and creativity, mediated by complex belief systems, including about the 'proper' way for children to develop. What a cultural approach emphasizes is that there is nothing natural about the environment for childcare, whether in school, or at home or in day care centres. The environment for child development is always shaped by human action, always social, and at all times mediated by cultural processes. This acknowledges the 'diversity of childhoods' shaped by culture-specific patterns of nurturance, communication and teaching which are an intrinsic part of the developmental process, in so far as the child engages with and participates in these processes from the very

Why Should We Rethink 'Child' and 'Development' in Psychology? **307**

start. The cultural approach, unlike a cross-cultural approach, doesn't operate within the logic of universalist paradigm. It makes it explicit that the culture-specific descriptions of Euro-American, white, middle-class childhood have been accepted as a universal standard for the goals, processes and expectations of child development that exclude a wide variety of childhoods the world over.

3. Goodnow (2011) points to the cultural contexts such as religious institutions that have been left out in Bronfenbrenner's (1979) model of development. She also deepens the original model by highlighting the overlap among contexts, such as family and work. These omissions reflect the dominance of Euro-American cultural and gendered assumptions of religion as personal faith and the rigid distinction between private and public domains of life in middle-class urban lifestyles. Finally, she introduces the possibility that the ordering of nested contexts depends on culture. Drawing on research showing that ethnic minority children often have an early awareness of broader societal conditions and which opportunities are open to them (Raffaelli et al., 2005), Goodnow (2011) proposes that 'we might well reverse the usual arrangement of layers placing the "outside world" at the centre and asking how effects radiate out to family life' (p. 82). Goodnow's proposals exemplify a new way to configure theories, as shifting Venn diagrams rather than an immobile nested doll.

The Cultural Critique of Sociocultural Theory

The Vygotskian perspective on culture provides a significant understanding of the way individuals master the linguistically mediated aspects of their culture and the way they are changed in that process. However, it is also limited and biased. It is limited because Vygotsky took a narrow view of culture as referring to counting, writing and language (speech in his terms) while ignoring other aspects of culture such as law, moral thinking, religion, art, kinship systems, etc. It is also inadequate in explaining the transmission of non-linguistically mediated aspects of cultural heritage. It is biased because using these limited aspects of culture, Vygotsky argued that different cultures could be rank-ordered with the Western conceptual scientific system at the top. This allowed him to say that the non-Western people should be introduced to the Western conceptual scientific system which would cause a progressive shift in their thinking. Rather than being a cultural relativist, Vygotsky operated within the universalist paradigm in which the non-Western ways of thinking were regarded as lower or less developed.

REVIEW QUESTION

'The contextual model of development is limited in its understanding of context.' Discuss.

308 Why Should We Rethink 'Child' and 'Development' in Psychology?

What Are the Critiques of Developmental Theory from the Social Constructionist/Post-Structuralist/Critical Psychological Perspective?

1. *Focus on 'childhood' rather than 'the child'*: These approaches push for a radical change from the study of the a-historical, decontextualized, universal child to the study of childhood as historically, socially and culturally constructed. This marks the distinction between the conception of a 'socially developing psychological child' and 'socially constructed and historically variable conceptions of childhood'. In the former, the maturational and socialization processes are extensively investigated in order to describe, explain and optimize development. In the latter, childhood becomes a unit of analysis. Childhood is studied as 'an actively negotiated set of social relationships within which the early years of human life are constituted' (James & Prout, 1997, p. 7). These social relationships are culturally mediated and historically variable. Ariès (1962) argues that in medieval society there was lack of awareness of the nature of childhood, i. e., the awareness of the features that distinguish adults from children. In various forms of artwork, children were portrayed as miniature adults with no representative acknowledgement of the differences in physical attributes between adults and children (Archard, 2004). In these historical periods, they were miniature adults.

2. *Rethinking developmental change*: The meta-theories of 'organism' and 'contextualism' which form the meta-narrative of mainstream developmental psychology see development as an intra-organismic change in the service of pragmatic adaptation to society, i.e., serving the best interests of maintaining social stability. The diverse kinds of developmental theories describe the culturally valued goals (of Western societies) such as psychological autonomy, logical and abstract thinking, identity formation, postconventional morality, gender binarism as the signposts of healthy development. The socialization theory leans on the maturational emphasis in developmental theories to emphasize the 'internalization' of social constraints under external regulation (in the 'hard' version of the socialization theory) or 'transactional negotiation' (in the 'soft' version of the socialization theory) in a bid to attain the goals prescribed by the society.

   In the alternative framework, development is not about improvement of the capacities of an individual but a change of collective nature. Drawing on the radical interpretation of Vygotskian work which has its roots in Marxism, it is argued that development is not about adaptation; rather it is about people collectively transforming the world, and through this transformation, also changing themselves and gaining their own status and their essence, which also appears as ineluctably social (i.e. collaborative and collective; see Vygotsky, 1997). It is argued that while Vygotsky (1987) accepted adaptation as 'the fundamental and universal law of development

Why Should We Rethink 'Child' and 'Development' in Psychology? **309**

and life of organisms' (p. 57) for lower mental functions, he deemed the framework of Darwinian adaptation insufficient to explain fully the emergence of 'higher mental functions' in human evolution. The higher mental functions represent a qualitative change or 'leap' in human cognition. The 'leap' in human cognition, Vygotsky believed, was directly connected to social interaction and collaboration with others in particular material and sociocultural contexts. For Vygotsky, children develop and learn as they actively change the world they live in, simultaneously changing themselves and gaining knowledge of themselves and of the world through changing the world – all in the process of transformative collaborative practices with other people. Claiming Vygotsky to be a Marxist, Newman and Holzman (1993) state that human beings do not merely respond to stimuli, acquire societally determined and useful skills, and adapt to the determining environment. The uniqueness of human social life is that we ourselves transform the determining circumstances. Human development is not an individual accomplishment but a sociocultural activity. They present Vygotsky as a forerunner to their viewpoint 'a new psychology of becoming', in which people experience the social nature of their existence and the power of collective creative activity in the process of making new tools for growth (Holzman, 2009).

3. *Development as social rather than natural*: The logic of evolution is very intricately interwoven with the idea of development in mainstream developmental psychology (see section on 'developmentalism in developmental psychology' on p. 000 for a detailed discussion). This is especially strong for the infancy period which is a period where experience has not begun to have its effect. Infants are said to be governed by biology, children and adults by culture. Theories of infant development assume quite specific caretaking conditions, but treat them as universal, thus as natural. An example of this is assuming that the sensitive responsiveness of the mother to the child is a universal and natural feature of childcare. The theories posit nurturant and facilitating others are necessary to the facilitation of a natural sequence of development in the child. But this understanding of (m)other is believed to be naturally endowed rather than repeatedly struggled for. To ignore that mothering, unavoidably implied in all accounts of infant development, is a set of practices and desires which is socially constituted, is to oppress mothers and negate the complexity of development. Even where the infant–mother dyad is considered, the focus on interpersonal dyadic parties leaves out of the picture the wider social structural relations of power and thus correspondingly works to obscure the ways in which those wider structural relations enter into and are (re) produced within micro-social relations Infant/child development treats change actually produced socially as natural.

On a different note, Bradley (1989) argues that natural descriptions of babies, of their competencies and development are exercises in interpretation.

They reflect the socially agreed-upon suppositions of human nature in general which is that humans develop from biological to social beings.

The understanding of 'social' is also of a qualitatively different nature than 'social effects' (see the discussion on dualism of the individual and the social in Chapter 3). 'Social' is not to be reduced to an independent variable impacting a developmental outcome, rather the very possibility of development and individuals is premised upon a particular social formation. Any stage of development is irrevocably linked to other variables, such as class, gender, or ethnicity. Comparative and cross-cultural analysis reveals a variety of childhoods rather than a single and universal phenomenon. As Frønes (1993) argues: 'There is not one childhood, but many formed at the intersection of different cultural, social and economic systems, natural and man-made physical environments. Different positions in society produce different experiences' (p. 18).

4. *Child-centric rather than adult-centric*: The critical thrust in the alternative framework is not how children function in an adult-constructed world, i.e., how children negotiate the institution of childhood, but rather how they construct their own reality and assign meaning to their lives. The concern is, therefore, not children as constructed by adults, but rather the roles that children play and the meanings they themselves attach to their lives (James & Prout, 1997). In this respect, it is advocated that children are and must be seen as active in the construction and determination of their own social lives, the lives of those around them and the societies they live in. 'Children are not just passive subjects of social structures and processes' (James & Prout, 1997, p. 8). Child culture is not seen as a rehearsal of adult life, rather as a form of social practice in itself.

5. *Value-laden enterprise of developmental psychology*: Child/developmental psychology is not a value-neutral field of study. It itself is shaped by larger social forces. Bradley (1989) emphasizes that scientific descriptions are never arbitrary; they always emerge from particular circumstances for particular reasons. Universal stages proposed by developmental theories can be no more than bodies of knowledge, forms of scientific, professional and lay discourse. Many examples attest to this. Decontextualized mediated action came to be seen as the feature of any rational, intellectually advanced thinking because by the mid-twentieth century, mandatory schooling was established for all children and industrial production expanded into all spheres of human life in the Western world. Moreover, alongside the external colonization of traditional societies, the internal colonization, i.e., the transformation of a traditional lifestyle based on contextualized activities in non-Western societies into an industrial lifestyle based on decontextualized activities, was also taking place. International organizations and colonizer governments started establishing schools in colonies so lifestyles based on contextual activities rapidly shrank.

Adrienne Harris (1987) argues that the cognitive model of the infant as problem-solver mirrors that of the assembly worker, with research privileging those activities and products which will enhance performance. As a result, the indeterminate, ambiguous and non-instrumental features of infant behaviours are suppressed.

Attending to the 'active infant' narrative in infant research, Kessen (1993) argued that locating previously undiscovered skills and qualities within the child serves an additional function of warding off contemporary anxiety about the adequacy of conditions and care in which we are rearing children. He states:

The assignment of cognitive capabilities to the new infant frees the baby of dependence on environmental – specifically cultural and parental – influences; his intellectual growth is safe regardless of variations in his surrounding context. Whether or not western culture is the epitome of historical evolution, whether or not American child-rearing patterns are optimal, the child contains shielded knowledge that will exist independently of his nation or handling ...

(Kessen, 1993, p. 424)

6. *Standardized methods create a standardized theory*: It is often missed that the methodological imperatives shape the phenomena under consideration. Inge Bretherton (1992) speaks about the method centredness of attachment theory. She states that attachment theory and the Strange Situation Procedure are synonymous. Heidi Keller (2021) shared that because she studied relationship development in cultural context using ethnographic methods rather than Strange Situation Procedure, she often heard that she was not an attachment theorist. Similarly, Gilligan (1982) argues that women's characteristic form of thinking will emerge only when such real-life dilemmas will be used which encompass their lives. This is the reason why Gilligan made use of the issue of birth control and abortion because this is a personally relevant issue in which the woman has a right to choose for herself and also such choice also brings her into conflict with the conventions of femininity, particularly the equation of goodness with self-sacrifice. This conception of morality is concerned with the activity of care and centres on the understanding of relationships and responsibility. It differs from the Kohlbergian conception of morality in Heinz's dilemma as fairness tied to the understanding of rights and rules.

Final Comments

The philosophy of human development in current times is best summarized by lifespan development theory as the "study of individual development from conception to old age" (Baltes et al., 2006, p. 569). The important objectives of the theory are to offer an organized account of the overall structure and sequence of development across the lifespan and to delineate the biological, psychological, social, and environmental factors and mechanisms which are the foundation of lifespan development. This widely accepted paradigm in developmental psychology is critiqued by the cultural and post-structuralist/critical psychological frameworks on various counts: dualism of organism and context, focus on adaptation, restricted understanding of context, development as naturally regulated and limited range of possible developmental trajectories for individuals. Child/lifespan development perspectives have to seriously contend with the cultural dimensions of the subject. There are two distinct aspects of this issue. First, children's development is fundamentally cultural. These cultural dimensions apply both to the universal and to variable features of children's experience of growth and learning. Second, the study of child development is a fundamentally cultural activity in so far as developmental psychologists are also cultural members. They also have to address how development is embedded at the intersection of macro socio-structural relations of gender, class, rural-urban, race, caste, etc. Consideration of questions such as: What were children in the past?, What are children in different cultures? How do the contexts of family, school, work inter-mesh for a working-class child as compared to a middle-class child?, open up radical apertures to rethink the claim for a generic human condition across time and place. The ideological construction of the body of knowledge related to child development is self-evident. It needs to be recognized that it is a form of expert knowledge partly constituted by schooling practices which call for expert knowledge about children in general. Besides, beliefs and expectations of parents and children themselves also play a part in the constitution of ideas about development.

REFERENCES

Abrams, D. (2010). Processes of prejudice: Theory, evidence and intervention. *Equality and Human Rights Commission Research*, 56. Retrieved from http://www.equality humanrights.com (accessed 10 June 2017).

Acker, J. (1990). Hierarchies, jobs, bodies: A theory of gendered organizations. *Gender & Society*, 4(2), 139–158.

Addis, M. E., & Cohane, G. H. (2 005). Social scientific paradigms of masculinity and their implications for research and practice in men's mental health. *Journal of Clinical Psychology*, 61(6), 633–647.

Aguinaldo, J. P. (2004). Rethinking validity in qualitative research from a social constructionist perspective: From is this valid research? To what is this research valid for? *The Qualitative Report*, 9(1), 127–136.

Ajzen, I., & Fishbein, M. (1975). *Belief, attitude, intention and behaviour.* Addison-Wesley.

Alavi, S. B., & McCormick, J. (2007). Measurement of vertical and horizontal idiocentrism and allocentrism. *Small Group Research*, 38(4), 556–564.

Allport, F. H. (1924). *Social psychology.* Houghton Mifflin Company.

Allport, G. W. (1935). Attitudes. In C. Murchison (Ed.), *Handbook of social psychology* (pp. 798–844). Clark University Press.

Allport, G. W. (1954). The historical background of modern social psychology In G. Lindzey (Ed.), *Handbook of social psychology* (1st ed., vol. 1, pp. 3–56). Addison-Wesley.

Allport, G. W. (1956). *The nature of prejudice.* Addison-Wesley.

APA (American Psychological Association). (2013). *DSM-5 diagnostic and statistical manual of mental disorders.* American Psychological Association.

Archard, D. (2004). The moral and political status of children. *Philosophical Quarterly*, 54(216), 490–492.

Ardila, R. (1982). International psychology. *American Psychologist*, 37(3), 323–329.

Argyle, M. (2001). The development of social psychology at Oxford. In G. C. Bunn, A. D. Lovie, & G. D. Richards (Eds.), *Psychology in Britain: Historical essays and personal reflections* (pp. 333–343). BPS Books.

314 References

Argyle, M., & Dean, J. (1965). Eye-contact, distance and affiliation. *Sociometry*, 28(3), 289–304.

Ariès, P. (1962). *Centuries of childhood: A social history of family life*. Knopf.

Augoustinos, M.*et al.* (2014). *Social cognition: An integrated introduction* (3rd ed.) Sage.

Avotri, J. Y., & Walters, V. (1999). You just look at our work and see if you have any freedom on earth: Ghanaian women's accounts of their work and health. *Social Science & Medicine*, 48, 1123–1133.

Azuma, H. (1984). Psychology in a non-western country. *International Journal of Psychology*, 19(1), 45–55.

Bakan, D. (1966). *The duality of human existence: An essay on psychology and religion*. Rand McNally.

Baltes, P. B. (1979). On the potential and limits of child development: Life-span developmental perspectives. *Newsletter of the Society of Research in Child Development*, 1–4.

Baltes, P. B. (1983). Life-span developmental psychology: Observations on history and theory revisited. In R. M. Lerner (Ed.), *Developmental psychology: Historical and philosophical perspectives* (pp. 79–111). Erlbaum.

Baltes, P. B., Lindenberger, U., & Staudinger, U. M. (2006). Life span theory in developmental psychology. In R. M. Lerner & W. Damon (Eds.), *Handbook of child psychology: Theoretical models of human development* (pp. 569–664). John Wiley & Sons, Inc.

Bandura, A. (1986). *Social foundations of thought and action: A social cognitive theory*. Prentice Hall.

Bandura, A. (1997). *Self-efficacy: The exercise of control*. W H Freeman/Times Books Henry Holt & Co.

Bandura, A., & Walters, R. H. (1963). *Social learning and personality development*. Holt, Rinehart & Winston.

Bardwick, J. M. (1971). *Psychology of women: A study of bio-cultural conflicts*. Harper & Row.

Baron, R. A., Byrne, D., & Branscombe, N. R. (2007). *Mastering social psychology*. Pearson.

Barrett, R. J. (2004). Kurt Schneider in Borneo: Do first rank symptoms apply to the Iban? In *Cambridge Studies in Medical Anthropology* (pp. 87–109). Cambridge University Press.

Baumrind, D. (1964). Some thoughts on ethics of research: After reading Milgram's 'behavioral study of obedience'. *American Psychologist*, 19(6), 421–423.

Baumrind, D. (1985). Research using intentional deception: Ethical issues revisited. *American Psychologist*, 40(2), 165–174.

Beall, A. E., & Sternberg, R. J. (Eds.). (1993). *The psychology of gender*. Guilford Press.

Becker, D., & Lamb, S. (1994). Sex bias in the diagnosis of borderline personality disorder and posttraumatic stress disorder. *Professional Psychology: Research and Practice*, 25(1), 55.

Becker, H. S. (1953). Becoming a marihuana user. *The American Journal of Sociology*, 59(3), 235–242.

Bell, R. Q. (1968). A reinterpretation of the direction of effects in studies of socialization. *Psychological Review*, 75, 81–95.

Bell, R. Q., & Harper, L. V. (1977). *Child effects on adults*. Erlbaum.

Bem, S. L. (1974).The measurement of psychological androgyny. *Journal of Consulting and Clinical Psychology*, 42(2), 155–162.

Bem, S. L. (1976). Probing the promise of androgyny. In A. Kaplan & J. P. Bean (Eds.), *Beyond sex-role stereotypes: Readings toward a psychology of androgyny*. Little, Brown & Co.

Bem, S. L. (1981). Gender schema theory: A cognitive account of sex typing. *Psychological Review*, 88, 354–364.

Bem, S. L. (1993). *The lenses of gender: Transforming the debate on sexual inequality*. Yale University Press.

Bem, S. L. (1995). Dismantling gender polarization and compulsory heterosexuality: Should we turn the volume down or up? *Journal of Sex Research*, 32(4), 329–334.

Bem, S. L. (2008). Transforming the debate on sexual inequality: From biological difference to institutionalized androcentrism. In J. C. Chrysler, C. Golden, & P. D. Rozee (Eds.), *Lectures on the psychology of women* (4th ed., pp. 2–15). McGraw-Hill.

Benjamin, J. (1995). Recognition and destruction: An outline of intersubjectivity. In J. Benjamin (Ed.), *Like subjects, love objects*. Yale University Press.

Benjamin, J. (1998). *The shadow of the other: Intersubjectivity and gender in psychoanalysis*. Routledge.

Bentall, R. P., Jackson, H. F., & Pilgrim, D. (1988). Abandoning the concept of 'schizophrenia': Some implications of validity arguments for psychological research into psychotic phenomena. *British Journal of Clinical Psychology*, 27(4), 303–324.

Berger, I. E. (1992). The nature of attitude accessibility and attitude confidence: A triangulated experiment. *Journal of Consumer Psychology*, 1, 103–123.

Berlin, I. (1976). *Vico and Herder: Two studies on the history of ideas*. The Hogarth Press.

Berry, J. W. (1974). Canadian psychology: Some social and applied emphases. *Canadian Psychologist/Psychologie canadienne*, 15(2), 132–139.

Berry, J. W. (2004). An ecocultural perspective on the development of competence. In R. J. Sternberg & E. L. Grigorenko (Eds.), *Culture and competence: Contexts of life success* (pp. 3–22). American Psychological Association.

Berry, J. W., Poortinga, Y. H., Pandey, J., Dasen, P. R., Saraswathi, T. S., Segall, M. H., & Kağitçibaşi, Ç. (Eds.). (1997). *Handbook of cross-cultural psychology* (2nd ed., vols. 1–3). Allyn and Bacon.

Berry, J. W., Poortinga, Y. H., Segall, M. H., & Dasen, P. (1992). *Cross-cultural psychology: Research and application*. Cambridge University Press.

Berry, J. W., Poortinga, Y. H., Segall, M. H., & Dasen, P. (2002). *Cross cultural psychology: Research and application* (2nd ed.). Cambridge University Press.

Berry, J. W., & Sam, D. (1997). Acculturation and adaptation. In J. W. Berry, M. H. Seagull, & Ç. Kağitçibaşi (Eds.), *Handbook of cross-cultural psychology: Social behavior and applications* (vol. 3, pp. 291–326). Allyn & Bacon.

Berry, J. W., Van de Koppel, J. M. H., Senechel, C., Annis, R. C., Bahuchet, C., Cavalli-Sforza, L. L., & Witkin, H. A. (1986). *On the edge of the forest: Cultural adaptation and cognitive development in Central Africa*. Swets and Zeitlinger.

Bhabha, H. (1994). *Location of culture*. Routledge.

Bhatia, S. (2007). Rethinking culture and identity in psychology: Towards a transnational cultural psychology. *Journal of Theoretical and Philosophical Psychology*, 27(2), 301–321.

Bhattacharya, K. C. (1954) Swaraj in ideas. *Visvabharati Quarterly*, 20, 103–114. (Original lecture delivered 1931.)

Blalock, H. M. (1970). *An introduction to social research*. Prentice Hall.

Bleuler, E. ([1911] 1958). *Dementia praecox or the group of schizophrenias*. International Universities Press.

Blumer, H. (1948). Public opinion & public opinion polling. *American Sociological Review*, 13(5), 542–549.

Blumer, H. (1954). What is wrong with social theory? *American Sociological Review*, 19(1), 3–10.

316 References

Blumer, H. (1969). *Symbolic interactionism*. Prentice Hall.

Bockoven, J. S. (1956). Moral treatment in American psychiatry. *Journal of Nervous and Mental Disease*, 124, 167–194.

Boesky, D. (2002). Why don't our institutes teach the methodology of clinical psychoanalytic evidence? *Psychoanalytic Quarterly*, 71, 445–475.

Bolton, D. (2010). Conceptualisation of mental disorder and its personal meanings. *Journal of Mental Health*, 19(4), 328–336.

Boring, E. G. (1951). The women problem. *American Psychologist*, 6, 679–682.

Borrell-Carrió, F., Suchman, A. L., & Epstein, R. M. (2004). The biopsychosocial model 25 years later: Principles, practice, and scientific inquiry. *The Annals of Family Medicine*, 2(6), 576–582.

Boudon, R. (1984). *La Place du désordre*. Presses Universitaires de France.

Boudon, R. (1986). *Theories of social change*. Polity Press.

Bradley, B. (1989). *Visions of infancy*. Blackwell.

Breakwell, G. M. (1993). Social representations and social identity. *Papers on Social Representations*, 2(8), 198–217.

Bretherton, I. (1992). The origins of attachment theory: John Bowlby and Mary Ainsworth. *Developmental Psychology*, 28(5), 759–775.

Brewer, M. B., & Gardner, W. (1996). Who is this "we"? Levels of collective identity and self-regulations. *Journal of Personality and Social Psychology*, 71, 89–93.

Bridgman, P. (1927). *The logic of modern physics*. Macmillan.

Briley, D. A., Morris, M. W., & Simonson, I. (2000). Reasons as carriers of culture: Dynamic versus dispositional models of cultural influence on decision making. *Journal of Consumer Research*, 27, 157–178.

Brim, O. G., Jr., & Kagan, J. (1980). Constancy and change: A view of the issues. In O. G. Brim, Jr. & J. Kagan (Eds.), *Constancy and change in human development* (pp. 1–25). Harvard University Press.

Britt, S. H. (1937). Past and present trends in the methods and subject matter of social psychology. *Social Forces*, 15, 462–469.

Bronfenbrenner, U. (1979). *The ecology of human development*. Harvard University Press.

Bronfenbrenner, U. (1989). Ecological systems theory. In R. Vasta (Ed.), *Annals of child development: Six theories of child development—Revised formulations and current issues* (pp. 187–249). JAI Press.

Bronfenbrenner, U., & Morris, P. (1998). The ecology of developmental process. In W. Damon & R. M. Lerner (Eds.), *Handbook of child psychology* (vol. 1, pp. 993–1028). John Wiley & Sons, Inc.

Broughton, J. M. (1987). An introduction to critical developmental psychology. In J. M. Broughton (Ed.), *Critical theories of psychological development* (pp. 1–30). Plenum Press.

Broughton, J. (1988). The masculine authority of the cognitive. In B. Inhelder (Ed.), *Piaget today* (pp. 111–125). Psychology Press.

Broverman, I. K., Vogel, S. R., Broverman, D. M., Clarkson, F. E., & Rosenkrantz, P. S. (1972). Sex-role stereotypes: A current appraisal. *Journal of Social Issues*, 28(2), 59–78.

Bruner, J. S. (1957). On perceptual readiness. *Psychological Review*, 64(2), 123–152.

Bruner, J. S. (1990). *The Jerusalem-Harvard lectures: Acts of meaning*. Harvard University Press.

Bruner, J. S. (1993). Explaining and interpreting: Two ways of using mind. In G. Harman (Ed.), *Conceptions of the human mind: Essays in honor of George A. Miller* (pp. 123–137). Lawrence Erlbaum Associates.

Bryman, A. (2004). *Quantity and quality in social research*. Taylor & Francis e-library.

Burman, E. (Ed.). (1998). *Deconstructing feminist psychology*. Sage.

Burman, E. (2008). *Deconstructing developmental psychology* (2nd ed.). Routledge.

Burman, E. (2017). *Deconstructing developmental psychology* (3rd ed.). Routledge.

Burr, V. (1998). *Gender and social psychology*. Routledge.

Buss, D. M., & Kenrick, D. T. (1998). Evolutionary social psychology. In D. T. Gilbert, S. T. Fiske, & G. Lindzey (Eds.), *The handbook of social psychology* (pp. 982–1026). McGraw-Hill.

Butler, J. (1990). *Gender trouble: Feminism and the subversion of identity*. Routledge.

Cakal, H., Hewstone, M., Schwar, G., & Heath, A. (2011). An investigation of the social identity model of collective action and the 'sedative' effect of intergroup contact among Black and White students in South Africa. *British Journal of Social Psychology*, 50(4), 606–627.

Calkins, M. W. (1896). Association. *Psychological Review*, 3, 32–49.

Campbell, D. T. (1957). Factors relevant to the validity of experiments in social settings. *Psychological Bulletin*, 54(4), 297–312.

Cantor, N., & Mischel, W. (1977). Traits as prototypes: Effects on recognition memory. *Journal of Personality and Social Psychology*, 35(1), 38–48.

Chamberlain, K. (2000). Methodolatry and qualitative health research. *Journal of Health Psychology*, 5(3), 285–296.

Chekroun, P., & Brauer, M. (2002). The bystander effect and social control behavior: The effect of the presence of others on people's reactions to norm violations. *European Journal of Social Psychology*, 32, 853–867.

Cheung, F. M., & Leung, K. (1998). Indigenous personality measures: Chinese examples. *Journal of Cross-Cultural Psychology*, 29, 233–248.

Ching, C. C. (1984). Psychology and the four modernizations in China. *International Journal of Psychology*, 19, 57–63.

Chodorow, N. (1974). Family structure and female personality. In M. Z. Rosaldo & L. Lamphere (Eds.), *Women, culture and society* (pp. 43–66). Stanford University Press.

Chodorow, N. (1978). *The reproduction of mothering: Psychoanalysis and the sociology of gender*. University of California Press.

Chodorow, N. (1997). The psychodynamics of family. In L. J. Nicholson (Ed.), *The second wave: A reader in feminist theory* (pp. 181–197). Routledge.

Choi, S.-C., Kim, U., & Choi, S.-H. (1993). Indigenous analysis of collective representations: A Korean perspective. In U. Kim & J. W. Berry (Eds.), *Indigenous psychologies: Research and experience in cultural context* (pp. 193–210). Sage.

Clearfield, M. W., & Nelson, N. M. (2006). Sex differences in mothers' speech and play behavior with 6-, 9-, and 14-month-old infants. *Sex Roles*, 54(1–2), 127–137.

Clifton, A. K., McGrath, D., & Wick, B. (1976). Stereotypes of woman: A single category? *Sex Roles*, 2(2), 135–148.

Cohen, D., Vandello, J., Puente, S., & Rantilla, A. (1999). When you call me that, smile! How norms for politeness, interaction styles, and aggression work together in Southern culture. *Social Psychology Quarterly*, 62(3), 257–275.

Cole, M. (1988). Cross-cultural research in the sociohistorical tradition. *Human Development*, 31, 137–157.

Cole, M. (1990). Cultural psychology: A once and future discipline? In J. J. Berman (Ed.), *Nebraska Symposium on Motivation, 1989: Cross-cultural perspectives* (vol. 37, pp. 279–336). University of Nebraska Press.

Cole, M. (1992). Context, modularity, and the cultural constitution of development. In L. T. Winegar & J. Valsiner (Eds.), *Children's development within social context. Vol. 1: Metatheory and theory. Vol. 2: Research and methodology* (pp. 5–31). Lawrence Erlbaum Associates, Inc.

318 References

Cole, M. (1996). *Cultural psychology: A once and future discipline.* Harvard University Press.

Cole, M., & Engeström, Y. (1993). A cultural historical approach to distributed cognition. In G. Salomon (Ed.), *Distributed cognitions: Psychological and educational considerations* (pp. 1–46). Cambridge University Press.

Cole, M., Gay, J., Glick, J. A., Sharp. D. W., Ciborowski, T., Frankel, F., Kellemu J., & Lancy, D.(1971). *The cultural context of learning and thinking.* Basic Books.

Collins, P. H. (1990). *Black feminist thought: Knowledge, consciousness, and the politics of empowerment.* Routledge.

Constantinople, A. (1973). Masculinity-femininity: An exception to a famous dictum? *Psychological Bulletin,* 80(5), 389–407.

Cooley, C. H. (1902). *Human nature and the social order.* Charles Scribner's Sons.

Cooter, R. J. (1976). Phrenology and British alienists, c. 1825–1845. Part I: Converts to a doctrine. *Medical History,* 20(1), 1.

Corbetta, P. (2003). *Social research: Theory, methods and techniques.* Sage.

Crawford, M. (1995). *Talking difference.* Sage.

Crawford, M., & Marecek, J. (1989). Psychology reconstructs the female: 1968–1988. *Psychology of Women Quarterly,* 13(2), 147–165.

Crenshaw, K. (1989). Demarginalizing the intersection of race and sex: A Black feminist critique of antidiscrimination doctrine, feminist theory and antiracist politics. *University of Chicago Legal Forum,* 140, 139–167.

Cronbach, L. J. (1975). Beyond the two disciplines of scientific psychology. *American Psychologist,* 30(2), 116 127.

Cronbach, L. J., & Drenth, P. J. (Eds.). (1972). *Mental tests and cultural adaptation.* Mouton Publishers.

Dalal, A. K., & Misra, G. (2010). The core and context of Indian psychology. *Psychology and Developing Society,* 22(1), 121–155.

Danziger, K., & Dzinas, K. (1997). How psychology got its variables. *Canadian Psychology,* 38, 43–48.

Davies, B., & Harré, R. (1990). Positioning. *Journal for the Theory of Social Behaviour,* 20(1), 43–63.

Dawkins, R. (1976). *The selfish gene.* Oxford University Press.

Deacon, B. J. (2013). The biomedical model of mental disorder: A critical analysis of its validity, utility, and effects on psychotherapy research. *Clinical Psychology Review,* 33(7), 846–861.

Deaux, K., & Major, B. (1987). Putting gender into context: An interactive model of gender-related behavior. *Psychological Review,* 94(3), 369–389.

De Beauvoir, S. (1949). *The second sex.* Gallimard.

Denzin, N. (1970). *The research act in sociology.* Aldine.

Denzin, N. (1971). *The research act: A theoretical introduction to sociological methods.* Butterworth.

Deregowski, J. B. (1972). Pictorial perception and culture. *Scientific American,* 227, 82–88.

Descartes, R. (2013). *Discours de la Méthode/Discourse on method* [French/English bilingual text]. Jiahu Books. (Original work published 1637.)

Deutsch, M. (1975). Equity, equality, and need: What determines which value will be used as the basis of distributive justice? *Journal of Social Issues,* 31(3), 137–149.

Dewey, J., & Bentley, A. F. (1948). *Knowing and the known.* Beacon Press.

Dhar, A., & Siddiqui, S. (2013). At the edge of (critical) psychology. In *Critical psychology in a changing world II: Building bridges and expanding the dialogue. Annual Review of Critical Psychology,* 10, 506–548.

Díaz-Guerrero, R. (1977). A Mexican psychology. *American Psychologist,* 32(11), 934–944.

Dilthey, W. (1883). *Introduction to the human sciences*. Princeton University Press.

Dixon, J., Tropp, L. R., Durrheim, K., & Tredoux, C. (2010). Let them eat harmony. Prejudice reduction strategies and attitudes of historically disadvantaged groups. *Current Directions in Psychological Science*, 19(2), 76–80.

Doi, T. (1973). *The anatomy of dependence*. (Trans. John Bester). Kodansha International.

Doise, W. (1986). *Levels of explanation in social psychology*. Cambridge University Press.

Draguns, J. G. (1973). Comparisons of psychopathology across cultures: Issues, findings, directions. *Journal of Cross-Cultural Psychology*, 4(1), 9–47.

Dryden, C. (1999). *Being married, doing gender: A critical analysis of gender relationships in marriage*. Routledge.

DuBois, W. E. B. (1903). *The souls of Black folks: Essays and sketches*. McClurg and Co.

Durojaiye, M. A. O. (1993). Indigenous psychology in Africa. In U. Kim & J. W. Berry (Eds.), *Indigenous psychologies: Research and experience in cultural context*. Sage.

Durrheim, K., Hook, D., & Riggs, D. (2009). Race and racism. In D. Fox., I. Prilleltensky, & S. Austin (Eds.), *Critical psychology: An introduction* (2nd ed.). Sage.

Eagly, A. H., & Kite, M. E. (1987). Are stereotypes of nationalities applied to both women and men? *Journal of Personality and Social Psychology*, 53(3), 451–462.

Eagly, A. H., Wood, W., & Diekman, A. B. (2000). Social role theory of sex differences and similarities: A current appraisal. In T. Eckes & H. M. Trautner (Eds.), *The developmental social psychology of gender* (pp. 123–174). Erlbaum.

Earley, C. (1989). Social loafing and collectivism: A comparison of the United States and People's Republic of China. *Administrative Science Quarterly*, 34, 565–581.

Ebbinghaus, H. ([1885] 1964). *Memory: A contribution to experimental psychology* (Trans. H. A. Ruger & C. E. Bussenius). Dover.

Eccles, J. S. (1987). Gender roles and women's achievement-related decisions. *Psychology of Women Quarterly*, 11(2), 135–171.

Eccles, J. S. (1994). Understanding women's educational and occupational choices: Applying the Eccles et al. model of achievement-related choices. *Psychology of Women Quarterly*, 18(4), 585–609.

Eccles, J. S. (2011). Gendered educational and occupational choices: Applying the Eccles et al. model of achievement-related choices. *International Journal of Behavioral Development*, 35(3), 195–201.

Eccles, J. S., Adler, T. F., Futterman, R., Goff, S. B., Kaczala, C. M., Meece, J. L., & Midgley, C. (1983). Expectancies, values, and academic behaviors. In J. T. Spence (Ed.), *Achievement and achievement motivation* (pp. 75–146). W. H. Freeman.

Ekman, P., & Friesen, W. V. (1986). A new pan-cultural facial expression of emotion. *Motivation and Emotion*, 10(2), 159–168.

Elder, G. H., Jr. (1974). *Children of the Great Depression*. University of Chicago Press.

Elder, G. H., Jr. (1999). *Children of the Great Depression: Social change in life experience*. (25th anniversary ed.). Westview Press.

Elkin, F. (1960). *The child and society*. Random House.

Elliott, R., Fischer, C. T., & Rennie, D. L. (1999). Evolving guidelines for publication of qualitative research studies in psychology and related fields. *British Journal of Clinical Psychology*, 38, 215–229.

Ellis, H. (1894). *Man and woman: A study of human secondary sexual characters*. Walter Scott.

Elms, A. C. (1975).The crisis of confidence in social psychology. *American Psychology*, 30(10), 967–976.

Emmerich, W. (1968). Personality development and concepts of structure. *Child Development*, 39, 671–690.

320 References

Engel, G. L. (1977). The need for a new medical model: A challenge for biomedicine. *Science*, 196(4286), 129–136.

Enriquez, V. G. (1977). Filipino psychology in the Third World. *Philippine Journal of Psychology*, 10(1), 3–18.

Enriquez, V. G. (1993). Developing a Filipino psychology. In U. Kim & J. W. Berry (Eds.), *Indigenous psychologies: Research and experience in cultural context* (Cross-cultural research and methodology series, vol. 17, pp. 152–169). Sage.

Epstein, C. F. (1988). *Deceptive distinctions: Sex, gender, and the social order.* Yale University Press.

Erikson, E. (1968). *Identity: Youth and crisis.* W. W. Norton & Company.

Ernster, V., Kaufman, N., Nichter, M., Samet, J., & Yoon, S. Y. (2000). Women and tobacco: Moving from policy to action. *Bulletin of the World Health Organization*, 78, 891–901.

Evered, R., & Louis, M. R. (1981). Alternative perspectives in the organizational sciences, 'enquiry from the inside' and 'inquiry from the outside'. *Academy of Management Review*, 6(3), 385–395.

Fausto-Sterling, A. (2000). *Sexing the body: Gender politics and the construction of sexuality.* Basic Books.

Feshbach, S. (1989). The bases and development of individual aggression. In J. Groebel & R. A. Hinde (Eds.), *Aggression and war: Their biological and social bases* (pp. 78–90). Cambridge University Press.

Feyerabend, P. (1962). Explanation, reduction and empiricism. In H. Leigl & G. Maxwell (Eds.), *Scientific explanation: Space and time* (Minnesota Studies in Philosophy of Science, vol. III, pp. 28–97). University of Minneapolis Press.

Feyerabend, P. (1963). How to be a good empiricist: A plea for tolerance in matters epistemological. In B. Baumrin (Ed.), *Philosophy of science: The Delaware Seminar* (vol. 2, pp. 3–39). Interscience Publishers.

Feyerabend, P. (1964). Realism and instrumentalism: Comments in the logic of factual support. In M. Bunge (Ed.), *Critical approaches to science and philosophy* (pp. 260–308). The Free Press.

Feyerabend, P. (1965). Problems of empiricism. In R. G. Colodny (Ed.), *Beyond the edge of certainty: Essays in contemporary science and philosophy* (pp. 145–260). Prentice-Hall.

Feyerabend, P. (1975). *Against method.* New Left Books.

Fine, M., & Gordon, S. M. (1989). Feminist transformations of/despite psychology. In M. Crawford & M. Gentry (Eds.), *Gender and thought: Psychological perspectives* (pp. 146–174). Springer Verlag.

First, M. B., Regier, D. A., & Kupfer, D. J. (2002). *A research agenda for DSM-V.* American Psychiatric Association.

Fishbein, M., & Ajzen, I. (1975). *Belief, attitude, intention, and behavior: An introduction to theory and research.* Addison-Wesley.

Flick, U. (1998). *The psychology of the social.* Cambridge University Press.

Foot, K. A. (2014). Cultural-historical activity theory: Exploring a theory to inform practice and research. *Journal of Human Behavior in the Social Environment*, 24(3), 329–347.

Foucault, M. (1965). *Madness and civilization: A history of insanity in the age of reason.* Pantheon Books.

Foucault, M. (1971). *Madness and civilization: A history of insanity in the age of reason,* (Trans. R. Howard). Tavistock.

Foucault, M. (1982). The subject and power. *Critical Inquiry*, 8(4), 777–795.

Fox, D., Prilleltensky, I., & Austin, S. (Eds.). (2009). *Critical psychology: An introduction*. (2nd ed.). Sage.

Fraser, C., & Gaskell, G. (Eds.). (1990). *Attitudes, beliefs and representations: The social psychological study of widespread beliefs*. Clarendon Press.

Freud, S. (1923). The infantile genital organization (An interpolation into the theory of sexuality). In J. Strachey (Ed.), *The standard edition of the complete psychological works of Sigmund Freud* (vol. 19, pp. 139–146). The Hogarth Press and the Institute of Psychoanalysis.

Freud, S. (1924). The dissolution of the Oedipus Complex. In J. Strachey (Ed.), *The standard edition of the complete psychological works of Sigmund Freud* (vol. 19, pp. 171–180). The Hogarth Press and the Institute of Psychoanalysis.

Freud , S. (1925). Some psychical consequences of the anatomical distinction between the sexes. In J. Strachey (Ed.), *The standard edition of the complete psychological works of Sigmund Freud* (vol. 19, pp. 243–258). The Hogarth Press and the Institute of Psychoanalysis.

Freud, S. (1931). Female sexuality. In J. Strachey (Ed.), *The standard edition of the complete psychological works of Sigmund Freud* (vol. 21, pp. 221–244). The Hogarth Press and the Institute of Psychoanalysis.

Freud, S. (1933). New introductory lecture on psycho-analysis. In J. Strachey (Ed.), *The standard edition of the complete psychological works of Sigmund Freud* (vol. 22, pp. 1–182). The Hogarth Press and the Institute of Psychoanalysis.

Frønes, I. (1993). Changing childhood. *Childhood*, 1(1), 1–2.

Frosh, S. (2003). Psychosocial studies and psychology: Is a critical approach emerging? *Human Relations*, 56(12), 2–23.

Funk, L., Scheidecker, G., Chapin, B. L., Schmidt, W. J., Quardani, C. E., & Chaudhary, N. (2023). Feeding, bonding, and the formation of social relationships: Ethnographic challenges to attachment theory and early childhood interventions. *Elements in Psychology and Culture*. Online.

Gallimore, R., & Goldenberg, C. (1993). Activity setting of early literacy: Home and school factors in children's emergent literacy. In E. Forman, N. Minick, & C. A. Stone (Eds.), *Contexts for learning: Sociocultural dynamics in children's development* (pp. 315–335). Oxford University Press.

Galupo, M. P., Pulice-Farrow, L., & Ramirez, J. L. (2017). "Like a constantly flowing river": Gender identity flexibility among nonbinary transgender individuals. In *Identity flexibility during adulthood* (pp. 163–177). Springer.

Gardner, W. L., Gabriel, S., & Lee, A. Y. (1999). "I" value freedom, but "we" value relationships: Self-construal priming mirrors cultural differences in judgment. *Psychological Science*, 10(4), 321–326.

Garfinkel, H. (1967). *Studies in ethnomethodology*. Prentice Hall.

Geary, D. C. (1995). Reflections of evolution and culture in children's cognition: Implications for mathematical development and instruction. *American Psychologist*, 50(1), 24.

Geertz, C. (1966). Religion as a cultural system. In M. Banton (Ed.), *Anthropological approaches to the study of religion* (pp. 1–46). Tavistock.

Geertz, C. (1973). *The interpretation of cultures: Selected essays*. Basic Books.

Gergen, K. J. (1973). Social psychology as history. *Journal of Personality and Social Psychology*, 26(2), 309–320.

Gergen, K. J. (1994). *Realities and relationships: Soundings in social constructionism*. Harvard University Press.

Gergen, K. J., & Gergen, M. M. (1988). It's a love story. *Psychology Today*, 22(12), 48–49.

322 References

Gergen, K. J., Massey, A. L., Gulerce, A., & Misra, G. (1996). Psychological science in cultural context. *American Psychologist*, 51(5), 496–503.

Gergen, M. M. (1988). Toward a feminist metatheory and methodology in the social sciences. In M. M. Gergen (Ed.), *Feminist thought and the structure of knowledge* (pp. 87–104). New York University Press.

Gesell, A. (1971). *Studies in child development*. Greenwood Press.

Gillespie, M. (2005). *Media audiences*. Open University Press.

Gilligan, C. (1982). *In a different voice: Psychological theory and women's development*. Harvard University Press.

Gilman, C. P. (1911). *The man made world; Or, our androcentric culture*. Charlton Company.

Giorgi, A. (1994). A phenomenological perspective on certain qualitative research methods. *Journal of Phenomenological Psychology*, 25(2), 190–220.

Giroux, H. A. (2005). *Border crossings: Cultural workers and the politics of education*. Routledge.

Glaser, B. G., & Strauss, A. L. (1967). *The discovery of grounded theory: Strategies for qualitative research*. Aldine.

Goffman, E. (1959). *The presentation of self in everyday life*. Doubleday.

Goffman, E. (1974). *Frame analysis: An essay on the organization of experience*. Harvard University Press.

Gollin, E. S. (1981). Development and plasticity. In E. S. Gollin (Ed.), *Developmental plasticity: Behavioral and biological aspects of variations in development* (pp. 231–251). Academic Press.

Good, B. J., & Kleinman, A. M. (1985). Culture and anxiety: Cross-cultural evidence for the patterning of anxiety disorders. In A. H. Tuma & J. D. Maser (Eds.), *Anxiety and the anxiety disorders* (pp. 297–323). Lawrence Erlbaum Associates, Inc.

Goodenough, W. H. (1961). Comment on cultural evolution. *Daedalus*, 90, 521–528.

Goodenough. W. H. (1971). *Culture, language, and society* (McCaleb Module in Anthropology). Addison-Wesley.

Goodnow, J. J. (2011). Merging cultural and psychological accounts of family contexts. In L. A. Jensen (Ed.), *Bridging cultural and developmental approaches to psychology: New syntheses in theory, research, and policy* (pp. 73–91). Oxford University Press.

Goodwin, D. W. (1968). Sex and gender: On the development of masculinity and femininity. *JAMA*, 206(6), 1310.

Gottlieb, G. (1997). *Synthesizing nature–nurture: Prenatal roots of instinctive behavior*. Erlbaum.

Graumann, C. F.(Ed.). (1972). *Sozialpsychologie*. Hogrefe.

Greenfield, P. M. (1997). You can't take it with you: Why ability assessments don't cross cultures. *American Psychologist*, 52(10), 1115–1124.

Greenfield, P. M. (2000). Three approaches to the psychology of culture: Where do they come from? Where can they go? *Asian Journal of Social Psychology*, 3(3), 223–240.

Grunbaüm, A. (1984). *The foundations of psychoanalysis: A philosophical critique*. University of California Press.

Guba, E. G., & Lincoln, Y. S. (1982). Epistemological and methodological bases of naturalistic inquiry. *Educational Communication & Technology Journal*, 30(4), 233–252.

Guba, E. G., & Lincoln, Y. S. (1994). Competing paradigms in qualitative research. In N. K. Denzin, & Y. S. Lincoln (Eds.), *Handbook of qualitative research* (pp. 105–117). Sage.

Gupta, A., & Ferguson, J. (1992). Beyond culture: Space, identity and the politics of difference. *Cultural Anthropology*, 7(1), 6–23.

Hacker, H. M. (1951). Women as a minority group. *Social Forces*, 30, 60–69.

References **323**

Hall, E. T. (1966). *The hidden dimension.* Doubleday.

Han, S., & Northoff, G. (2008). Culture-sensitive neural substrates of human cognition: A transcultural neuroimaging approach. *Nature Reviews Neuroscience,* 9(8), 646–654.

Harré, R. (1979). *Social being: A theory for social psychology.* Blackwell.

Harris, A. (1987). The rationalisation of infancy. In J. Broughton (Ed.), *Critical theories of psychological development* (pp. 31–60). Plenum Press.

Harris, J. R. (1998). *The nurture assumption: Why children turn out the way they do.* Free Press.

Harrison, S. I. (1967). Individual psychotherapy. In A. M. Friednan & H. I. Kaplan (Eds.), *Comprehensive textbook of psychiatry* (pp. 1453–1463). Williams and Wilkins.

Haslam, J. (1810). *Illustrations of madness: Exhibiting a singular case of insanity and a no less remarkable difference in medical opinion: developing the nature of assailment, and the manner of working events; with a description of the tortures experienced by bomb-bursting, lobster-cracking, and lengthening the brain.* G. Hayden for Rivingtons.

Hastie, R., & Kumar, P. A. (1979). Person memory: Personality traits as organizing principles in memory for behaviors. *Journal of Personality and Social Psychology,* 37(1), 25–38.

Hathaway, S. R., & McKinley, J. C. (1940). A multiphasic personality schedule (Minnesota): I. Construction of the schedule. *The Journal of Psychology,* 10(2), 249–254.

Heider, F. (1958). *The psychology of interpersonal relations.* John Wiley & Sons, Ltd.

Heilman, M. E., Wallen, A. S., Fuchs, D., & Tamkins, M. M. (2004). Penalties for success: Reactions to women who succeed at male gender-typed tasks. *Journal of Applied Psychology,* 89(3), 416–427.

Helgeson, V. S. (2012). *The psychology of gender* (4th ed.). Pearson Education Inc.

Henriques, J., Hollway, W., Urwin, C., Venn, C., & Walkerdine, V. (1984). *Changing the subject: Psychology, social regulation and subjectivity.* Methuen.

Henwood, K. L., & Pidgeon, N. F. (1992). Qualitative research and psychological theorizing. *British Journal of Psychology,* 83(1), 97–112.

Hermans, H. J. M., & Kempen, H. J. G. (1998). Moving cultures: The perilous problems of cultural dichotomies in a globalizing society. *American Psychologist,* 53(10), 1111–1120.

Hiles, D. (2001). Rethinking paradigms in research in psychology [PDF document]. Retrieved from https://is.muni.cz/el/1423/podzim2011/PSY401/um/Hiles.pdf.

Ho, D. Y. F. (1982). Asian concepts in behavioral science. *Psychologia,* 25, 228–235.

Ho, D. Y. F. (1993). Relational orientation in Asian social psychology. In U. Kim & J. W. Berry (Eds.), *Indigenous psychologies: Research and experience in cultural context* (Cross-cultural research and methodology series, vol. 17, pp. 240–259). Sage.

Hochschild, A. R. (1989). *The second shift.* Avon Books.

Hofstede, G. (1980). *Culture's consequences: International differences in work-related values.* Sage.

Hofstede, G. (2001). *Culture's consequences: Comparing values, behaviors, institutions, and organizations across nations* (2nd ed.). Sage.

Hogg, M. A., & Vaughan, G. M. (1998). *Social psychology.* Prentice Hall.

Hollingworth, L. S. (1914a). *Functional periodicity: An experimental study of the mental and motor abilities of women during menstruation* (No. 69). Teachers College, Columbia University.

Hollingworth, L. S. (1914b). Variability as related to sex differences in achievement: A critique. *American Journal of Sociology,* 19(4), 510–530.

Hollway, W. (2004). Editorial. Special issue on psycho-social research. *International Journal of Critical Psychology,* 10, 5–12.

Hollway, W. (2006). Towards a psycho-social account of self in family relationships: The legacy of 20th century discourses. *Theory and Psychology,* 16(4), 465–482.

324 References

Hollway, W. (2010). Conflict in the transition to becoming a mother: A psychosocial approach. *Psychoanalysis, Culture and Society*, 15(2), 136–155.

Hollway, W., & Jefferson, T. (2000). *Doing qualitative research differently*. Sage.

Hollway, W., & Jefferson, T. (2005). Panic and perjury: A psychosocial exploration of agency. *British Journal of Social Psychology*, 44, 147–163.

Hollway, W., & Jefferson, T. (2010). *Doing qualitative research differently: Free association, narrative and the interview method*. Sage.

Hollway, W., Lucey, H., & Phoenix, A. (2010). *Social psychology matters*. Tata McGraw Hill Edition

Holmes, S., Drake, S., Odgers, K., & Wilson, J. (2017). Feminist approaches to anorexia nervosa: A qualitative study of a treatment group. *Journal of Eating Disorders*, 5(1), 36.

Holzman, L. (2009). *Vygotsky at work and play*. Taylor & Francis.

Hong, Y. Y., Benet-Martínez, V., Chiu, C., & Morris, M. W. (2003). Boundaries of cultural influence: Construct activation as a mechanism for cultural differences in social perception. *Journal of Cross-Cultural Psychology*, 34, 453–464.

Hong, Y. Y., & Chiu, C. Y. (2001). Toward a paradigm shift: From cross-cultural differences in social cognition to social-cognitive mediation of cultural differences. *Social Cognition*, 19(3), 181–196.

Hong, Y. Y., Morris, M. W., Chiu, C. Y., & Benet-Martínez, V. (2000). Multicultural minds. A dynamic constructivist approach to culture and cognition. *American Psychologist*, 55(7), 709–720.

Horney, K. (1936). Culture and neurosis. *American Sociological Review*, 1, 221–235.

Horney, K. (1939). *New ways in psychoanalysis*. Norton.

Horney, K. (1967). *Feminine psychology*. Ed. H. Kelman. Norton.

House, J. S. (1977). The three faces of social psychology. *Sociometry*, 40(2), 161–177.

Howarth, C. (2006). How social representations of attitudes have informed attitude theories. *Theory & Psychology*, 16(5), 691–714.

Howitt, D., Billig, M., & Cramer, D. (1989). *Social psychology: Conflicts and continuities: An introductory textbook*. McGraw-Hill Education.

Howitt, D., & Cramer, D. (2011). *Introduction to research methods in psychology* (3rd ed.). Pearson Education Limited.

Hsu, F. L. K.(Ed.). (1961). *Psychological anthropology*. Dorsey Press.

Hughes, P. (2006). Beyond the medical model of gender dysphoria to morphological self-determination. *Lahey Clinic Medical Ethics Journal*, Winter, 10–11.

Husserl, E. (1927). Phenomenology. In *Encyclopaedia Britannica* (14th ed., pp. 699–702). Available at: www.britannica.com

Hyde, J. S. (2005). The gender similarities hypothesis. *American Psychologist*, 60(6), 581–592.

Hyde, J. S., & McKinley, N. M. (1997). Gender differences in cognition: Results from meta-analyses. In P. J. Caplan, M. Crawford, J. S. Hyde, & J. R. E. Richardson (Eds.), *Gender differences in human cognition* (pp. 30–51). Oxford University Press.

Ingraham, C. (1994). The heterosexual imaginary: Feminist sociology and theories of gender. *Sociological Theory*, 12(2), 203–219.

Irigaray, L. ([1977] 1985). *This sex which is not one* (Eng. trans. 1985). Cornell University Press.

Irigaray, L. (1984). *An ethics of sexual difference*. Cornell University Press.

Irvine, S. H. (1979). The place of factor analysis in cross-cultural methodology and its contribution to cognitive theory. In L. Eckensberger, W. Lonner, & Y. H. Poortinga (Eds.), *Cross-cultural contributions to psychology* (pp. 300–341). Swets and Zeitlinger.

Jahoda, G. (1990). Our forgotten ancestors. In J. J. Berman (Ed.), *Nebraska Symposium on Motivation: Cross-cultural perspectives* (pp. 1–40). University of Nebraska Press.

Jahoda, G. (1992a). Foreword. In J. W. Berry, Y. H. Poortinga, M. H. Segall, & P. R. Dasen (Eds.), *Cross-cultural psychology: Research and applications* (pp. x–xii). Cambridge University Press.

Jahoda, G. (1992b). *Crossroads between culture and mind: Continuities and change in theories of human nature*. Harvard University Press.

Jahoda, G. (1993). The colour of a chameleon: Perspectives on concepts of 'culture'. *Cultural Dynamics*, 6, 277–287.

James, A., & Prout, A. (1997). A new paradigm for the sociology of childhood? Provenance, promise and problems. In A. James & A. Prout (Eds.), *Constructing and reconstructing childhood: Contemporary issues in the sociological study of childhood* (pp. 7–32). Falmer Press.

James, W. ([1907] 1975). Pragmatism: A new name for some old ways of thinking. In F. H. Burkhardt, F. Bowers, & I. K. Skrupskelis (Eds.), *The works of William James* (vol. 1, pp. 1–144). Harvard University Press.

Janesick, V. J. (1994). The dance of qualitative research design: Metaphor, methodolatry and meaning. In N. K. Denzin & Y. S. Lincoln (Eds.), *Strategies of qualitative inquiry* (pp. 209–235). Sage Publications.

Jaspers, K. (1963). *General psychopathology* (trans. J. Hoenig & M. Hamilton). University of Chicago Press.

Johnstone, L. (2006). Controversies and debates about formulation. In *Formulation in psychology and psychotherapy: Making sense of people's problems* (pp. 208–235). Routledge.

Johnstone, L., & Dallos, R. (2013). *Formulation in psychology and psychotherapy: Making sense of people's problems* (2nd ed.). Routledge.

Jørgensen, M., & Phillips, L. (2002). *Discourse analysis as theory and method*. Sage.

Judith, P. B. (2004). *Undoing gender*. Routledge.

Kachele, H., Schachter, J., & Thomäs, H. (2009). *From psychoanalytic narrative to empirical single case research: Implications for psychoanalytic practice*. Routledge.

Kağitçibaşi, Ç. (1984). Socialization in traditional society: A challenge to psychology. *International Journal of Psychology*, 19, 145–157.

Kakar, S. (1978). *The inner world*. Oxford University Press.

Kakar, S. (1982). *Shamans, mystics and doctors: A psychological inquiry into India and its healing traditions*. Oxford University Press.

Kanter, R. M. (1977). *Men and women of the corporation*. Basic Books.

Kashima, Y., & Kashima, E. (2003). Individualism, GNP, climate, and pronoun drop: Is individualism determined by affluence and climate, or does language use play a role? *Journal of Cross-Cultural Psychology*, 34(1), 125–134.

Kearney, R. N., & Miller, B. D. (1985). The spiral of suicide and social change in Sri Lanka. *The Journal of Asian Studies*, 45(1), 81–101.

Keesing, R. M. (1974). Theories of culture. *Annual Review of Anthropology*, 3(1), 73–97.

Keller, H. (2007). *Cultures of infancy*. Lawrence Erlbaum.

Keller, H. (2021). *Themyth of attachment theory: A critical understanding for multicultural societies*. Routledge.

Kelley, H. (1992), Common-sense psychology and scientific psychology. *Annual Review of Psychology*, 43, 1–23.

Kelley, H. H. (1971). *Attribution in social interaction*. General Learning Press.

Kessen, W. (1993). Avoiding the emptiness: The full child. *Theory and Psychology*, 3(4), 415–427.

Kidder, L. H., & Fine, M. (1987). Qualitative and quantitative methods: When stories converge. *New Directions for Evaluation*, 35, 57–75.

326 References

Kim, U., & Berry, J. W. (1993). *Indigenous psychologies: Experience and research in cultural context.* Sage.

Kim, U., Yang, K.-S., & Hwang, K.-K. (2006). Contributions to indigenous and cultural psychology: Understanding people in context. In U. Kim, K.-S. Yang, & K.-K. Hwang (Eds.), *Indigenous and cultural psychology: Understanding people in context* (pp. 3–25). Springer Science + Business Media.

King, D. K. (1988). Multiple jeopardy, multiple consciousness: The context of a Black feminist ideology. *Signs,* 14(1), 42–72.

Kirmayer, L. J. (1998). The fate of culture in DSM-IV. *Transcultural Psychiatry,* 35(3), 339–342.

Kirsten, A. F. (2014). Cultural-historical activity theory: Exploring a theory to inform practice and research. *Journal of Human Behavior in the Social Environment,* 24(3), 329–347.

Kitayama, S., Markus, H. R., Matsumoto, H., & Norasakkunkit, V. (1997). Individual and collective processes in the construction of the self: Self-enhancement in the United States and self-criticism in Japan. *Journal of Personality and Social Psychology,* 72, 1245–1267.

Kitayama, S., & Park, J. (2010). Cultural neuroscience of the self: Understanding the social grounding of the brain. *Social Cognitive Affective Neuroscience,* 5(2–3), 111–129.

Kitayama, S., & Rarasawa , M. (1997). Implicit self-esteem in Japan: Name letters and birthday numbers. *Personality and Social Psychology Bulletin,* 23(7), 736–742.

Kite, M. E., Deaux, K., & Haines, E. L. (2008). Gender stereotypes. In F. L. Denmark & M. A. Paludi (Eds.), *Women's psychology: Psychology of women: A handbook of issues and theories* (pp. 205–236). Praeger Publishers/Greenwood Publishing Group.

Kleinman, A. (1988). *The illness narratives: Suffering, healing, and the human condition.* Basic Books.

Kleinman, A., Anderson, J. M., Finkler, K., Frankenberg, R. J., & Young, A. (1986). Social origins of distress and disease: Depression, neurasthenia, and pain in modern China. *Current Anthropology,* 24(5), 499–509.

Kleinman, A., Das, V., & Lock, M. M. (Eds.). (1997). *Social suffering.* University of California Press.

Kleinman, A., & Good, B. (Eds.). (1986). *Culture and depression: Studies in the anthropology and cross-cultural psychiatry of affect and disorder* (vol. 16). University of California Press.

Koenig, A. M., Eagly, A. H., Mitchell, A. A., & Ristikari, T. (2011). Are leader stereotypes masculine? A meta-analysis of three research paradigms. *Psychological Bulletin,* 137(4), 616–642.

Kofsky Scholnick, E. (2000). Engendering development: Metaphors of change. In P. Miller & E. Kofsky Scholnick (Eds.), *Towards a feminist developmental psychology* (pp. 11–28). Routledge.

Kohlberg, L. (1958). The development of modes of moral thinking in the years ten to sixteen. [Unpublished doctoral dissertation]. University of Chicago.

Kohlberg, L. (1981). *The philosophy of moral development.* Harper and Row.

Kohlberg, L., & Kramer, R. (1969). Continuities and discontinuities in childhood and adult moral development. *Human Development,* 12(2), 93–120.

Kohlberg, L., Levine, C., & Hewer, A. (1983). Moral stages: A current formulation and a response to critics. In J. A. Mecham (Ed.), *Contributions to human development* (vol. 10, p. 174). Karger.

Kohler, W. (1969). *The task of Gestalt psychology.* Princeton University Press.

Kraepelin, E. (1883). *Compendium der Psychiatrie.* Abel.

Kraepelin, E. ([1896] 1971). Psychiatrie. In *Dementia praecox and paraphrenia* (8th ed., Trans. R. M. Barclay). Robert E. Kreiger.

Kroeber, A. L., & Kluckhohn, C. (1952). *Culture: A critical review of concepts and definitions*. Peabody Museum.

Kuhn, T. S. (1962). *The structure of scientific revolutions*. University of Chicago Press.

Kuper, L. E., Nussbaum, R., & Mustanski, B. (2012). Exploring the diversity of gender and sexual orientation identities in an online sample of transgender individuals. *Journal of Sex Research*, 49(2–3), 244–254.

Kupfer, D. J., First, M. B., & Regier, D. A. (2002). Introduction. In D. J. Kupfer, M. B. First, & D. A. Regier (Eds.), *A research agenda for DSM-V* (pp. xv–xxiii). American Psychiatric Association.

Kvale, S. (1994). Ten standard objections to qualitative research interviews. *Journal of Phenomenological Psychology*, 25, 147–173.

Kwon, T. H. (1979). Seminar on Koreanizing Western approaches to social sciences. *Koreajournal*, 19, 20–25.

Lacombe, A. C., & Gay, J. (1998).The role of gender in adolescent identity and intimacy decisions. *Journal of Youth and Adolescence*, 27(6), 795–802.

Laing, R. D. (1960). *The divided self: An existential study in sanity and madness*. Penguin.

Laing, R. D. (2010). *The divided self: An existential study in sanity and madness*. Penguin UK.

Lamb, M. E. (1978). Qualitative aspects of mother- and father-infant attachments. *Infant Behavior and Development*, 1, 265–275.

Larson, R., & Wilson, S. (2004). Adolescence across place and time: Globalization and the changing pathways to adulthood. In R. M. Lerner & L. Steinberg (Eds.), *Handbook of adolescent psychology* (2nd ed., pp. 299–330). John Wiley & Sons.

Leahey, T. H. (2013). *A history of psychology: Antiquity to modernity* (New International Edition). Pearson.

Le Bon, G. ([1895] 1977). *The crowd: A study of the popular mind*. Penguin.

Lee, B. (1973). A cognitive-developmental approach to filiality development. [Unpublished master's dissertation]. Committee on Human Development. University of Chicago.

Leff, J., Wig, N. N., Menon, D. K., Bedi, H., Kuipers, L., Ghosh, A., & Jablensky, A. (1987). Expressed emotion and schizophrenia in North India: III. Influence of relatives—expressed emotion on the course of schizophrenia in Chandigarh. *The British Journal of Psychiatry*, 151(2), 166–173.

Lemke, J. L. (1990). *Talking science: Language, learning and values*. Ablex.

Lerner, R. M. (1976). *Concepts and theories of human development*. Addison-Wesley.

LeVine, R. A., Dixon, S., LeVine, S.*et al*. (1994). *Child care and culture: Lessons from Africa*. Cambridge University Press.

Lévi-Strauss, C. (1963). *Structural anthropology* (Trans. Claire Jacobson & Brooke Grundfest Schoepf). Basic Books.

Levitt, H. M. (1997). A semiotic understanding of eating disorders: The impact of media portrayal. *Eating Disorders*, 5(3), 169–183.

Lewin, K. (1943). Defining the "field at a given time." *Psychological Review*, 50, 292–310.

Lewin, K. (1948). *Resolving social conflicts: Selected papers on group dynamics*. Harper and Row.

Lewin, M., & Wild, C. L. (1991). The impact of the feminist critique on tests, assessment, and methodology. *Psychology of Women Quarterly*, 15(4), 581–596.

328 References

Lewis, M., & Rosenblum, L. A. (1974). The effect of the infant on its caregivers: An Introduction. In M. Lewis & L. A. Rosenblum (Eds.), *The effect of the infant on its caregivers* (pp. xv–xxiv). John Wiley & Sons.

Lin, K. M., Kleinman, A., & Lin, T. Y. (1981). Overview of mental disorders in Chinese cultures: review of epidemiological and clinical studies. In *Normal and abnormal behavior in Chinese culture* (pp. 237–272). Springer.

Lin, T. Y., & Lin, M. C. (1981). Love, denial and rejection: Responses of Chinese families to mental illness. In *Normal and abnormal behavior in Chinese culture* (pp. 387–401). Springer.

Lincoln, Y. S., & Guba, E. G. (1985). *Naturalistic inquiry*. Sage.

Littlewood, R., & Lipsedge, M. (1987). The butterfly and the serpent: Culture, psychopathology and biomedicine. *Culture, Medicine and Psychiatry*, 11(3), 289–335.

Locksley, A., & Colten, M. E. (1979). Psychological androgyny: A case of mistaken identity? *Journal of Personality and Social Psychology*, 37(6), 1017–1031.

Longino, H. E. (1996). Cognitive and non-cognitive values in science: Rethinking the dichotomy. In L. H. Nelson & J. Nelson (Eds.), *Feminism, science, and the philosophy of science* (pp. 39–58). Springer.

Lonner, W. J., & Adamopoulos, J. (1997). Culture as antecedent to behavior. In J. W. Berry, Y. H. Poortinga, & J. Pandey (Eds.), *Handbook of cross-cultural psychology* (2nd ed., pp. 43–83). Allyn & Bacon.

Looft, W. R. (1973). Socialization and personality throughout the life-span: An examination of contemporary psychological approaches. In P. B. Baltes & K. W. Schaie (Eds.), *Life-span developmental psychology: Personality and socialization* (pp. 25–52). Academic Press.

Lorde, A. (1984). *Sister outsider: Essays and speeches*. Crossing Press.

Lowell, A. L. (1934). *At war with academic traditions in America*. Harvard University Press.

Lukes, S. (1973). *Individualism: Key concepts in the social sciences* (Wolfson College Lectures). Harper and Row.

Luria, A. R. (1928). The problem of the cultural development of the child. *Journal of Genetic Psychology*, 41, 255–259.

Maccoby, E. E., & Jacklin, C. N. (1974). *The psychology of sex differences*. Stanford University Press.

Mach, E. (1960). *The science of mechanics: A critical and historical account of its development* (6th English ed.). Open Court.

Madill, A., Jordan, A., & Shirley, C. (2000). Objectivity and reliability in qualitative analysis: Realist, contextualist and radical constructionist epistemologies. *British Journal of Psychology*, 91(1), 1–20.

Marcia, J. E. (1993). The status of the statuses: Research review. In J. E. Marcia, D. R. Matteson, J. L. Orlofsky, A. S. Waterman, & S. L. Archer (Eds.), *Ego identity: A handbook for psychosocial research* (pp. 22–41). Springer Verlag.

Marecek, J. (2001). After the facts: Psychology and the study of gender. *Canadian Psychology*, 42(4), 254–267.

Markus, H. R., & Hamedani, M. G. (2007). Sociocultural psychology: The dynamic interdependence among self systems and social systems. In S. Kitayama & D. Cohen (Eds.), *Handbook of cultural psychology* (pp. 3–39). Guilford Press.

Markus, H. R., & Kitayama, S. (1991). Culture and the self: Implications for cognition, emotion, and motivation. *Psychological Review*, 98, 224–253.

Marsella, A. J., & Scheuer, A. (1993). *Coping: Definitions, conceptualizations, and issues*. Integrative Psychiatry.

Marsella, A. J., & Yamada, A. M. (2007). Culture and psychopathology: Foundations, issues, and directions. In S. Kitayama & D. Cohen (Eds.), *Handbook of cultural psychology* (pp. 797–818). Guilford Press.

Martin, P. Y. (2004). Gender as social institution. *Social Forces*, 82(4), 1249–1273.

Matsumoto, D. (1996). *Culture and psychology*. Brooks Cole.

Matsumoto, D. (1999). Culture and self: An empirical assessment of Markus and Kitayama's theory of independent and interdependent self-construals. *Asian Journal of Social Psychology*, 2(3), 289–310.

Matsumoto, D. (2007). Culture, context and behaviour. *Journal of Personality*, 75(6), 1285–1320.

May, R. (1971). Letters to the Editor. *New York Times Magazine*, April 18, p. 100.

McClelland, D. C. (1961). *The achieving society*. University of Illinois at Urbana-Champaign's Academy for Entrepreneurial Leadership, Historical Research Reference in Entrepreneurship.

McCrae, R. R., & Costa, P. T. (1985). Updating Norman's "adequacy taxonomy": Intelligence and personality dimensions in natural language and in questionnaires. *Journal of Personality and Social Psychology*, 49, 710–721.

McGuire, W. J. (1986). The vicissitudes of attitudes and similar representational constructs in twentieth century psychology. *European Journal of Social Psychology*, 16(2), 89–192.

McKeown, S., & Dixon, J. (2017). The 'contact hypothesis': Critical reflections and future directions. *Social and Personality Psychology Compass*, 11(1), 1–13.

Mead, G. H. (1934). *Mind, self and society*. University of Chicago Press.

Mehta, P. (1973). *Election campaign*. National Publishing House.

Menon, N. (2012). *Seeing like a feminist*. Penguin/Zubaan.

Mesquita, B., Karasawa, M., Haire, A., Izumi, K., Hayashi, A., Idzelis, M., *et al.* (2005). What do I feel? The role of cultural models in emotion representations. Unpublished manuscript, Wake Forest University.

Middleton, D., & Edwards, D. (Eds.). (1990). *Inquiries in social construction: Collective remembering*. Sage.

Milgram, S. (1974). *Obedience to authority: An experimental view*. Harper and Row.

Miller, J. G. (1984). Culture and development of everyday social explanation. *Journal of Personality and Social Psychology*, 46(5), 961–978.

Miller, P. J., & Goodnow, J. J. (1995). Cultural practices: Toward an integration of culture and development. *New Directions for Child and Adolescent Development*, 67, 5–16.

Mischel, W. (1966). Theory and research on the antecedents of self-imposed delay of reward. *Progress in Experimental Personality Research*, 3, 85–132.

Misra, G., & Gergen, K. J. (1993) The place of culture in psychological science. *International Journal of Psychology*, 38, 225–253.

Misra, G., & Tripathi, L. B. (1980). *Psychological consequences of prolonged deprivation*. National Psychological Corporation.

Mixon, D. (1972). Instead of deception. *Journal of the Theory of Social Behavior*, 2(2), 145–177.

Mixon, D. (1976). Studying feignable behavior. *Representative Research in Social Psychology*, 7(2), 89–104.

Mixon, D. (1989). *Obedience and civilization: Authorized crime and the normality of evil*. Pluto Press.

Moede, W. (1915). The mass and social psychology in the critical overview. *Journal of Educational Psychology and Experimental Pedagogy*, XVI.

330 References

Moede, W. (1920). *Experimentelle Massenpsychologie*. Hirzel.

Moghaddam, F. M. (1987). Psychology in the three worlds: As reflected by the crisis in social psychology and the move toward Indigenous Third-World psychology. *American Psychologist*, 42(10), 912–920.

Moghaddam, F. M. (2010). Commentary: Intersubjectivity, interobjectivity, and the embryonic fallacy in developmental science. *Culture & Psychology*, 16(4), 465–475.

Moghaddam, F. M., & Harré, R. (1992). Rethinking the psychology laboratory. *American Behaviorist Scientist*, 36(1), 22–38.

Money, J., Hampson, J. G., & Hampson, J. L. (1955). An examination of some basic sexual concepts. The evidence of human hermaphroditism. *Bulletin of the Johns Hopkins Hospital*, 97(4), 301–319.

Morawski, J. G. (1994). *Critical perspectives on women and gender: Practicing feminisms, reconstructing psychology: Notes on a liminal science*. University of Michigan Press.

Morgan, T., Williams, L. A., & Gott, M. (2016). A feminist quality appraisal tool: Exposing gender bias and gender inequities in health research. *Critical Public Health*, 27(2), 263–274.

Morling, B., Kitayama, S., & Miyamoto, Y. (2002). Cultural practices emphasize influence in the United States and adjustment in Japan. *Personality and Social Psychology Bulletin*, 28(3), 311–323.

Morris, A. S., Treat, A., Hays-Grudo, J.*et al*. (2018). Integrating research and theory on early relationships to guide intervention and prevention. In A. S. Morris (Ed.), *Building early social and emotional relationships with infants and toddlers* (pp. 1–25). Springer.

Morris, B. (1991). *Western conceptions of the individual*. Berg.

Morris, M. W., & Peng, K. (1994). Culture and cause: American and Chinese attributions for social and physical events. *Journal of Personality and Social Psychology*, 67(6), 949–971.

Moscovici, S. (1963). Attitudes and opinions. *Annual Review of Psychology*, 14, 231–260.

Moscovici, S. (1972). Society and theory in social psychology. In J. Israel & H. Tajfel (Eds.), *The context of social psychology: A critical assessment*. Academic Press.

Moscovici, S. (1982).The coming era of social representations. In J. P. Codol & J. P. Leyens (Eds.), *Cognitive approaches to social behaviour* (pp. 115–150). Nijhoff.

Moscovici, S. (1984). The phenomenon of social representations. In R. M. Farr & S. Moscovici (Eds.), *Social representations* (pp. 3–69). Cambridge University Press.

Moscovici, S., & Zavalloni, M. (1969).The group as a polarizer of attitudes. *Journal of Personality and Social Psychology*, 12(2), 125–135.

Moss-Racusin, C. A., Phelan, J. E., & Rudman, L. A. (2010). When men break the gender rules: Status incongruity and backlash against modest men. *Psychology of Men & Masculinity*, 11(2), 140–151.

Mulkay, M. (1979). *Science and the sociology of knowledge controversies in sociology* (vol. 8). George Allen & Unwin.

Munroe, R. H., Munroe, R. L., & Whiting, B. B. (Eds.). (1972). *Handbook of cross-cultural human development*. Garland.

Muralidharan, R. (1971). *Developmental norms of Indian children: 2 years to 5 years*. NCERT.

Murdock, G. P. (1975). *Outline of world cultures*. Human Relations Area Files.

Murdock, G. P., & Douglas, R. W. (1975). *Outline of cultural materials*. Human Relations Area Files.

Murphy, G., & Murphy , L. B. (1931). *Experimental social psychology*. Harper.

Myers, S., & Spencer, D. G. (2006). *Social psychology* (3rd ed.). McGraw-Hill Ryerson.

Nagel, T. (1986). *The view from nowhere*. Oxford University Press.

Nakajima, M., & Al'Absi, M. (2012). Predictors of risk for smoking relapse in men and women: A prospective examination. *Psychology of Addictive Behaviors*, 26(3), 633–637.

Nandy, A. (1972). Defiance and conformity in science: The identity of Jagadis Chandra Bose. *Science Studies*, 2(1), 31–85.

Nandy, A. (1974). The non-paradigmatic crisis of Indian psychology: Reflections on a recipient culture of science. *Indian Journal of Psychology*, 49(1), 1–20.

Nandy, A. (1980). *Alternative sciences: Creativity and authenticity in two Indian scientists*. Allied Publishers Pvt. Ltd.

Nandy, A. (2004). *Bonfire of creeds: The essential Ashis Nandy*. Oxford University Press.

Neki, J. S. (1973). Guru-chela relationship: The possibility of a therapeutic paradigm. *American Journal of Orthopsychiatry*, 43, 755–766.

Neuman, W. L. (2006). *Social research methods: Qualitative and quantitative approaches*. Pearson.

Nevers, C. C., & Calkins, M. W. (1895). Wellesley College Psychological Studies: Dr. Jastrow on community of ideas of men and women. *Psychological Review*, 2(4), 363–367.

Newman, F., & Holzman, L. (1993). *Lev Vygotsky: Revolutionary scientist*. Routledge.

Nichter, M. (1981). Idioms of distress: Alternatives in the expression of psychosocial distress: A case study from South India. *Culture, Medicine and Psychiatry*, 5(4), 379–408.

Nightingale, D. J., & Cromby, J. (2001). Critical psychology and the ideology of individualism. *Journal of Critical Psychology, Counselling and Psychotherapy*, 1(2), 117–128.

Nisbett, R. E., & Cohen, D. (1996). *Culture of honor: The psychology of violence in the South*. Westview Press.

Nsamenang, A. B. (1995). Theories of developmental psychology for a cultural perspective: A view from Africa. *Psychology and Developing Societies*, 7(1), 1–19.

Nsamenang, A. B. (2000). Critical psychology: A Sub-Saharan African voice from Cameroon. In T. Sloan (Ed.), *Critical psychology: Voices for change* (pp. 91–102). St. Martin's Press.

Olson, C. B. (1988). *The influence of context on gender differences in performance attributions: Further evidence of a "feminine modesty" effect*. Paper presented at the Annual Meeting of the Western Psychological Association, San Francisco.

Orbach , S. (1986). *Hunger strike: The anorectic's struggle as a metaphor for our time*. Faber & Faber.

Orlofsky, J. L. (1993). Intimacy status: Theory and research. In E. Marcia, D. R. Matteson, J. L. Orlofsky, A. S. Waterman, & S. L. Archer (Eds.), *Ego identity: A handbook for psychosocial research* (pp. 111–133). Springer Verlag.

Orne, M. T. (1962). On the social psychology of the psychological experiment with particular reference to demand characteristics and their implications. *American Psychologist*, 17, 776–783.

Oudshoorn, N. (1994). *Beyond the natural body: An archaeology of sex hormones*. Routledge.

Overton, W. F. (1978). Klaus Riegel: Theoretical contribution to concepts of stability and change. *Human Development*, 21, 360–363.

Overton, W. F. (2015). Process and relational developmental systems. In W. F. Overton & P. C. M. Molenaar (Eds.), *Handbook of child psychology and developmental science*. Vol. 1 *Theory and method* (7th ed., pp. 9–62). Wiley.

Oyewumi, O. (1997). *The invention of women: Making an African sense of western gender discourses*. University of Minnesota Press.

Oyserman, D., Coon, H. M., & Kemmelmeier, M. (2002). Rethinking individualism and collectivism: Evaluation of theoretical assumptions and meta-analyses. *Psychological Bulletin*, 128(1), 3–72.

332 References

Oyserman, D., & Lee, S. W. S. (2007). Priming 'culture': Culture as situated cognition. In S. Kitayama & D. Cohen (Eds.), *Handbook of cultural psychology* (pp. 255–279). Guilford Press.

Pande, N., & Naidu, R. K. (1992). Anāsakti and health: A study of non-attachment. *Psychology and Developing Society*, 4(1), 89–104.

Pareek, U., & Rao, T. V. (1974). *A status study of population research in India: Behavioural science*. McGraw-Hill.

Parker, I. (1989). *The crisis in modern social psychology, and how to end it*. Routledge.

Parker, I. (1990). Discourse: Definitions and contradictions. *Philosophical Psychology*, 3(2), 187–204.

Parker, I. (2007). Critical psychology: What it is and what it is not. *Social and Personality Psychology Compass*, 1(1), 1–15.

Parsons, T., & Bales, R. F. (1955). *Family, socialization and interaction process*. Free Press.

Peirce, C. S. ([1903] 1997). Lecture VII. MS 315. In *Harvard lectures on pragmatism*. Ed. P. A. Turrisi. State University of New York.

Pepper, S. C. (1942). *World hypotheses: A study in evidence*. University of California Press.

Peshkin, A. (1993). The goodness of qualitative research. *Educational Researcher*, 22(2), 23–29.

Piaget, J. (1932). *The moral judgment of the child*. The Free Press.

Piaget, J. (1966). *The psychology of intelligence* (Trans. M. Pierce & D. Berlyne). Littlefield, Adams & Co. (Original work published 1947.)

Piker, S. (1994).Classical culture and personality. In P. K. Bock (Ed.), *Psychological anthropology* (pp. 1–17). Praeger Publishers/Greenwood Publishing Group.

Pleck, J. H. (1981). *The myth of masculinity*. Pluto Press.

Poortinga, Y. H., & van de Vijver, F. J. R. (1987). Explaining cross-cultural differences: Bias analysis and beyond. *Journal of Cross-Cultural Psychology*, 18(3), 259–282.

Poortinga, Y. H., van de Vijver, F. J. R., Joe, R. C., & van de Koppel, J. M. H. (1987). Peeling the onion called culture: A synopsis. In Ç. Kağitçibaşi (Ed.), *Growth and progress in cross-cultural psychology* (pp. 22–34). Swets & Zeitlinger.

Popper, K. (1959). *The logic of scientific discovery*. Hutchinson & Co. (Original published in 1935.)

Popper, K. (1963). *Conjectures and refutations*. Routledge and Kegan Paul.

Potter, J. (1998). Discursive social psychology: From attitudes to evaluative practices. *European Review of Social Psychology*, 9(1), 233–266.

Potter, J., & Wetherell, M. (1987). *Discourse and social psychology: Beyond attitudes and behaviour*. Sage.

Potter, J., & Wetherell, M. (2003). Unfolding discourse analysis. In C. Seale (Ed.), *Social research methods: A reader* (pp. 350–356). Routledge.

Prentice, D. A., & Carranza, E. (2002). What women and men should be, shouldn't be, are allowed to be, and don't have to be: The contents of prescriptive gender stereotypes. *Psychology of Women Quarterly*, 26(4), 269–281.

Prown, J. D. (1982). Mind in matter: An introduction to material culture theory and method. *Winterthur Portfolio*, 17(1), 1–19.

Pryzgoda, J., & Chrisler, J. C. (2000). Definitions of gender and sex: The subtleties of meaning. *Sex Roles*, 43(7–8), 553–569.

Rabinow, P. (1984). *The Foucault reader*. Pantheon Books.

Raffaelli, M., Carlo, G., Carranza, M. A., & González-Kruger, G. E. (2005). Understanding Latino children and adolescents in the mainstream: Placing culture at the center of the developmental models. In R. Larson & L. Jensen (Eds.), *New horizons in developmental research: New directions for child and adolescent development* (pp. 23–32). Jossey-Bass.

Rao, A. V. (1973). Depressive illness and guilt in Indian culture. *Indian Journal of Psychiatry*, 15, 231–236.

Rao, S. K. R. (1983). The concept of stress in Indian thought: The theoretical aspect of stress in Samkhya and Yoga systems. *NIMHANS Journal*, 2, 115–121.

Reese, H. W., & Overton, W. F. (1970). Models of development and theories of development. In L. R. Goulet & P. B. Baltes (Eds.), *Lifespan developmental psychology: Research and theory* (pp. 115–145). Academic Press.

Reicher, S. (2000). Against methodolatry: Some comments on Elliott, Fischer, and Rennie. *British Journal of Clinical Psychology*, 39(1), 1–6.

Reicher, S., & Hopkins, N. (2001). *Self and nation: Categorization, contestation and mobilization.* Sage.

Ridgeway, C. L. (2011). *Framed by gender: How gender inequality persists in the modern world.* Oxford University Press.

Riegel, K. F. (1975). Toward a dialectical theory of human development. *Human Development*, 18, 50–64.

Riley, D. (1983). *War in the nursery: Theories of child and mother.* Virago.

Ring, K. (1967). Experimental social psychology: Some sober questions about some frivolous values. *Journal of Experimental Social Psychology*, 3(2), 113–123.

Risman, B. J. (1998). *Gender vertigo: American families in transition.* Yale University Press.

Risman, B. J. (2004). Gender as a social structure: Theory wrestling with activism. *Gender & Society*, 18(4), 429–450.

Robertson, J., & Fitzgerald, L. F. (1990). The (mis)treatment of men: Effects of client gender role and life-style on diagnosis and attribution of pathology. *Journal of Counseling Psychology*, 37(1), 3.

Robinson, D. N. (1986). *An intellectual history of psychology* (rev. ed.). University of Wisconsin Press.

Robinson, M. D., Johnson, J. T., & Shields, S. A. (1998). The gender heuristic and the database: Factors affecting the perception of gender-related differences in the experience and display of emotions. *Basic and Applied Social Psychology*, 20(3), 206–219.

Rogoff, B. (1990). *Apprenticeship in thinking: Cognitive development in social context.* Oxford University Press.

Rogoff, B. (1995). Observing sociocultural activity on three planes: Participatory appropriation, guided participation, and apprenticeship. In J. V. Wertsch, P. del Rio, & A. Alvarez (Eds.), *Sociocultural studies of mind* (pp. 139–164). Cambridge University Press.

Rogoff, B. (2003). *The cultural nature of human development.* Oxford University Press.

Roland, A. (1998). *Cultural pluralism and psychoanalysis: The Asian and North American experience.* Routledge.

Rose, N. (1990). *Governing the soul: The shaping of the private self.* Routledge.

Rose, T. (2016). *The end of average: How we succeed in a world that values sameness.* HarperCollins.

Rosen, N. (1989). *John and Anzia: An American romance.* Dutton.

Rosenberg, M. J. (1965). When dissonance fails: On eliminating evaluation apprehension from attitude measurement. *Journal of Personality and Social Psychology*, 1(1), 28–42.

Rosenthal, R. (1965). The volunteer subject. *Human Relations*, 18, 389–406.

Rosenthal, R., & Fode, K. L. (1963). The effect of experimenter bias on the performance of the albino rat. *Systems Research and Behavioral Science*, 8(3), 183–189.

Rosenthal, R., & Rosnow, R. L. (Eds.). (1969). *Artifact in behavioural research.* Academic Press.

Ross, E. A. (1908). *Social psychology: An outline and source book.* Macmillan Company.

334 References

Ross, L., & Nisbett, R. E. (1991). *The person and the situation: Perspectives of socialpsychology*. McGraw-Hill.

Ross, L., & Ward, A. (1996). Naive realism in everyday life: Implications for social conflict and misunderstanding. In T. Brown, E. Reed, & E. Turiel (Eds.), *Values and knowledge* (pp. 103–135). Erlbaum.

Rossiter, M. W. (1993). The Matthew Matilda effect in science. *Social Studies of Science*, 23(2), 325–341.

Rudman, L. A., & Glick, P. (2001). Prescriptive gender stereotypes and backlash toward agentic women. *Journal of Social Issues*, 57(4), 743–762.

Rudman, L. A., & Mescher, K. (2013). Penalizing men who request a family leave: Is flexibility stigma a femininity stigma? *Journal of Social Issues*, 69(2), 322–340.

Rudman, L. A., Moss-Racusin, C. A., Phelan, J. E., & Nauts, S. (2012). Status incongruity and backlash effects: Defending the gender hierarchy motivates prejudice against female leaders. *Journal of Experimental Social Psychology*, 48(1), 165–179.

Rust, J., Golombok, S., Hines, M., Johnston, K., Golding, J., & ALSPAC Study Team. (2000). The role of brothers and sisters in the gender development of preschool children. *Journal of Experimental Child Psychology*, 77(4), 292–303.

Salazar, J. M. (1984). The use and impact of psychology in Venezuela. *International Journal of Psychology*, 19, 113–122.

Sameroff, A. (Ed.). (2009). *The transactional model of development: How children and contexts shape each other*. American Psychological Association.

Sampson, E. E. (1988). The debate on individualism: Indigenous psychologies of the individual and their role in personal and societal functioning. *American Psychologist*, 43(1), 15–22.

Samy, J. (1978). Development and research for the Pacific, and session on theory and methods. In A. Marma & G. McCall (Eds.), *Paradise postponed: Essays on research and development in the South Pacific*. Pergamon.

Scheidecker, G. (2023). Parents, caregivers, and peers: Patterns of complementarity in the social world of children in rural Madagascar. *Current Anthropology*, 64(3).

Schutz, A. (1962). *The problem of social reality: Collected papers* (vol. 1, Eds. M. A. Natanson & H. L. Van Brenda). Martinus Nijhoff.

Schutz, A. (1967). *The phenomenology of the social world*. Northwestern University Press.

Schwartz, S. H. (1992). Universals in the content and structure of values: Theoretical advances and empirical tests in 20 countries. In M. Zanna (Ed.), *Advances in experimental social psychology* (vol. 25, pp. 1–65). Academic Press.

Schwartz, S. H. (1994). Studying human values. In A. Bouvy, F. J. R. Van de Vijver, P. Boski, & P. Schmitz (Eds.), *Journeys into cross-cultural psychology* (pp. 239–254). Swets and Zeitlinger.

Schwartz, S. H. (2004). Mapping and interpreting cultural differences around the world. In H. Vinken, J. Soeters, & P. Ester (Eds.), *Comparing cultures: Dimensions of culture in a comparative perspective* (pp. 43–73). Brill.

Scull, A. T. (1979). Moral treatment reconsidered: Some sociological comments on an episode in the history of British psychiatry. *Psychological Medicine*, 9(3), 421–428.

Scull, A. T. (1982). *Museums of madness: The social organization of insanity in nineteenth century England*. Allen Lane.

Segall, M. H., Campbell, D. T., & Herskovits, M. J. (1966). *The influence of culture on visual perception*. Bobbs-Merrill.

Serpell, R. (1984). Commentary: The impact of psychology on Third World development. *International Journal of Psychology*, 19(1–2), 179–192.

Shadish, W., Cook, T. D., & Campbell, D. T. (2002). *Experimental and quasi-experimental designs for generalized causal inference.* Wadsworth Cengage Learning.

Sherif, C. W. (1998). Bias in psychology. *Feminism & Psychology,* 8(1), 58–75.

Sherman, J. A. (1971). *On the psychology of women: A survey of empirical studies.* Thomas.

Shields, S. (1975). Functionalism, Darwinism, and the psychology of women. *American Psychologist,* 30(7), 739–754.

Shields, S. A., & Bhatia, S. (2009). Darwin on race, gender, and culture. *American Psychologist,* 64(2), 111–119.

Shildkrout, E. (1978). Age and gender in Hausa society: Socio-economic roles of children in urban Kano. In J. S. La Fontaine (Ed.), *Sex and age as principles of social classification* (pp. 109–137). Academic Press.

Shore, B. (1996). *Culture in mind: Cognition, culture, and the problem of meaning.* Oxford University Press.

Shweder, R. A. (1990). Cultural psychology—what is it? In J. W. Stigler, R. A. Shweder, & G. H. Herdt (Eds.), *Cultural psychology: Essays on comparative human development* (pp. 1–44). Cambridge University Press.

Shweder, R. A. (1991). *Thinking through cultures: Expeditions in cultural psychology.* Harvard University Press.

Shweder, R. A. (1995). The confessions of a methodological individualist. *Culture and Psychology,* 1(1), 115–122.

Shweder, R. A. (2000). The psychology of practice and the practice of the three psychologies. *Asian Journal of Social Psychology,* 3(3), 207–233.

Shweder, R. A. (2001). *A polytheistic conception of the science and the virtue of deep variety in unity of knowledge.* New York Academy.

Shweder, R. A., Goodnow, J., Hatano, G., Levine, R., Markus, H., & Miller, P. (2006). The cultural psychology of development: One mind, many mentalities. In W. Damon (Ed.), *Handbook of child psychology.* John Wiley & Sons, Ltd.

Shweder, R. A., Mahapatra, M., & Miller, J. G. (1990). Culture and moral development. In J. W. Stigler, R. A. Shweder, & G. Herdt (Eds.), *Cultural psychology: Essays on comparative human development* (pp. 130–204). Cambridge University Press.

Shweder, R. A., & Sullivan, M. A. (1993). Cultural psychology: Who needs it? *Annual Review of Psychology,* 44, 497–523.

Sikanartey, T., & Eaton, W. W. (1984). Prevalence of schizophrenia in the Labadi district of Ghana. *Acta Psychiatrica Scandinavica,* 69(2), 156–161.

Silverman, I. (1971). Crisis in social psychology: The relevance of relevance. *American Psychologist,* 26(6), 583–584.

Singh, A. K. (1981). Development of religious identity and prejudice in Indian children. In D. Sinha (Ed.), *Socialization of the Indian child* (pp. 87–100). Concept.

Sinha, D. (1969). *Indian villages in transition: A motivational analysis.* Associated Publishing House.

Sinha, D. (1986). *Psychology in a Third World country: The Indian experience.* Sage.

Sinha, D. (1990). Concept of psychological well-being: Western and Indian perspectives. *National Institute of Mental Health and Neurosciences Journal,* 8, 1–11.

Sinha, D. (1997). Indigenizing psychology. In J. W. Berry, Y. H. Poortinga, & J. Pandey (Eds.), *Handbook of cross-cultural psychology: Theory and method* (vol. 1). Allyn & Bacon.

Sinha, J. (1958). *Indian psychology* (vols 1 & 2). Jadunath Sinha Foundation.

Sinha, J. (1962). *A manual of ethics* (7th ed.). Sinha Publishing House.

Sinha, J. B .P. (1980). *Nurturant task leader.* Concept.

336 References

Small, R., Astbury, J., Brown, S., & Lumley, J. (1994) Depression after childbirth. Does social context matter? *Medical Journal of Australia*, 161, 473–477.

Smedsland, J. (1984). The invisible obvious: Culture in psychology. In *Psychology in the 1990s* (pp. 443–452). Elsevier.

Smith, M. B. (1973). Is psychology relevant to new priorities? *American Psychologist*, 28 (6), 463–471.

Smith, P. B., & Schwartz, S. H. (1997). Values. In J. W. Berry, M. H. Segall, & Ç. Kağitçibaşi (Eds.), *Handbook of cross-cultural psychology* (2nd ed., vol. 3, pp. 77–118). Allyn & Bacon.

Snyder, M. (1979). Self-monitoring processes. In L. Berkowitz (Ed.), *Advances in experimental social psychology* (vol. 12, pp. 85–128). Academic Press.

Spade, D. (2006). Mutilating gender. In S. Stryker & S. Whittle (Eds.) *The transgender reader*. Routledge.

Spettigue, W., & Henderson, K. A. (2004). Eating disorders and the role of the media. *The Canadian Child and Adolescent Psychiatry Review*, 13(1), 16–19.

Spivak, G. C. (1993). More on power knowledge. In G. C. Spivak, *Outside in the teaching machine* (pp. 27–57). Routledge.

Spivak, G. C. (2000). *A critique of postcolonial reason: Towards a history of the vanishing past*. Harvard University Press.

Stainton Rogers, R., Stenner, P., & Gleeson, K. (1995). *Social psychology: A critical agenda*. John Wiley & Sons.

Stainton Rogers, W. (2003). *Social psychology: Experimental and critical approaches*. UK Higher Education. Oxford University Press.

Stake, R. E. (1994). Case studies. In N. K. Denzin & Y. S. Lincoln (Eds.), *Handbook of qualitative research* (pp.236–247). Sage.

Stevens, G., & Gardner, S. (1982). *The women of psychology: Pioneers and innovators* (vol 1). Schenkman Publishing Company.

Stevens, S. S. (1939). *On the problem of scales for the measurement of psychological magnitudes*. Paper presented at the Fifth International Congress for the Unity of Science at Cambridge, MA, USA.

Stoller, R. J. (1968). *Sex and gender*. Science House.

Strakowski, S. M., Lonczak, H. S., Sax, K. W., West, S. A., Crist, A., Mehta, R., & Thienhaus, O. J. (1995). The effects of race on diagnosis and disposition from a psychiatric emergency service. *The Journal of Clinical Psychiatry*, 56(3), 101–107.

Strauss, A., & Corbin, L. (1990). *Basics of grounded theory methods*. Sage.

Sully, J. (1881). Illusions. *Mind*, 6(23),413–421.

Sumner, W. G. (1906). Education, history. In W. G. Sumner (Ed.), *Folkways: A study of the sociological importance of usages, manners, customs, mores, and morals* (pp. 1553–1578). The Athenaeum Press.

Tajfel, H. (1969). Social and cultural factors in perception. In G. Lindzey & E. Aronson (Eds.), *The handbook of social psychology* (vol. 3). Addison-Wesley.

Tajfel, H., & Turner, J. C. (1979). An integrative theory of intergroup conflict. In W. G. Austin & S. Worchel (Eds.), *The social psychology of intergroup relations* (pp.33–37). Brooks/Cole.

Tarde, G. (1890). *Les lois de l'imitation*. Félix Alcan.

Tavris, C. (1992). *The mismeasure of woman: Why women are not the better sex, the inferior sex, or the opposite sex*. Simon & Schuster.

Tavris, C. (1993). The mismeasure of woman. *Feminism & Psychology*, 3(2), 149–168.

Taylor, J. M., Gilligan, C., & Sullivan, A. M. (1995). *Between voice and silence: Women and girls, race and relationship*. Harvard University Press.

References **337**

Teo, T. (2013). Backlash against American psychology: An Indigenous reconstruction of the history of German critical psychology. *History of Psychology*, 16(1), 1–18.

Terman, L. M. (1916). *The measurement of intelligence*. Houghton Mifflin.

Terman, L. M., & Miles, C. C. (1936). *Sex and personality: Studies in masculinity and femininity*. McGraw-Hill.

Thomas, W. J. (1931). *The unadjusted girl*. Little, Brown.

Thompson, H. B. (1903). *The mental traits of sex: An experimental investigation of the normal mind in men and women*. University of Chicago Press.

Tolman, C. W. (1994). *Psychology, society and subjectivity: An introduction to German critical psychology*. Routledge.

Trafimow, D., Triandis, H. C., & Goto, S. G. (1991). Some tests of the distinction between the private self and the collective self. *Journal of Personality and Social Psychology*, 60, 649–655.

Triandis, H. C. (1964). Cultural influences upon cognitive processes. In *Advances in experimental social psychology* (pp.1–48). Elsevier.

Triandis, H. C. (1972). *The analysis of subjective culture*. Wiley-Interscience.

Triandis, H. C. (1980). Values, attitudes, and interpersonal behavior. In *Nebraska symposium on motivation*. University of Nebraska Press.

Triandis, H. C. (1990). Cross-cultural studies of individualism and collectivism. In J. Berman (Ed.), *Nebraska symposium on motivation* (pp. 41–133). University of Nebraska Press.

Triandis, H. C. (1993). Collectivism and individualism as cultural syndromes. *Cross-Cultural Research*, 27(3–4), 155–180.

Triandis, H. C. (1994). *Culture and social behaviour*. McGraw-Hill.

Triandis, H. C. (1995). *Individualism and collectivism*. Westview Press.

Triandis, H. C. (2001). Individualism and collectivism: Past, present, and future. In D. Matsumoto (Ed.), *Handbook of culture and psychology* (pp. 35–50). Oxford University Press.

Triandis, H. C., Bontempo, R., Villareal, M. J., Asai, M., & Lucca, N. (1988). Individualism and collectivism: Cross-cultural perspectives on self-in-group relationships. *Journal of Personality and Social Psychology*, 54(2), 323–338.

Triandis, H. C., & Gelfand, M. J. (1998). Converging measurement of horizontal and vertical individualism and collectivism. *Journal of Personality and Social Psychology*, 74(1), 118–128.

Triandis, H. C., Leung, K., Villareal, M., & Clack, E. L. (1985). Allocentric vs. idiocentric tendencies: Convergent and discriminant validation. *Journal of Research in Personality*, 19, 395–415.

Triandis, H. C., & Vassiliou, V. (1972). Interpersonal influence and employee selection in two cultures. *Journal of Applied Psychology*, 56(2), 140–145.

Tudge, J. R. H., Mokrova, I., Hatfield, B. E., & Karnik, R. B. (2009). Uses and misuses of Bronfenbrenner's bioecological theory of human development. *Journal of Family Theory & Review*, 1(4), 198–210.

Turner, J. C., Hogg, M. A., Oakes, P. J., Reicher, S. D., & Wetherell, M. S. (1987). *Rediscovering the social group: A self-categorization theory*. Basil Blackwell.

Tyrer, P. (2010).Categories and continuums. In C. Morgan & D. Bhugra (Eds.), *Principles of social psychiatry*. Online (pp. 31–37). Wiley.

Unger, R. K. (1979). Toward a redefinition of sex and gender. *American Psychologist*, 34 (11), 1085–1094.

Unger, R. K. (1998). *Resisting gender: Twenty-five years in/of feminist psychology*. Sage.

338 References

Vahali, H. O. (2009). *Lives in exile: Exploring the inner world of Tibetan refugees.* Routledge.

Van de Vijver, F. J. (2009). Types of comparative studies in cross-cultural psychology. *Online Readings in Psychology and Culture*, 2(2).

Van de Vliert, E. (2006). Autocratic leadership around the globe: Do climate and wealth drive leadership culture? *Journal of Cross-Cultural Psychology*, 37(1), 42–59.

Van Fraassen, B. C. (1980). *The scientific image.* Oxford University Press.

Van IJzendoorn, M. H., & Kroonenberg, P. M. (1998). Cross-cultural patterns of attachment: A meta-analysis of the Strange Situation. *Child Development*, 59, 147–156.

Vernon, P. E. (1969). *Intelligence and cultural environment.* Methuen.

Vygotsky, L. S. (1978). *Mind in society: The development of higher psychological processes.* Harvard University Press.

Vygotsky, L. S. (1981). The genesis of higher mental function. In J. V. Wertsch (Ed.), *The concept of activity in Soviet psychology* (pp. 144–188). Sharp.

Vygotsky, L. S. (1987). *The collected works of L. S. Vygotsky.* Vol. 1. *Problems of general psychology* (Eds. R. W. Rieber & A. S. Carton). Plenum.

Vygotsky, L. S. (1997). The historical meaning of the crisis in psychology: A methodological investigation. In R. W. Rieber & J. Wollock (Eds.), *The collected works of L. S. Vygotsky.* Vol. 3. *Problems of the theory and history of psychology* (pp. 233–343). Plenum.

Wagner, W., Duveen, G., Farr, R. M., Jovchelovitch, S., Lorenzi-Ciuoli, F., Markova, I., & Rose, D. (1999). Theory and method of social representation. *Asian Journal of Social Psychology*, 2(1), 95–125.

Walkerdine, V. (1988). *The mastery of reason: Cognitive development and the production of rationality.* Routledge.

Wallerstein, R. S. (2009). What kind of research in psychoanalytic science? *The International Journal of Psychoanalysis*, 90(1), 109–133.

Watson, J. B. (1919). *Psychology from the standpoint of a behaviourist.* Lippencott.

Waxler, N. E. (1979). Is outcome for schizophrenia better in nonindustrial societies? The case of Sri Lanka. *Journal of Nervous and Mental Disease*, 167(3), 144–158.

Weber, M. (1904). *The Protestant ethic and the spirit of capitalism.* Scribner's Press.

Weber, M. (1949). The meaning of ethical neutrality in sociology and economics. In E. A. Shuls & H. A. Finch (Eds. and Trans.), *Methodology of the social sciences.* Free Press (Original work published 1917.)

Weber, S. J., & Cook, T. P. (1972). Subject effects in laboratory research: An examination of subject roles, demand characteristics, and valid inference. *Psychological Bulletin*, 77, 273–295.

Weinstein, N. (1993). Psychology constructs the female; or the fantasy life of the male psychologist (with some attention to the fantasies of his friends, the male biologist and the male anthropologist). *Feminism and Psychology*, 3(2), 194–210.

Werner, H., & Kaplan, B. (1963). *Symbol formation: An organismic-developmental approach to language and the expression of thought.* John Wiley & Sons, Ltd.

Wertsch, J. V. (1979). From social interaction to higher psychological processes: A clarification and application of Vygotsky's theory. *Human Development*, 22(1), 1–22.

Wertsch, J. V. (1991). *Voices of the mind: A sociocultural approach to mediated action.* Harvester Wheatsheaf.

West, C., & Zimmerman, D. H. (1987). Doing gender. *Gender & Society*, 1(2), 125–151.

Wetherell, M. (2003). Paranoia, ambivalence and discursive practices: Concepts of position and positioning in psychoanalysis and discursive psychology. In R. Harré & F.

Moghaddam, (Eds.), *The self and others: Positioning individuals and groups in personal, political and cultural contexts*. Praeger/Greenwood Publishers.

Wetherell, M., Hilda, S., & Potter, J. (1987). Unequal egalitarians: A preliminary study of discourses concerning gender and employment opportunities. *British Journal of Social Psychology*, 26(1), 59–71.

Whiting, B. B., & Whiting, J. W. M. (1975).*Children of six cultures: A psycho-cultural analysis*. Harvard University Press.

Whiting, J. M., & Child, I .L. (1953). *Child training and personality: A cross-cultural study*. Yale University Press.

Wicker, A. W. (1969). Attitudes versus actions: The relationship of verbal and overt behavioural responses to attitude objects. *Journal of Social Issues*, XXV(4), 41–78.

Wigginton, B. (2017). Reimagining gender in psychology: What can critical psychology offer? *Social and Personality Psychology Compass*, 11(6), 1–14.

Wilkinson. S. (1997). Feminist psychology. In D. R. Fox & L. Pricelessly (Eds.), *Critical psychology: An introduction* (pp. 247–264). Sage.

Williams, J. E., & Best, D. L. (1986). Sex stereotypes and intergroup relations. In W. Austin & S. Weichel (Eds.), *Psychology of intergroup relations*. Nelson Hall.

Willig, C. (2013). *Introducing qualitative research in psychology*. McGraw-Hill Education.

Willig, C., & Stainton Rogers, W. (2008). *The SAGE handbook of qualitative research in psychology*. Sage.

Witkin, H. A., & Berry, J. W. (1975). Psychological differentiation in cross-cultural perspective. *Journal of Cross-Cultural Psychology*, 6(1), 4–87.

Widmer, L. (1907). Clinical psychology. *Psychologica Clinic*, 1, 1–6.

Wood, W., & Eagly, A. H. (2002). A cross-cultural analysis of the behavior of women and men: Implications for the origins of sex differences. *Psychological Bulletin*, 128(5), 699–727.

Woolley, H. T. (1910). A review of the recent literature on the psychology of sex. *Psychological Bulletin*, 7(10), 335–342.

Worell, J. (2000). Feminism in psychology: Revolution or evolution? *The Annals of the American Academy of Political and Social Science*, 571(1), 183–196.

Yang, K. (1981). Social orientation and individual modernity among Chinese students in Taiwan. *Journal of Social Psychology*, 113(2), 159–170.

Yang, K-S. (1986). Chinese personality and its change. In M. H. Bond (Ed.), *The psychology of the Chinese people* (pp. 106–170). Oxford University Press.

Yang, K-S. (2000). Monocultural and cross-cultural indigenous approaches: The royal road to the development of balanced global psychology. *Asian Journal of Social Psychology*, 3(3), 241–263.

Yin, R. K. (1994).*Case study research: Design and methods*. Sage.

Zahn-Waxler, C., & Plancha, N. (2004). All things interpersonal. In M. Puntillas & K. L. Bierman (Eds.), *Aggression, antisocial behavior, and violence among girls: A developmental perspective* (pp. 48–70). Guilford Press.

Zisouk, S., Curable, E., Duan, N., Iglewicz, A., Karam, E. G., Lanouette, N., Lebowitz, B., Pies, R., Reynolds, C., Seay, K., Shear, M. K., Simon, N., & Tal Young, I. (2012). The bereavement exclusion and DSM-5. *Depression and Anxiety*, 29(5), 425–443.

INDEX

abduction 118–119
adaptation 291–292, 308
agency-structure 11, 131
androcentrism 7, 222
antecedent-consequent 294–296
anti realists 26
attitudes 112, 117, 122–126

bicultural 178, 179
big q 75
binary/binarism 6, 190–191, 193, 224–225, 240–241
bio-ecological 293, 302–303, 306,
biomedical model/psychiatry 255–256, 281, 286
biopsychiatry 259
biopsychosocial model 255–257, 286

capitalism 1, 66
categorical classification 253
causality 20–21, 62, 294
CHAT 183–185
child 288–292
collective constructionist 180–183,
common sense 10, 13, 17, 108, 110, 117
complementarity 240–241
conditions of possibility, 2
contextualism 294, 300–302, 308
critical social science 70–71
cross-cultural psychology 141–142, 144–165, 169
cultural deviance 253, 266
cultural equivalence 146–147,

cultural explanation 137–138
cultural relativism 160
cultural syndromes 148, 152–153
culture as a variable 150, 153–155, 159, 162, 176
culture as ideational 133
culture as material 133
culture complex 174, 175
culture in mind 134
culture-psyche 149, 150, 153

deconstruction, 2, 3, 8
deductive 18, 23
dependability 82
derived etic 146, 169
determinism 6, 19, 41
development change 298, 302–303, 308
developmentalism 292, 309
diagnosis 257–258, 261, 265–267
discourse 2, 11
discourse analysis 2, 72, 112–114, 124–126
dramaturgical sociology 109
dualism 10, 14, 56, 71, 95, 168, 199, 303
dynamic constructivist approach 143

ecocultural approach 155, 157
ecological fallacy 149
embryonic fallacy 303
emic 146
empiricism 21–22, 30, 41, 53, 61, 198
ethnocentrism 7
ethnomethodology 68, 108
European social psychology 110–111

Index **341**

evolution 98, 204
evolutionary theory 6, 203, 222, 288
experimental social psychology 90–93,
  112–113, 122
external colonization 310
external validity 62, 82, 140

falsification 22–23, 26, 29,
femininity 191, 193, 195–198
feminism 192
frame switching 178, 179
Freudian psychoanalysis 200, 205,
  229–230, 233–235, 241–242

gender as a variable 190, 211, 218, 220–221
gender binary 250
gender difference 211–212, 217–219, 221,
gender schema 208–209, 247–248
generalization 47,62, 82–83, 147–148

holism 296
horizontal collaboration 132
human science model, 17–18, 139,
hypothetico deductive 59, 63, 131, 191

idioms of distress 280–281, 286
illness narrative 276
illness narratives 276
imposed etic 146
incommensurability 27, 32, 171
indigenization 167, 169–170
indigenous psychology 165–169
individualism 5–6, 63, 90, 100, 152, 155, 218
individual–society 95, 119
inductive 18, 23, 66, 75
information processing 100–101
intentional 45, 173
interactionism 298–299
internal colonization 310
internal validity 62, 79,
interpretive repertoires 126
interpretivism 66.69, 71
intersectional 216
intersubjective 11, 99, 121, 243, 253

logical positivism 19, 53–54

mad doctors 262
masculinity 212–213, 229–231, 234,
  240–241
mechanist 295–297
mechanistic/organismic model 294,
  296–297
medical/bio medical model 5, 255
member checking 75

meta – theory 303, 308
methodological individualism 5
moral therapy 263
multidirectional 293–294

natural science model, 6, 17–18, 25–26,
  138–139
nature-nurture 202, 294, 297–298
neutrality 6, 52–54, 265–266
normal science 30–32

object relational 237, 239
objectivity 6, 21, 25, 56, 71, 74, 78, 83
operationalism 53–54, 56, 62
organismic 295–297

phenomenology 67, 165,
positivism/positivist science 19–20, 43–44,
  52, 54, 56, 61
post positivism 19, 55–56
post structuralist 292, 308, 312,
postcolonial 161, 188
predetermined epigenesis 298
priming 179, 180
probabilistic epigenesis 299
psychiatric diagnosis 266–267, 275–276
psychic unity 139, 141, 146, 164, 174, 188,
  238, 304
psychoanalysis, 14, 30, 42–43, 229,
psychological formulation 276
psychological individualism 5
psychological social psychology 88 – 89
psychology of gender 195–199
psychology of the social 116
psychology of women 196–198,
psycho-social/psychosocial 6, 11, 120–121,

quantification 51–52, 56 – 57, 78, 87, 221

radical empiricism 384
realists 25–26
reductionism 45
reflexivity 6, 71, 75–76,
relational 10, 115, 168, 177, 239
relational meta-theory 293
reliability 82–83, 272–273
replicability 62, 148

sameness 230, 241–242
scientific explanation 20
scientific method 18, 23, 35, 41, 64, 74, 93,
scientism 6, 90, 92,
sex difference 196, 198, 204, 216–225
sex differences 216–224
sexism 7, 213 – 214

342 Index

sexual difference 229–230, 233, 240–243
shared culture 134
small q 75
social categorization 127–128
social explanation 97–98
social representation 110–111, 123–124, 126–127
social situation 88–89, 93 – 96, 137, 182, 213
social suffering 282, 286
socialization theory 206–207, 291, 308
sociobiology 203–204, 217
sociological social psychology 88, 106
socio-structural explanation 137–138
split meta-theory 293
statistical deviance 253, 266
stereotypes 126, 196–197, 213, 245–246, 248–249

structure-function 294, 296–297
subjectification 255
subjectivity 4, 10, 74, 78, 128, 131, 172,
symbolic interactionism 66. 68–69, 107–108

thick descriptions 72, 81
transferability 82–83
transformative change 296
triangulation 80, 86

unit of analysis 114, 148, 175, 292, 308
universalism 160, 167, 177,
unreason 260–262

variable 14, 58 – 62,
variational change 296
verification/ 26, 30, 81
verstehen 65–67

Milton Keynes UK
Ingram Content Group UK Ltd.
UKHW031500071224
451979UK00015B/168